Soviet and Russian Military Aircraft in the Middle East

Soviet and Russian Military Aircraft in the Middle East

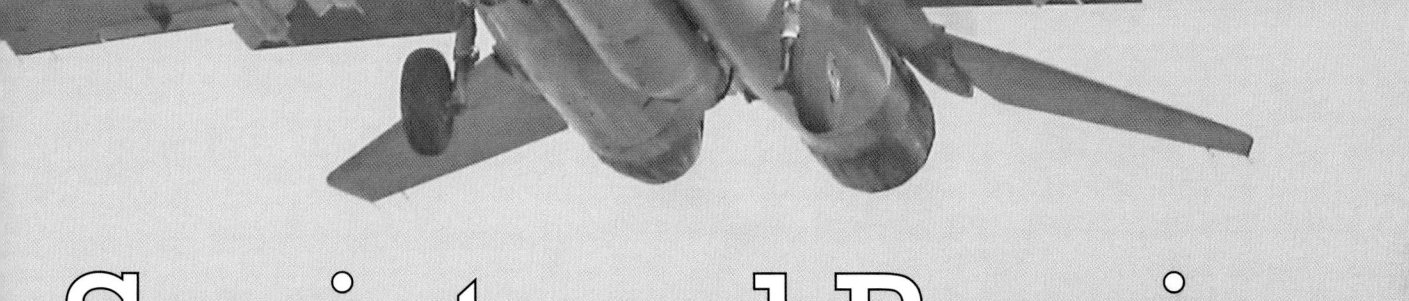

Yefim Gordon & Dmitriy Komissarov

First published in 2013 by
Hikoki Publications Ltd
1a Ringway Trading Est
Shadowmoss Rd
Manchester
M22 5LH
England

Email: enquiries@crecy.co.uk
www.crecy.co.uk

Layout by Polygon Press Ltd., Moscow

Colour profiles: Mikhail Bykov, Aleksandr Gavrilov, Sergey Ignat'yev, Viktor Mil'yachenko, Aleksander Rusinov, Sergey Yershov, Andrey Yurgenson.

ISBN 9 781902 109282

Printed in China

Contents

Acknowledgements

Special thanks go to Chris Lofting, Patrick Roegies, Peter Davison, Detlev Grass, Sergey Burdin and the Russian Aviation Research Trust (especially Nigel Eastaway), who have contributed invaluably to the selection of illustrations for this book. The authors would also like to apologise, and express their gratitude at the same time, to the persons whose names are unknown to the authors but whose photos have been included due to their obvious value for the reader.

This book is illustrated with photos by Max Bryanskiy, Igor' Bubin, Sergey Burdin, Alexander Datsenko, Sergey Krivchikov, Peter Davison, Zdeněk Dvořak, Detlev Grass, Svetozar Jokanović, Ferdinand C. W. Käsmann, Chris Lofting, Amir Mahdavi, Hassan Mousavi, Martin Novak, Dmitriy Pichugin, Ali Rafiei, Patrick Roegies, Alireza Sotakbar and Rouhollah Vahdati, Helmut Walther as well as photos from the archives of Yefim Gordon, RART, MEHR, FARS News Agency, IRNA News Agency, ISNA News Agency.

Additionally, photos from the following sources have been used: www.planes.cz, www.elhangardetj.blogspot.com, www.irna.ir, www.benwilhelmi.com, www.xairforces.com, www.irandefence.net, www.aerospacetalk.ir, www.defence-arab.com, www.historicflight.cz www.photozagros.com, www.aviaforum.ru, www.russianplanes.net, www.forcesdz.com, www.siregar.deviantart.com, www.taknaz.ir www.spotters.net.ua, homepage.eircom.net, www.avijacijabezgranica.com.

Two Islamic Republic of Iran Air Force Su-24MK bombers shown on final approach. The first one is Russian-supplied and fitted with overwing flare dispensers; the other one is an ex-Iraqi aircraft.

Introduction

In the second half of the 1950s the Soviet Union started supplying weaponry to the Arab nations. Egypt, whose president Gamal Abdel Nasser had struck ties with the Soviet leaders, was the first to receive Soviet weapons. Now, there had been animosity between Egypt and Israel ever since the latter state emerged in 1948, the first Arab-Israeli war breaking out that very year. Both the East and the West were implicitly involved in the Arab-Israeli conflicts; the western powers supplied Israel with weapons, including combat aircraft, while the Soviet Union provided Egypt with Mikoyan/Gurevich MiG-15 jet fighters (NATO reporting name *Fagot*), which had made their mark in the Korean War, and subsequently more advanced fighters, tactical and medium jet bombers and heavy transport helicopters. Additionally, groups of Soviet military advisors and instructors were sent to the Middle East to help the Arabs master their new hardware and the tactics of using it. In the 1960s Syria and Iraq, too, started taking delivery of Soviet combat and transport aircraft. Co-operation with Egypt in defence matters continued until 1976 when there was a rift between Moscow and Cairo on political grounds (Nasser began persecuting the Egyptian Communists, which Moscow could not tolerate), and the Soviet military personnel in Egypt were expelled; from then on, Egypt switched allegiance to the West as an arms supplier. On the other hand, Soviet co-operation with Syria and Iraq broadened, these countries receiving progressively more advanced weaponry, including combat aircraft and helicopters.

The Arabs were denied the chance to put their Soviet aircraft to the test in the Six-Day War of 5th-11th June 1967 because the greater part of the fleet was destroyed on the ground by Israeli air strikes on the opening day of the hostilities. The Soviet Union had to make good the losses by supplying new (and more modern) aircraft. On the other hand, in the next Arab-Israeli war – the Yom Kippur War of October 1973 – and in the period leading up to it, which was characterised by incessant skirmishes, the Soviet aircraft operated by the Arab nations were used very actively, showing their worth. They made up the backbone of the air forces of Egypt and Syria – Israel's main adversaries.

It deserves mention that some aircraft ostensibly wearing Egyptian Air Force insignia were in fact owned and operated by the Soviet Air Force or the Soviet Navy. Most of them were operated by the 90th Independent Long-Range Reconnaissance Squadron – an *ad hoc* outfit temporarily deployed to Egypt in 1968-72 in order to 'extend help to a friendly nation' (actually it operated in the interests of both nations). The squadron operated such assorted types as Antonov An-12R *Cub* and Tupolev Tu-16R *Badger-E/F* reconnaissance aircraft, An-12BK-PP and Tu-16P *Badger-J* electronic countermeasures aircraft, Beriyev Be-12 *Mail* and Il'yushin IL-38 *May* anti-submarine warfare aircraft, all of which returned to the Soviet Union. Others were Mikoyan MiG-21 *Fishbed* fighters which were flown by Soviet pilots from a different unit for a while before the Soviet airmen left in 1972, turning the fighters over to the Egyptians.

In the 1970s and 1980s large-scale deliveries of Soviet weaponry, including combat and military transport aircraft, were made to Iraq; in the course of the last 20 years Soviet and Russian weapons have also been supplied to Yemen and Iran. Iraq used its Soviet combat aircraft against Iran in the 1980-88 war, losing many of them in the process. More Iraqi Air Force aircraft were destroyed by Coalition force strikes during the First Gulf War in 1991, and still others sought refuge in Iran and were appropriated by the latter at the end of that war. Thus, Iran actually obtained Soviet military hardware *thanks to* its opponent – the western world, despite the latter's efforts to prevent this.

This book is a follow-up to *Soviet and Russian Military Aircraft in Africa*. It contains the information the authors have collected on Soviet and Russian military aircraft and helicopters operated in the Middle East and on the Arabian Peninsula. It also includes Egypt, which had been omitted from the previous book, on the grounds that all wars in which Egypt has participated were fought in the Middle East. Furthermore, the authors have deemed it expedient to include information on Soviet/Russian military aircraft in Iran in this book, even though geographically Iran is outside the Middle East. By analogy with *Soviet and Russian Military Aircraft in Africa* the book includes certain Chinese derivatives of Soviet types.

The book features fleet list tables of Soviet/Russian combat and military transport aircraft operated in the Middle East, on the Arabian Peninsula and in Iran. The authors have done their best to update and correct the available information, part of which has been published in previous books, magazine features and on the Internet. The authors will be grateful for any reader feedback that will make it possible to correct possible errors or fill in gaps in the information contained here.

Four Egyptian Air Force Chengdu F-7Bs pass overhead in echelon starboard formation.

Unmarked and partly under wraps, these Iraqi Air Force MiG-21*bis* fighters have been sitting at the Moma Stanojlović aircraft repair plant in Batajnica, Serbia. The conical radomes are missing from three of the four aircraft in the picture.

Egyptian Air Force Mi-8TV helicopters, including 1429 Black, undergoing refurbishment.

Egypt

Egypt, which had been under British control since 1882 and a British protectorate since 1914, was formally declared an independent kingdom in 1922; the Suez Canal zone, however, remained under British control. On 2nd November 1930 King Fuad I decreed the formation of an Egyptian Army Air Force which, in 1937, became the autonomous Royal Egyptian Air Force. On 23rd July 1952 King Farouk I was overthrown in a military coup led by Gamal Abdel Nasser. After the declaration of the Arab Republic of Egypt on 18th June 1953, with Nasser as President, the Egyptian Air Force (EAF, or *al Quwwat al-Jawwiya al-Jomhouriya il-Misriya*) was created.

The new government's independent political course angered Great Britain, which was the primary arms supplier to Egypt, and new aircraft deliveries to the EAF dried up. Financial constraints forced Egypt to buy outdated aircraft, such as Gloster Meteors and de Havilland Vampires, and even this was not easy. Seeking new allies in the Eastern Bloc, Nasser turned to Czechoslovakia for help. A contract for the delivery of various weapons (mainly aircraft, tanks and air defence radars) was signed in August 1955.

On 1st February 1958 Syria and Egypt formed a union called the United Arab Republic (UAR); a month later this was joined by the Kingdom of Yemen (North Yemen) to create the Union of Arab States. Hence the joint Egyptian/Syrian air arm was known as the United Arab Republic Air Force (UARAF). The union proved to be short-lived – Syria seceded on 28th September 1961; nevertheless, Egypt persisted with the UAR name until 1971. Accordingly the EAF name was restored in 1971.

Egypt was the first Arab nation to operate the Mikoyan/Gurevich MiG-15*bis Fagot-B* fighter and the UTI-MiG-15 *Midget* trainer. The first of 110 Czechoslovak-built *Fagot-Bs* (Aero S-103s) delivered to the EAF arrived in October 1955. Incidentally, Czech sources say the fighters were flown to Egypt, while other sources state they were delivered to the Mediterranean seaport of Alexandria by Soviet freighters (the first batch arrived aboard M/S *Stalingrad*). 80 aircraft were delivered in 1955, followed by 28 in 1956 and the final two in 1957. Only 60 MiGs were reportedly in service by March 1956. The fighters were operated by the No.1 Sqn consecutively based at Cairo-Almaza AB, El Qabrit AB and Cairo-West AB (with 12 aircraft), (reportedly) No.5 Sqn at Inshas (15 aircraft, inoperative; converted to the MiG-17F in 1957), No.18 Sqn consecutively based at Cairo International airport, Abu Sueir and El Arish, No.20 Sqn consecutively based at Deversoir, El Qabrit and Inshas (with 12 and 13 aircraft respectively), No.24 Sqn at Cairo-West AB and El Sur, and No.30 Sqn at Deversoir, El Qabrit and Cairo-West (Abu Sueir was also reported; 15 aircraft). During the Suez Crisis (26th October – 7th November 1956) most of them did not take part in the fighting; however, three *Fagot-Bs* were shot down in air-to-air combat – one on 30th October and two on 31st October.

After 1956, a total of 42 factory-fresh Czechoslovak-built UTI-MiG-15s (Aero CS-102s) were delivered to Egypt to supplement those supplied earlier. Most of the

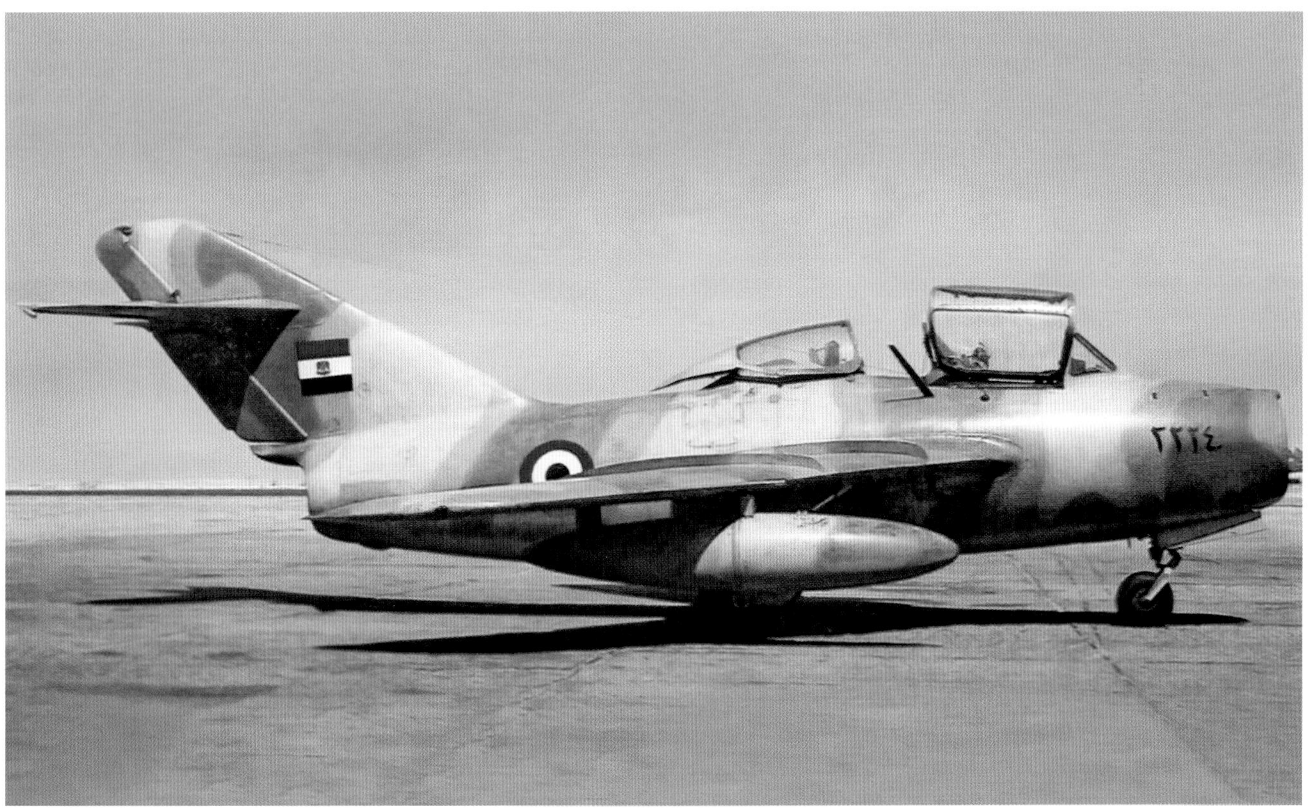

Seen here with 400-litre drop tanks, camouflaged Egyptian Air Force UTI-MiG-15 '2224 Black' wears post-UARAF insignia.

Above: Egyptian Air Force ground crew pull a wooden dummy MiG-15. Considerable numbers of these were built and used by the EAF as false targets to fool the Israelis – with scant success.

Below: The MiG-15*bis* of Abdel Rahman Muharram is salvaged by the Israelis after ditching in Lake Bordavil on the Sinai on 31st October 1956.

Bottom: Another view of the same aircraft as it is lifted out of the water by a crane.

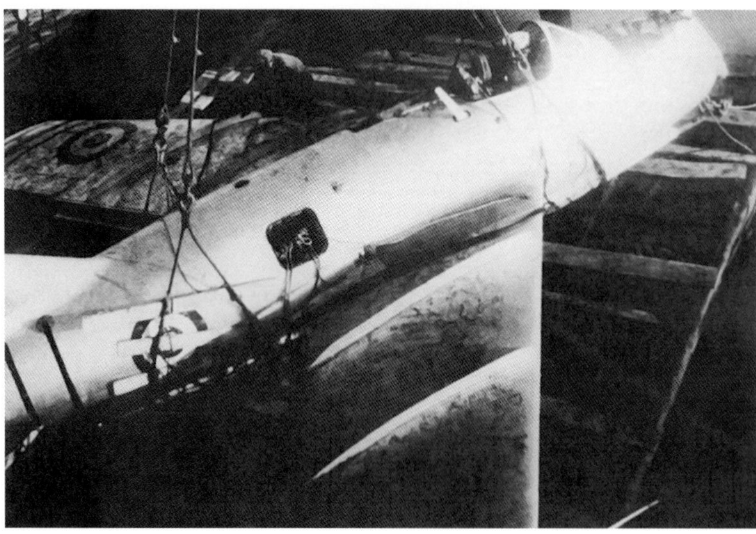

MiG-15s that survived the earlier conflict were destroyed on the ground during the Six-Day War (5th-11th June 1967).

Egyptian (UARAF) MiG-15s initially flew in natural metal finish and wore twin black identification stripes around the rear fuselage and triple stripes on the wingtips in addition to roundels. A sand/brown/green camouflage was hastily introduced after the Six-Day War in 1967, in which heavy losses had been incurred due to the high conspicuity of natural metal aircraft, among other things.

The first 12 Soviet-built Mikoyan/Gurevich MiG-17F *Fresco-C* fighters were delivered to the Egyptian Air Force in the autumn of 1956 to bolster its fighter arm in view of the growing political tension in the Suez Canal area. None of them had reached operational status when the Suez Crisis fighting broke out; eventually, however, they did take part in the conflict, operating from El Qabrit AB. At least one of them was shot down during the conflict (on 31st October 1956). 15 more *Fresco-Cs* arrived after the withdrawal of British and French troops from the Suez Canal area, starting in March 1957; by late June the EAF had nearly 100 MiG-17Fs based at Almaza AB near Cairo and other places. In the 1960s, many UARAF *Fresco-Cs* were transferred to ground attack units and retrofitted with two or four double launch rails for four or eight 76-mm Oerlikon unguided rockets (manufactured locally under the name Sakr) outboard of the drop tank hardpoints. Some aircraft also had bomb racks on the forward fuselage for carrying two 250-kg (551-lb) bombs. The upgrade was performed by the maintenance facility in Helwan.

In the early 1960s the UARAF received a small number of MiG-17PF *Fresco-D* radar-equipped all-weather interceptors. These were operated by the No.31 Sqn.

Again, originally the Egyptian MiG-17Fs flew in natural metal finish and wore no serials, making individual aircraft identification impossible. Four-digit serials were introduced by May 1967 but the aircraft were still unpainted. This changed fast after the Six-Day War of June 1967 – a three-tone desert camouflage was hastily introduced. Also in 1967, the EAF started taking delivery of 50 *Fresco-Cs* transferred from the East German Air Force as military aid – 17 Soviet-built MiG-17Fs manufactured by the Komsomol'sk-on-Amur aircraft factory and 33 Polish-built PZL Lim-5s; deliveries were completed in October 1968. One aircraft crashed on 21st April 1970. According to *Interavia*, 60 MiG-17F fighter-bombers were

The same MiG-15*bis* in a rather undignified position as a gate guard at the IDF/AF base at Hatzor. The aircraft was shot down by an Israeli Defence Force/Air Force Dassault Mystère piloted by 101 Sqn Deputy CO Yaakov Nevo (note the damage to the starboard aileron). The identification stripes are clearly visible here.

Abdel Rahman Muharram's aircraft was carefully studied by the Israelis but they could not make it airworthy again. Here it is seen being worked on at Hatzor AB.

Another view of the captured Egyptian MiG-15*bis*. The aircraft carried pre-United Arab Republic green/white insignia.

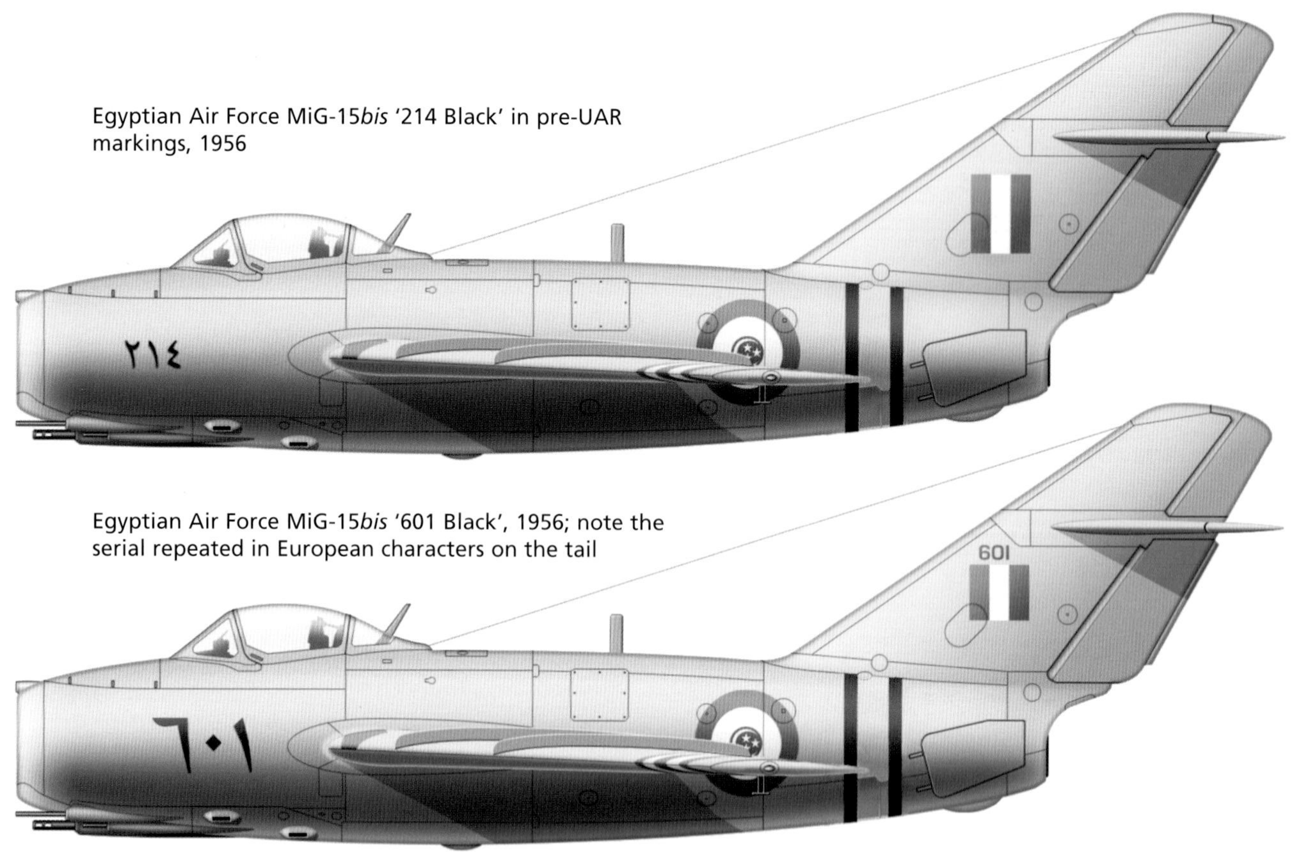

Egyptian Air Force MiG-15*bis* '214 Black' in pre-UAR markings, 1956

Egyptian Air Force MiG-15*bis* '601 Black', 1956; note the serial repeated in European characters on the tail

still in service with the EAF in early 1987 but were being withdrawn.

When Israel fielded its first supersonic fighter – the Dassault Super Mystère B.2 (known as the Sa'ar in Israeli service) – in 1959, the United Arab Republic Air Force decided to match this capability by ordering the Mikoyan/Gurevich MiG-19S *Farmer-C* day fighter. The first UARAF pilots were sent to the Soviet Union in the summer of 1960 to take their training; a year later the Soviet Union began deliveries of 80 MiG-19S day fighters. The first Egyptian MiG-19 squadron (No.27 Sqn at Fayeed AB) was commissioned in the spring of 1961; a second unit, No.29 Sqn at Hurghada, followed in 1962. (Some sources claim that 100 *Farmer-Cs* had been delivered by June 1962!)

A number of EAF MiG-19s (as many as 40 aircraft) were transferred to the Syrian Air Force before 1967. During the Six-Day War of 1967 the Egyptian MiG-19 force was hard hit: 17 aircraft were destroyed on the ground by Israeli air raids and another 12 shot down (these included the aircraft supplied to Syria). After the war the USSR delivered another 50 or 60 *Farmer-Cs* to the EAF as attrition replacements; some aircraft from this second shipment stayed in service until 1985.

When relations between Cairo and Moscow soured in 1976, Egypt initially looked to the West as an arms supplier but western aircraft were found to be expensive. Egypt turned to China for spares support. China was

Pre-1958 Egyptian Air Force roundel and fin flash.

Six Egyptian MiG-15*bis* fighters in pre-UAR markings make a formation flypast over Cairo during a military parade.

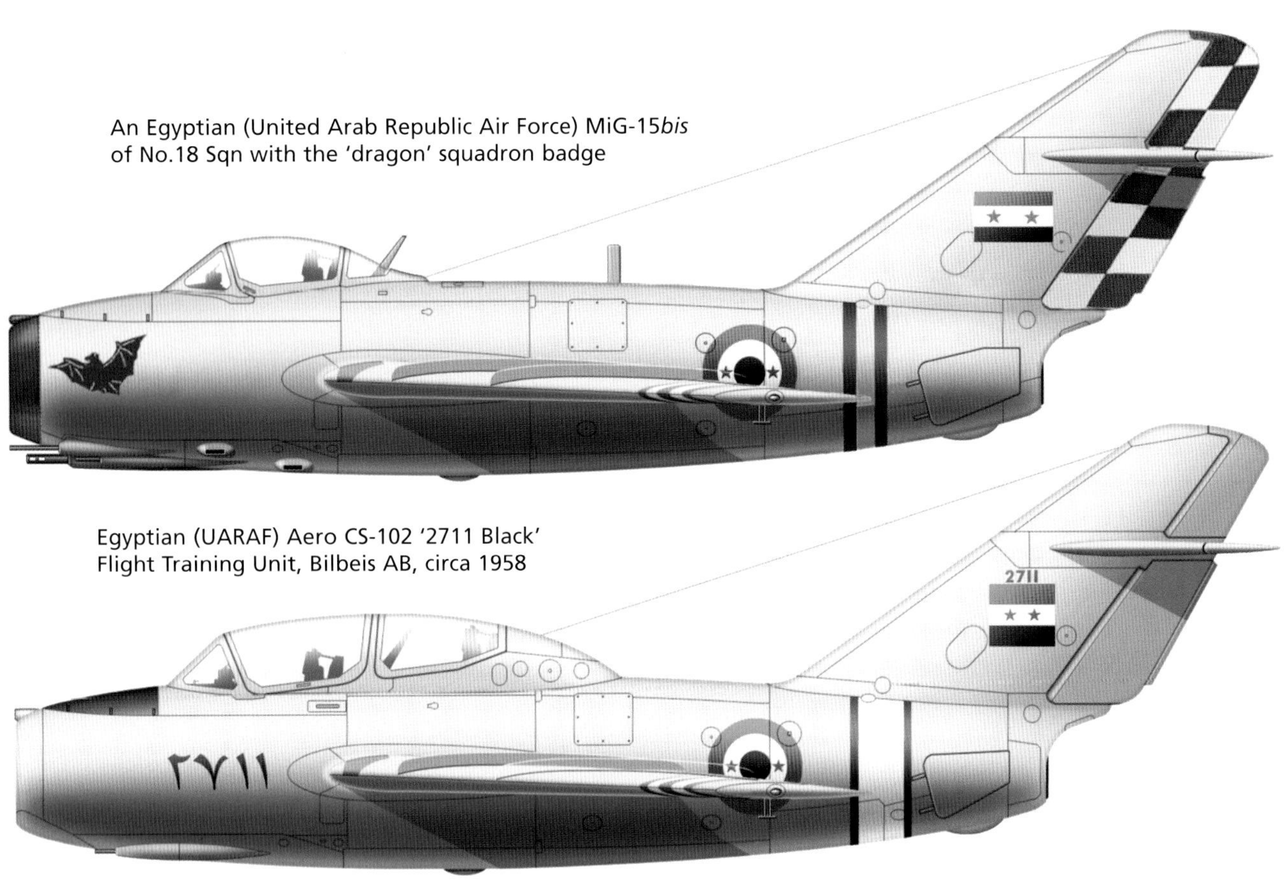

An Egyptian (United Arab Republic Air Force) MiG-15*bis* of No.18 Sqn with the 'dragon' squadron badge

Egyptian (UARAF) Aero CS-102 '2711 Black' Flight Training Unit, Bilbeis AB, circa 1958

The Egyptian (United Arab Republic Air Force) roundel and fin flash.

A trio of Egyptian MiG-15*bis* fighters with drop tanks fly in a loose V formation during a military parade.

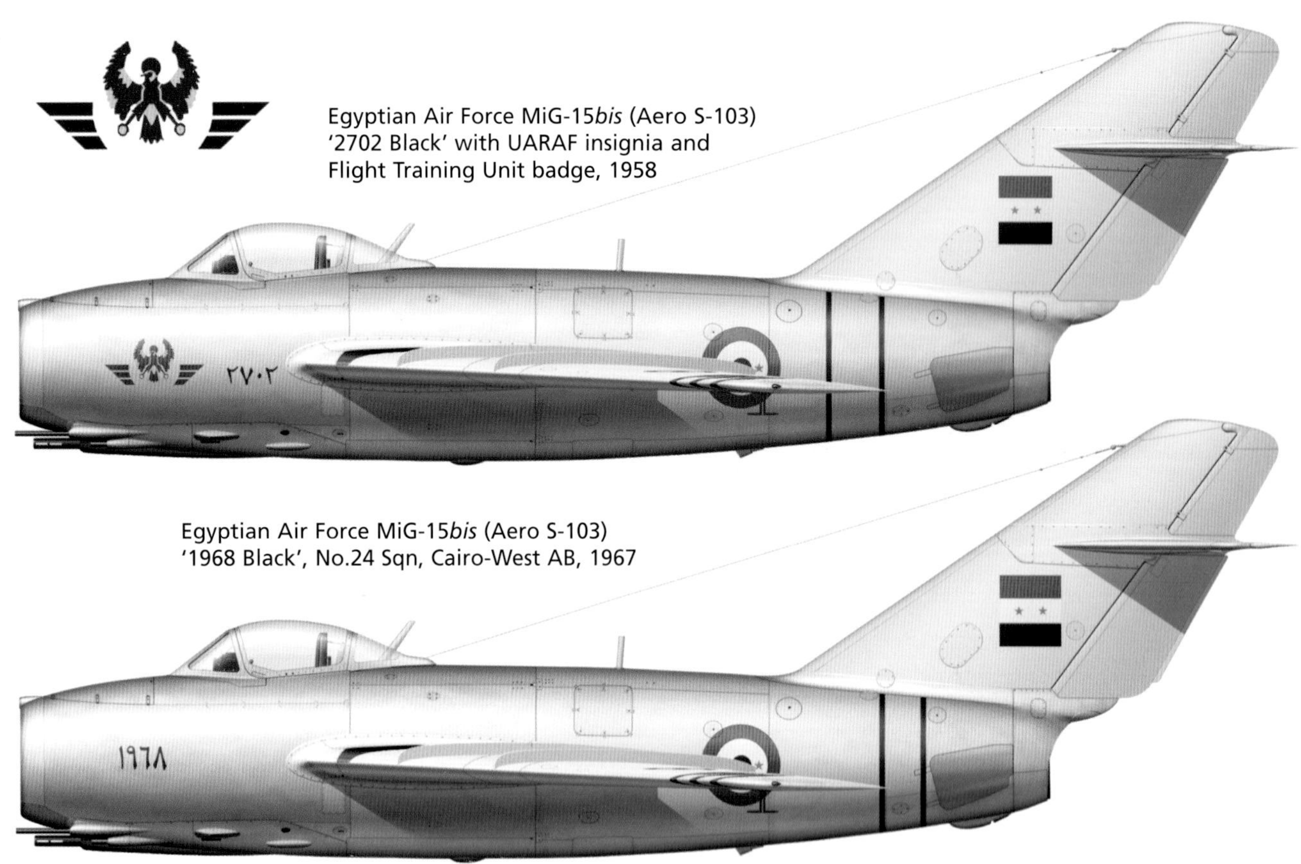

Egyptian Air Force MiG-15*bis* (Aero S-103) '2702 Black' with UARAF insignia and Flight Training Unit badge, 1958

Egyptian Air Force MiG-15*bis* (Aero S-103) '1968 Black', No.24 Sqn, Cairo-West AB, 1967

quick to sense the opportunity, selling about 40 Shenyang F-6C fighter-bombers (a Chinese version of the MiG-19S) and FT-6 trainers (a Chinese derivative with no Soviet counterpart) to the EAF; these were reportedly traded in for a few MiG-23MSs (see below), which were of interest to China from a technology standpoint. According to *Interavia*, however, Egypt had no fewer than 100 Shenyang F-6C fighter-bombers and FT-6 trainers equipping two air brigades – No.241 at Bilbeis-East AB and No.242 at Beni Sueif AB – in early 1987. *Flight International* reported that 72 F-6s and six FT-6s remained in late 1991.

The F-6Cs were fitted with pylons for carrying two 100-kg or 250-kg (220-lb or 551-lb) bombs, ORO-57 FFAR pods or 212-mm (8.34-in.) rockets. Some aircraft had non-standard trapezoidal gun blast panels. A number of EAF F-6Cs was reportedly upgraded with French Matra R550 Magic IR-homing AAMs.

The first Mikoyan MiG-21F-13 (*izdeliye* 74) *Fishbed-C* fighters arrived in June and July 1962 and equipped one fighter brigade (equivalent to a USAF Fighter Wing) comprising three squadrons. Another 80 were ordered in 1963. In 1965 the EAF underwent a reorganisation; the brigades and squadrons were renumbered. By the start of the Six-Day War on 6th June 1967, the EAF had received 235 MiG-21 fighters and 40 trainers; actually, according to Israeli sources, accident attrition and transfers to other Arab air forces had reduced the number to an estimated 102 (Arab sources suggest 108). During this war the EAF lost, according to most well informed sources, nearly 100 MiG-21 fighters of which about 70 were destroyed while on the ground.

It is believed that 120 MiG-21F-13s were delivered before the Six-Day War, serving with the 5th, 7th and 9th Air Brigades (the numbers are those in use before the 1965 renumbering). Most of these aircraft were destroyed in the conflict. After this, the Warsaw Pact countries made an effort to replenish the Egyptian stock of MiG-21s as soon as possible; to this end Czechoslovakia transferred 26 *Fishbed-Cs* (built locally under licence as the Aero S-106) from Czechoslovak Air Force stocks.

The *Fishbed-Cs* were augmented by 40 MiG-21PF (*izdeliye* 76 Version A) *Fishbed-D* all-weather interceptors delivered in 1964 and 75 MiG-21PFM (*izdeliye* 94A) *Fishbed-F* all-weather interceptors delivered in 1966 to equip four squadrons. Again, by the end of 1967 almost all of them were either lost in

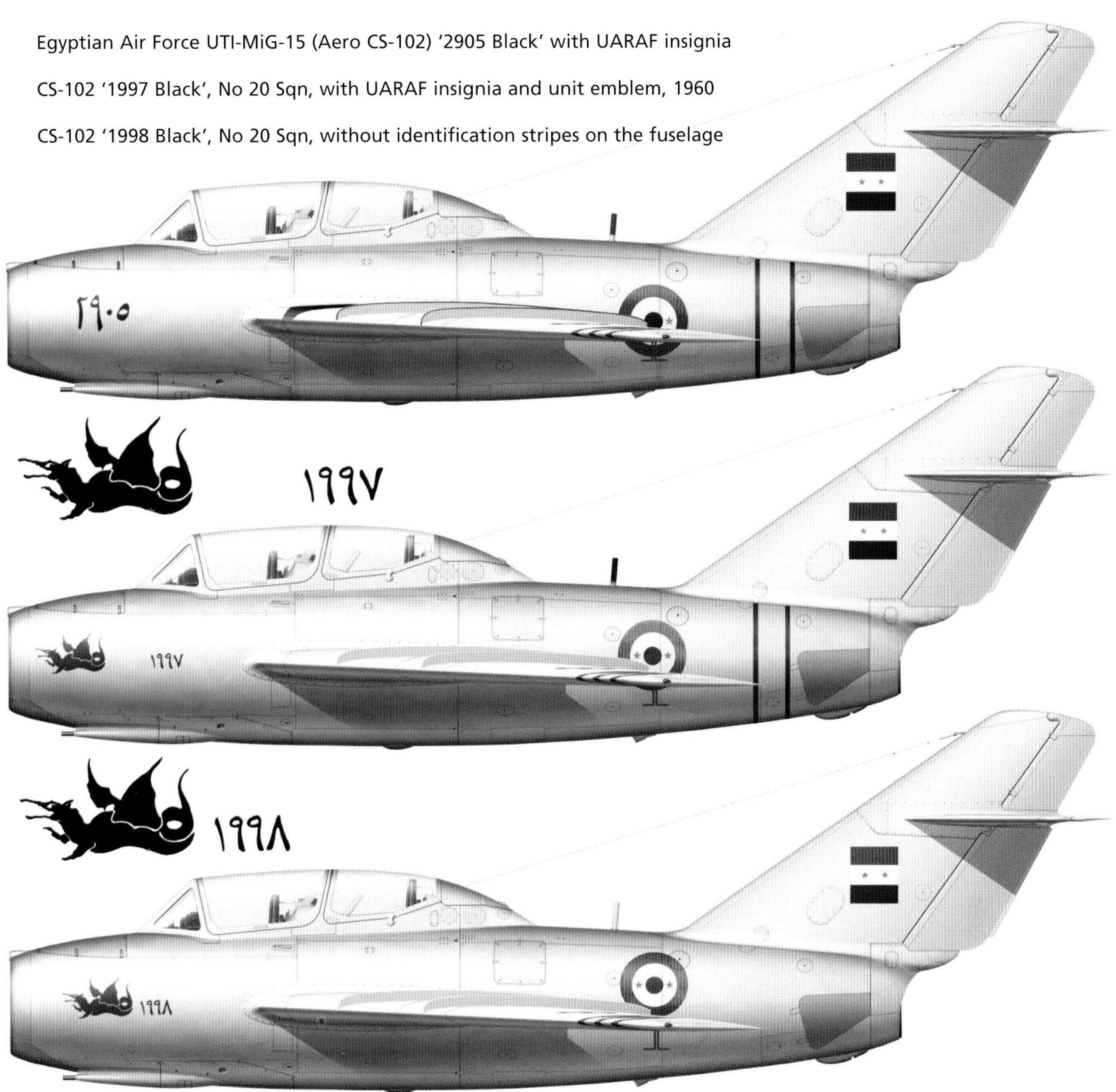

Egyptian Air Force UTI-MiG-15 (Aero CS-102) '2905 Black' with UARAF insignia

CS-102 '1997 Black', No 20 Sqn, with UARAF insignia and unit emblem, 1960

CS-102 '1998 Black', No 20 Sqn, without identification stripes on the fuselage

accidents or destroyed in the Six-Day War, after which no more than ten of the total of 235 MiG-21s delivered were still extant. Further deliveries took place after the Six-Day War; unfortunately there is no guarantee that the MiG-21PFMs were correctly identified.

The Soviet Union and its allies made strenuous efforts to resupply the EAF; a number of MiG-21PFS (*izdeliye* 94A) *Fishbed-D* fighters – reportedly 75 – were delivered around 1970. This version was actually an intermediate step from the MiG-21PF to the MiG-21PFM, combining the latter's dorsally-mounted brake parachute housing with the former model's forward-hinged one piece canopy and having blown flaps but no cannon armament.

At least six MiG-21RF (*izdeliye* 94R) *Fishbed-H* tactical reconnaissance aircraft were supplied in 1971. They saw service with the No.64 Squadron.

The Six-Day War and the ensuing so-called War of Attrition left the EAF very short of aircraft and pilots qualified to fly MiG-21. Among the first replacements to arrive were 12 MiG-21M (*izdeliye* 96) *Fishbed-J* fighters delivered in 1972-73, a downgraded export version of the MiG-21SM; some reputable sources suggest they were MiG-21MFs (*izdeliye* 96F). These fighters were particularly welcome as they had a built-in 23-mm cannon. Additionally, to help protect Egyptian cities and airfields against Israeli raids the

Soviet Union despatched five (some reputable sources state two) regiments of MiG-21MFs in early 1970. The aircraft wore Egyptian Air Force markings for appearance's sake, and when the Soviets left in July 1972 the surviving 94 (?) fighters were turned over to the Egyptians. More MiG-21MFs were delivered to the EAF itself, starting in 1970 or 1971, and 110 were reported to have arrived over the next few years, some after July 1972. The MiG-21MFs served with a fighter brigade stationed at Aswan, as well as the No.45 Sqn and No.49 Sqn of the 104th Fighter Brigade at Al Mansoura. Also, a detachment of MiG-21MFs was normally based at Hurghada.

40 MiG-21U (*izdeliye* 66) *Mongol-A* trainers were acquired in 1964 but it is not known whether they were *izdeliye* 66-400s with narrow-chord fins or *izdeliye* 66-600s with wide-chord fins. Other deliveries followed around 1970, including a substantial number (24?) of MiG-21US (*izdeliye* 68) *Mongol-Bs*; some sources suggest some trainers in this batch were MiG-21UM (*izdeliye* 69) *Mongol-Bs*. Originally delivered in green/dark green/sand camouflage with black serials, they later received a grey/green/black camouflage with high-visibility orange markings on the outer wings, vertical tail and fuselage spine and white serials.

In 1980 an order was placed with China for 80 Chengdu F-7B fighters based on the MiG-21F-13. These were delivered in 1982, equipping the No.22 Sqn of the 104th Fighter Brigade and the No.26 Sqn of the Tactical Fighter Brigade at Mersa Matruh. Despite being reported under the same designation, the fighters represent two distinct sub-variants with the old one-piece forward-hinged canopy copied from the *Fishbed-C* and the new two-

Still in natural metal finish, UARAF UTI-MiG-15 '2752 Black' is preserved in a city park in Egypt.

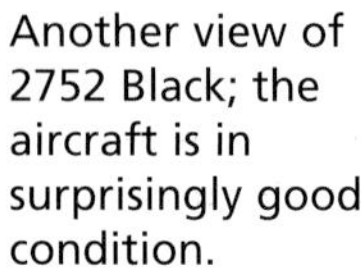

Another view of 2752 Black; the aircraft is in surprisingly good condition.

Egyptian Air Force UTI-MiG-15 (Aero CS-102) '2224 Black' with post-UARAF insignia

piece sideways-hinged canopy designed in China (they are equivalent to the 'domestic' J-7 II and J-7 IIA respectively). The F-7Bs wear a two-tone grey camouflage with the same orange markings.

In 1974 the Egyptian Air Force took delivery of eight Mikoyan MiG-23MS *Flogger-E* fighters and four MiG-23UB *Flogger-C* trainers; the aircraft were based at Mersa Matruh. Some sources claim that more advanced MiG-23MF *Flogger-B* fighters were also delivered. However, the break with Moscow in 1976 meant that no more *Flogger* deliveries followed. The ones already in Egypt were subsequently placed in storage and later sold to places as far apart (both geographically and ideologically) as the USA and China. The latter purchased two MiG-23MSs, two MiG-23UBs and some air-to-surface missiles in return for spares and technical support for the Egyptian MiG-17s and MiG-21s. The USA, eager to evaluate Soviet equipment, received six MiG-23MSs and other types of Soviet aircraft and weapons In exchange for AIM-9J Sidewinder air-to-air missiles and other weapons.

The Egyptian Air Force was the first non-WarPac operator of the Sukhoi Su-7 – and the largest foreign operator as well. Up to 1972 Egypt purchased no fewer than 158 Su-7BMK *Fitter-A* fighter-bombers and 20 Su-7UMK *Moujik* trainers. The first 14 Su-7BMKs were

Another view of UTI-MiG-15 '2224 Black', seen here minus drop tanks.

No.1 Sqn CO Sqn Ldr Mustafa Shalabi el-Hinnawy, the future Air Vice-Marshal and Egyptian Air Force Commander-in-Chief, inspects the unit's brand-new MiG-17Fs in 1956. The nearest aircraft is c/n 8047.

shipped off to Egypt in the summer of 1966, but for reasons unknown they did not reach their destination until April 1967. The aircraft operated from Fayeed AB right next to the Suez Canal. All 14 aircraft were wiped out in the Six-Day War two months later, but these losses were more than made good in later years. The Su-7s saw service with the Nos. 55, 202 and 204 Sqns (the latter two were based at Bilbeis).

After the Six-Day War, Egypt set about rebuilding its ravaged air force with renewed effort. Three squadrons of Su-7s (the reborn No.55 Sqn, No.202 Sqn and No.204 Sqn) were activated at Bilbeis. From 1969 onwards the Su-7BMKs were retrofitted locally with two additional wing pylons. Another mid-life upgrade focusing on the aircraft's avionics suite was initiated in 1976 but three years later the programme was scrapped. A mere 40 Su-7s of both versions were still active with the EAF in 1984.

In 1986 the Egyptians succeeded in foisting about 30 Su-7BMKs on Iraq; the machines were in such poor condition that the EAF had no use for them anyway. Three more *Fitter-As* were sold to the USA for evaluation.

In addition, the Egyptian Air Force took delivery of 16 'swing-wing' Su-17K *Fitter-Cs* and a number of Su-20 *Fitter-Cs*; the flyaway cost was US$ 2 million per aircraft at the 1975 exchange rate. 20 examples were reportedly still in service at the end of 1986. Two Su-20s were sold to West Germany and the USA for evaluation. There were also press reports of examples of Egyptian Su-20s being supplied to China, also for evaluation purposes.

In 1974 Egypt received eight Mikoyan MiG-23BN *Flogger-H* fighter-bombers; like the fighter and trainer MiG-23s, they were based at Mersa Matruh. Again, after the rift with the USSR these aircraft were withdrawn from service and eventually sold. It has been reported that two were sold to China and six to the USA (exactly the same figures as for the fighters); apparently there is a good deal of confusion as to how many of each variant were delivered and where they went.

The Egyptian Air Force ordered about 50 Il'yushin IL-28 *Beagle* bombers and IL-28U *Mascot* bomber trainers from Czechoslovakia (where they were known as the B-228 and CB-228 respectively), taking delivery of the first aircraft in December 1955. Three squadrons of *Beagles* were formed, albeit only one of them was operational in October 1956; the aircraft were initially based at Cairo-West AB. After the Suez Crisis of 1956, in which at

The wreck of Egyptian (UARAF) MiG-17F '2235 Black' destroyed on the ground at El Arish AB by the first Israeli air raid on 5th June 1967. Note the chequered rudder, the identification stripes on the wings and fuselage, and the launch rails for Sakr unguided rockets.

least seven of these bombers were lost, President Gamal Abdel Nasser launched a major programme to re-equip his armed forces; this included the acquisition of more *Beagles*. In March 1957 three Romanian ships brought the first ten IL-28s to Alexandria, among other things; by late June the EAF had about 40 on strength.

In his speech on 25th July 1957 on the occasion of Nasser's fifth anniversary as President, Egyptian Air Force Chief of Staff Air Vice-Marshal Mohammed Sidqi stated that the EAF's first-line assets had doubled as compared to the time immediately before the Suez Crisis. To add weight to his words, a formation of no fewer that 100 combat jets was to pass over Cairo same day. However, the show of force fizzled because the tech staff had managed to prepare only 42 aircraft for the display – eleven MiG-15*bis*, eighteen MiG-17Fs and thirteen IL-28s. The spectators went wild all the same, but the message was clear: it would take the EAF years to become fully combat-capable.

When the United Arab Republic was created, the EAF IL-28s were included into the assets of the UARAF. in addition to the basic bomber and trainer versions, the UARAF reportedly operated IL-28R tactical photo reconnaissance aircraft and Chinese-built Harbin H-5 (or B-5) copies of the *Beagle*. Egypt reclaimed most of these aircraft in September 1961 after the dissolution of the UAR.

Reports on the total number of Egyptian IL-28s vary widely, some sources stating as many as 72 aircraft in 1966. These included four second-hand IL-28T torpedo-bombers bought from the Soviet Navy in 1962 with a supply of 90 RAT-52 torpedoes. Other sources claim that 27 of 30 (!?) aircraft on strength in 1967 were destroyed on the ground by Israeli air strikes during the Six-Day War (5th-11th June 1967). Considering that two IL-28s were resold to Nigeria and six to Syria, it makes you wonder where the remaining 34 aircraft went! Anyway, by the outbreak of the Yom Kippur War (6th October 1973) Egypt had 35 to 40 IL-28s in four bomber squadrons and one reconnaissance squadron with IL-28Rs. The *Beagles* were now based at Aswan. Two aircraft were written off on 25th April 1970 under unknown circumstances (possibly in a collision). No more than four or five IL-28s remained airworthy by 1983.

In 1963 about 20 Tupolev Tu-16KS *Badger-B* missile carriers were supplied to the Egyptian

A lower view of an Egyptian MiG-17F in wrap-around camouflage. Note that the camouflage is not applied to the drop tanks and the inboard main gear doors. The silver spot under the port wing root is the landing light.

Egyptian MiG-17Fs attack an Israeli convoy near Romani in the north of the Sinai Peninsula on 6th June 1967. An M4 Sherman tank has just taken a hit, bursting into flames.

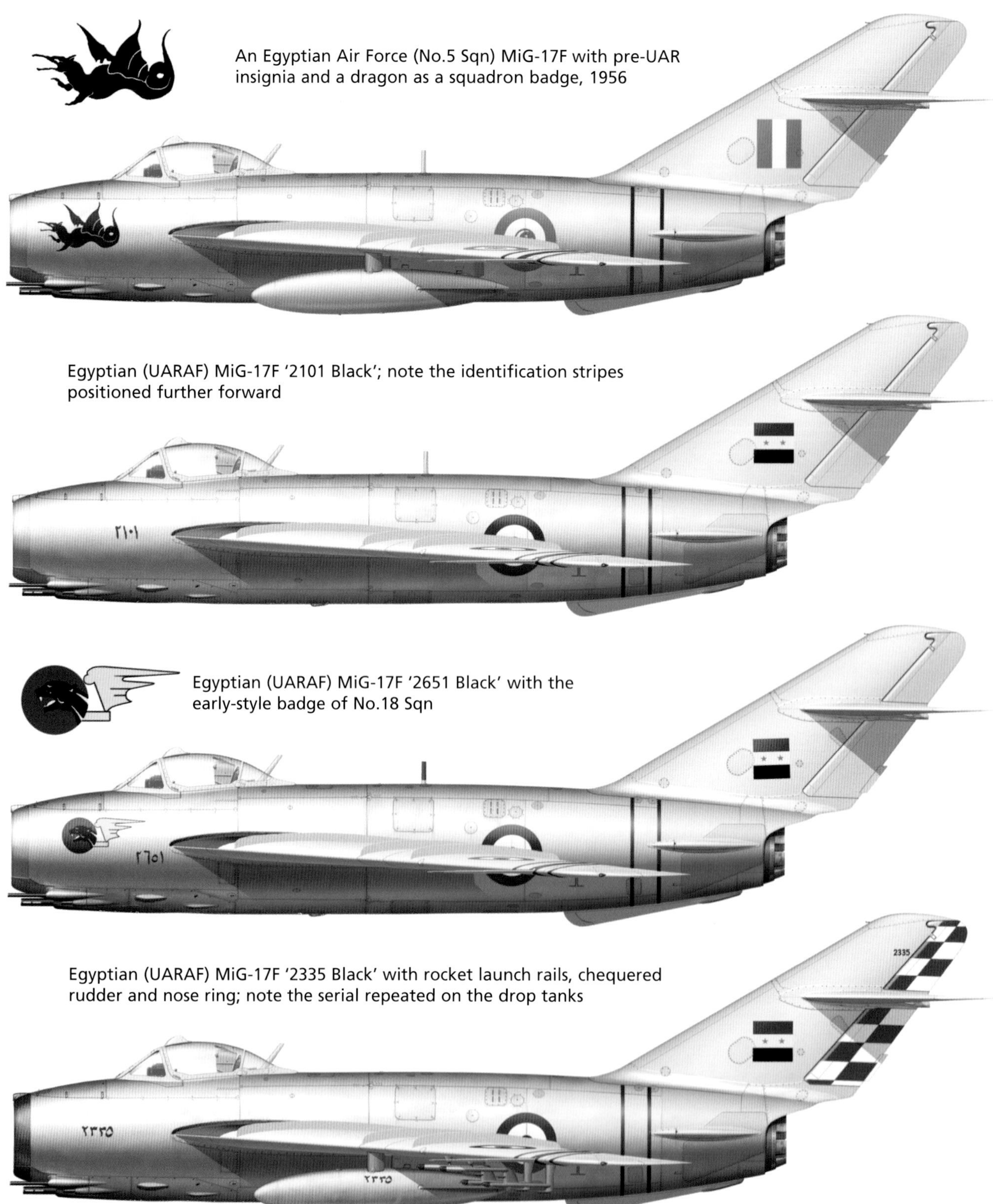

An Egyptian Air Force (No.5 Sqn) MiG-17F with pre-UAR insignia and a dragon as a squadron badge, 1956

Egyptian (UARAF) MiG-17F '2101 Black'; note the identification stripes positioned further forward

Egyptian (UARAF) MiG-17F '2651 Black' with the early-style badge of No.18 Sqn

Egyptian (UARAF) MiG-17F '2335 Black' with rocket launch rails, chequered rudder and nose ring; note the serial repeated on the drop tanks

Air Force where they formed two squadrons. The aircrews were trained in the USSR and Soviet specialists took part in their service induction in Egypt. A while later, on 26th January 1966, the Soviet government approved the delivery of six Tu-16T *Badger-A* torpedo-bombers to Egypt. In June 1967, in the first hours of the Six-Day War, they were destroyed by Israeli air raids before they could take part in the action.

After the war, in the autumn of 1971, the USSR supplied Egypt with about 20 further Tu-16KSR-2A and Tu-16KSR-2-11 *Badger-G* missile carriers, as well as a stock of KSR-2

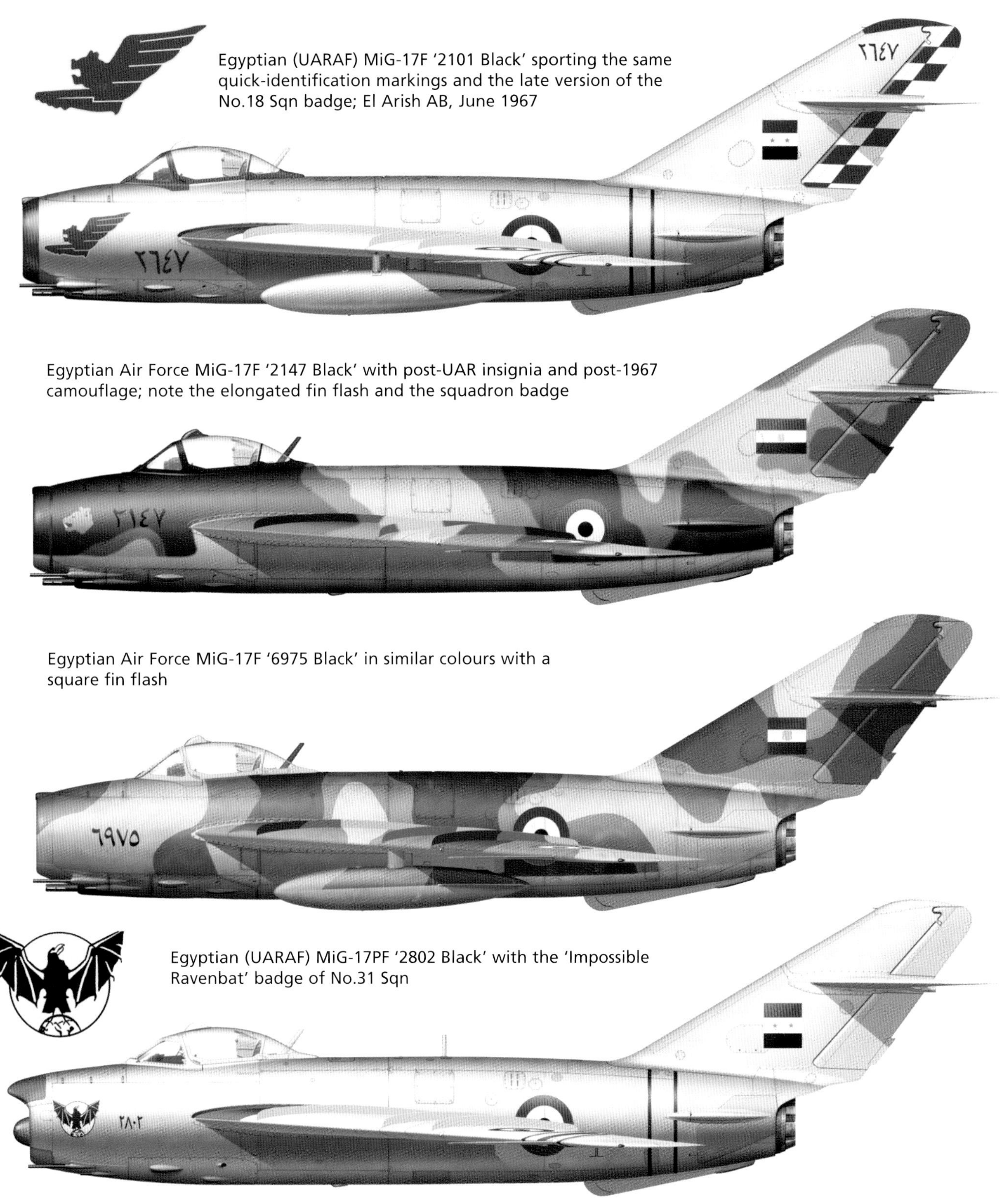

Egyptian (UARAF) MiG-17F '2101 Black' sporting the same quick-identification markings and the late version of the No.18 Sqn badge; El Arish AB, June 1967

Egyptian Air Force MiG-17F '2147 Black' with post-UAR insignia and post-1967 camouflage; note the elongated fin flash and the squadron badge

Egyptian Air Force MiG-17F '6975 Black' in similar colours with a square fin flash

Egyptian (UARAF) MiG-17PF '2802 Black' with the 'Impossible Ravenbat' badge of No.31 Sqn

(AS-2 *Kelt*) air-to-surface missiles. The aircraft were ferried in pairs via Hungary and Yugoslavia to Cairo-West AB, entering service with the newly formed No.36 Sqn. Soviet Naval Aviation/Black Sea Fleet crews made the ferry flights, and the Egyptian personnel were trained *in situ* by Soviet instructors. The *Badgers* equipped two squadrons which were heavily involved in operations during the Yom Kippur War of October 1973. During this round of hostilities the Egyptian Tu-16s launched some 25 missiles against Israeli targets on the Sinai Peninsula, destroying two radar sites and a field supply depot.

Egyptian Air Force MiG-17F '2034 Black' wearing post-UAR markings and three-tone camouflage. The Ural-375 lorry in the background is probably an APA-5 ground power unit.

'2728 Black', another Egyptian MiG-17F, wears a different (two-tone) camouflage and a bolder serial. Note the locally installed bomb racks on the centre fuselage.

Mindful of the experience gained from the Six-Day War, the Egyptian Tu-16s were now based at airfields south of Sinai, beyond the reach of the Israeli Defence Force/Air Force (IDF/AF). According to the Egyptians, their Tu-16s suffered no losses, although the Israelis claimed one bomber destroyed.

In addition, several Soviet Navy Tu-16R *Badger-E*/*-F* reconnaissance aircraft with SRS-1 and SRS-3 SIGINT kits and Tu-16P *Badger-J* ECM aircraft were on detachment in Egypt in keeping with an agreement signed in March 1968, gathering intelligence for both nations. The North Fleet Tu-16Rs arrived in 1968, being superseded by Black Sea Fleet aircraft in 1970, and the Baltic Fleet Tu-16Ps (at least four) followed in 1971. Although wearing EAF markings like the rest, they were Soviet-operated, serving with the 90th Independent Special Mission Long-Range Reconnaissance

Egyptian (post-UAR) Air Force MiG-17F '2147 Black' carrying 250-kg (551-lb) bombs on the extra fuselage hardpoints

Egyptian Air Force MiG-17F '2355 Black' with rocket launch rails and fuselage hardpoints

Squadron (90th ODRAE ON – *ot**del'**naya **dahl'**nyaya raz**ved**yvatel'naya **a**viaeskad**ril'**ya o**sob**ovo nazna**che**niya*). Originally the detachment was based at Cairo-West, a major EAF base; later some of the aircraft moved to Mersa Matruh AB.

After the rift between Egypt and the USSR, the Soviets cut off spares supplies for the military equipment they had provided. Striving to maintain their machines in operational condition, the Egyptians turned to China, which was building the Tu-16 under licence as the Xian H-6 (B-6). In April 1976 an agreement was signed whereby China furnished Egypt with spares for their *Badgers*. In early 1990 the EAF still operated sixteen Tu-16 and B-6D missile carriers which formed a bomber brigade based in the south of the country.

Despite its name, the 90th ODRAE ON included several anti-submarine warfare aircraft – again masquerading in Egyptian markings and operating for both nations. These included three Black Sea Fleet Beriyev Be-12 Chaika (*Mail*) amphibians deployed from 19th August 1968 and North Fleet Il'yushin IL-38 *May* shore-based long-range ASW aircraft. Originally two IL-38s were deployed in the autumn of 1970, flying sorties over the Mediterranean. On the pretext of filling the need for more sophisticated equipment they were supplemented in June 1971 by two more aircraft, while the Be-12s returned to the USSR. In the course of their operations from

Silver-painted MiG-17F '2355 Black' preserved in Egypt. Again, the aircraft has extra fuselage hardpoints and launch rails for Sakr rockets. Note the omission of the 'spread eagle' crest on the fin flash.

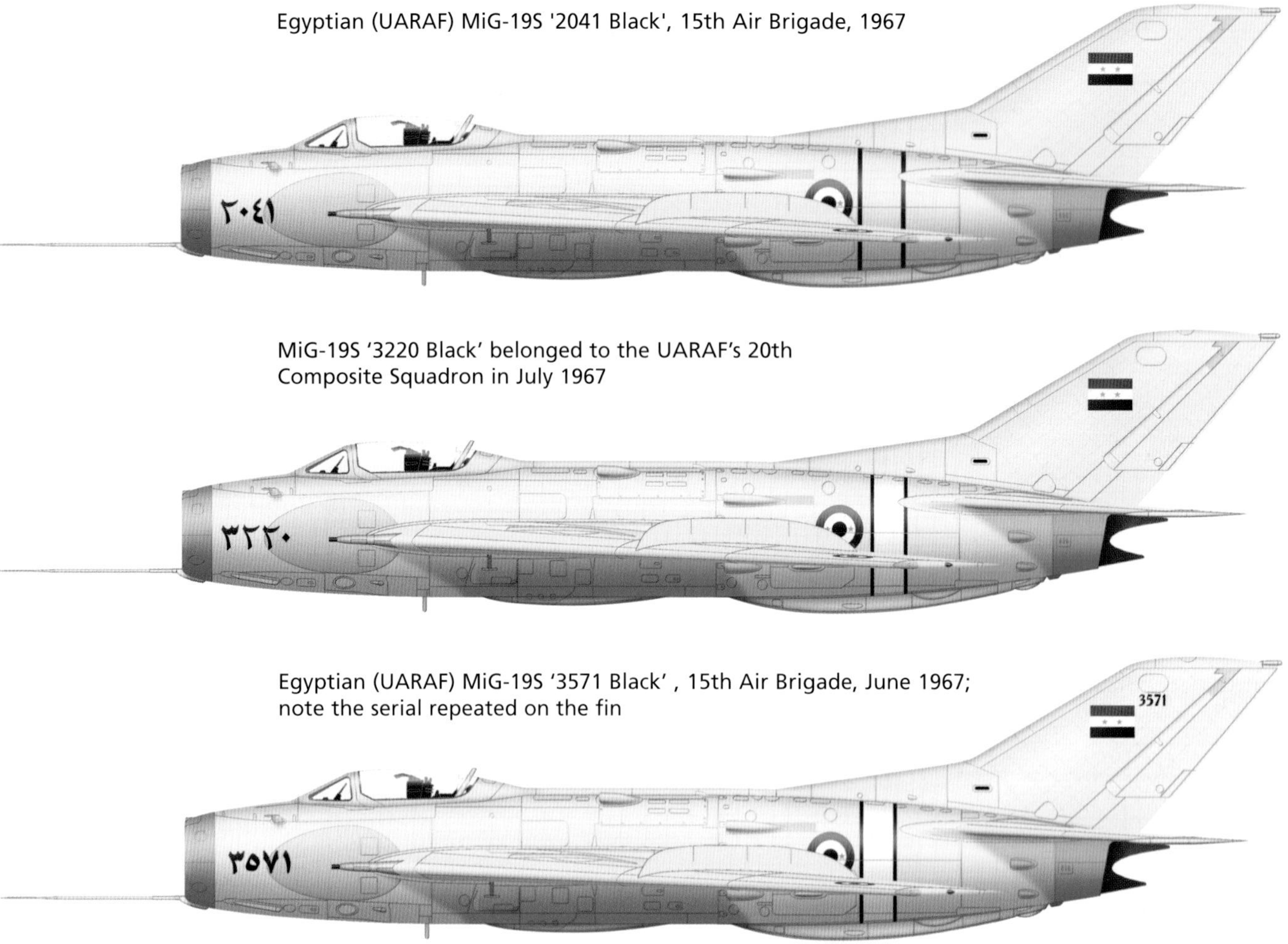

Egyptian (UARAF) MiG-19S '2041 Black', 15th Air Brigade, 1967

MiG-19S '3220 Black' belonged to the UARAF's 20th Composite Squadron in July 1967

Egyptian (UARAF) MiG-19S '3571 Black' , 15th Air Brigade, June 1967; note the serial repeated on the fin

Mersa Matruh the *Mays* had 20 reported contacts with submarines.

An unknown number of Antonov An-2 *Colt* utility biplanes were delivered to the Egyptian Air Force. Only two examples wearing a beige/grey colour scheme akin to that worn by Soviet and East European An-2R agricultural aircraft are known; one of them, sporting old UARAF markings, was used for geophysical survey (possibly ore prospecting) with a towed sensor 'bird' under the fuselage.

The Egyptian Air Force operated 25 Antonov An-12 *Cub* medium transports, including 15 Voronezh-built An-12Bs delivered in 1964-67 and ten Tashkent-built An-12BPs purchased in 1966-72. The aircraft saw service with a single squadron (No.16?) based at Cairo-West AB. At first they wore a restrained civil-style colour scheme with EAF serials and large Egyptian flag fin flashes but no roundels on the fuselage. Civil registrations were added soon afterwards, and these were changed from time to time on some aircraft – apparently for security reasons.

In 1962 one of the An-12Bs, serialled 1223 Black, became a flying testbed for the 4,800-kgp (10,580-lbst) E-300 afterburning turbojet developed by the German engineer Dr. Ferdinand Brandner for Egypt's Helwan HA-300 light fighter. The development engine was mounted in place of the No.2 AI-20 turboprop in a compact nacelle on a short pylon attached to a suitably modified engine bearer. However, the flight-cleared engine was never installed in the HA-300; the two prototypes, the first of which entered flight test on 7th March 1964, were powered by Bristol Orpheus B.Or. 12 turbojets. Eventually the ambitious programme was cut short by financial problems and closed down in 1968. As for the An-12, it was reconverted to standard configuration, serving on until finally retired.

Additionally, at least three Soviet Air Force An-12s wearing Egyptian markings for appearance's sake served with the 90th ODRAE ON from late 1969 to 1972. They included at least one An-12BK-PP *Cub-C* ECM aircraft and an An-12R ELINT aircraft.

Two of the An-12s were destroyed in the Six-Day War. Starting in 1976, the *Cubs* were supplemented and gradually replaced by 23 Lockheed C-130H Hercules, the last of which arrived in 1982 (later augmented by three 'stretched' C-130H-30s); this was in line with Egypt's new allegiance to the West. The last of the An-12s reportedly remained in service until the early 1990s; eventually, however, all the *Cubs* were retired and progressively scrapped.

In post-Soviet days the Egyptian Air Force ordered a batch of Antonov An-74TK-200A *Coaler-B* convertible STOL tactical transports from the Khar'kov State Aircraft Manufacturing Co. in the Ukraine. The first of the three aircraft was delivered in September 2005; the An-74s wear a sand/brown camouflage scheme, sporting both civil registrations and EAF serials (which were added later).

The Egyptian Air Force (UARAF) had a sizeable number of Il'yushin IL-14 *Crate* airliners/transports, which included Tashkent-built, Moscow-built and even East German-built examples. Some of them were IL-14S VIP aircraft operated by the Presidential Flight. In late October 1956 one such aircraft (1101 Black) went to Syria and Jordan, carrying a delegation of the Egyptian High Commission (= government). This did not pass unnoticed by the Israeli intelligence service Mossad, which decided to assassinate the members of the delegation in the belief that the Egyptian Minister of Defence Field Marshal Abdel Hakim Amer was aboard (which he was not). On the night of 29th October, when the IL-14S headed back to Egypt, it was intercepted and shot down by an IDF/AF (119 Sqn) Gloster Meteor NF.13 night fighter piloted by the unit's CO Yoash 'Chatto' Ziddon, with Eliashive Brosh as radar intercept operator. The airliner's crew and 16 passengers died in this dastardly shootdown, which remained a classified operation until 1989. Some UARAF IL-14s were equipped for ELINT duties. In addition to direct deliveries from the Soviet Union, 19 IL-14Ps were purchased from the East German airline Interflug and the East German Air Force in 1964-67 (although one of them crashed en route to Egypt and another was shot down by 'friendly fire' on the delivery flight). The EAF serials were supplemented by civil registrations on some of the IL-14s, and a few were quasi-civil.

For the purpose of providing *ab initio* training for its pilots the EAF ordered huge numbers of the Yakovlev Yak-11 *Moose*. 106 of these primary trainers built under licence in Czechoslovakia as the Let C-11 arrived in 1956-57. Later the Yak-11 was replaced by its more modern tricycle-gear stablemate – the Yakovlev Yak-18A *Max*. By 1970 the C-11s had been withdrawn, sitting in storage at El-Akha, and would have been scrapped, had it not been for the French warbird collector Jean-Baptiste Salis, who bought 41 of them in 1984, bringing them to his base at La Ferté-Alais, along with a few Yak-18As.

Starting in late 1955, at least 18 (possibly 20) Mil' Mi-1 *Hare* light helicopters were delivered to the EAF, serving in the liaison (No.42 Sqn at Dikhelia) and search & rescue (No.12 Sqn) roles. At the same time Egypt received 40 Mil' Mi-4 *Hound* transport helicopters. After the civil war in Yemen in 1962-70 some of the Mi-4s were transferred to North Yemen. Of the 21 that remained by June 1967, all but one were lost in the Six-Day War.

Starting in late June 1967, the Egyptian Air Force took delivery of 68 Mil' Mi-8T *Hip-C* helicopters in transport/assault configuration, Mi-8PS *Hip-C* VIP helicopters and at least one Mi-9 (Mi-8IV) *Hip-G* tactical airborne command post. The helicopters operated from Cairo-West AB and wore a uniform sand camouflage scheme. Some of them were retrofitted with air intake filters supplied by the British company APME (Aircraft Porous Media Equipment); the common boxy filter served both engines. Later, deliveries were curtailed with Egypt's new allegiance to the West; not until post-Soviet times did the type make a comeback in these parts when Kazan' Helicopters began deliveries of 20 Mi-17-1V *Hip-H* transport/assault helicopters. A few of these are operated by the Egyptian police and equipped accordingly, with loud-hailers and a high-powered searchlight attached to the weapons outriggers. In 2009 Egypt placed an additional order for 20 Mi-17V-5 *Hip-H* transport/assault helicopters.

Heavier transport missions were performed by Mil' Mi-6 *Hook* helicopters. Initial deliveries comprised a batch of 12 helicopters, which were based at Bir Thamada and Bir Gifgafa. Ten of them were destroyed on the ground by Israeli air strikes on 5th June 1967. However, the Soviet Union supplied additional Mi-6s as attrition replacements, and a squadron of them was operational in October 1973. 18 Egyptian/UARAF Mi-6s have been identified; one of them was sold to the USA for evaluation.

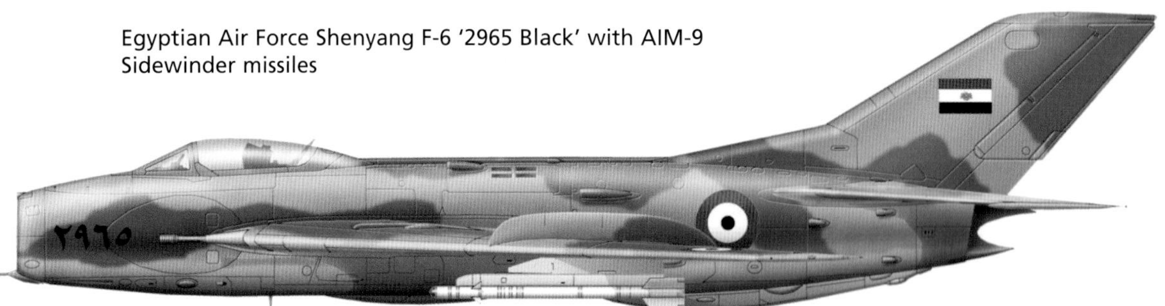

Egyptian Air Force Shenyang F-6 '2965 Black' with AIM-9 Sidewinder missiles

The EAF in action: The Suez Crisis

During the first 20 years of its existence the Egyptian/United Arab Republic Air Force went to war on multiple occasions, and the first of these was as early as 1956, when the Suez Crisis (26th October – 7th November) developed. As mentioned earlier, Great Britain was thoroughly displeased with Gamal Abdel Nasser's independent political course; when Egypt nationalised the Suez Canal on 26th July 1956, this was the last straw. Fearing (with good reason) that the canal would be closed to western ships, Great Britain teamed up with France and with Egypt's arch-enemy, Israel, to take action. According to the plan, Israel would start an armed conflict with Egypt, then Great Britain and France would interfere on the pretext of ensuring the safety of international traffic in the Suez Canal and occupy the area. Stage 1, Operation *Kadesh* ('cleansing' in

A camouflaged Egyptian Air Force Shenyang F-6C in post-UAR markings serialled 2808 Black is just about to touch down. Note the open airbrakes and the odd shape of the gun blast plates.

An unusual line-up of ex-Egyptian Air Force fighters, including MiG-17F '2975 Black', an F-6C and a MiG-21MF, in the USA where they were sold for evaluation, with a McDonnell Douglas F-4 Phantom II and a Grumman F-14 Tomcat to keep them company.

Egyptian F-6C '3872 Black' taxies out for a sortie.

Hebrew), was scheduled for 29th October – 1st November and Stage 2, Operation *Musketeer*, for 1st-7th November. As planned, on 29th October the Israelis attacked, launching an assault by the 202nd Airborne Division that secured a bridgehead near the Mitla Pass. At the time, Israeli incursions into Egyptian airspace were the order of the day, and it took the Egyptians a while to realise that this time it was war.

Only 69 of the EAF's 160 (some sources say 178) combat aircraft were serviceable at the beginning of the conflict. These included two squadrons of MiG-15*bis* (about 30 aircraft, that is, half of those on strength). The MiGs drew first blood at daybreak on 30th October when they intercepted four RAF English Electric Canberra PR.7 reconnaissance aircraft at 10,000-13,000 m (32,810-42,650 ft), damaging one of them (serialled WH801); Flt Lt Sayd

Maintenance in progress on a sister ship serialled 3878 Black.

Two views of an Egyptian Air Force Shenyang FT-6 trainer serialled 3953 Black. The aircraft wears the standard overall white finish.

el-Qadi scored the hit. At 0915 hrs same day four Egyptian MiG-15s followed in short order by four de Havilland Vampire FB.52s strafed and bombed the positions of the Israeli 890th Airborne Regiment on the Mitla Pass, causing heavy casualties; at the same time more MiG-15s attacked Israeli troops at El Thamad, killing 40 paratroopers and destroying six vehicles. An IDF/AF Piper PA-18 Super Cub liaison aircraft serialled 47 White that had landed at the eastern entrance to the Mitla Pass was strafed and sent up in flames. Soon after midday the attack on the Mitla Pass was repeated by two EAF Gloster Meteor F.8 fighter-bombers escorted by six MiGs. This time they were counterattacked by six Israeli Dassault Mystère IVAs

A quartet of Egyptian MiG-21F-13s in UARAF markings, complete with stripes. Unfortunately the serials are too small to be legible. Two of the fighters wear unit badges on the nose.

An air-to-air of a UARAF MiG-21F-13. The serial appears to have been retouched by the military censor.

of the 101st Sqn from Hatzor, the Israelis claiming two MiGs shot down; still, the MiGs succeeded in keeping the Mystères away from the Meteors, which did their job. The Israelis lost one aircraft, Binyamin Peled gaining the distinction of being the first IDF/AF pilot to use the ejection seat. (Some sources claim the Egyptians had no losses over the Mitla Pass on 30th October, but later that day six 101st Sqn Mystères led by Capt. Yaakov Nevo attacked six MiGs taking off from El Qabrit AB. Lt. Yosef Tzuk shot down a MiG-15*bis* flown by Fuad Kamal, but immediately afterwards 12 more MiGs appeared on the scene, and a frightful free-for-all began in which Tzuk's aircraft was seriously damaged by a MiG-15*bis* flown by Capt. Hussein Sidqi.)

The air war peaked on 31st October; dogfights mostly took place over the roads along which Israeli troops advanced and over Egyptian defensive positions. Six Egyptian MiGs attacked and dispersed two Mystères, but not before the latter had shot down three of the four unescorted Vampires strafing Israeli troops on the Mitla Pass. Shortly after noon same day two Mystères flown by Yaakov Nevo and his wingman Yosef Tzuk had a tussle with seven MiG-15s between Bir Gifgafa and Bir Hama, with no losses for either side. Several minutes later they were bounced by two more *Fagot-Bs* near El Arish in the north of the Sinai Peninsula. In the dogfight Nevo succeeded in damaging a MiG-15*bis* flown by Abdel Rahman Muharram but ran out of ammunition before he could finish it off. The

An Egyptian pilot on quick-reaction alert in the cockpit of his MiG-21F-13 '5172 Black'. Note the ground power cable.

UARAF MiG-21F-13s (including 5001 Black) on the flight line – still in natural metal finish.

MiG ditched in the shallows of Lake Bordavil (also rendered as Bardawil), known to the Israelis as Lake Sirbon; it was recovered and studied by the Israelis but not restored to flying condition.

At about 1600 hrs same day six MiGs escorted several Meteors sent to strafe Israeli troops in the Hittan Creek, engaging a pair of Mystères summoned to the rescue but without success. On the way home they spotted two Israeli Dassault Ouragans strafing an Egyptian armoured convoy and attacked them, damaging both aircraft. One Ouragan force-landed in the Sinai Desert while the other made it back to base.

Here, in contrast, is an Egyptian MiG-21F-13 in two-tone camouflage and post-UAR markings.

MiG-21F-13 '5843 Black' of the EAF's 26th Fighter Sqn takes off; note the unit badge.

This view of the same aircraft firing its cannon gives an idea of the camouflage colours.

Egyptian Air Force MiG-21F-13 '5843 Black', 26th Fighter Squadron, Mersa Matruh AB, 1969

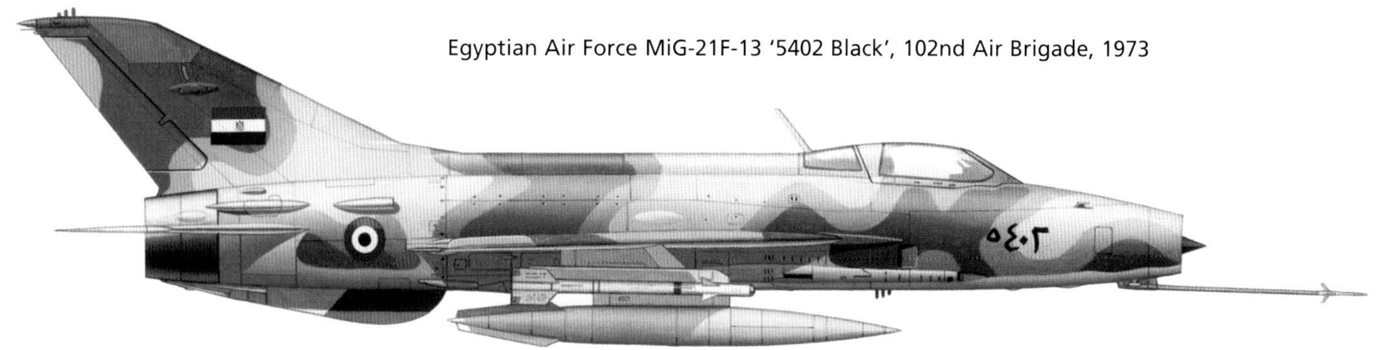

Egyptian Air Force MiG-21F-13 '5402 Black', 102nd Air Brigade, 1973

At the beginning of the conflict the Egyptian Air Force had only twelve MiG-17Fs based at El Qabrit AB, which were being made operational at the time. The first encounter between the *Fresco-C* and its French equivalent, the Dassault Mystère IVA, was the abovementioned skirmish over El Qabrit AB on 30th October when a group of 12 MiGs, including a solitary MiG-17F flown by Flt Lt Mustafa Shalabi el-Hinnawy, jumped the six Mystères attacking the base. Later, in an interview for an American newspaper, President Nasser maintained that three MiG-17s *'attacked a large group of Mystères, shooting down three of them and putting the rest to flight'*! As with any war, 'kills' statistics are notoriously optimistic...

At 1210 hrs on 31st October the two abovementioned 101st Sqn Mystère IVAs piloted by Yaakov Nevo and Yosef Tzuk spotted and attacked three MiG-17Fs flying below them near El Arish. Nevo recalled that two of the Egyptians panicked and fled, leaving their buddy to deal with the Israelis as best he could – one sought cover in the nearest cloud while the other hightailed it towards the Suez Canal. Lt. Tzuk dived straight at the third MiG, but he was not in a position to fire. Ordering him to break off the attack, Nevo applied the airbrakes to stay behind the MiG and pulled his Mystère into a climb in order to take aim. Only then did he realise that he was up against the newer and more dangerous MiG-17F, not a MiG-15*bis*. Anyway, Nevo put his aiming pipper on the target and fired a short burst from the port cannon at about 180 m (590 ft) range; the starboard cannon had jammed. He could see his 30-mm shells hitting the MiG – seemingly with no effect at first; then the enemy fighter abruptly rolled inverted and went down like a brick. At about 3,000 m (10,000 ft) after trying unsuccessfully to level out the Egyptian pilot ejected, but apparently his parachute did not open and he was killed. This was the first-ever MiG-17 to be lost in combat.

At about 1600 hrs on 1st November a pair of Mystère IVAs patrolling over the Mitla Pass attacked a group of EAF Vampires escorted by MiG-17Fs which continued their attacks on Israeli 202nd Airborne Division positions. One Egyptian aircraft was shot down, but it is not known whether it was a Vampire or a MiG.

By the time the Suez Crisis began the Egyptian Air Force had about 50 IL-28 bombers equipping three squadrons, but only one squadron operating 12 aircraft was fully combat-capable. Consequently the IL-28 was used in the conflict on a small scale. For instance, on the night of 31st October one of the *Beagles* bombed an Israeli kibbutz named Gezer in retaliation for the attack on El Qabrit. An IDF/AF Gloster Meteor NF.13 night fighter took off to intercept the intruder but missed the target. Same day a group of IL-28s raided Lod airbase near Tel Aviv but the bombs missed their target, exploding near the Jewish settlement of Ramat-Rachel. One more mission against Israeli ground troops near Be'er-Sheba had to be called off, however, because the MiG-17s did not have enough range to escort the bombers all the way from Cairo-Almaza and back.

Meanwhile, Great Britain and France were growing concerned about the possibility of Israeli troops reaching the Suez Canal and Egypt calling for a ceasefire, which would ren-

The current roundel and fin flash of the Egyptian Air Force.

This EAF MiG-21F-13, 5402 Black, wears a rather different three-tone camouflage scheme.

Another view of 5843 Black. The transparency aft of the cockpit reveals this is a Soviet-built example.

der the planned occupation of the Canal Zone – the whole point of the operation – impossible. Hence on 30th October they issued an ultimatum to the belligerents, demanding that the latter withdraw their troops from the Canal Zone – Egypt to the west and Israel to the east. This would mean an obviously unfair deal for Egypt, as the Israeli troops would make a major advance into Egyptian territory. Of course, Egypt rejected the ultimatum, giving Great Britain and France a 'legitimate' cause for intervention.

The Egyptian top commanders were fully aware that, with not enough qualified crews

Gaudily camouflaged Egyptian MiG-21PFS '8070 Black'. Oddly, the canopy frame and the saddle tank are not painted – as if to tell Israeli fighter pilots where to aim.

Another view of the same aircraft. The rear airbrake is partly open but the forward ones are not.

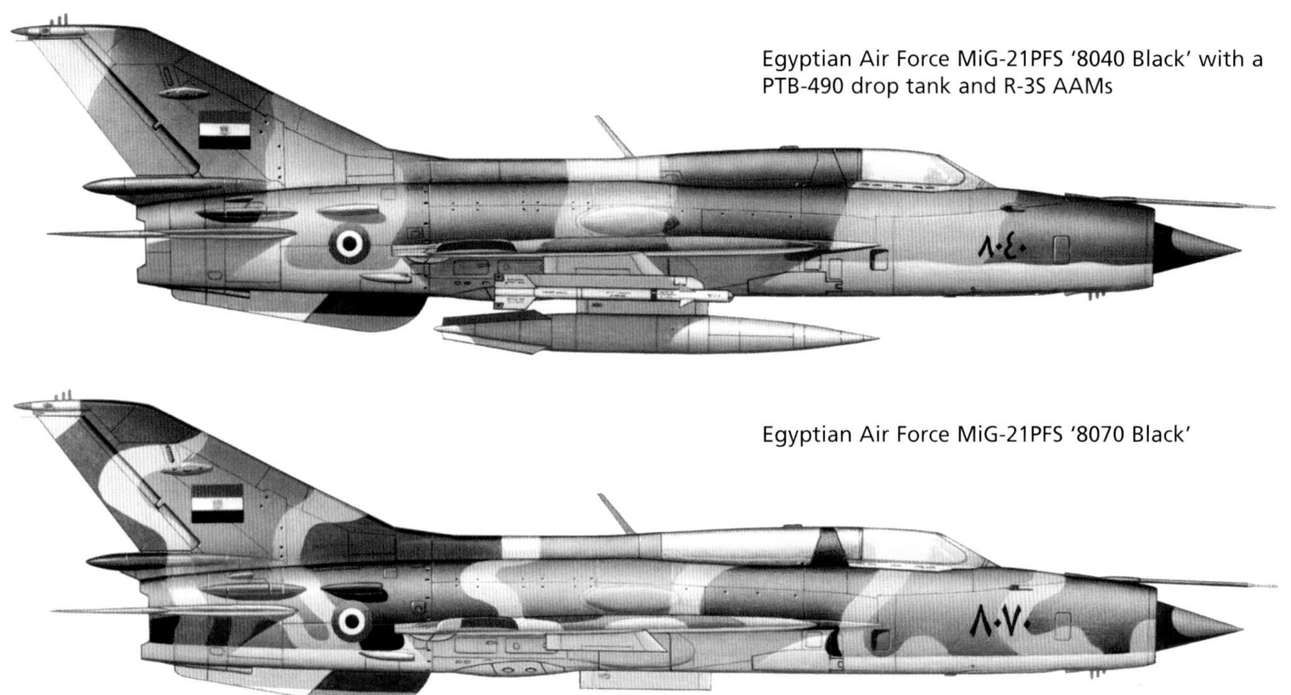

Egyptian Air Force MiG-21PFS '8040 Black' with a PTB-490 drop tank and R-3S AAMs

Egyptian Air Force MiG-21PFS '8070 Black'

to fly them, the EAF aircraft would be sitting ducks and a lucrative target for the Anglo-French strike force. Hence after the above-mentioned ultimatum Nasser wisely ordered the EAF assets dispersed to remote bases or relocated to safe havens in Syria and Saudi Arabia. It was just as well, for on the night of 1st November Great Britain and France launched Operation *Musketeer* as planned. RAF bombers deployed to Luqa, Malta, and Royal Navy strike aircraft from the carriers HMS *Albion*, HMS *Eagle* and HMS *Bulwark* attacked Egyptian airbases in the Suez Canal area. However, post-attack reconnaissance

Below: Egyptian MiG-21s – a 'PFS (left) and a 'PFM (centre) – are readied for a mission at Nile Delta AB in October 1973. The camouflage patterns on the Egyptian MiGs varied widely.

Bottom: An Egyptian MiG-21PFM over the Sinai Desert.

Egyptian Air Force MiG-21RF '8501 Black' in three-tone camouflage carrying a Type R ELINT pod and R-3S AAMs for self-defence.

revealed shockingly low results: the bases were almost empty. Twenty IL-28s had been flown to the Royal Saudi Air Force (RSAF) base at Riyadh by Soviet and Czech pilots; the other 24 or 28 *Beagles* moved to Luxor, Egypt's southernmost airbase, which was supposed to be safe. This assumption out to be wrong; on 4th November RAF Canberras bombed Luxor, forcing the evacuation of eight more IL-28s to Saudi Arabia. That same day the base was attacked by French Air Force Republic F-84F Thunderjet fighter-bombers; the French claimed the destruction of every single aircraft at the base but the EAF acknowledged the loss of only seven bombers. (When the British and French troops left the Suez Canal area in January 1957, not only did these 'expatriates' come back but a major re-equipment programme was launched.) The Royal Navy had more success on 1st November, destroying 27 newly delivered Syrian MiG-15*bis* fighters and UTI-MiG-15 trainers at Abu Sueir, where Syrian

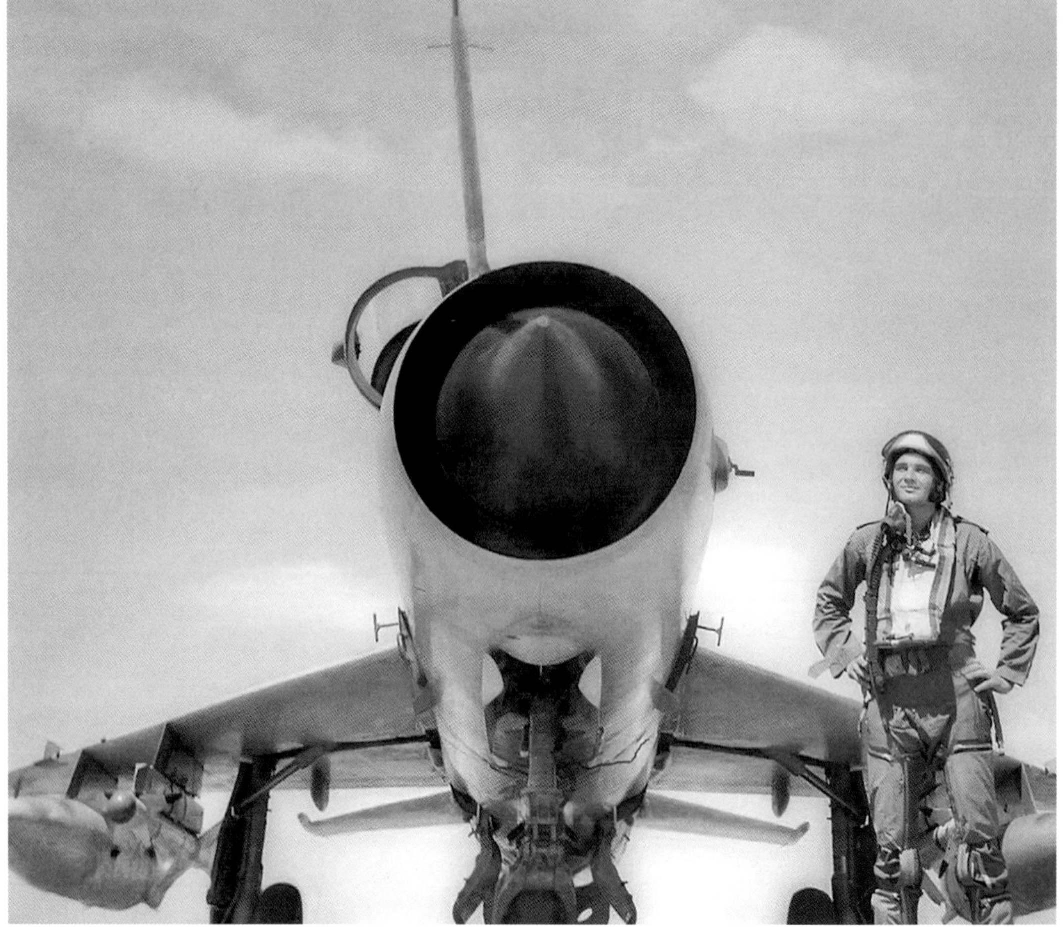
Egyptian Air Force Maj. Ahmed Kamal poses with his MiG-21RF on 15th February 1973. The aircraft carries R-3S AAMs inboard and 490-litre PTB-490 drop tanks outboard.

pilots were taking their training (the Syrian MiGs did not take part in the fighting).

Interestingly, the Egyptians had foreseen the possibility of air strikes, for they went so far as to build large numbers of wooden MiG-15 mock-ups for use as false targets! It is not known whether any such 'wooden wonders' were actually destroyed, but Western sources say this ploy did not work the mock-ups were given away by the lack of wear and tear and by their unrealistic positions too close to the runway.

After that, EAF activity dropped sharply; in the next five days the MiGs succeeded only in damaging two RAF Canberras and bombing British assault troops near Ghamil. They had more success on 6th November, shooting down another Canberra over Syria. When the conflict ended, Egypt had lost four to eight MiG-15s shot down by the Israelis and another eight destroyed on the ground. On the credit side, Egyptian MiGs had shot down two Israeli aircraft, damaging two more and destroying one on the ground. These unimpressive results are accounted for primarily by the Egyptian pilots' poor training.

Sporadic clashes between Egypt and Israel continued after the Suez Crisis. Combat aircraft took part in these operations; for example, UARAF IL-28Rs flew several night reconnaissance missions over the Israeli seaport of Eilat in December 1958.

In 1962 Nasser sent a large military force supported by aircraft (including MiG-15s, MiG-17Fs, MiG-19S, IL-28s and Mi-4s) to North Yemen, extending aid to the Republicans (who had overthrown Imam al-Badr) in the eight-year Yemeni civil war; this was known as 'Mission 9000'. Great Britain, Jordan and Saudi Arabia supported the Royalists, sending their aircraft to Yemen, but the opposing sides rarely met in air-to-air combat. In March 1963 Egyptian MiG-17Fs had a few encounters with RAF Hawker Hunter FGA.9s. Generally, however, the MiGs were tasked with ground attack; a few were shot down by ground fire. Among other things, they hit a number of targets in South Yemen, which was a British protectorate at the time (probably by accident, as the North-South Yemeni border was ill-defined). The IL-28s attacked the Royalists' positions and flew reconnaissance sorties; the Western press reported that they were flown by both Yemeni and Soviet crews. Occasionally the bombers attacked the Saudi towns of Dhahran and Najran located next to the Yemeni border. In June 1966 a solitary UARAF *Beagle* escorted by UARAF MiG-17Fs bombed the Saudi airbase at Khamis Mushayt; same month IL-28Rs flew reconnaissance missions over the Saudi seaport of Qizan. In 1967, however, the Egyptian troops had to leave Yemen because the situation was bad enough back at home.

On 23rd December 1964 there was an unfortunate incident that went down in history as the first-ever 'kill' scored by a MiG-21 and almost caused Egypt and the USA to break off diplomatic relations. A civil-registered Fairchild C-82A-35-FA Packet twin-engine transport (N128E, c/n 10164) owned by the John Mechan Oil Co. and captained by none other than the company's head was en route from Libya to Jordan via Israel and Egypt. Unfortunately Mechan had neglected to obtain the required overflight clearance from the Egyptian authorities, and when the aircraft entered Egyptian airspace at 1005 hrs a pair of UARAF MiG-21F-13s scrambled from Cairo-West AB to intercept the intruder. Here the circumstances conspired against the American crew. Firstly, the Packet shared the high-wing, twin-boom layout of the Nord Noratlas transport which was in service with the IDF/AF since 1956. Secondly, at that time the IDF/AF had stepped up its reconnaissance operations against Egypt; since the C-82A came from the direction of Eilat, it was unsurprisingly misidentified as an Israeli N-2501IS Noratlas. Calling the crew on international frequencies, the fighter pilots demanded that the transport follow them to Cairo International airport. Mechan's radio was out of order, so he could not hear them, but he could see their hand signals and pretended to comply, extending the landing gear and setting course for Cairo. However, on final approach to Cairo International he foolishly decided to make a dash to escape, retracting the gear and heading for Alexandria. After firing warning shots across the C-82A's path the MiGs nailed it with cannon fire; the transport crashed near the village of Halek al-Gamil, killing the crew of three.

Until 1967 Israel continuously provoked its Arab neighbours. For example, on 20th December 1958 two Mystère IVAs piloted by the 101st Sqn's new CO Maj. Aharon Yoelli and the commander of Hatzor AB Mordechai 'Moti' Hod entered Egyptian airspace near El Arish. Circling and gradually retreating towards the border, they lured the two MiG-17Fs sent to intercept the intruders into an ambush set by another pair of Mystères,

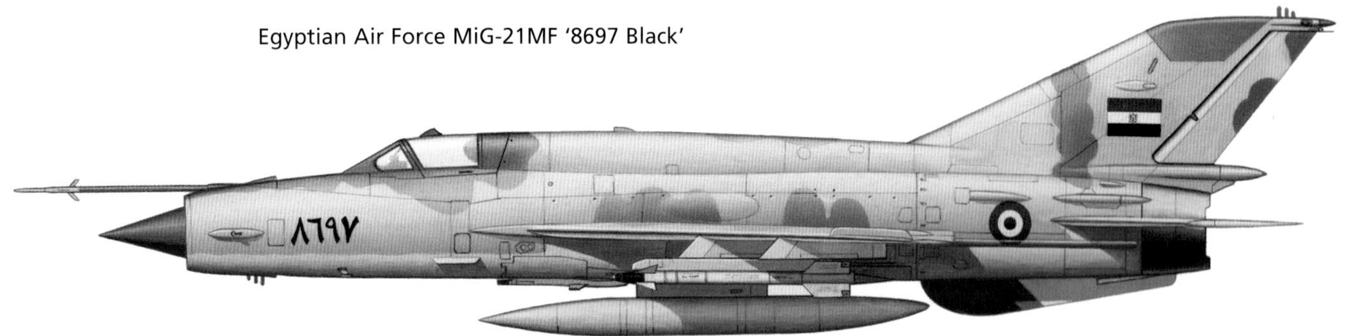

Egyptian Air Force MiG-21MF '8697 Black'

the leader of which, Capt. Yaakov Nevo, added another MiG 'kill' to his score. Still, such provocative tactics did not always work out. On 4th November 1959 a Super Mystère B.2 flown by Maj. David Ivri (who eventually became IDF/AF C-in-C) lost control and crashed during a dogfight with EAF MiG-17s.

In November 1959 a pair of Super Mystère B.2s entered Egyptian airspace over the Gaza Strip and attacked two MiG-17Fs patrolling the area, damaging one of them. Sometimes the Arabs answered in kind; on 25th May 1960 two Egyptian MiG-17Fs penetrated deep into Israeli airspace in the same area. They were intercepted by two IDF/AF fighters piloted by Capt. Agaron and 1st Lt. Yadin; Agaron managed to damage one of the intruders. Five days later a dogfight took place between four MiGs and two Super Mystères;

An Egyptian Air Force MiG-21MF manoeuvres in full afterburner. This was the principal MiG-21 version used by Egypt against the Israelis in the 1970s.

Egyptian Air Force MiG-21MF '8460 Black' carries a red eagle's head as a squadron badge beneath the cockpit.

Very weathered EAF MiG-21RF '8501 Black' shows the ventral camera fairing characterising this version. The paintwork below the cockpit sill has been scuffed away to bare metal by the boarding ladder.

Egyptian Air Force MiG-21RF '8506 Black' carrying three PTB-490 drop tanks

Egyptian Air Force MiG-21MF '6751 Black' with a drop tank from a MiG-23

according to Israeli reports, one of the Egyptian fighters was damaged.

On 28th April 1961 a pair of Super Mystère B.2s again met with a pair of UARAF MiG-17Fs near the Egyptian border. In the ensuing dogfight, pilot error caused one of the MiGs to go into a spin. After unsuccessful attempts at recovery the Egyptian pilot ejected; unfortunately for him, he did so over Israeli territory and was taken prisoner. Another battle occurred on 23rd July 1963 over the Negev Desert in Israel; the IDF/AF pilots claimed two MiGs shot down but, since both aircraft crashed in Egyptian territory, this could not be proved beyond doubt and the 'kills' were not credited.

The first air-to-air engagement by UARAF MiG-19s was on 29th November 1966, when two *Farmer-Cs* flown by Lt. Khalid el-Daly and Lt. Mohammad Abdel Moneim attempted to intercept an Israeli Piper L-4 Cub observation aircraft that had intruded into Egyptian airspace. They were attacked by two Israeli Dassault Mirage IIICJs which destroyed both MiGs, one of them with a Matra R.530F AAM; Moneim was killed but el-Daly, whose aircraft was downed by cannon fire, ejected safely.

The Six-Day War

In 1967, the relations between Israel and its Arab neighbours worsened after Egypt compelled the United Nations Emergency Force to leave the Sinai Peninsula, closed the Straits of Tiran to Israeli ships, rendering the port of Eilat unusable, and proposed united Arab action against Israel. The Israeli response was a preemptive attack against Egypt, Syria and Iraq (in that order) triggering the third Arab-Israeli war, commonly referred to as the Six-Day War (5th-10th June 1967).

Unlike the Arabs, Israel had been planning this war long and carefully – right down to building five mock Egyptian airbases in the Negev Desert where they constantly practiced raids against the real thing. Within a year all IDF/AF combat squadrons had passed a training course at these facilities. Building on the results of this training, the Israeli high command developed a 'first strike' plan known as Operation *Moked*. The combined air forces of the Arab nations outnumbered the IDF/AF almost three times (Egypt, Syria, Jordan, Lebanon and Iraq had some 800 combat aircraft at the start of the war), so it was decided to destroy them on the ground rather than tangle with them in the air; this would ensure air superiority and demoralise the enemy. The 49 to 56 Egyptian, Iraqi and Syrian IL-28s and the 36 Tu-16 bombers (mostly in Egypt, plus six in Iraq) were considered priority targets during the planned air strikes.

The first attack was targeted at 19 airfields deep inside Egypt, but it was decided to spare the runways at the four bases on the Sinai Peninsula so that Israeli aircraft could use

An Egyptian Air Force MiG-21RF serialled 8506 Black in reasonably good condition, with R-3S AAMs on the inboard pylons. Note the open camera port.

One more view of 8506 Black with three PTB-490 drop tanks and two AAMs.

Three-quarters rear view of the same aircraft.

A rather weathered and faded Egyptian Air Force MiG-21MF serialled 8692 Black.

5642 Black, an Egyptian Air Force MiG-21US trainer. Again, note the scuffed paintwork below the front cockpit.

them, once the peninsula had been occupied. Four waves of strike aircraft were to destroy the greater part of the Egyptian Air Force on the ground by 1400 hrs; after that, the attacks would be redirected at airbases in Syria, Jordan and Iraq.

(Note: Of this total of 800 combat aircraft, the EAF had about 100 MiG-21F-13s and MiG-21PFs, 40 MiG-19Ss, 150 MiG-15*bis* and MiG-17F fighters, 35 IL-28s and 30 Tu-16s. The 14 Su-7BMK fighter-bombers and Su-7U trainers delivered in April were not yet operational. The Iraqi Air Force had some 30 (*sic*) first-line aircraft. The MiG-21F-13 made up the backbone of the fighter force, serving alongside the MiG-17F/PF, MiG-19 and Hawker Hunter; there were also a few BAC Strikemaster attack aircraft and 16 IL-28 and Tu-16 bombers. Syria had about 40 MiG-21PFs and 60 MiG-17Fs. The Royal Jordanian Air Force had 24 Hunter F.6s and 16 Vampire FB.9 fighter-bombers, which could be augmented by the few Lebanese military aircraft.)

By the spring of 1967 it became clear that war was imminent; skirmishes on the Israeli-Syrian border in which both sides used heavy weapons and aircraft were becoming increasingly more frequent. On 17th May Egypt started concentrating troops on the Israeli border; four days later Egypt and Israel called a mobilisation of the army reserve, and on 22nd May President Nasser declared the Suez Canal closed for Israeli ships as well.

On the morning of 5th June the Israelis launched a massive assault against Arab airbases. The first wave of 170 strike aircraft launched at 0714-0828 hrs Israeli time (0814-0928 hrs Egyptian time), and the first jets swept in at 0845 hrs ET from the direction of the sea, staying below radar cover, to attack ten airbases. The time was chosen because the Egyptian fighters were not expected to be out on combat air patrol and the base commanders were usually not on site that early, which would prevent the Egyptians form organising an effective defence. The Egyptians were taken completely by surprise. True, expecting an attack, they did patrol the Israeli border with a squadron of MiG-21s and a squadron of MiG-17Fs, but only between 5 AM and 8 AM; no one could even suppose that the Israelis would have the nerve to attack in broad daylight.

Close-up of the nose art carried by MiG-21US '5642 Black'.

The Israelis claimed 196 Egyptian jets destroyed on the ground and a further eight in dogfights, including seven MiG-21s, for the loss of ten aircraft (four or five shot down by MiG-21PFs). In particular, the MiG-21F-13s of Nos. 45 and 47 Sqns were destroyed at Meliz Ab and Fayeed AB respectively. 28 IL-28s were destroyed at Ras-Banas AB and Luxor. One more *Beagle* and its fighter escort were shot down by Mystère IVs while attacking Israeli troops advancing on el-Arish. Eight Tu-16s were destroyed at Cairo-West AB and another 12 at Beni Sueif. An IL-14S landing at Fayeed AB in the midst of the attack was destroyed as well, Egyptian Vice-President Hussein el-Shafei and an Iraqi delegation headed by Prime Minister Yahya el-Tahir barely escaping with their lives. Another IL-14 equipped for ELINT duties was shot down over the Sinai; Egypt lost a total of 19 IL-14s in the war.

Egyptian Air Force MiG-21RF '8506 Black', 21 Reconnaissance Sqn, Salihiya AB, 1969-70

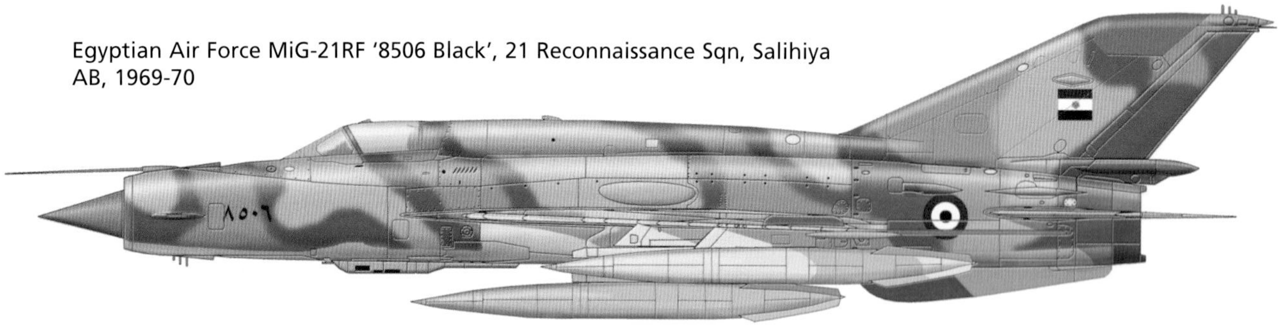

MiG-21MF '8692 Black', Soviet AF Task Force in Egypt, 135th Fighter Regiment, Beni Sueif AB, 1970

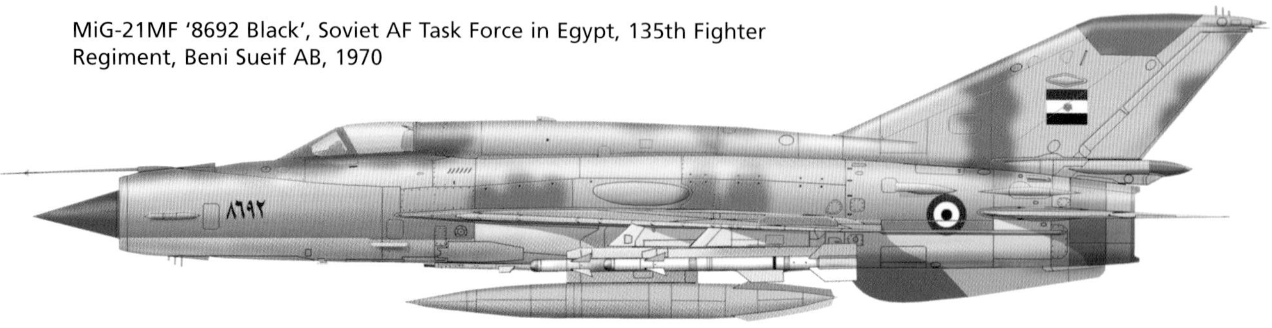

MiG-21R '4799 Black' with Type D camera pod, Soviet AF Task Force in Egypt, Independent Fighter Sqn, Sayyah AB, 1970

The second wave of about 100 IDF/AF aircraft launched at 0933-1155 hrs (1033-1255 hrs) and swept in at 1100 hrs ET, again attacking ten airbases. This time the Israelis claimed 107 aircraft destroyed on the ground and eight in the air (including four MiG-21s) for the loss of just one fighter. The Egyptian losses occurred when a mixed force of 20 MiG-19s and MiG-21s from Hurghada on the Red Sea defended their base.

The third wave of 100 aircraft launched at 1215-1410 hrs (1315-1510 hrs) and attacked ten airbases in Egypt, Syria, Iraq and Jordan, starting at 1350 hrs ET. For the loss of four of their own fighters, the Israelis claimed 61 Syrian, 30 Jordanian, 12 Iraqi and at least two Egyptian aircraft destroyed on the ground and 12 in air-to-air combat (including two Syrian and one Iraqi MiG-21s). The fourth wave launched at 1415-1540 hrs (1515-1640 hrs);

Egyptian Air Force MiG-21UM '5654 Black', 104th Air Brigade, El Mansourah AB, 1970

Egyptian Air Force MiG-21MF '3823 Black', 104th Air Brigade, El Mansourah AB, 1970

the fifth and last wave of over 50 Israeli fighter-bombers attacked five airbases in Egypt and Syria from 1720 hrs.

In particular, four Israeli fighters raided Jebel Libni AB, destroying 13 MiG-17Fs and MiG-19Ss; they also shot down the pair of MiG-17Fs on quick-reaction alert (QRA) duty scrambling to intercept them. It was the same story at El Arish where six *Fresco-Cs* were destroyed on the ground; another MiG-17F was lost in a dogfight with 105th Sqn fighters. On the credit side, several MiG-21s managed to scramble from Hurghada and shot down two Super Mystère B.2s bombing Abu Sueir. Another flight of four Super Mystères led by the now famous Capt. Yaakov Nevo attacked El Qabrit AB. Leaving several MiG-15s and MiG-17Fs and two IL-14T transports burning on the ground, they made for home at low altitude. Two MiG-17Fs scrambled and gave chase; attempting to get away, two of the Israeli fighters lost control and hit the ground.

The Israelis met almost no resistance. Only at Luxor, where the memory of the French air strikes of 1956 was still fresh, the Egyptians met the attackers with a hail of AA fire. One Sud-Ouest SO.4050 Vautour bomber was shot down, but little good did it do because the stricken aircraft fell squarely on the flight line, destroying four MiG-17Fs. In fairness, the Israeli plan did not entirely succeed; a good many Egyptian aircraft, including more than a squadron's worth of MiG-19s, MiG-21s and Su-7s, were well hidden and survived. Also, at least five Egyptian fighter pilots who did manage to scramble shot down at least eight Israeli jets; six more were lost to the Syrian air defences.

At 1020 hrs IT came the first retaliatory action on the part of the Arabs: RJAF Hunters attacked the Israeli section of Jerusalem and Kefar Sirkin AB where four fighters were present. By 1400 hrs, however, all but three of the 24 Jordanian Hunters had been destroyed; this ended the air war on this front. Next, the action shifted north where a lone Egyptian Tu-16 bombed the Israeli coastal town of Netanya and was shot down by the air defences.

By 1500 hrs the IDF/AF aircraft turned their attention to Syrian and Iraqi airbases. In Iraq

An air-to-air of an Egyptian MiG-21MF wearing Dayglo orange quick identification markings on the wings, tail and fuselage spine. The markings are vaguely reminiscent of those worn by Israeli Defence Force/Air Force Dassault Mirage IIICJs.

Seen on the apron of the Odesavia-remservis aircraft repair plant in Odessa, the Ukraine, MiG-21US '5650 White' displays the latest camouflage worn by the type in Egyptian service. Note the Yemeni MiG-21*bis*'s, Ukrainian MiG-23MLDs and Aero L-39Cs, and Angolan MiG-23UB in the background.

Also pictured at Odessa, Egyptian AF MiG-21MF '8360 White' wears the same camouflage scheme. Note how the roundels on the wings straddle the colour division line of the high-visibility markings.

they annihilated nine MiG-21F-13s, five Hunters and two IL-14s. The fighting in Syria was more intense, and the Syrian losses were accordingly higher – no fewer than 32 MiG-21s, 23 MiG-15*bis* and MiG-17Fs, two IL-28s and three Mi-4 helicopters. Some of the MiG-17Fs were downed while strafing Israeli army positions. The Israelis also lost a few aircraft, including two Mystères shot down over Damascus.

After noon the Egyptians managed to get their air defence (AD) radars working so that the ground controlled intercept system could be brought into play. By then the Israeli land offensive had started, and on 6th June the remnants of the EAF were put into action against enemy ground troops. In the afternoon of 6th June Egyptian MiG-17Fs strafed an Israeli armoured convoy advancing towards Ismailiya, 12 km (7.5 miles) from the canal. Super Mystères were summoned to the rescue, and the MiGs downed one of them. On 9th June two groups of Syrian MiGs attacked more tanks and the airfield at Bir Gifgafa on the Golan Heights, again destroying one of the counterattacking Mystères. It was a different story near Ismailiya where Israeli Mirage IIICJs shot down three of the MiG-17Fs still hammering away at the advancing troops.

After that, Egyptian MiGs attacked the enemy with a do-or-die resolve that even the Israelis acknowledged. In the final hours of the battle all available aircraft were flung into the fray to cover the Egyptian troops retreating from the Suez Canal. At the cost of 13 fighters lost the Egyptians managed to check the Israeli onslaught for a few hours. Eventually the Israelis seized all of the Sinai Peninsula and reached the Suez Canal, where the offensive stopped.

Meanwhile, up north Syrian artillery shelled Israeli territory, including IDF/AF bases. Since the Syrian Air Force had taken a less serious battering compared to the EAF, the Syrian MiGs made a few post-attack reconnaissance sorties over Israel. Those were their last sorties in the war; after that, they stayed on the ground until the ceasefire.

The results were devastating for the Arabs: the Israelis claimed 374 aircraft as destroyed (286 in Egypt, 52 in Syria, 27 in Jordan and nine in Iraq); however, Egypt acknowledged the loss of only 176 aircraft. For example, of an estimated 102 to 108 MiG-21s the Egyptians had at the start of this war, only ten (!) were left to fight another day. About 70 of the *Fishbeds* were destroyed on the ground. This was because no lessons had been learned from the Suez Crisis – despite the imminent danger of attack, no attempts had been made to disperse the aircraft at the bases; they were neatly lined up on the flight lines, and the shiny natural metal finish made them a target that could be seen for miles.

Another reason was inappropriate battle tactics. The MiG-21 pilots had only been trained by the Soviets to fly and fight at high altitudes, but the Six-Day War was been fought at low altitudes. Also, while the older MiG-17 had potent gun armament, the MiG-21F-13 had just one 30-mm cannon with only 40 rounds, and the MiG-21PF and early MiG-21PFMs had no cannons at all, relying on the inaccurate and troublesome R-3S AAMs. Fortunately for them, the missiles used by the Israelis at the time were not much better; on the other hand, all IDF/AF fighters were armed with cannons as well.

By the outbreak of the Six-Day War the Egyptian Air Force had taken delivery of its first Su-7BMK fighter-bombers. Like the other EAF aircraft, these were parked in the open and presented an easy target. First, the Israeli SO.4050 Vautour bombers cratered the runway at Fayeed AB and then concentrated on the flight line; most of the *Fitters* were destroyed or damaged (a few were subsequently repaired). The base's air defences was caught by surprise and did not offer any resistance; the Israelis lost only a single Vautour which was hit by splinters from its own bombs.

The participation of the Egyptian Mi-6 in the Six-Day War (marking the start of the type's combat career) turned out to be more than deplorable: by nightfall on 5th June ten of the EAF's 12 helicopters of this type had been destroyed on the ground at Bir Thamada and Bir Gifgafa by Israeli air strikes.

On the morning of 6th June, when hasty repairs had been made to the runway, two pairs of Su-7BMKs took off to raid el-Arish, which had been seized by the Israelis. The actual target was a concentration of Israeli armour and other vehicles on the roads near the base; the HQ of the Israeli 7th Armour Brigade was also there. However, the first pair expended all their 57-mm rockets to little avail (they proved useless against the Centurion tanks) and returned home. The second pair was intercepted by IDF/AF Dassault Mirage IIICJ fighters before it had a chance to begin the attack; Mirage pilot Yitzhak Barzilay claimed both of them shot down. Actually,

2232
51
31
٥٦٥٠

٨٣٦٠

2232
51
31
٨٣٦٠

MiG-21UM '5658 White' in the same colour scheme is seen here at its home base.

Egyptian Air Force MiG-21US '5642 Black' in early three-tone camouflage

Egyptian Air Force MiG-21UM '5658 White' in late colours

only one Su-7 was lost in an off-field crash landing, killing the pilot; the other one was hit but landed safely. The following day, Oded Sagee flying a Mirage shot down a Su-7; Giora Aven (Epstein) downed another on 8th June. During the remainder of the war (6th-10th June) the surviving Egyptian MiG-17Fs, MiG-19Ss, MiG-21s, Su-7s and IL-28s deliv-

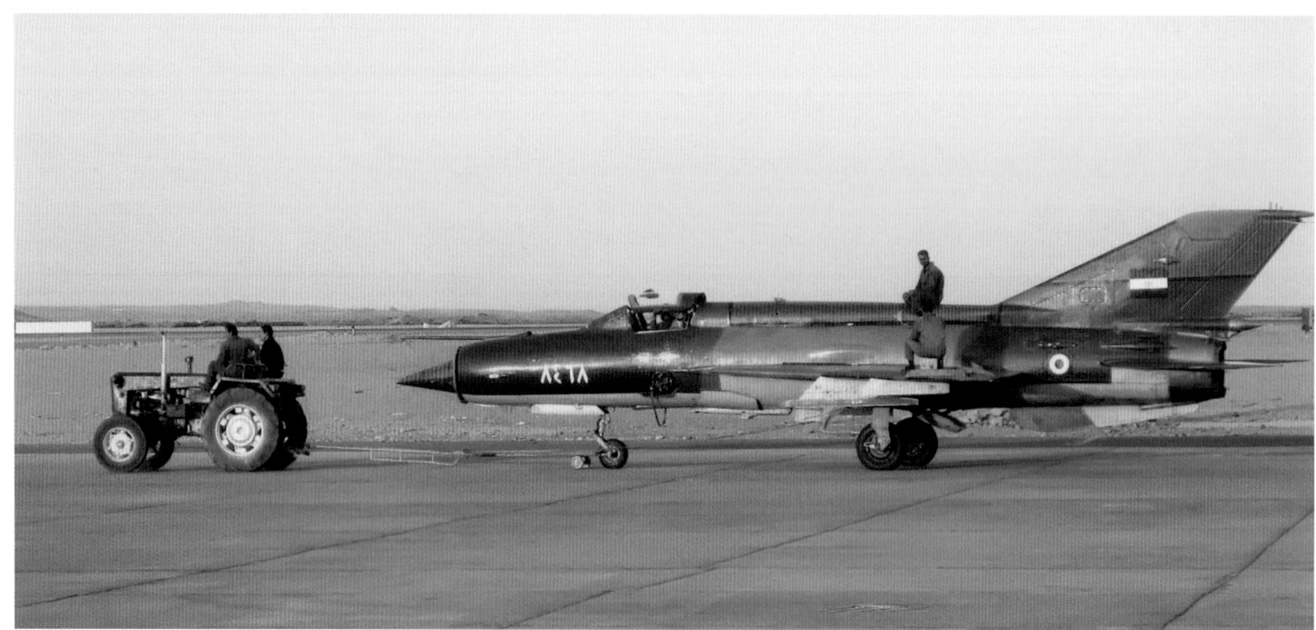

Identically camouflaged MiG-21MF '8468 White' is towed by a tractor at Luxor.

Egyptian Air Force MiG-21MF '8676 White' with orange identification markings and R-13M AAMs

ered strikes against Israeli ground forces, protecting the Egyptian ground troops evacuating the Sinai Peninsula in accordance with a misguided order by a panicky Field Marshal Hakim Amer. Unguided rockets were the main weapons. The UARAF suffered further losses from IDF/AF interceptors in so doing; for example, four MiG-19s, three Su-7s and one

Here, '8468 White' is seen undergoing maintenance in the dispersal area at Luxor. With the engine shut down and no hydraulic pressure, all three airbrakes have 'bled' down.

Another view of the same machine on the taxiway at Luxor, with a power cart parked alongside and hardened aircraft shelters in the background.

Egyptian Air Force Chengdu F-7B '1023 Black' in early camouflage colours

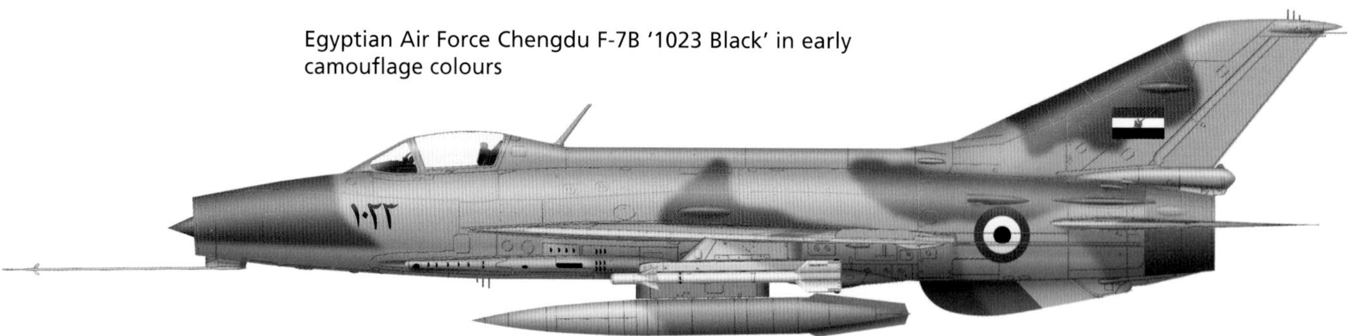

MiG-21 were lost on 6th June, and four more MiG-19s on 7th June. One of the IL-28s was shot down on 8th June.

It was not until 8th June that the Egyptian leaders realised their position was hopeless and agreed to a ceasefire proposed by the UN. A truce was brokered on 11th June 1967 on an *uti possidetis* basis, with Israel retaining most of its territorial gains, namely the Golan Heights and Sinai. By the end of June the UARAF had regained its pre-war strength thanks to massive deliveries of replacement aircraft from the Soviet Union, Algeria and East Germany. It also had a tough new C-in-C, Air Marshal Abu al-Ezz, who resolutely set about rebuilding the air force; this included tougher training based on lessons learned from the July defeat.

'4510 Black' and '4519 Black', a pair of EAF F-7Bs in late grey camouflage with high-viz markings.

However, while holding in principle, the ceasefire was broken by skirmishes every now and then, as the Israelis kept taunting the Egyptians and the latter were eager for revenge. For example, camera-equipped MiG-21F-13s reconnoitred an Israeli camp at el-Qantara on the Sinai on 8th-9th July 1967. The first Egyptian post-war loss occurred on 11th July 1967 Israeli fighters intercepted a strike group over the Suez Canal and a Su-7BMK was downed by a Mirage IIICJ piloted by Yoram Agmon; one more was downed four days later in similar circumstances. On 14th July Egyptian MiG-17Fs intercepted a pair of Mystère IVAs intruding into Egyptian airspace near the Suez canal and shot down one of them; the following day four out of six Mirage IIICJs launching from Refidim AB (formerly Bir Gifgafa) were shot down by MiG-21s in similar circumstances. Offensive activity in the form of commando raids continued for the rest of the year. On 1st July 1968, the Egyptian Air Force was reorganised along Soviet lines and an Air Defence Command was split off, operating two brigades of interceptors plus SAM and radar sites.

Skirmishes between Israel and Egypt continued unabated after the Six-Day War. On 8th February 1969 a flight of Su-7BMKs led by Capt. Ghali made a successful 'hit-and-run' strike against an Israeli stronghold near the Suez Canal, rapidly returning to friendly territory at low level. After this raid, attacks against Israeli ground targets in the Canal Zone continued; AAA positions and SAM sites were

Here, '4510 Black' acts as wingman to '4518 Black'. Note the different serial presentation.

Below: This view of early F-7B '4505 Black' streaming its brake chute shows details of the colour scheme and the old-style one-piece canopy.

Bottom: Two EAF F-7Bs, including '4504 Black', at Luxor.

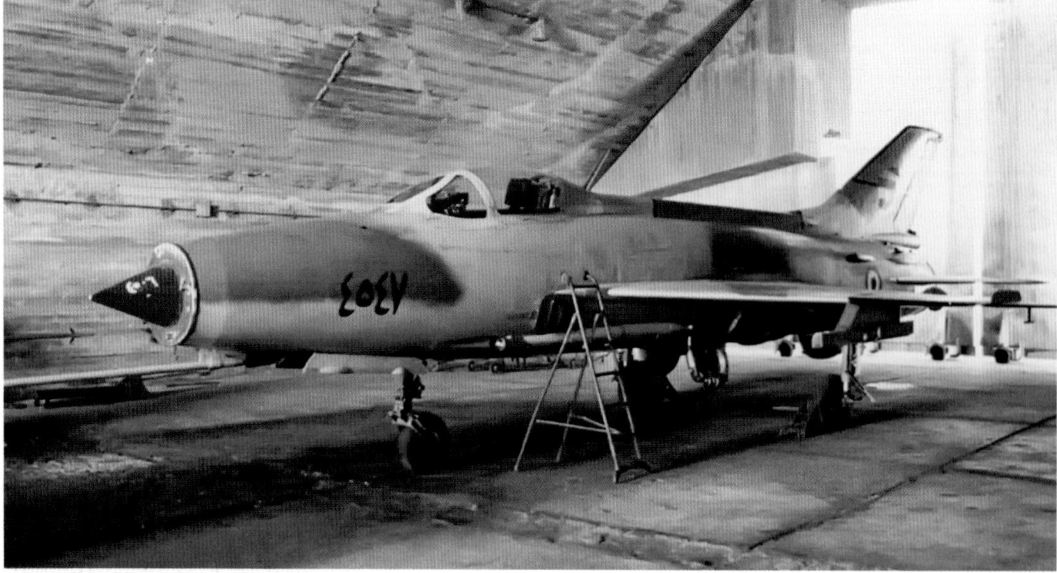

In contrast, '4547 Black' pictured here inside a HAS is a late-production F-7B with a two-piece aft-hinged canopy.

Below: Late F-7B '4533 Black' in echelon starboard formation with a sister ship.

attacked particularly often. On 12th February a pair of Su-7s led by Capt. Darvish attacked AAA positions in the region of Ismailiya, using S-5K unguided rockets and HE bombs. The following day the scenario was repeated by another pair led by the same Capt. Ghali. On the return leg of their flight, both pairs came under fire from SAMs but managed to outmanoeuvre them. On 18th April four Su-7BMKs, each toting four 500-kg (1,102-lb) bombs, and 16 MiG-17F fighter-bombers made strikes against two Raytheon MIM-23 Hawk SAM sites, troops and artillery positions in the Canal Zone. Cover was provided by three flights of MiG-21s, as well as ground ECM stations whose job was to jam Israeli AD radars.

On 2nd April 1969 two Su-7BMKs were shot down over the Sinai Peninsula. The IDF/AF

Egyptian Air Force MiG-23UB '9091 Black' is depicted here at the moment of rotation.

enjoyed air superiority thanks to extensive radar coverage and the capabilities of its fighters. The Sukhoi pilots, on the other hand, had to rely solely on their eyes and the rear warning radar; small wonder they preferred to hotfoot it back to Egyptian airspace if they encountered Israeli jets. One such episode took place in September 1968; a Su-7BMK piloted by Hussain Izzat flying a photo reconnaissance mission over the Sinai successfully dodged all missile and gunfire attacks by a pair of Mirages and got away unscathed.

Between the end of the Six-Day War and the start of the War of Attrition, Israeli Mirage IIICJs shot down six confirmed Egyptian MiG-21s. In return, the EAF MiG-21 pilots claimed two confirmed 'kills' and three probables.

EAF IL-28s participated actively in these clashes, flying reconnaissance missions over Israeli territory; two of them were shot down between 10th July and 1st August 1970. One more example was lost in a 'friendly fire' incident in March 1970 when an IL-28BT target tug towing a sleeve-type target was destroyed by an S-125 Koob (Cube; NATO SA-3 *Gainful*) SAM battery manned by a Soviet crew. Of course a scandal erupted; to make matters worse, one of the IL-28's crewmembers killed in the shootdown was a member of one of the Arab royal families. However, using the SAM system's data recording equipment, the battery commander N. M. Kootyntsev provided proof that the air defence crews had not been informed of the bomber's mission and the IL-28's IFF transponder was out of order. Furthermore, four Israeli McDonnell Douglas F-4E Phantom IIs had crossed the Suez Canal, formating with the *Beagle*, then heading back at ultra-low level. As a result, the missile team misidentified the IL-28 as the leader of an Israeli strike group and opened fire. The Egyptians had to admit the Soviet officer was right.

The crew chief of an Egyptian MiG-23MS reports to the pilot that the aircraft is mission ready.

The 'War of Attrition'

On 21st April 1969 President Nasser announced a 'war of attrition' against Israel. The aim was to sap the enemy's resources and recapture the ground lost in the Six-Day War and, ideally, annihilate Israel utterly ('dump them into the sea', as the Arabs were wont to put it). Egyptian artillery lost no time in launch-

An Egyptian MiG-23MS taxies with the wings in intermediate position. Note the odd placement of the roundel (on the nose rather than on the air intake trunk).

An Egyptian Air Force MiG-23BN fighter-bomber

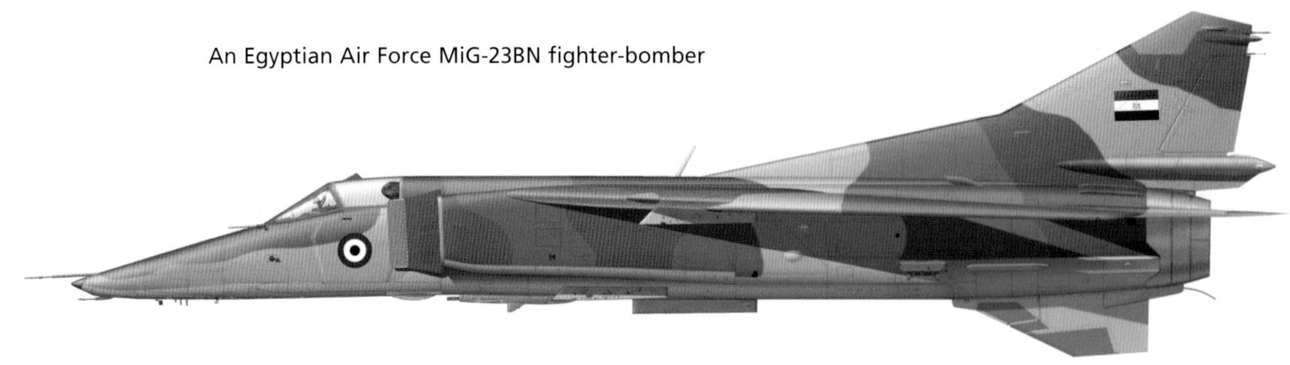

An Egyptian MiG-23BN at rest with a tarpaulin over the cockpit.

A quartet of EAF MiG-23BNs in flight.

ing a massive bombardment of the Bar-Lev Line – an Israeli line of fortifications along the East Bank of the Suez Canal. No full-scale Egyptian attack over the Nile took place; the intention was to make raids into Israeli held territory to inflict casualties even if their own losses were greater. The reasoning was that Israel, with its smaller population, could not tolerate huge losses.

On 19th July 1969 the IDF/AF made the first major raid on Egyptian targets after the Six-Day War, attacking air defence installations west of the Suez Canal. The next day the Egyptians mounted a retaliatory strike, using all the aircraft they could muster. In the course of this operation two more Su-7BMKs were shot down by Mirage IIICJs (Israeli sources say one aircraft was shot down).

EAF fighter-bomber operations at this stage were well planned. Several targets would be attacked simultaneously by one or two flights of Su-7BMKs or MiG-17Fs each, forcing the Israelis to split resources. The aircraft would either fan out to attack the target from different directions or makes consecutive attacks from the same direction. The mission plan defined the time en route, headings and waypoints were calculated literally down to the second. This was the only reliable method in a desert with next to no visible landmarks (except the Suez Canal). The group would approach the target at ultra-low level (30-50 m/100-164 ft) as a stream of flights or pairs, with a horizontal separation of 600-800 m (1,970-2,620 ft) and a lateral interval of 150-200 m (490-660 ft); inside each pair the separation and lateral interval were 200 m and 75 m (250 ft) respectively, allowing the aircraft to manoeuvre. Initially some of the *Fitters* were assigned the top cover role; later this function was assigned to MiG-21s armed with R-3S AAMs.

The attack tactic and number of passes depended on the nature of the target and on the air defence assets in the area. If the Su-7BMK carried two FAB-500M62 low-drag bombs, these were released on the first pass, whereupon the aircraft strafed the target with its cannons. If two 250-kg (551-lb) HE/fragmentation or incendiary bombs and two

A camouflaged (and well-worn) Egyptian Air Force Su-7BMK serialled 7649 Black. The original natural metal finish is showing through the paint in some places.

A ground crew-man loads cannon ammunition into an Egyptian Air Force Su-7BMK serialled 7732 Black.

EAF Su-7BMKs wore differing camouflage schemes, as illustrated by 7025 Black and 7671 Black shown here. Note the four wing pylons.

7912 Black, another EAF Su-7UMK, shows the most common colour scheme of the Egyptian Sukhois.

Top: An Egyptian Su-7BMK undergoes maintenance.

Above: Camouflage colours quickly became weathered and faded under the hot desert sun. This EAF Su-7BMK appears to be serialled 7721 Black.

Below: This view of Su-7BMK '7732 Black' shows how the areas of dark grey colour were edged in green on the tan-coloured background.

UB-16-57 rocket pods were carried, the bombs were dropped first, then the Su-7 would fire 57-mm unguided rockets and use the cannons. Occasionally four 250-kg bombs were carried and released in a single pass in order to shorten the exposure to anti-aircraft fire; larger S-24 unguided rockets were also used. However, such cases were rare – the pilots were reluctant to fly without drop tanks. In the course of combat operations the Egyptians managed to remedy this shortcoming by installing two additional wing pylons with the aid of West German specialists.

On 20th July 1969 a large group of up to 20 Su-7BMKs and MiG-17Fs protected by ten MiG-21 raided several radars sites and AAA positions on the east side of the canal. Caught off guard, the Israelis did not manage to open fire before the Sukhois unloaded their 500-kg bombs, scoring direct hits, and made off with impunity. The *Frescos* were less lucky: two MiG-17Fs crashed when attempting to get away, pursued by IDF/AF fighters after an attack on the radar at Ismailiya. The Israelis, too, lost two Mirages which were downed by the escorting MiG-21s.

Four days later four flights of Su-7BMKs and two flights of MiG-17Fs attacked Israeli positions. The first pair of *Fitters* appeared at 1415 hrs, dropping two 500-kg bombs each on the Israeli air defence command post at Ismailiya without any opposition; the next pair toting four OFAB-250-270 bombs each was greeted with AA machine-gun fire and came back with bullet holes. Then, however, the plan started going off the rails. Two more

flights of bombed-up *Fitters* led by Maj. Munib attacked an AD command post and Hawk SAM sites near the Suez Canal. The first pair messed up the approach and attacked the target almost at right angles to the desired track. When the next flight came in, they were warned that Israeli Mirages were on the way; the lead pair dropped their bombs hastily and

Su-7BMK '7706 Black' in three-tone camouflage; note the serial applied in large digits.

Su-7UMK '7904 Black' in a two-tone camouflage and again with a very bold serial.

Two views of the same Su-7UMK in a different camouflage scheme and with the serial applied in smaller digits.

Egyptian Air Force Su-7BMK '7649 Black'

made off, while the other pair were ordered to turn back. The return flight was more of a disorderly retreat; the Mirages managed to catch up with one of the *Fitters* and shoot it down. The others crossed the Suez Canal wherever they chanced to, not caring about the designated routes agreed with the Egyptian air defences; as a result, one more Su-7 was downed in a 'friendly fire' incident.

A further flight of *Fitters* attacked a nest of AA guns at 1417 hrs. Avoiding ground fire, the group was attacked on the way back by Israeli Mirages that happened to be nearby. Still, the fighter-bombers managed to shake off the pursuit and escape across the canal, aided by the combat air patrol MiG-21s which engaged the attackers.

The losses of the fighter-bombers were too high, and the Egyptians changed their tactics. Now each target was to be attacked in a single pass, minimising the exposure to enemy air defences; also, the attack was always made from the east so that the aircraft exited towards the Suez Canal. The typical ordnance load was four 500-kg bombs or two 500-kg bombs and two drop tanks. The aircraft always carried a full cannon ammunition complement and, even though the risk of interception by IDF/AF fighters on the way back was reduced, the pilots were instructed to save one-third of the ammunition for such a situation.

If the target was heavily defended, the tactic was to attack it simultaneously by two

Top: Another Egyptian *Fitter-A* returns from a mission (note the open brake parachute housing doors).

Above: One more view of Su-7UMK '7904 Black' parked in front of a HAS.

Left: Israeli soldiers pose with the charred wreckage of a downed EAF Su-7BMK. The brake parachute must have opened when the aircraft was hit.

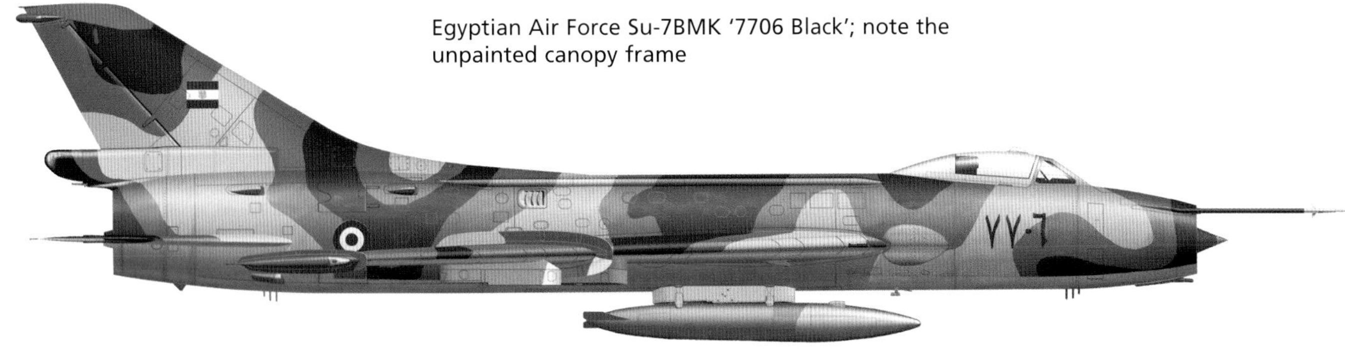

Egyptian Air Force Su-7BMK '7706 Black'; note the unpainted canopy frame

Egyptian Su-7BMK '7025 Black' shares the flight line with MiG-17F fighter-bombers.

A dogfight over the Sinai as a Mirage IIICJ (with quick-identification orange triangle markings on the wings) chases a Su-7BMK. The latter has been hit, flames belching from the damaged afterburner; looks like the fight is over for the Arab pilot.

Left: Not shot down, but nevertheless lost: this Su-7BMK (with UARAF insignia) dismantled for major repairs was captured by Israeli troops at Fayeed AB. The captors have already 'tagged' their booty in Hebrew.

A pair of Egyptian Su-7BMKs (the wingman is serialled 7689 Black) on a mission.

flights in a single pass. Accelerating to 1,100 km/h (683 mph), the fighter-bombers climbed to an altitude of 1,500 m (4,920 ft), did a wingover and dived at the target from different directions at an angle of 20-30°. After the attack they escaped across the canal at no more than 30 m (100 ft).

Target approach was usually made at a speed of 850 km/h (528 mph) and an altitude of 30-50 m (100-160 ft), to avoid detection by radar; in the immediate vicinity of the target the aircraft engaged their afterburners, accelerating to 1,100 km/h (683 mph) and climbing abruptly to 1,000-1,200 m (3,280-3,940 ft). Bomb or rocket attacks were then delivered in a shallow dive while strafing the target with the two 30-mm cannons for good measure.

On 11th September 1969 the EAF mounted a massive raid involving 100 aircraft which attacked in three waves at three-hour intervals. The AD radar at Port Said was the first to be hit by a flight of Su-7BMKs led by Maj. Makarim at 1000 hrs. Two pairs attacking from different directions unleashed volleys of S-5K FFARs; overwhelmed by the sudden attack, the Israelis had no time to put up any

Two Egyptian Su-7BMKs, 7271 Black and 7166 Black, in echelon port formation. Note the variance in camouflage colours.

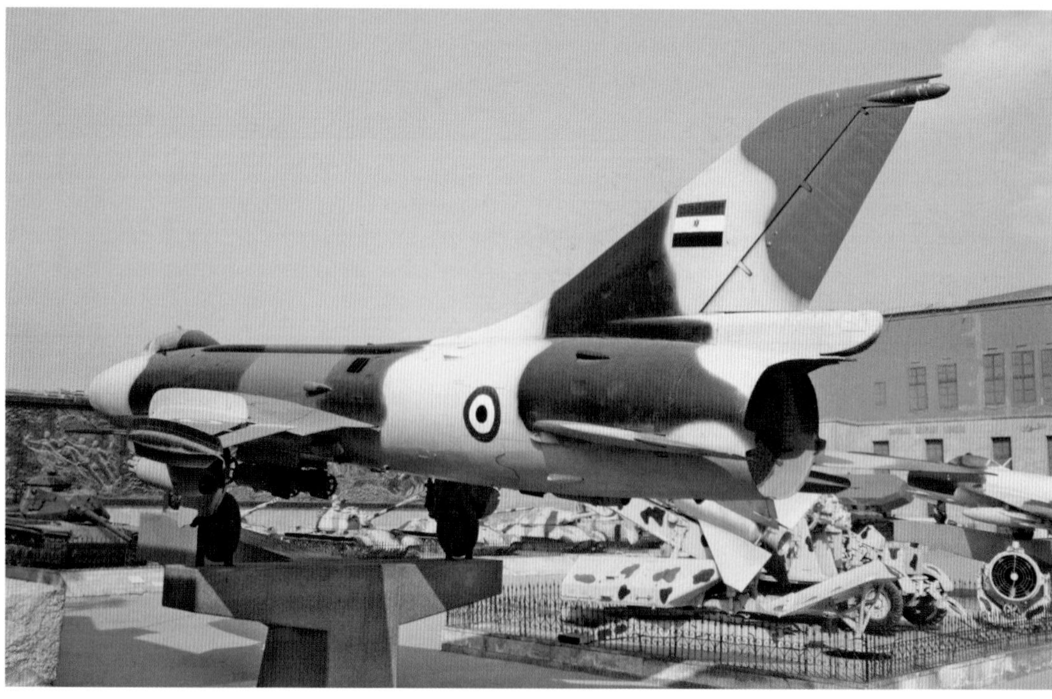

Now repainted and devoid of a serial, this Su-7BMK (originally 7320 Black) is on display at the Egyptian Army Museum in Cairo's Saladin Citadel.

Egyptian Air Force Su-17K '1256 Black'

1256 Black, one of the 16 Su-17Ks delivered to Egypt, survived the wars and is now preserved in this overall silver finish.

Egyptian Air Force Su-20 '7789 Black' in two-tone camouflage. The 'Danger, jet intake' stencils are in English.

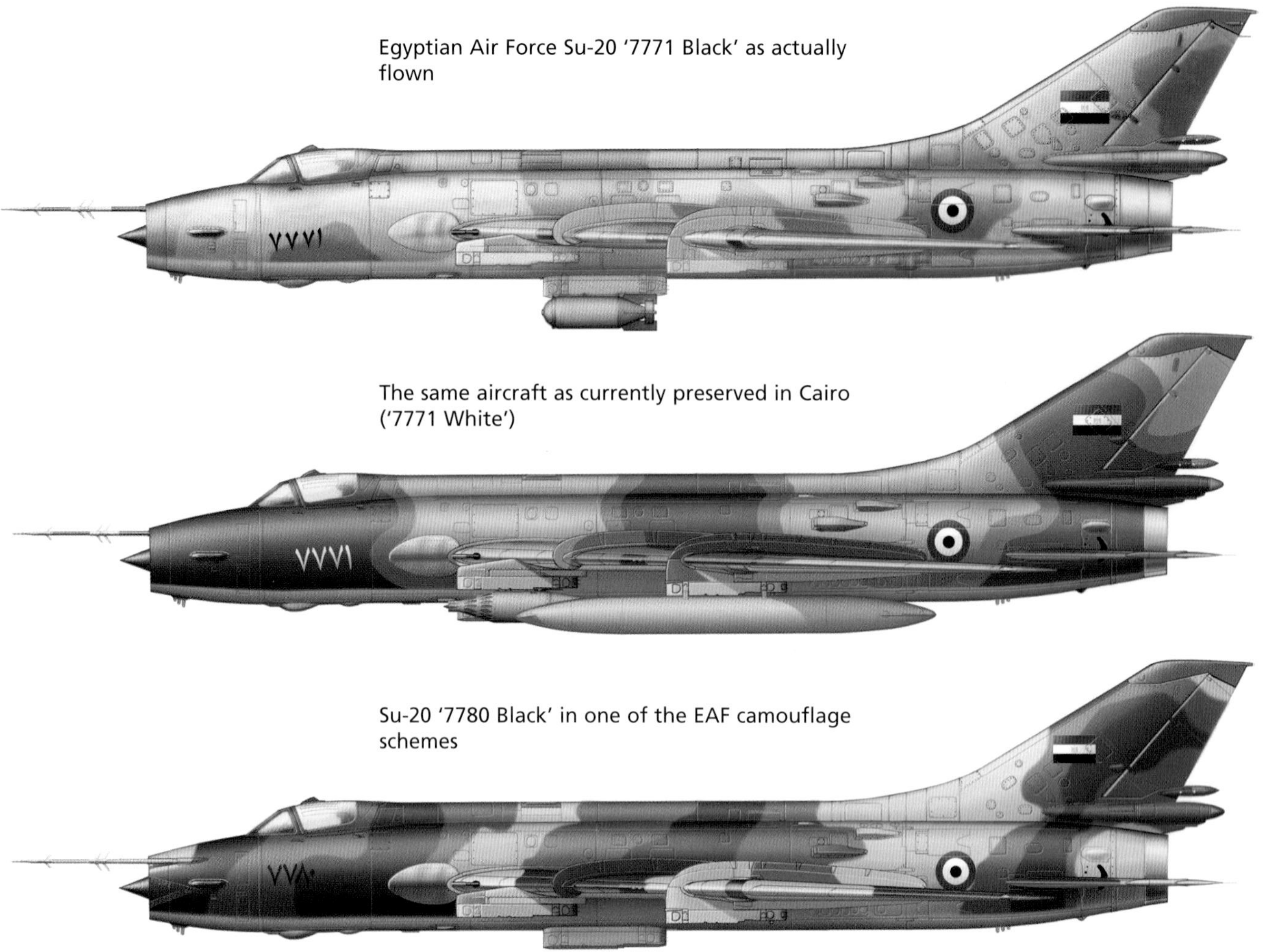

Egyptian Air Force Su-20 '7771 Black' as actually flown

The same aircraft as currently preserved in Cairo ('7771 White')

Su-20 '7780 Black' in one of the EAF camouflage schemes

resistance. At 1300 hrs a second flight of *Fitters* blasted another AD radar near Suez (El Suweis) at the southern end of the canal with 250-kg bombs; this time two IDF/AF Mirage IIICJs were on the scene and the wingman's Su-7 in the tail-end pair was destroyed by an AAM. Dumping the drop tanks, his flight leader broke into the threat and managed to dodge the missile that was fired at him; nevertheless, a well-aimed burst of cannon fire from one of the Mirages found its mark, and the Egyptian pilot had to eject immediately after crossing the canal.

Meanwhile, the lead pair of Sukhois from the same flight was making for home at top speed, following the valleys and creeks to escape interception. Knowing that the Egyptians' route would inevitably take them to the canal, the Israeli pilots decided to ambush them there. Soon they saw the westbound Su-7s on their radars and gave chase, trying to cut them off before they reached home ground. However, just when the target was within range, the Mirages found themselves counterattacked by the flight of MiG-21s which had been standing by to provide top cover. The MiGs crossed the canal, and a dogfight ensued in which the lead Mirage was destroyed by a direct hit of an R-3S missile; the pilot ejected and became a prisoner of war.

In the meantime, the third wave of the attack was coming in; at 1600 hrs two flights of Su-7s attacked one more AD radar, Israeli fortifications and a tank group near Musala. The aircraft were armed with 250-kg bombs and FFARs, and did some strafing as well. By then, however, the Israelis had regained their wits and met the attackers with a barrage of Hawk SAMs which destroyed one of the Su-7s, killing the pilot. The Egyptians had miscalculated, not counting on SAMs being deployed there.

Speaking of which, the Egyptians' first experience with the Raytheon Hawk led the Moscow-based Soviet Air Force Engineering Academy named after Nikolay Ye. Zhukovskiy to develop anti-Hawk tactics. The Hawk had a large funnel-shaped blind spot directly above

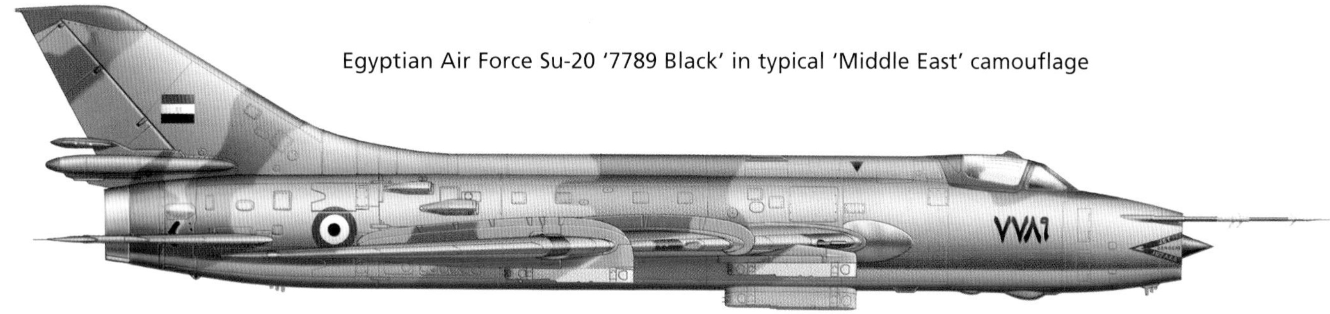
Egyptian Air Force Su-20 '7789 Black' in typical 'Middle East' camouflage

the rotating launcher where target tracking was impossible. Additionally, certain evasive manoeuvres of the target would cause the missile to lose lock-on; it took 25-50 seconds to re-lock on, which was sufficient for the aircraft to attack the SAM site. These tactics were soon used by the Egyptian pilots.

On 6th October 1969 the experienced pilot Lt.-Col. Abu Agur led two flights of Su-7BMKs on a SAM hunt mission. Either the intelligence had been incorrect or the SAM battalions had swiftly redeployed; anyway, when the formation reached the designated area it found nothing and had to use its bombs and rockets for destroying an alternate target. On 31st October and 10th November the Su-7s were fired upon by Hawk missiles, which missed their target. However, the EAF preferred to use the vintage MiG-17F for such missions; the more nimble *Fresco* could stay inside the blind spot without any trouble.

Hostilities continued unabated in 1970, with groups of four Su-7BMKs raiding Israeli positions on 6th, 18th, 24th and 28th January 1970. On 7th January the EAF lost another *Fitter-A* which was downed by small-calibre AAA. This was the only Su-7 loss of the kind, even though the Israelis made wide use of 20-mm and 40-mm AAA.

Occasionally the Su-7BMKs and MiG-17Fs operated as a mixed group. This was the case on 9th February 1970 when four MiGs and four Sukhois attacked targets near the Suez Canal, with four MiG-21s flying top cover.

In January 1970 the more experienced Egyptian pilots started flying 'free chase' missions, attacking targets of opportunity (enemy communications) near Ismailiya. Apart from the lack of information on predesignated targets, the task was all the more complicated

Egyptian Su-20s fly in V formation during a military parade.

Su-20 '7771 White' is part of the Sinai War Memorial in Cairo.

An Egyptian Air Force IL-28 in natural metal finish and pre-UAR markings at Cairo-Almaza AB. The gunner's entry hatch is open and the navigator's hatch cover appears to be missing.

because of the sandy mist found at low altitudes, which forced the pilots to make periodic hops to higher altitude in order to look around – and hence run the risk of revealing themselves. Such missions were always flown in pairs, the aircraft carrying FFARs which could be used against soft-skinned vehicles and armour alike. Flying at 20-30 m (65-100 ft), the pair moved in a scissors pattern – the wingman periodically changed formation from echelon port to echelon starboard and back to get a better view of the surroundings. On detecting a target the fighter-bombers would 'hop' to higher altitude and attack the target in a dive.

The second such mission on 8th January resulted in the destruction of a SAM site 12 km (7.45 miles) beyond the Suez Canal. The Israelis fired two SAMs at the attacking pair, which missed. On 10th January 1970 one more Hawk SAM site in the Sinai Desert was destroyed. The Israelis refuted this and claimed, in turn, the destruction of two Su-7s (some sources give the date as 9th January).

On 24th January four Su-7BMKs led by Capt. Sofiyi crossed the canal and split into two pairs to conduct 'free chase'. Pretty soon the first pair found an Israeli armoured convoy, dropped their bombs accurately and made off. The other pair, however, stuck around a little longer and suddenly found itself in the kill zone of a Hawk SAM site. Realising the danger, the pilots started making evasive manoeuvres but the SAM crew nevertheless launched a missile which scored a hit on the wingman's aircraft. With its tail unit shot to shreds and the crippled engine smoking and vibrating violently, the barely controllable aircraft made it across the canal; then, assured that he was out of Indian ground, the pilot chose to eject.

The Egyptians also used the Su-7BMK for tactical reconnaissance. For this purpose several aircraft were fitted with British-made Vinten cameras. Within one month in the win-

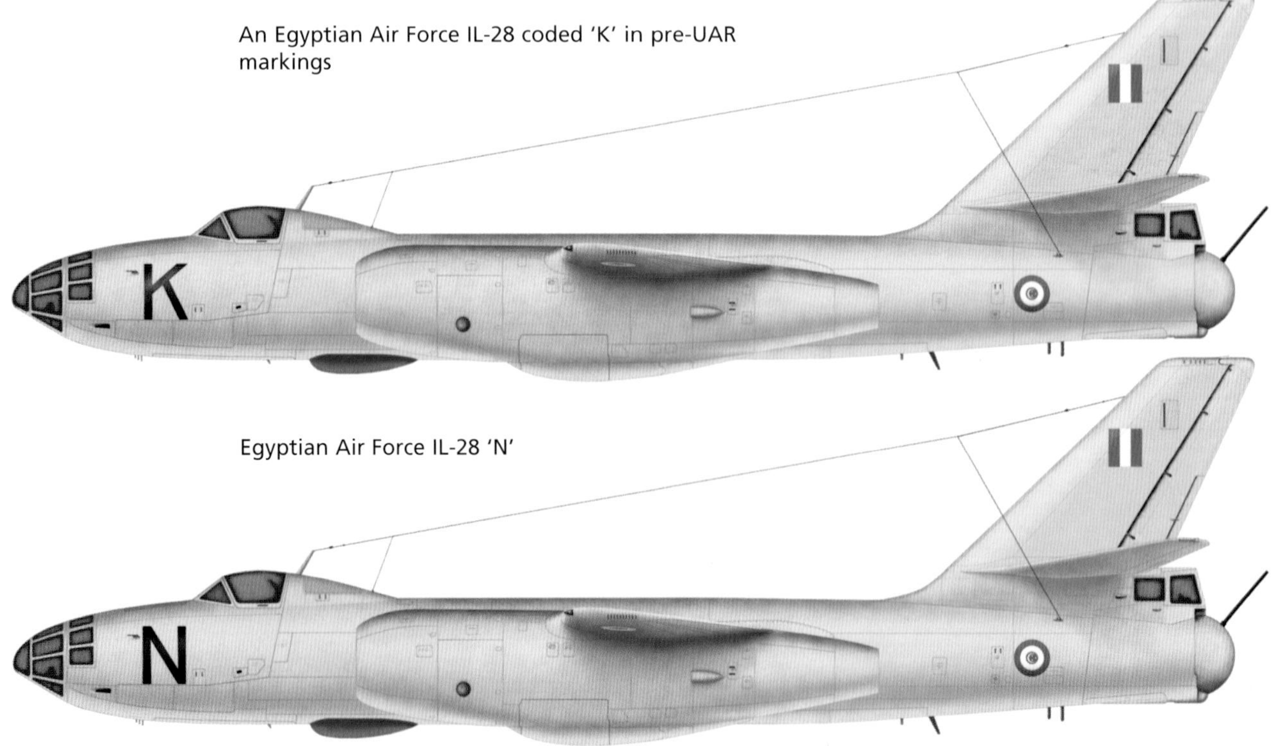

An Egyptian Air Force IL-28 coded 'K' in pre-UAR markings

Egyptian Air Force IL-28 'N'

Another view of the same IL-28 as part of an aircraft display at Almaza staged in 1957 to mark the EAF's 25th birthday. Also featured are two MiG-15s, two Mi-1 helicopters and a Zlin Z-26 Trener trainer.

Egyptian IL-28 crews lined up for a parade, with their mounts in the background. The letter codes include P, U, L, R, N, S, J and A.

ter of 1968, they flew 54 reconnaissance sorties with impunity. On 11th September 1970, however, a Su-7BMK on a reconnaissance sortie was shot down by ground fire over Sinai.

By 1st February 1970 the EAF had lost 14 fighter-bombers, including eleven Su-7BMKs. Of these, five were shot down by Mirage IIICJs on the way back to base; three were downed by Hawk SAMs (interestingly, not a single MiG-17F was lost in this way!) and one was shot down by AAA. Additionally, one *Fitter-A* crashed fatally due to pilot error and another was shot down by Egyptian air defences as mentioned earlier. This was not the only red-on-red incident in the war: two more Su-7s were damaged by 9K32 *Strela* (Arrow; SA-7 *Grail*) shoulder-launched SAMs fired by the Egyptians. The latter category was caused by poor co-ordination and notification in the Egyptian Army.

Analysis shows that that in most cases the aircraft were lost while making repeat attacks (when enemy fighters showed up) or on the return leg of the flight. This was due to loss of vigilance (when pilots felt confident that they were out of danger, realising too late that they were under attack) and piloting errors at low level as a result of inept manoeuvring in close formation.

In the months that followed, the Su-7s became increasingly active; between 25th April and 5th June 1970 they made 11 raids

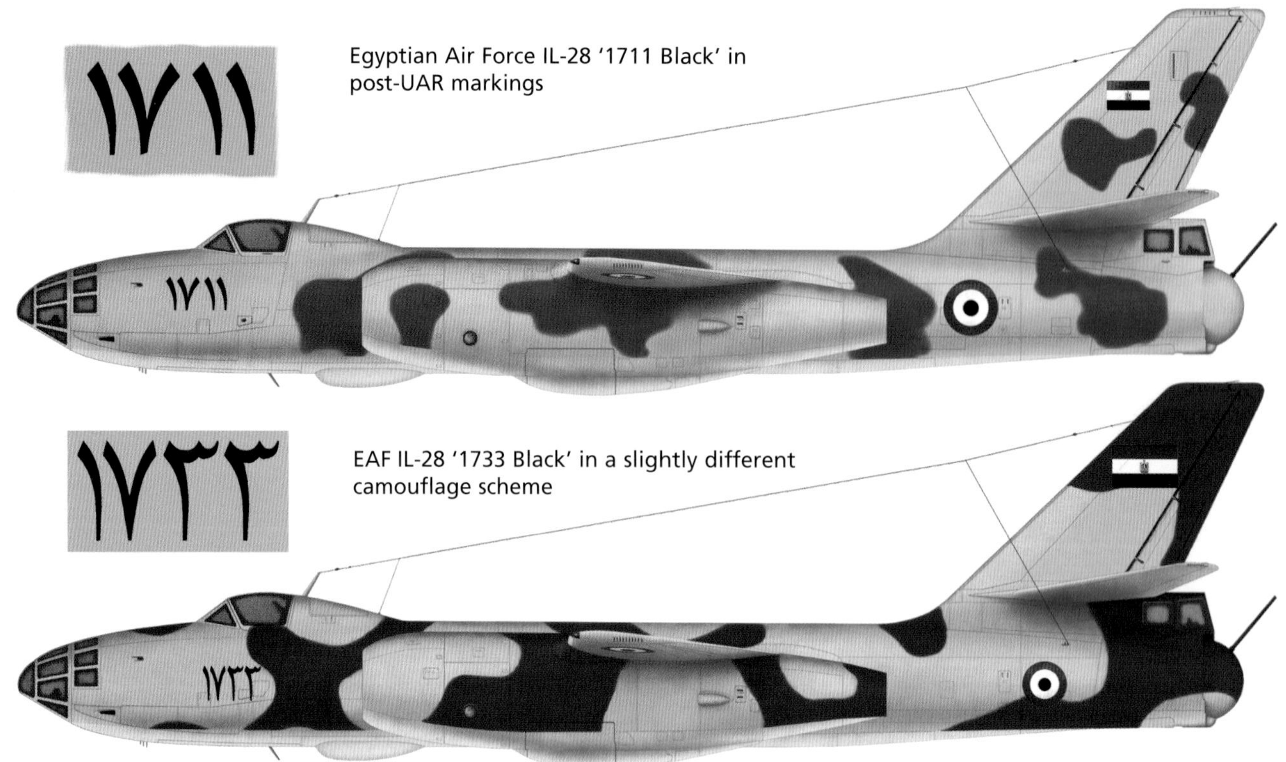

Egyptian Air Force IL-28 '1711 Black' in post-UAR markings

EAF IL-28 '1733 Black' in a slightly different camouflage scheme

on Israeli positions. By August 1970 two more Su-7BMKs had been lost in action; thus, total EAF *Fitter-A* losses in the 'War of Attrition' stand at 13.

The reasons of the fairly high losses included the Egyptians' tactical inflexibility and their inability to maintain security when it came to planning operations. This, together with the Israelis' very efficient intelligence service, meant that the adversary was well informed about the Egyptians' plans, and when the fighter-bombers approached the target the air defences would be ready to 'greet' them.

IL-28 '1711 Black' about to depart on a routine sortie.

Pristine-looking Egyptian IL-28 '1733 Black' sits in a concrete-lined revetment.

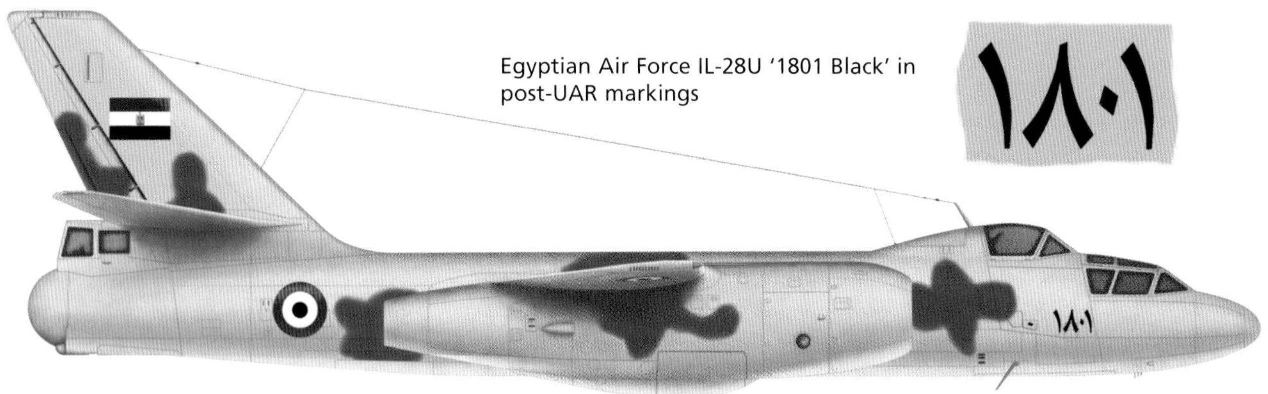

Egyptian Air Force IL-28U '1801 Black' in post-UAR markings

The successes of the Israelis forced President Nasser to extend a plea to the Soviet government that Soviet pilots and SAM crews be dispatched to Egypt in addition to the advisors and supplies of materiel. His wish was granted. The 135th IAP (Fighter Regiment) of the Soviet Air Defence Force, along with an independent fighter squadron (both flying MiG-21MFs painted in Egyptian insignia for appearance's sake), arrived in Egypt in June 1970 to protect Egyptian cities against Israeli

This Egyptian IL-28 wears a different camouflage of sand, green and brown. The serial appears to be 1771 Black.

The sand base colour prevails on this IL-28U trainer serialled 1801 Black.

This EAF IL-28 (1774 Black) has a camouflage scheme of sand and two shades of green.

Appearances are deceptive! Though wearing Egyptian (UARAF) markings, 4378 Black is a Soviet Navy Tu-16R *Badger-E* reconnaissance aircraft operated by the 90th ODRAE ON (Independent Long-Range Special Mission Recce Squadron) at Cairo-West.

4380 Black, another quasi-Egyptian (90th ODRAE ON) Tu-16R – this time a *Badger-F*, as indicated by the underwing pods of the SRS-4 ELINT system. Note the open port of the oblique camera.

Quasi-Egyptian Tu-16R *Badger-E* '4376 Black' is shadowed by a US Navy F-4J Phantom over the Mediterranean.

air attacks, acting in concert with three brigades of S-125 SAMs and radar sites. All of these were manned by Soviet personnel, of whom there were now about 12,000 in Egypt; this mission was known in the USSR as Operation *Kav**kaz*** (Caucasus). The Soviet pilots were carefully selected for the mission – they needed to have at least Pilot 2nd Class airmanship rating and several thousand hours' total flying time. Before departing on their tour of duty they took special training at a facility in Central Asia where the climatic conditions were as close to Egypt as you could get in the USSR. At first the instructors training the selected pilots were wont to capitalise on the strengths of the MiG-21MF and the perceived weaknesses of the Israeli jets, but the trainees did not buy this approach because enough

4381 Black, another 90th ODRAE ON *Badger-E*.

Soviet airmen seconded to the 90th ODRAE pose with Tu-16R *Badger-E* '438... Black' at Cairo-West.

Tu-16R *Badger-E* '4392 Black' seen from a shadowing US Navy F-4J.

Tu-16R *Badger-E* '4376 Black', Soviet Navy/90th ODRAE ON, Cairo-West AB, 1970

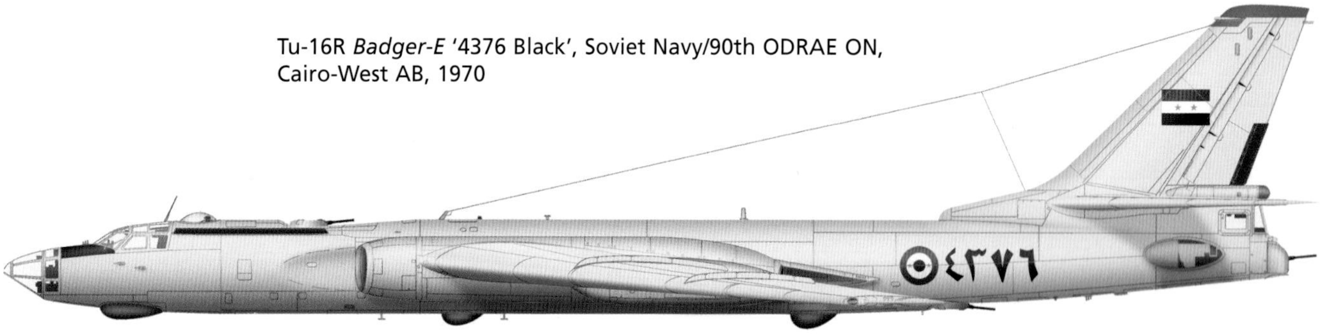

Tu-16R *Badger-F* '4380 Black', Soviet Navy/90th ODRAE ON, Cairo-West AB, 1970

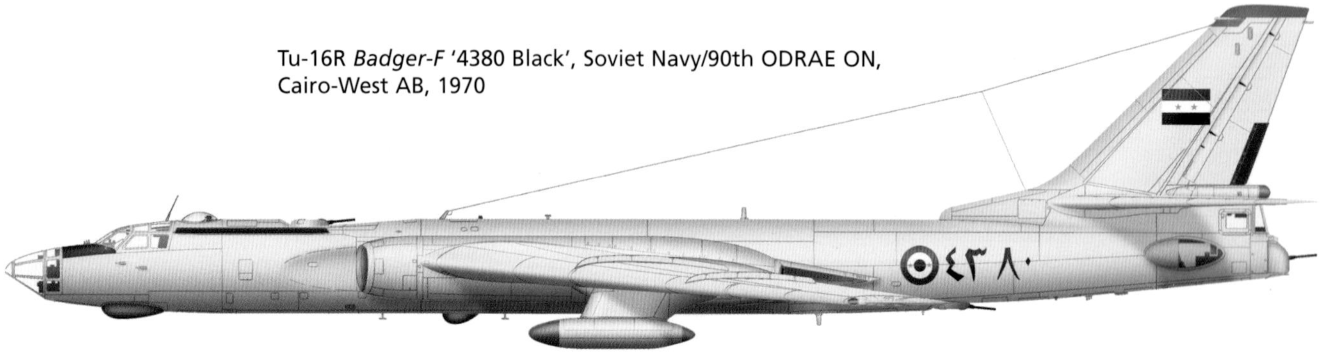

Tu-16R *Badger-E* '4393 Black', Soviet Navy/90th ODRAE ON, Cairo-West AB, 1970

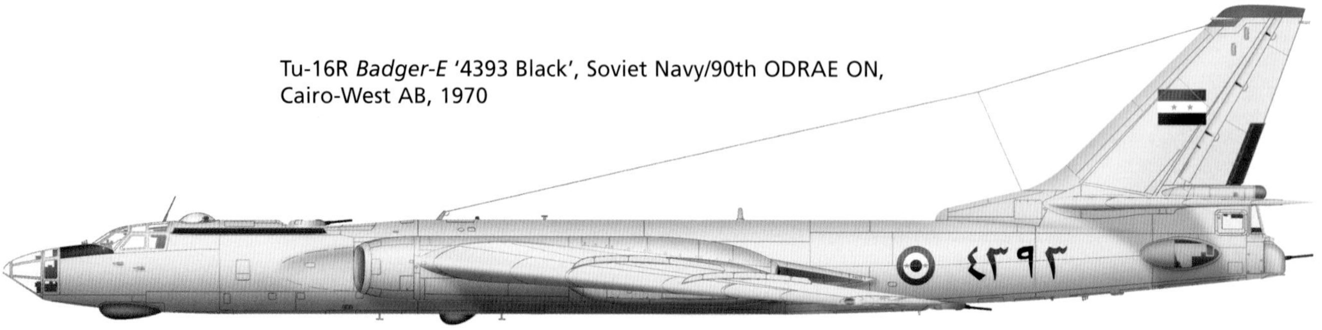

objective information was available to tell them that the adversary was not to be treated lightly.

On arrival the Soviet pilots familiarised themselves with the area they were to defend. The 135th IAP commanded by Col. Konstantin Korotyuk covered the Egyptian territory south of the Helwan-Suez line; the independent fighter squadron commanded by Col. Yuriy Nastenko covered the Egyptian part of the Mediterranean and the area between Cairo, Alexandria and the Suez Canal, while Cairo itself was defended by Soviet and Egyptian SAM crews. The Soviet fighter units were stationed within 200 km (124 miles) of the Suez Canal, but the Soviet pilots were expressly forbidden to cross the canal.

The Israeli intelligence service immediately became aware of the newly arrived reinforcements. Before long, the fact that Soviet fighter

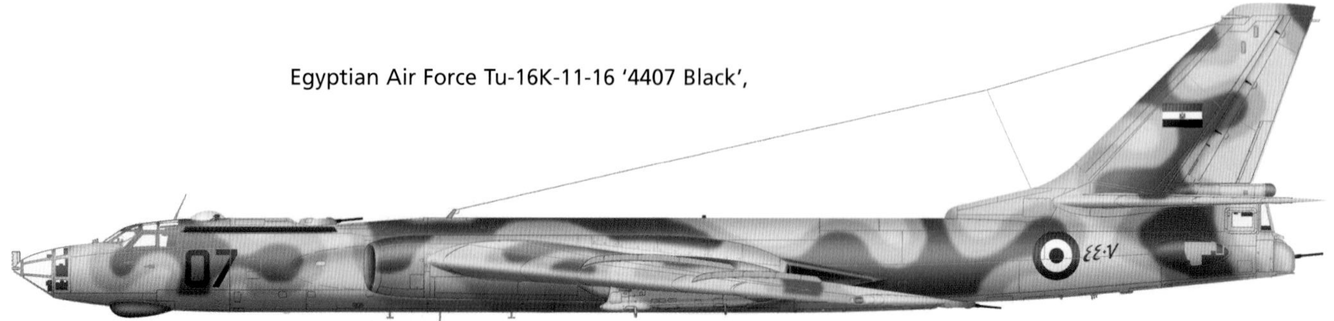

Egyptian Air Force Tu-16K-11-16 '4407 Black',

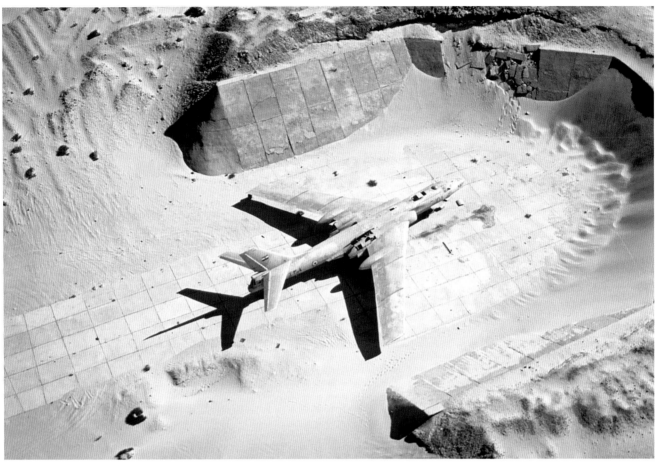

units were deployed in Egypt had made the headlines all over the world. The Soviet Union, however, denied this fact, stating adamantly that it had sent only advisors to Egypt.

This one's Egyptian all right. Camouflaged Tu-16 '4301 Black' sits unserviceable in a revetment at Cairo-West partly filled with sand.

EAF Tu-16K-11-16s taxiout. Note the wrecked example on the left.

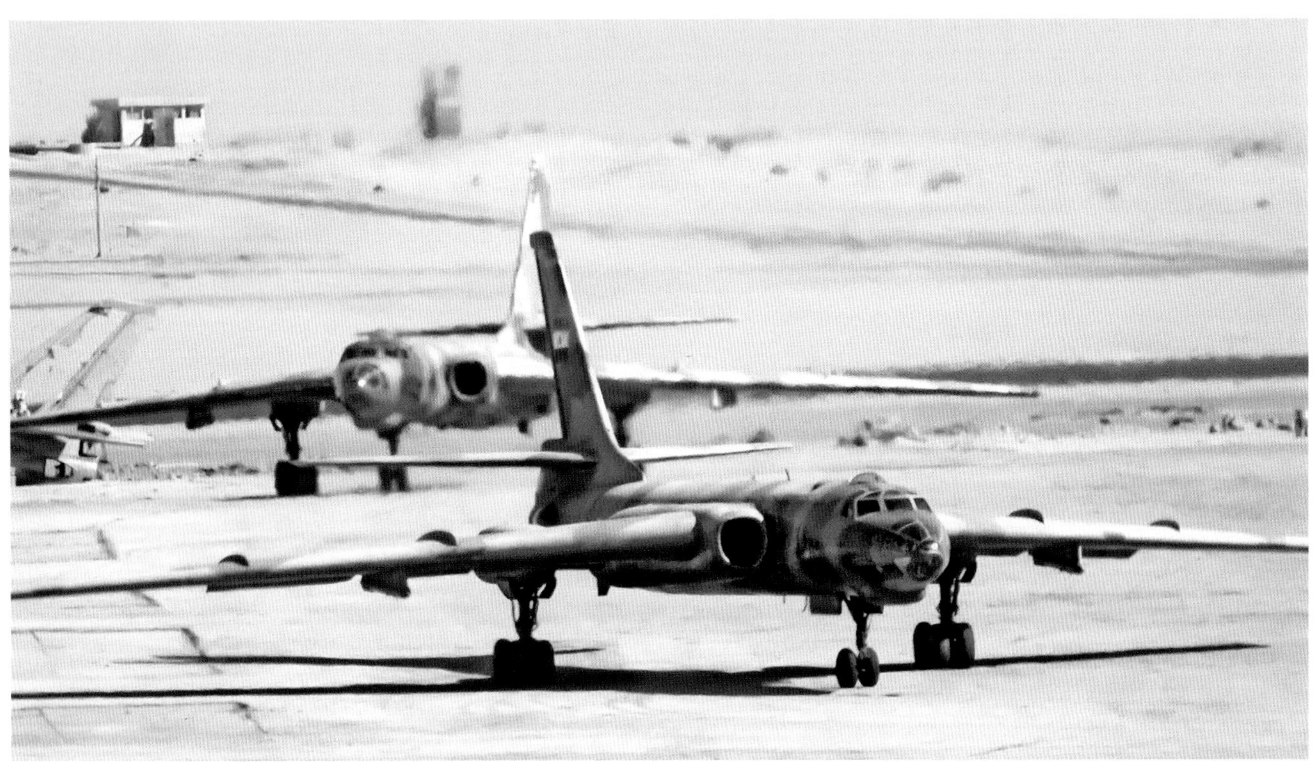

Tu-16KSR-2-11 '4406 Black' resting between missions with the entry hatches open.

This view of the same aircraft shows the camouflage colours. Note that the last two digits of the Arabic serial on the rear fuselage are repeated in European characters on the nose.

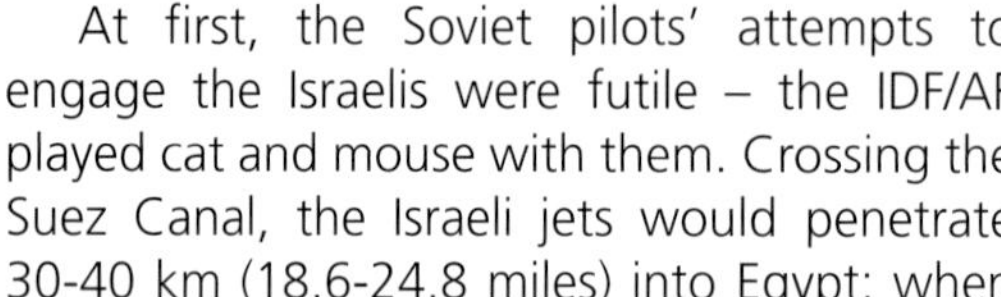

At first, the Soviet pilots' attempts to engage the Israelis were futile – the IDF/AF played cat and mouse with them. Crossing the Suez Canal, the Israeli jets would penetrate 30-40 km (18.6-24.8 miles) into Egypt; when

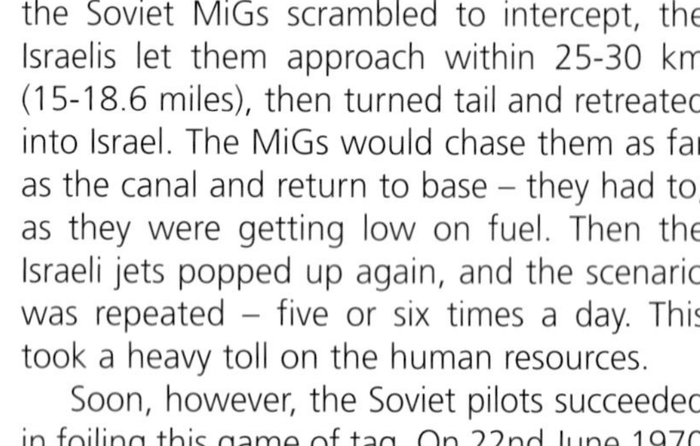

the Soviet MiGs scrambled to intercept, the Israelis let them approach within 25-30 km (15-18.6 miles), then turned tail and retreated into Israel. The MiGs would chase them as far as the canal and return to base – they had to, as they were getting low on fuel. Then the Israeli jets popped up again, and the scenario was repeated – five or six times a day. This took a heavy toll on the human resources.

Soon, however, the Soviet pilots succeeded in foiling this game of tag. On 22nd June 1970 Egyptian AD radars near Janaklis AB detected a group of Douglas A-4E Skyhawk attack aircraft escorted by Mirage IIICJs heading across the Suez Canal towards Ismailiya at low altitude. Several flights of MiG-21MFs from Nastenko's squadron scrambled immediately and lured the Mirages into a dogfight, forcing them to abandon their charges. Meanwhile, a pair of MiGs slipped through unnoticed to Ismailiya, flying at 100 m (330 ft), and pounced on the Skyhawks.

Tu-16KSR-2A '4404 Black' in flight carrying a pair of KSR-2 missiles. Note the different placement of the serial.

A 90th ODRAE ON Be-12 amphibian in a revetment at Cairo-West. Note the tarpaulins draped across the wings.

Another 90th ODRAE ON Be-12 is readied for a sortie. The UARAF roundels on the wings are visible here.

One of the A-4s was shot down, crashing west of the Suez Canal.

After that, the IDF/AF halted the deep penetration raids into Egypt for a week. When the incursions resumed, the Israelis exercised greater care, but the Soviet pilots used the same tactic successfully on three more occasions. After the shootdown of yet another A-4E on 25th July, the Israelis decided to set a trap for them. The plan involved 12 seasoned IDF/AF pilots with a total of some 60 'kills' between them.

On 30th July 1970 a flight of four F-4E Phantom IIs crossed the Suez Canal, following

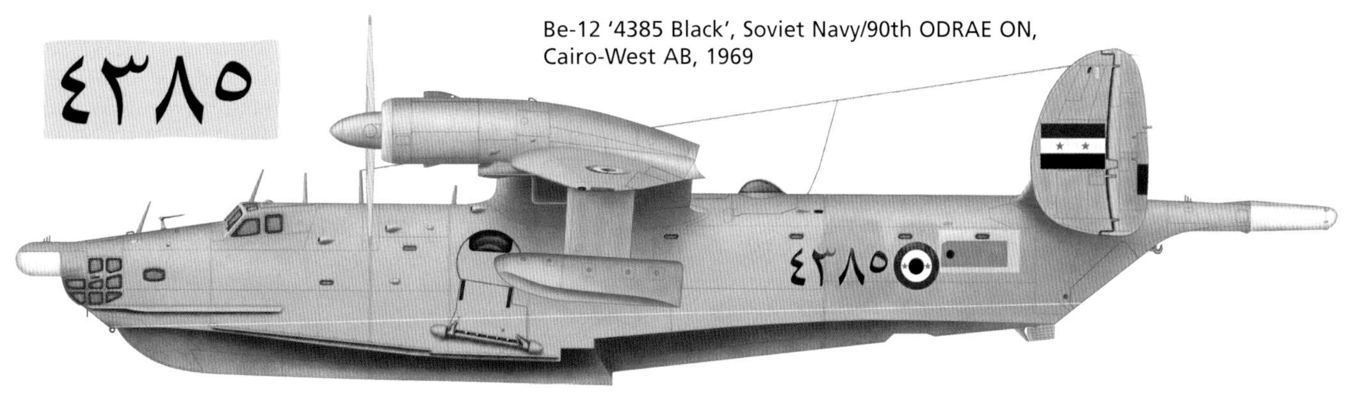

Be-12 '4385 Black', Soviet Navy/90th ODRAE ON, Cairo-West AB, 1969

Soviet advisors in civilian clothes pose with a 90th ODRAE ON Be-12 at Cairo-West AB, 1969. Note that the main gear units, including the wheel wells, are covered with tarpaulins while the aircraft is parked.

A fine in-flight study of the same aircraft.

A 90th ODRAE ON IL-38 starts up the engines at Cairo-West AB in 1970.

IL-38 '4399 Black' seen from the top of the revetment wall. The light-coloured ZiL-130 is an APA-50 ground power unit; the olive drab one with the van body may be a test equipment van.

The same aircraft cruising over the Mediterranean during a sortie.

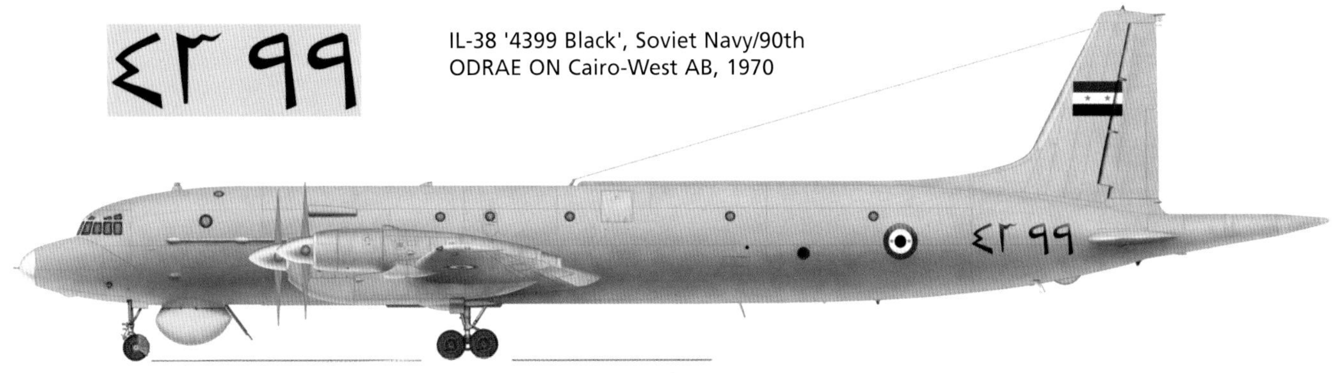

IL-38 '4399 Black', Soviet Navy/90th ODRAE ON Cairo-West AB, 1970

Pristine-looking Yak-11 (C-11) '590 Black' in a hangar. The aircraft was light grey overall, with the serial on a yellow band.

Another view of the same aircraft. The fairing on top of the windshield is a gun camera.

the avenue of approach usually taken by the Skyhawks and keeping the same formation. Immediately eight Soviet-flown MiG-21MFs led by Capt. N. Kamenev took off and attacked, taking no precautions against a possible ambush. This was exactly what the Israelis were expecting and in a flash, two flights of four Mirage IIICJs that were lurking unseen over the Sinai Desert jumped them. In the ensuing mêlée four of the MiGs were shot down (interestingly, the Egyptians stated afterwards that five Soviet aircraft had been destroyed!) for no loss to themselves. Phantom pilots Avihu Ben-Nun and Avie Stella shot down one aircraft each (with AIM-7 and AIM-9 missiles respectively), while the other two 'kills' were scored by Mirage pilots – Asher Smir, who downed a MiG with cannon fire, and an unidentified pilot who launched a Shafrir AAM. Three of the Soviet pilots (Capt.

Wearing the beige/grey colour scheme usually applied to agricultural examples, this An-2 in UARAF insignia serialled 95... Black is equipped for geophysical survey with a towed magnetometer 'bird'. The V-509A-D9 propeller with straight wooden blades and spinner shows this is a Soviet-built machine.

Another Egyptian Air Force An-2, 951 Black, in post-UAR markings. The propeller has no spinner and may be an AV-2, suggesting Polish production. Note the concrete tie-down weights.

Zhuravlyov, Capt. Yurchenko and Capt. Yakovlev) were killed; the fourth pilot ejected and survived. Another pair of MiGs piloted by V. Kolosov and Yu. Pushkaryov scrambled to the rescue, but too late – the Israeli fighters had gone.

It was an embarrassing situation for the Soviets, who up to that point had had some success in drawing Israeli aircraft onto nests of SAMs. However, the S-125 SAM batteries persistently presented a very real problem to the Israelis, as their missiles could destroy low-flying aircraft by diving down upon them.

After President Nasser died on 28th September 1970 and was succeeded by Anwar al-Sadat, a peace agreement was reached – but not for long. Sadat, who pursued the same confrontation policy towards Israel, wisely decided not to continue with the policy of attrition but rather, to plan and husband resources for a pre-emptive strike across the Nile. Thus, barely three months after the ceasefire the skirmishes resumed and one more Su-7BMK was lost in action on 11th September 1971. Sadat made another surprising but very popular decision in 1972; he

Grey-painted Egyptian (UARAF) IL-14T '1142 Black' taxies past a USAF Douglas C-124 Globemaster.

Anyway, the 'War of Attrition' was damaging to both sides, sapping their resources. Worried about possible escalation of the conflict, both the Soviet Union and the USA had been urging the Egyptian government since January 1970 to stop the pointless war. On 7th August 1970 Egypt and Israel finally concluded a ceasefire. The 21 IDF/AF aircraft destroyed by the Soviet fighter pilots and SAM crews were undoubtedly one of the factors that prompted Israel to sign the ceasefire agreement.

1101 Black is an IL-14S VIP aircraft with 'United Arab Republic' titles in English and Arabic. This aircraft was shot down by an Israeli Gloster Meteor on the night of 29th October 1956.

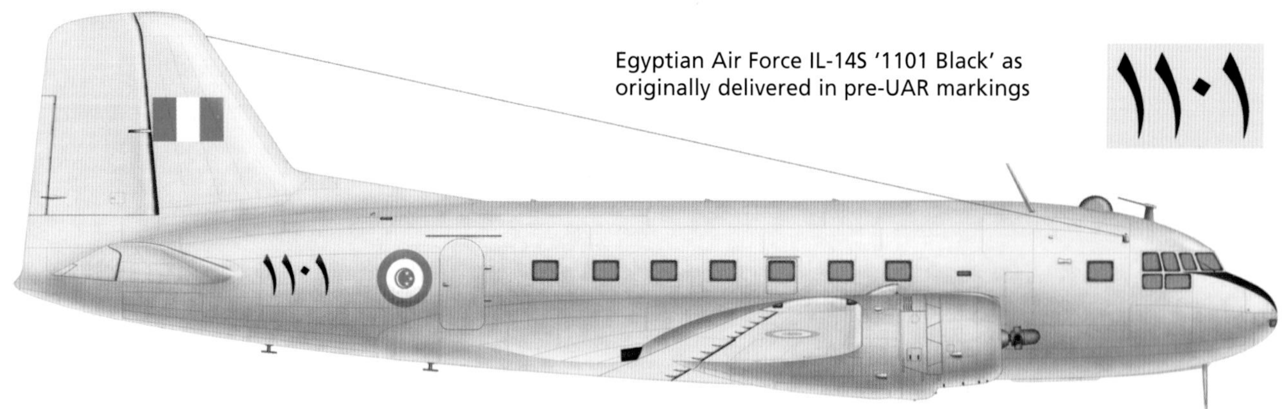

Egyptian Air Force IL-14S '1101 Black' as originally delivered in pre-UAR markings

requested the withdrawal of Soviet military advisors and pilots, except for a small number with specialised technical skills. He was dissatisfied with the quality of the advisors and the standard and arrogance of their advice, particularly on tactics and training.

During the War of Attrition, Israel chalked up 56 confirmed Egyptian MiG-21 'kills', while the MiG-21s claimed 14 confirmed 'kills' and 12 probables. There were many reasons for these high Egyptian losses, including their role as escort to MiG-17F fighter-bombers, but the most likely cause is that the Arabs were simply outclassed by the Israeli pilots with their superior training, experience and first-rate mission planning and tactical shrewdness. These factors were acknowledged by the Arabs, who strove to remedy the faults in time for the 1973 aggression. Replicas of the principal Israeli targets were created in the Libyan Desert, and Egyptian pilots honed their skills alongside volunteers from Algeria, Pakistan, Iraq, Jordan, Libya and North Korea, many of whom brought their own aircraft. To remedy the range problem of the MiG-21, emergency landing strips were built in the desert, allowing pilots to refuel.

Furthermore, the Arabs had an ace up their sleeve in the form of the S-125 SAMs missiles, which were a great threat to the Israelis. So effective were the missiles that Arab generals were reluctant to risk their soldiers in areas with no SAM cover, as will be seen in the next (fourth) Arab-Israeli war which began in 1973.

The Yom Kippur War

On 6th October 1973 large-scale military operations began again in the Suez Canal area. This time the roles were reversed: Egypt, aided by Syria and other Arab nations, acted as the aggressor, unleashing a new 'October War of Liberation' (better known in the West as the 'Holy Day War', or Yom Kippur War). The day was chosen carefully: firstly, 6th October was a Jewish religious holiday, Yom Kippur (the Day of Atonement), and the Arabs knew well that the Israelis don't fight on holidays. Secondly, it coincided with the 10th day of the Muslim holy month of Ramadan; hence the war is known in the Arab countries as the Ramadan War. Legend has it that on this day the prophet Mohammed began preparations for the battle of Badr, which he won and entered Mecca in triumph ten days later. Hence the offensive against Israel was codenamed Operation *Badr*. The Israelis knew of the

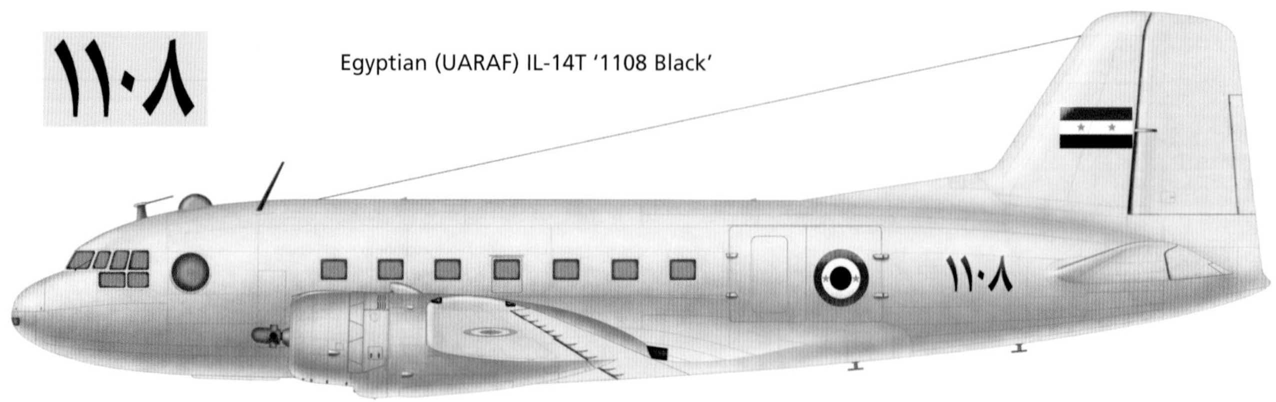

Egyptian (UARAF) IL-14T '1108 Black'

Arabs' plans but, on much deliberation, opted against a pre-emptive strike; after all, Israel had found itself in political isolation after the 1967 aggression against its Arab neighbours.

The Egyptian aviation in the Yom Kippur War was commanded by Lt.-Gen. Hosni Mubarak (who would become the next President of Egypt after Anwar Sadat's assassination in 1981). The EAF put up 240 aircraft which attacked Israeli positions on the Sinai Peninsula in two waves on 6th October, knocking out air defence assets and bases and destroying the barracks at El Tas. Large groups of MiG-17F and Su-7BMK fighter-bombers carried out a well-co-ordinated strike against the Bar-Lev Line, with MiG-21MFs from No.104 Fighter Wing flying top cover. In particular, the Su-7BMKs attacked the IDF/AF bases at Ophir (now known as Sharm el Sheikh) and Refidim. The EAF lost 28 aircraft on the opening day; among other things, pilot Irmi flying an IAI Nesher fighter (an Israeli derivative of the Mirage III) shot down two

The charred remains of two Egyptian (UARAF) IL-14s destroyed by an Israeli air raid at Fayeed AB on 5th June 1967 during the Six-Day War.

Two views of another pair of UARAF IL-14s that fell victim to Israeli air strikes.

Egyptian Air Force IL-14 '1148 Black' in post-UAR markings

Egyptian AIr Force An-12B SU-AOI shares the ramp at Berlin-Schönefeld with aircraft of the East German airline Interflug.

Below: SU-AOJ, another Egyptian An-12B in grey/white colours with the UAR flag.

Bottom: An-12B '1223 Black' was a testbed for the Brandner E-1 turbojet.

Top: Two EAF An-12Bs, including 1234 Black/SU-APX, at an East German airport.

Above: Another view of SU-AOI.

An-12BP '1251 Black'/SU-ARY with the post-UAR flag parked alongside an Iran Air Service Douglas DC-3 (EP-AEH).

Soviet Air Force/90th ODRAE ON An-12R
'4391 Black', Cairo-West AB, 1970

This grey-painted quasi-Egyptian example serialled 4391 Black is an An-12R ELINT aircraft operated by the 90th ODRAE ON, as revealed by the ventral antenna blisters and blade aerials.

Another fake Egyptian – an An-12BK-PP ECM aircraft serialled 4371 Black. Note the ventral Booket ECM packs, the tailcone housing an ASO-24 chaff dispenser and, the lateral heat exchanger air intakes/outlets.

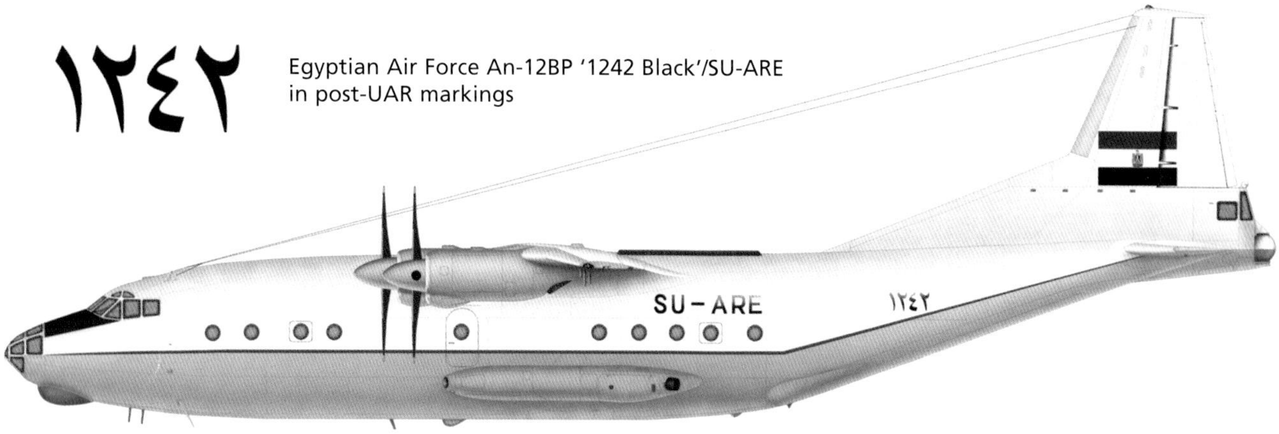

Egyptian Air Force An-12BP '1242 Black'/SU-ARE in post-UAR markings

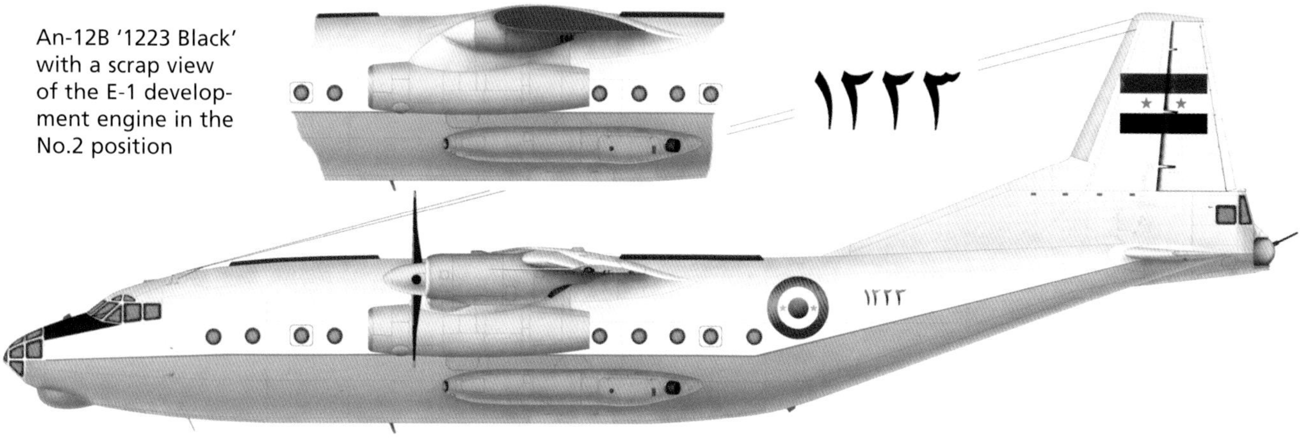

An-12B '1223 Black' with a scrap view of the E-1 development engine in the No.2 position

Su-7BMKs. MiG-21MFs of No.102 Fighter Wing were also in action as fighter-bombers, carrying either four 250-kg or two 500-kg bombs on their wing hardpoints. More often, however, MiG-21MFs and older MiG-21PFMs armed with cannons and missiles were used in conjunction with S-125 mobile SAM systems to deny the Israelis complete air superiority.

After the first Arab strike, the MiG-21s' mission was to protect the airfields in anticipation of a strong Israeli counterattack. It was not standard operational procedure to have standing patrols over bases, as the Israelis were masters of ambush; the Egyptians preferred to keep the pilots on high alert at the bases, quickly scrambling them when required. Once in the air, they adopted the strategy of intercepting attackers from below with the intention of breaking up the formations, separating the aircraft carrying ECM equipment and scattering the others over AAA and SAM nests. This tactic was intended to maximise the total number of kills but at the possible cost of an increase in the number of

Soviet Air Force/90th ODRAE ON An-12BK-PP '4371 Black', Cairo-West AB, 1970

An-12B '1220 Black'/SU-AOR seen on final approach with the flaps fully deployed.

Here an EAF An-12B is tended at an East German airport by a power cart and an articulated fuel truck (Minol was the brand of the local petroleum company).

1220 Black/SU-AOR parked at Cairo, with a support under the tail to prevent being tipped over by high winds.

An-12BP '1243 Black'/SU-ARD taxies at a wintry airport outside Egypt. The cannons in the tail barbette are fully raised.

Another view of the same aircraft; here the cannons have been removed.

A pair of EAF An-12BPs, 1241 Black/SU-ARA and 1254 Black/SU-AVB.

SU-AOI

SU-AOJ

SU-AVA ١٢٥٢

Opposite page, top to bottom:
An-12B SU-AOI seen visiting the UK in the late 1960s.

These views of An-12B SU-AOJ and An-12BP '1252 Black'/SU-AVA show detail differences, including a reduced number of windows on the latter (younger) aircraft.

Above: An-12BP '1254 Black'/SU-AVB was the last example delivered to the Egyptian Air Force. It is seen here during one of its foreign visits, probably to uplift spares for the Egyptian Air Force's western-made aircraft.

Below: Another aspect of 1254 Black/SU-AVB.

SU-BPM/1255 Black, the first of three An-74T-200A STOL transports delivered to the Egyptian Air Force.

Right and below: Wearing as yet no serial or registration, the same aircraft is seen at Khar'kov during pre-delivery tests.

own losses. In order to succeed, it required extreme vigilance in reporting the approach of enemy aircraft; to this end, the Egyptians provided nearly 500 radar units plus an army of observers to warn of attackers flying below the radar screen.

Simultaneously, the Syrians attacked Israeli positions on the Golan Heights, the land offensive being supported by Su-7BMK and Su-20 fighter-bombers. Iraq, too, joined the action on 7th October. The Israeli troops suffered serious losses, although the Arabs did not have things all their own way. Altogether, in this war the Su-7BMK made a reasonably good showing in combat.

The Egyptians rejoiced in the success of their first strike. As they had hoped, it had taken the Israelis completely by surprise. It was erroneously assumed that many bases in the Sinai Desert were out of action for a day or two; therefore, a second strike that day was cancelled. At the end of the first day, the EAF admitted the loss of ten aircraft but assessed Israeli losses to be 27, a figure that unsurprisingly proved too optimistic. The IDF/AF claimed 38 kills, of which only five were MiG-21s.

The following day, indeed, nearly 300 IDF/AF aircraft attacked Egyptian bases but were spotted in timely fashion, allowing over 60 MiG-21s to scramble. The area around the

An EAF An-74T-200A makes a 'low, slow, dirty' pass.

Nile Delta became the scene of a huge air battle. Few Israeli bombers got through to their targets, and Egyptian MiG-21s scored five confirmed 'kills' while losing seven of their own.

The Israelis tried to use the tactic which had worked well during the Six-Day War – that is, destroy the enemy's air forces on the ground. This time, however, they were in for a disappointment. The Egyptians and Syrians now kept their aircraft in hardened aircraft shelters (HASs) capable of withstanding a hit of a medium-calibre bomb, and the air defences around their bases were reinforced considerably. Then the Israelis tried bombing the runways at Egyptian and Syrian bases and mining them with the help of submunitions pods.

After a massive shelling the Egyptians breached the supposedly impregnable Bar-Lev line and secured bridgeheads on the eastern bank of the Suez Canal. By the second day of the war two corps of the Egyptian Army had crossed the Nile, advancing 15 km (9.3 miles) into Sinai without leaving the protective umbrella of the mobile SAM systems. On 8th October, an Israeli counter-attack was beaten off, after which each side waited for the other to attack.

Aerial warfare continued apace with determined Israeli attacks on Egyptian Air Force bases: five on Abu Hammad, four on Tanta and Mansourah, three on Salihiya, two on Abu Sueir and one each on Beni Sueif, Bir Arayida and Quwaysina. None of them succeeded in destroying any Egyptian aircraft on the ground or in putting the bases out of action for more than a few hours.

In an effort to take some of Israeli pressure off his struggling Syrian allies, President Sadat insisted that his generals go on the offensive. The attack began on 14th October with a full frontal thrust that failed miserably, allowing the Israeli army to counter-attack the next day. Deviating from customary practice, the Israelis infiltrated the Egyptian lines with their infantry taking out anti-tank defences and following with a divisional thrust to break through the line at the point where the Egyptian Second and Third Armies met. They crossed the Nile, advancing to within 101 km (62.76 miles) of Cairo before turning about to trap the Egyptian Third Army. By this time both sides were heavily dependent on massive airlifts to replace their losses in materiel. At this point, the United States persuaded the Israeli government to spare the Egyptian Third Army, thus assisting the negotiation of a United Nations-brokered ceasefire that came into effect on 26th October.

Interestingly, the Su-7 pilots included the President's half-brother Asaf Sadat, who was killed in action on the second day of the war when he was shot down by a Mirage IIICJ. Three Egyptian Su-7s fell to the guns of the Neshers on 8th October, and seven more on 10th October.

Neither side achieved major success until 16th October. That day the Israelis penetrated the Egyptian defences and seized a bridge-

An Egyptian Air Force Mi-6 serialled 885 Black in an overall tan finish. Note the position and size of the post-UAR insignia.

In contrast, this view of Mi-6 '820 White' shows the helicopter in early two-tone camouflage with large UARAF insignia positioned quite differently.

head on the west side of the Suez Canal. The airfield at Deversoir was captured and Israeli armoured groups approached Fayeed, which was only 100 km (62 miles) from Cairo. This came as a severe shock for the Egyptians; never before had the enemy succeeded in crossing the canal. The bridgehead and the temporary bridges leading to it were attacked by EAF fighter-bombers, which sustained heavy losses in so doing (ten aircraft were shot down on 17th October alone). The *Fitters*, however, suffered no further losses until 19th October when Giora Aven (Epstein) flying a Nesher had a particularly productive day,

This photo shows to advantage the late-style sand camouflage of Mi-6 '885 Black'.

One more view showing Mi-6 '885 Black' spooling up.

Left and below: EAF Mi-6 '882 Black' with the clamshell cargo doors open. Note the pale grey belly and the roundels on the underside of the stub wings.

Bottom: The wreckage of an Egyptian Mi-6 destroyed at Meliz AB by an Israeli air strike on 5th June 1967. Note the UARAF roundels.

claiming the destruction of two Su-7BMKs and two Su-20s. Encouraged by this success, on 22nd October the Israelis captured Fayeed and blocked the Suez-Cairo highway (despite the truce signed on 22nd October); not until the Soviet Union and the USA intervened did the belligerents back down.

In the Yom Kippur War the EAF lost 27 Su-7BMKs; the majority of these (16 aircraft) were shot down by Israeli air defences, five aircraft were downed by IDF/AF fighters and the rest (four aircraft) were 'friendly fire' incidents. Two Su-7s went missing. Also, the IDF/AF scored 73 confirmed victories over Egyptian MiG-21s, while the latter scored 27 confirmed 'kills' and claimed eight probables.

Despite its age, the MiG-17F fared well in the Yom Kippur War, which allowed it to remain in service for another ten years or so. Interestingly, in May 1976 the British magazine *Air International* questioned the advisability of designing specialised attack aircraft, given that the obsolete MiG-17F could still attack targets on the battlefield without the benefit of an automatic weapons control system, and without sustaining excessive losses at that.

Egyptian Air Force Mi-8TV '1465 Black' with Mi-8MT-style air intake filters and external cockpit armour

Zebras'R'Us: EAF Mi-8T '822 White' wears zebra-striped camouflage and has a common intake filter of western origin for both engines. Note the odd incline of the fin flash.

Mi-8TV '1465 Black' has been retrofitted not only with intake filters but also with Mi-8MTV-style bolt-on cockpit armour.

The Egyptian Air Force also operates the Mi-17-1V, exemplified by 3270 Black – again refitted with the boxy common intake filter of western origin.

By the outbreak of the Yom Kippur War the Egyptians had made good their losses of Mi-6s in the Six-Day War, possessing a combat-ready squadron of these helicopters. Unlike the Mi-8Ts, the lumbering Mi-6s were not used over the battlefield and in the enemy's immediate rear, being considered too vulnerable; they were used for airlifting materiel in the interests of the units of the second echelon.

As a result of their initial successes, Egypt and Syria were vindicated in their own eyes and those of the rest of the Islamic world for starting the war and excused their failures in 1967. The result was the Camp David Accord, whereby Sinai was returned to Egypt, the state of Israel became officially recognised by Egypt and ultimately, Egypt left the Soviet sphere of influence.

There was still friction leading to the occasional clash between Egyptian and Israeli fighters after 26th October 1973. For example, on 6th December of the same year, Egyptian MiG-23MFs claimed to have shot down an intruding F-4E, the Israelis denied the loss and

3286 Black, a Mi-172 VIP helicopter operated for the EAF top command.

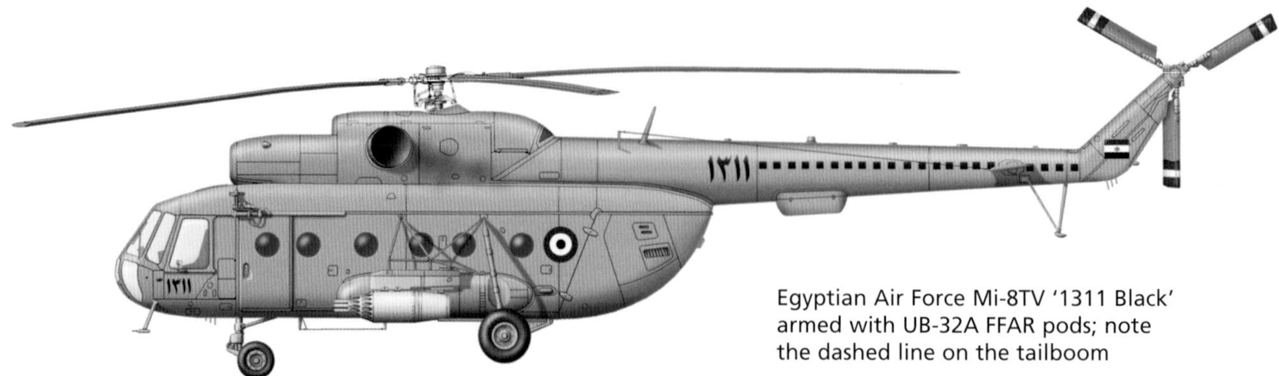

Egyptian Air Force Mi-8TV '1311 Black' armed with UB-32A FFAR pods; note the dashed line on the tailboom

for their part claimed to have destroyed a MiG-21MF, a loss denied by the Egyptians. MiG-25RBs of the Soviet Air Force remained in Egypt and continued their unmolested reconnaissance flights over Israel until 15th December 1973; they were escorted to and from the Israeli border by MiG-21MFs. The last Soviet 'advisor' left Egypt in August 1974.

Arab fratricide

The Egyptian Su-7BMKs were to see action once more in 1977. The US-brokered Camp David peace accord signed by President Anwar Sadat and Egypt's recognition of Israel were widely regarded as betrayal in the Muslim world, and Egypt found itself in isolation. Thousands of Libyan protesters instituted a 'March on Cairo' and the Libyan leader Col. Muammar Qaddafi decided to punish the renegade by military force. Hostilities began on 20th July and lasted five days. When Qaddafi ordered an attack on Egyptian border posts, in response an Egyptian armoured convoy headed for the border. Both sides flung artillery and aviation into the fray; on 21st July 1977 a group of Sukhoi Su-20 fighter-bombers escorted by MiG-21MFs bombed Libyan radar stations and army bases. Shortly afterwards, similar formations of Egyptian aircraft attacked al-Kurta AB and Gamal Abdel Nasser AB near Benghazi (the latter base had been named after the late Egyptian President when the countries were still on good terms). Seven Libyan Arab Air Force fighters were said to have been destroyed before they could take off. The following day a second attack on Nasser AB found the Libyans better prepared and two Dassault Mirage 5DE fighters shot down one of the escorting MiG-21MFs. On the same day and on 23rd July, LAAF aircraft engaged Egyptian targets and were jumped by MiG-21MFs which had been waiting for them; three (some sources suggest four) Libyan Mirages and one MiG-23MS were shot down. Shortly afterwards a ceasefire was agreed. A popular uprising against the government in Egypt did not take place, much to Colonel Gaddafi's chagrin.

As is often the case, there were several breakdowns in the ceasefire, the most significant of these taking place in 1979 when two Libyan MiG-23MSs had a dogfight with two Egyptian MiG-21MFs. However, the older MiG-21MFs had the advantage of carrying the latest US AIM-9P air-to-air missiles and Maj. Sal Mohammad shot down one MiG-23MS.

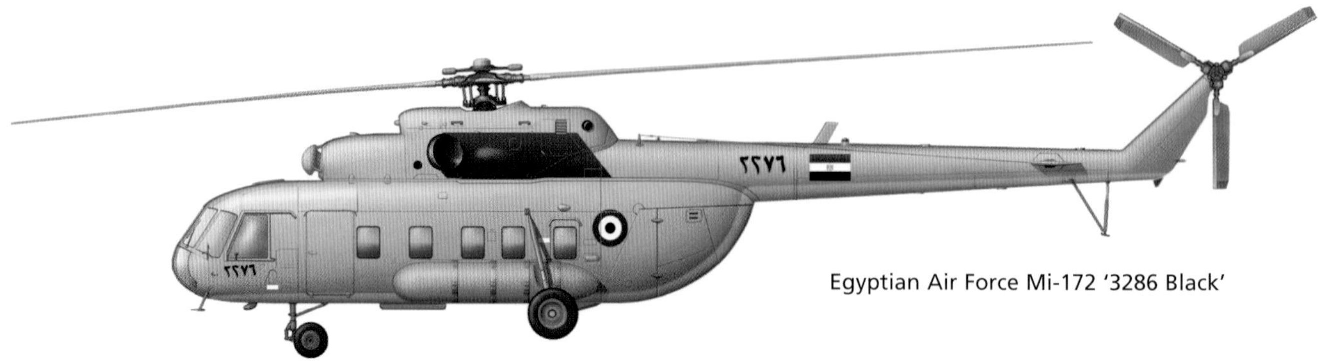

Egyptian Air Force Mi-172 '3286 Black'

Known Egyptian Air Force/United Arab Republic Air Force aircraft of Soviet origin				
Type	**Serial/registration**	**C/n**	**F/n**	**Notes**
An-2	951 Black	?		Beige/grey c/s, post-UAR insignia. Seen 11-1984
An-2	95* Black	?		Beige/grey c/s, UARAF insignia. Geophysical survey aircraft
An-12B (+)	1216 Black/SU-AOJ	402302		Voronezh-built. Registration confirmed worn in 1968; possibly to, see next line
	1216 Black/SU-AOS?			Registration reported in 1969 but unconfirmed!
An-12B (+)	1217 Black	402303?		Destroyed Cairo-West by Israeli air strikes 6-6-67?
An-12B (+)	1218 Black	402304?		Destroyed Cairo-West by Israeli air strikes 6-6-67?
An-12B (+)	1219 Black/SU-AOI	402305		
An-12B (+)	1220 Black/SU-AOR	402306		
An-12B (+)	1221 Black/SU-AOZ	402307?		
An-12B (+)	1222 Black/SU-APB	402308		
An-12B (+)	1223 Black/SU-AOS	402309		Was a testbed for the Brandner E-1 engine in 1962, later reconverted
An-12B (+)	1224 Black?/SU-AOP	402906		
An-12B (+)	1225 Black?/SU-AOJ	402907		
An-12B (+)	1226 Black/SU-AOI?	402908		Registration reported in 1966 but unconfirmed!
	1226 Black/SU-AOT			Registration confirmed
	1226 Black/SU-BAW			Registration confirmed
An-12B (+)	1227 Black/SU-APA	402909		
An-12B (+)	1228 Black/SU-AOI	402910		
	1228 Black/SU-APZ			
An-12B (+)	1229 Black/SU-AOK	402911?		
	1229 Black/SU-APC			
An-12B (+)	1231 Black?/SU-AOZ	402912		Not confirmed if carried EAF serial!
	1231 Black/SU-ARB			
An-12BP (+)	1233 Black/SU-ARC	6344107		Tashkent-built
An-12BP (+)	1234 Black/SU-AOR	6344108		
	1234 Black/SU-APX			
An-12BP (+)	1240 Black/SU-APY	9346706		
An-12BP (+)	1241 Black/SU-ARA	9346707		
An-12BP (+)	1242 Black/SU-ARE	9346709		
An-12BP (+)	1243 Black/SU-ARD	9346710		
An-12BP (+)	1251 Black/SU-ARY	02348209		
An-12BP (+)	1252 Black/SU-AVA	02348210		
An-12BP (+)	1253 Black/SU-ARZ	02348302		
An-12BP (+)	1254 Black/SU-AVB	02348305		
An-12BP (+)	4311 Black	?		90th ODRAE ON
An-12BK-PP	4371 Black	*34****		90th ODRAE ON
An-12R	4391 Black	?		90th ODRAE ON
An-74TK-200A	SU-BPM/1255 Black	365.470.98.977	1904	Ex-UR-CES (test and delivery registration); serial in European characters
An-74TK-200A	SU-BPN/1256 Black	365.470.98.979	1905	Serial in European characters
An-74TK-200A	SU-BPO/1257 Black	365.470.98.980	1906	Serial in European characters
Be-12	4380 Black	*60****		90th ODRAE ON
Be-12	4385 Black	*60****		90th ODRAE ON
Be-12	4386 Black	*60****		90th ODRAE ON
Be-12	438* Black	8601102		One of the above three (serial unknown)
Be-12	438* Black	8601202		One of the above three (serial unknown)
IL-14P	1092	?		Stored Cairo-Almaza
IL-14P	1096	?		
IL-14P	1097	?		Stored Cairo-Almaza
IL-14S	1101 Black	?		Shot down by Israeli fighter 29-10-1956

IL-14P	1102	?		
IL-14P	1103	?		
IL-14P	1104	?		
IL-14P	1105/SU-AJI	146001009		Moscow-built. Registration removed later
IL-14P	1106	?		
IL-14P	1107	?		
IL-14T	1108 Black	?		Light grey overall, UARAF markings
IL-14P	1109	?		
IL-14P	1111	?		
IL-14P	1113	?		
IL-14P	1116	?		
IL-14P	1118	?		
IL-14P	1120	?		
IL-14P	1121	?		Stored Cairo-Almaza
IL-14P	1122	?		Stored Cairo-Almaza
IL-14P	1133	?		
IL-14P	1124/SU-BBM	?		
IL-14P	1125/SU-BAE	?		
IL-14P	1126	147001444		Stored Cairo-Almaza until at least 1984
IL-14P	1127	?		
IL-14P	1128	?		
IL-14P	1130	?		
IL-14P	1131	?		
IL-14P	1133/SU-BEM	?		
IL-14P	1134	?		
IL-14P	1135	?		Stored Cairo-Almaza
IL-14P	1136	?		
IL-14P	1141	?		
IL-14T	1142 Black	?		Light grey overall, UARAF markings
IL-14P	1146	?		
IL-14P	1148 Black	?		Light grey overall, post-UAR markings
IL-14P	1161	?		
IL-14P	1200	?		
IL-14S	SU-AIP	?		D/D 1956, President Nasser's aircraft; natural metal finish
IL-14P	SU-ANE	?		
IL-14P	SU-AOE	?		
IL-14P	SU-AOF	?		
IL-14P	SU-AOH	?		
IL-14P	SU-BBF	?		
IL-14P	SU-BBN	?		
IL-14P	SU-BBO	?		
IL-14P	SU-BBT	?		
IL-14P	SU-BBU	?		
IL-14P	?	5340804		Tashkent-built. D/D 1964, ex-Interflug DM-SBX
IL-14P	?	5340809		D/D 1964, ex-Interflug DM-SBF
IL-14P	?	6341208		D/D 1966, ex-East German Air Force 461 Black (not 462 Black as sometimes reported)
IL-14P	?	6341403		D/D 1966, ex-Interflug DM-SBR
IL-14P	?	6341507		D/D 1964, ex-Interflug DM-SBW
IL-14P	?	6341509		D/D 1964, ex-Interflug DM-SBU
IL-14P	?	6341510		D/D 1966, ex-Interflug DM-SBV
IL-14P	?	6341601		D/D 1966, ex-Interflug DM-SBI
IL-14P	?	6341702		D/D 1964, ex-Interflug DM-SBE
IL-14P	?	6341704		D/D 1966, ex-Interflug DM-SBY
IL-14P	?	6341802		D/D 1956, ex-[East German] Deutsche Lufthansa DM-SBO
IL-14P	?	14803003		East German-built. D/D 1965, ex-East German Air Force 437 Black
IL-14T	?	14803005		East German-built, converted from IL-14P, ex-East German Air Force 491 Black.

				Sold 1965 but crashed on the delivery flight
IL-14P	?	14803007		East German-built, ex-East German Air Force 445 Black. Sold 1963 but shot down en route to Egypt
IL-14P	?	14803011		East German-built. D/D 1964, ex-Interflug DM-SAD
IL-14P	?	14803021		East German-built. D/D 1965, ex-East German Air Force 401 Black
IL-14P	?	14803075		East German-built. D/D 1964, ex-Interflug DM-SAM
IL-14P	?	14803077		East German-built. D/D 1964, ex-Interflug DM-SAN
IL-14P	?	14803080		East German-built. D/D 1964, ex-Interflug DM-SAO
IL-28	C_1	?		Natural metal finish, UARAF insignia
IL-28	E	?		Natural metal finish, UARAF insignia
IL-28	F	?		Natural metal finish, UARAF insignia
IL-28R	G	?		No.28 Ssn. Natural metal finish, UARAF insignia
IL-28	G_1	?		Natural metal finish, UARAF insignia
IL-28	H	?		Natural metal finish, UARAF insignia
IL-28	K	?		Natural metal finish, pre-UAR insignia, seen 1956
IL-28	L	?		Natural metal finish, UARAF insignia
IL-28	M	?		Natural metal finish, UARAF insignia
IL-28	N	?		Natural metal finish, UARAF insignia
IL-28	O	?		Natural metal finish, UARAF insignia
IL-28	O_1	?		Natural metal finish, UARAF insignia
IL-28	P	?		Natural metal finish, UARAF insignia
IL-28	Q	?		Natural metal finish, UARAF insignia
IL-28	R	?		Natural metal finish, UARAF insignia
IL-28	S	?		Natural metal finish, UARAF insignia
IL-28	T	?		Natural metal finish, UARAF insignia
IL-28	U	?		Natural metal finish, UARAF insignia
IL-28	V_1	?		No.8 Sqn. Natural metal finish, UARAF insignia
IL-28	V_2	?		Natural metal finish, UARAF insignia
IL-28	1714 Black	?		Natural metal finish
IL-28	1731	?		Natural metal finish
IL-28	1733	?		Sand/brown camouflage
IL-28	1772	?		Preserved Cairo-West AB
IL-28	1773	?		Reportedly used callsign SU-BAB
IL-28	1774	?		
IL-28	1778	?		Sand/brown camouflage
IL-28	1801	?		Natural metal finish
IL-28U	A	?		Natural metal finish, UARAF insignia
IL-38	4399 Black	08*01****		Wet-leased from Soviet Navy (90th ODRAE ON)
MiG-15*bis*	99	?		UARAF insignia; unusually low serial – ex-Syrian aircraft?
MiG-15*bis*	201?	?		UARAF insignia; serial may be 1201 or 1301. Shot down and ditched in Lake Bordavil 31-10-1956; now gate guard at Hatzor AB, Israel
MiG-15*bis*	214 Black	?		Pre-UAR insignia
MiG-15*bis*	601 Black	?		Pre-UAR insignia
MiG-15*bis*	1437	?		Last noted 1958
MiG-15*bis*	1475	?		Last noted 1973; WFU, used as a decoy at an Egyptian airbase
MiG-15*bis*	1900	?		Abu Sueir AB, last noted 1958
MiG-15*bis*	1968 Black	?		No.24 Sqn. UARAF insignia. Destroyed by Israeli air raid at el-Sur AB ?-6-67
MiG-15*bis*	1972	?		Abu Sueir AB, last noted 1958
MiG-15*bis*	2176 Black	?		Seen Cairo-Almaza AB
MiG-15*bis*	2600 (1)	?		Abu Sueir AB, last noted 1958; serial later reassigned to a MiG-17F
MiG-15*bis*	2655	?		Last noted 1963
MiG-15*bis*	2670	?		Last noted 1963
MiG-15*bis*	2702 Black	?		OTU, Abu Sueir AB, UARAF insignia and unit badge on nose; operational in 1958

MiG-15*bis*	2707	?		OTU, Abu Sueir AB, operational in 1955
MiG-15*bis*	2776	?		Last noted 1960
MiG-15*bis*	?	523824		Czechoslovak-built (Aero S-103). D/D 3-10-1955
MiG-15*bis*	?	523828		Czechoslovak-built (Aero S-103). D/D 3-10-1955
MiG-15*bis*	?	523829		Czechoslovak-built (Aero S-103). D/D 3-10-1955
MiG-15*bis*	?	523830		Czechoslovak-built (Aero S-103). D/D 3-10-1955
MiG-15*bis*	?	523831		Czechoslovak-built (Aero S-103). D/D 3-10-1955
MiG-15*bis*	?	523833		Czechoslovak-built (Aero S-103). D/D 3-10-1955
MiG-15*bis*	?	523834		Czechoslovak-built (Aero S-103). D/D 3-10-1955
MiG-15*bis*	?	523835		Czechoslovak-built (Aero S-103). D/D 3-10-1955
MiG-15*bis*	?	523836		Czechoslovak-built (Aero S-103). D/D 3-10-1955
MiG-15*bis*	?	523837		Czechoslovak-built (Aero S-103). D/D 3-10-1955
MiG-15*bis*	?	523838		Czechoslovak-built (Aero S-103). D/D 3-10-1955
MiG-15*bis*	?	523839		Czechoslovak-built (Aero S-103). D/D 3-10-1955
MiG-15*bis*	?	523840		Czechoslovak-built (Aero S-103). D/D 3-10-1955
MiG-15*bis*	?	523841		Czechoslovak-built (Aero S-103). D/D 3-10-1955
MiG-15*bis*	?	523842		Czechoslovak-built (Aero S-103). D/D 3-10-1955
MiG-15*bis*	?	523843		Czechoslovak-built (Aero S-103). D/D 3-10-1955
MiG-15*bis*	?	523844		Czechoslovak-built (Aero S-103). D/D 3-10-1955
MiG-15*bis*	?	523845		Czechoslovak-built (Aero S-103). D/D 3-10-1955
MiG-15*bis*	?	523846		Czechoslovak-built (Aero S-103). D/D 3-10-1955
MiG-15*bis*	?	523847		Czechoslovak-built (Aero S-103). D/D 6-11-1955
MiG-15*bis*	?	523848		Czechoslovak-built (Aero S-103). D/D 3-10-1955
MiG-15*bis*	?	523849		Czechoslovak-built (Aero S-103). D/D 6-11-1955
MiG-15*bis*	?	523850		Czechoslovak-built (Aero S-103). D/D 6-11-1955
MiG-15*bis*	?	523851		Czechoslovak-built (Aero S-103). D/D 6-11-1955
MiG-15*bis*	?	523852		Czechoslovak-built (Aero S-103). D/D 6-11-1955
MiG-15*bis*	?	523853		Czechoslovak-built (Aero S-103). D/D 6-11-1955
MiG-15*bis*	?	523854		Czechoslovak-built (Aero S-103). D/D 6-11-1955
MiG-15*bis*	?	523855		Czechoslovak-built (Aero S-103). D/D 6-11-1955
MiG-15*bis*	?	523856		Czechoslovak-built (Aero S-103). D/D 6-11-1955
MiG-15*bis*	?	523857		Czechoslovak-built (Aero S-103). D/D 7-11-1955
MiG-15*bis*	?	523858		Czechoslovak-built (Aero S-103). D/D 7-11-1955
MiG-15*bis*	?	523859		Czechoslovak-built (Aero S-103). D/D 7-11-1955
MiG-15*bis*	?	523860		Czechoslovak-built (Aero S-103). D/D 7-11-1955
MiG-15*bis*	?	523861		Czechoslovak-built (Aero S-103). D/D 7-11-1955
MiG-15*bis*	?	523862		Czechoslovak-built (Aero S-103). D/D 7-11-1955
MiG-15*bis*	?	523863		Czechoslovak-built (Aero S-103). D/D 7-11-1955
MiG-15*bis*	?	523864		Czechoslovak-built (Aero S-103). D/D 15-12-1955
MiG-15*bis*	?	523865		Czechoslovak-built (Aero S-103). D/D 12-11-1955
MiG-15*bis*	?	523866		Czechoslovak-built (Aero S-103). D/D 12-11-1955
MiG-15*bis*	?	523867		Czechoslovak-built (Aero S-103). D/D 12-11-1955
MiG-15*bis*	?	523869		Czechoslovak-built (Aero S-103). D/D 12-11-1955
MiG-15*bis*	?	523870		Czechoslovak-built (Aero S-103). D/D 12-11-1955
MiG-15*bis*	?	523871		Czechoslovak-built (Aero S-103). D/D 7-11-1955
MiG-15*bis*	?	523872		Czechoslovak-built (Aero S-103). D/D 12-11-1955
MiG-15*bis*	?	523873		Czechoslovak-built (Aero S-103). D/D 15-12-1955
MiG-15*bis*	?	523874		Czechoslovak-built (Aero S-103). D/D 15-12-1955
MiG-15*bis*	?	523875		Czechoslovak-built (Aero S-103). D/D 15-12-1955
MiG-15*bis*	?	523876		Czechoslovak-built (Aero S-103). D/D 15-12-1955
MiG-15*bis*	?	523877		Czechoslovak-built (Aero S-103). D/D 12-11-1955
MiG-15*bis*	?	523878		Czechoslovak-built (Aero S-103). D/D 12-11-1955
MiG-15*bis*	?	523880		Czechoslovak-built (Aero S-103). D/D 15-12-1955
MiG-15*bis*	?	523881		Czechoslovak-built (Aero S-103). D/D 15-12-1955
MiG-15*bis*	?	523882		Czechoslovak-built (Aero S-103). D/D 15-12-1955
MiG-15*bis*	?	523883		Czechoslovak-built (Aero S-103). D/D 15-12-1955
MiG-15*bis*	?	523884		Czechoslovak-built (Aero S-103). D/D 15-12-1955

MiG-15*bis*	?	523885		Czechoslovak-built (Aero S-103). D/D 15-12-1955
MiG-15*bis*	?	523886		Czechoslovak-built (Aero S-103). D/D 15-12-1955
MiG-15*bis*	?	523887		Czechoslovak-built (Aero S-103). D/D 15-12-1955
MiG-15*bis*	?	523888		Czechoslovak-built (Aero S-103). D/D 15-12-1955
MiG-15*bis*	?	523889		Czechoslovak-built (Aero S-103). D/D 15-12-1955
MiG-15*bis*	?	523890		Czechoslovak-built (Aero S-103). D/D 15-12-1955
MiG-15*bis*	?	523891		Czechoslovak-built (Aero S-103). D/D 15-12-1955
MiG-15*bis*	?	523892		Czechoslovak-built (Aero S-103). D/D 15-12-1955
MiG-15*bis*	?	523893		Czechoslovak-built (Aero S-103). D/D 15-12-1955
MiG-15*bis*	?	523894		Czechoslovak-built (Aero S-103). D/D 15-12-1955
MiG-15*bis*	?	523895		Czechoslovak-built (Aero S-103). D/D 15-12-1955
MiG-15*bis*	?	523896		Czechoslovak-built (Aero S-103). D/D 15-12-1955
MiG-15*bis*	?	523897		Czechoslovak-built (Aero S-103). D/D 15-12-1955
MiG-15*bis*	?	523898		Czechoslovak-built (Aero S-103). D/D 15-12-1955
MiG-15*bis*	?	523899		Czechoslovak-built (Aero S-103). D/D 15-12-1955
MiG-15*bis*	?	523601		Czechoslovak-built (Aero S-103). D/D 15-12-1955
MiG-15*bis*	?	523602		Czechoslovak-built (Aero S-103). D/D 15-12-1955
MiG-15*bis*	?	523603		Czechoslovak-built (Aero S-103). D/D 15-12-1955
MiG-15*bis*	?	523604		Czechoslovak-built (Aero S-103). D/D 15-12-1955
MiG-15*bis*	?	523605		Czechoslovak-built (Aero S-103). D/D 15-12-1955
MiG-15*bis*	?	523606		Czechoslovak-built (Aero S-103). D/D 15-12-1955
MiG-15*bis*	?	523607		Czechoslovak-built (Aero S-103). D/D 15-12-1955
MiG-15*bis*	?	523610		Czechoslovak-built (Aero S-103). D/D 15-12-1955
MiG-15*bis*	?	523616		Czechoslovak-built (Aero S-103). D/D 15-12-1955
MiG-15*bis*	?	523617		Czechoslovak-built (Aero S-103). D/D 15-12-1955
MiG-15*bis*	?	713031		Czechoslovak-built (Aero S-103). D/D 21-3-1957
MiG-15*bis*	?	713032		Czechoslovak-built (Aero S-103). D/D 21-3-1957
MiG-15*bis*	?	713033		Czechoslovak-built (Aero S-103). D/D 21-3-1957
MiG-15*bis*	?	713034		Czechoslovak-built (Aero S-103). D/D 21-3-1957
MiG-15*bis*	?	713035		Czechoslovak-built (Aero S-103). D/D 4-5-1956
MiG-15*bis*	?	713036		Czechoslovak-built (Aero S-103). D/D 3-5-1956
MiG-15*bis*	?	713037		Czechoslovak-built (Aero S-103). D/D 2-5-1956
MiG-15*bis*	?	713038		Czechoslovak-built (Aero S-103). D/D 3-5-1956
MiG-15*bis*	?	713039		Czechoslovak-built (Aero S-103). D/D 2-5-1956
MiG-15*bis*	?	713040		Czechoslovak-built (Aero S-103). D/D 3-5-1956
MiG-15*bis*	?	713041		Czechoslovak-built (Aero S-103). D/D 2-5-1956
MiG-15*bis*	?	713042		Czechoslovak-built (Aero S-103). D/D 4-5-1956
MiG-15*bis*	?	713044		Czechoslovak-built (Aero S-103). D/D 2-5-1956
MiG-15*bis*	?	713045		Czechoslovak-built (Aero S-103). D/D 4-5-1956
MiG-15*bis*	?	713046		Czechoslovak-built (Aero S-103). D/D 4-5-1956
MiG-15*bis*	?	713047		Czechoslovak-built (Aero S-103). D/D 3-5-1956
MiG-15*bis*	?	713048		Czechoslovak-built (Aero S-103). D/D 2-5-1956
MiG-15*bis*	?	713049		Czechoslovak-built (Aero S-103). D/D 4-5-1956
MiG-15*bis*	?	713050		Czechoslovak-built (Aero S-103). D/D 3-5-1956
MiG-15*bis*	?	713101		Czechoslovak-built (Aero S-103). D/D 3-5-1956
MiG-15*bis*	?	713102		Czechoslovak-built (Aero S-103). D/D 3-5-1956
MiG-15*bis*	?	713103		Czechoslovak-built (Aero S-103). D/D 3-5-1956
MiG-15*bis*	?	713104		Czechoslovak-built (Aero S-103). D/D 4-5-1956
MiG-15*bis*	?	713105		Czechoslovak-built (Aero S-103). D/D 2-5-1956
MiG-15*bis*	?	713106		Czechoslovak-built (Aero S-103). D/D 2-5-1956
MiG-15*bis*	?	713118		Czechoslovak-built (Aero S-103). D/D 4-5-1956
MiG-15*bis*	?	713119		Czechoslovak-built (Aero S-103). D/D 4-5-1956
MiG-15*bis*	?	713120		Czechoslovak-built (Aero S-103). D/D 4-5-1956
MiG-15*bis*	?	713121		Czechoslovak-built (Aero S-103). D/D 4-5-1956
MiG-15*bis*	?	713122		Czechoslovak-built (Aero S-103). D/D 4-5-1956
UTI-MiG-15	1405	?		Last noted 1962
UTI-MiG-15	1406	?		Operational 1957

UTI-MiG-15	1448	?		Operational 1957
UTI-MiG-15	1467	?		Last noted circa 1960
UTI-MiG-15	1996	?		Czechoslovak-built (Aero CS-102). Natural metal finish. Last noted circa 1960
UTI-MiG-15	1997 Black	?		Czechoslovak-built (Aero CS-102). No.20 Sqn, natural metal finish, UARAF insignia, dragon badge on nose. Seen circa 1960
UTI-MiG-15	1998 Black	?		Czechoslovak-built (Aero CS-102). No.20 Sqn, natural metal finish, UARAF insignia, dragon badge on nose. Seen circa 1960
UTI-MiG-15	2224 Black	?		Czechoslovak-built (Aero CS-102). Sand/green/brown camouflage, UARAF insignia
UTI-MiG-15	2357	?		Natural metal finish
UTI-MiG-15	2606 Black	?		Czechoslovak-built (Aero CS-102). No.31 Sqn; damaged 6-1967 but repaired
UTI-MiG-15	2711 Black	?		Czechoslovak-built (Aero CS-102). Natural metal finish, UARAF insignia
UTI-MiG-15	2752 Black	?		Czechoslovak-built (Aero CS-102). Natural metal finish, UARAF insignia; preserved in Egypt
UTI-MiG-15	2905 Black	?		Czechoslovak-built (Aero CS-102). Natural metal finish, UARAF insignia. Last noted in the mid-1970s
UTI-MiG-15	2906	?		Czechoslovak-built (Aero CS-102). Last noted 1973
UTI-MiG-15	2908	?		Czechoslovak-built (Aero CS-102). Last noted late 1967
UTI-MiG-15	2910	?		Czechoslovak-built (Aero CS-102). Last noted 1969
UTI-MiG-15	2912	?		Czechoslovak-built (Aero CS-102). Last noted 1963
UTI-MiG-15	2913	?		Czechoslovak-built (Aero CS-102). Last noted 1967
UTI-MiG-15	2919	?		Czechoslovak-built (Aero CS-102). Last noted 1967
UTI-MiG-15	3224	?		Czechoslovak-built (Aero CS-102). Three-tone camouflage
UTI-MiG-15	?	512200		Czechoslovak-built (Aero CS-102)
UTI-MiG-15	?	522523		Czechoslovak-built (Aero CS-102)
UTI-MiG-15	?	522531		Czechoslovak-built (Aero CS-102)
UTI-MiG-15	?	522532		Czechoslovak-built (Aero CS-102)
UTI-MiG-15	?	522538		Czechoslovak-built (Aero CS-102)
UTI-MiG-15	?	522540		Czechoslovak-built (Aero CS-102)
UTI-MiG-15	?	622970		Czechoslovak-built (Aero CS-102)
UTI-MiG-15	?	622971		Czechoslovak-built (Aero CS-102)
UTI-MiG-15	?	622980		Czechoslovak-built (Aero CS-102)
UTI-MiG-15	?	622982		Czechoslovak-built (Aero CS-102)
UTI-MiG-15	?	712125		Czechoslovak-built (Aero CS-102)
UTI-MiG-15	?	712159		Czechoslovak-built (Aero CS-102)
UTI-MiG-15	?	712160		Czechoslovak-built (Aero CS-102)
UTI-MiG-15	?	712161		Czechoslovak-built (Aero CS-102)
UTI-MiG-15	?	712162		Czechoslovak-built (Aero CS-102)
UTI-MiG-15	?	712165		Czechoslovak-built (Aero CS-102)
UTI-MiG-15	?	722515		Czechoslovak-built (Aero CS-102). D/D 1957
UTI-MiG-15	?	722516		Czechoslovak-built (Aero CS-102). D/D 1957
UTI-MiG-15	?	722517		Czechoslovak-built (Aero CS-102). D/D 1957
UTI-MiG-15	?	722518		Czechoslovak-built (Aero CS-102). D/D 1957
UTI-MiG-15	?	722519		Czechoslovak-built (Aero CS-102). D/D 1957
UTI-MiG-15	?	722520		Czechoslovak-built (Aero CS-102). D/D 1957
UTI-MiG-15	?	722531		Czechoslovak-built (Aero CS-102). D/D 1957
UTI-MiG-15	?	722545		Czechoslovak-built (Aero CS-102). D/D 1957
UTI-MiG-15	?	722546		Czechoslovak-built (Aero CS-102). D/D 1957
UTI-MiG-15	?	722554		Czechoslovak-built (Aero CS-102). D/D 1957
UTI-MiG-15	?	722565		Czechoslovak-built (Aero CS-102). D/D 1957
UTI-MiG-15	?	922237		Czechoslovak-built (Aero CS-102). D/D 1959
UTI-MiG-15	?	922238		Czechoslovak-built (Aero CS-102). D/D 1959
UTI-MiG-15	?	922239		Czechoslovak-built (Aero CS-102). D/D 1959
UTI-MiG-15	?	922240		Czechoslovak-built (Aero CS-102). D/D 1959
UTI-MiG-15	?	922241		Czechoslovak-built (Aero CS-102). D/D 1959
UTI-MiG-15	?	922242		Czechoslovak-built (Aero CS-102). D/D 1959

UTI-MiG-15	?	922243		Czechoslovak-built (Aero CS-102). D/D 1959
UTI-MiG-15	?	922244		Czechoslovak-built (Aero CS-102). D/D 1959
UTI-MiG-15	?	922245		Czechoslovak-built (Aero CS-102). D/D 1959
UTI-MiG-15	?	922246		Czechoslovak-built (Aero CS-102). D/D 1959
UTI-MiG-15	?	922247		Czechoslovak-built (Aero CS-102). D/D 1959
UTI-MiG-15	?	922248		Czechoslovak-built (Aero CS-102). D/D 1959
UTI-MiG-15	?	922249		Czechoslovak-built (Aero CS-102). D/D 1959
UTI-MiG-15	?	922250		Czechoslovak-built (Aero CS-102). D/D 1959
UTI-MiG-15	?	922255		Czechoslovak-built (Aero CS-102). D/D 1959
MiG-17F	72	?		UARAF markings; unusually low serial – ex-Syrian aircraft? Seen 7-1958
MiG-17F	1107	?		Operational in 1963-65
MiG-17F	2017	?		Last noted 1963
MiG-17F	2024	?		No.18 Sqn; four rocket launch rails and bomb racks on fuselage. Last noted in 1963
MiG-17F	2025 Black	?		Last noted 6-1967; transferred to Syria
MiG-17F	2028 Black	1447?		Falcon nose art. Last noted 1965
MiG-17F	2034 Black	?		Sand/green/brown camouflage, post-UAR markings, four rocket launch rails. Last noted 1973
MiG-17F	2038 Black	?		No.18 Sqn; last noted 1965
MiG-17F	2051	?		Transferred to Syria?
MiG-17F	2060	?		Last noted 1965
MiG-17F	2067	?		Last noted 1965
MiG-17F	2072	?		Last noted 1964
MiG-17F	2084 Black	?		Last noted 1967
MiG-17F	2101	?		No.18 Sqn; last noted in the mid-1960s
MiG-17F	2115 Black	?		Camouflaged, post-UAR markings, four rocket launch rails and bomb racks on fuselage. Last noted 1981
MiG-17F	2147	?		Leopard head nose art
MiG-17F	2162	?		Last noted 1981
MiG-17F	2182	?		Last noted 1958
MiG-17F	2195 Black	?		Black dragon nose art, four rocket launch rails. Destroyed El Arish AB 6-1967
MiG-17F	2214 Black	?		Natural metal, UARAF markings. Last noted 1961
MiG-17F	2216	?		To the USA for trials
MiG-17F	2224	?		Last noted 1960
MiG-17F	2225	?		Bat insignia. Destroyed El Arish AB 6-1967
MiG-17F	2235	1222		Destroyed El Arish AB 5-6-1967
MiG-17F	2248	?		To the USA for trials
MiG-17F	2250	?		Four rocket launch rails. Destroyed El Arish 6-1967
MiG-17F	2271 Black	?		Natural metal, UARAF markings, red/white chequered rudder, red ID bands on aft fuselage and wingtips; four rocket launch rails
MiG-17F	2300 Black	?		Transferred to Syria
MiG-17F	2302	?		Sold to the USA for trials
MiG-17F	'2355'	?		Preserved Luxor, fake serial
MiG-17F	2514	?		To the USA for trials
MiG-17F	2600 (2)	?		See MiG-15*bis*; last noted 1967
MiG-17F	2608	?		
MiG-17F	2609	?		Last noted 1973
MiG-17F	2613	?		Last noted 1973
MiG-17F	2621	?		Last noted 1973
MiG-17F	2647 Black	?		No.18 Sqn; four rocket launch rails
MiG-17F	2648 Black	?		No.18 Sqn; yellow late-style unit badge. Destroyed El Arish AB 5-6-1967
MiG-17F	2649	?		Last noted 1970
MiG-17F	2650	?		Last noted 1973
MiG-17F	2651 Black	?		No.18 Sqn. UARAF insignia, early-style unit badge; last noted 1973
MiG-17F	2665	?		No.18 Sqn; red late-style unit badge, four rocket launch rails. Destroyed El Arish AB 5-6-1967

MiG-17F	2680	?		Last noted Helwan 1977
MiG-17F	2695	?		Last noted 1974
MiG-17F	2728 Black	?		Green/brown camouflage, post-UAR markings, two hardpoints on the fuselage. Last noted in the early 1980s
MiG-17F	2782 Black	?		Camouflaged, post-UAR markings
MiG-17F	2851	?		Last noted 1973
MiG-17F	2858	?		Last noted 9-1967
MiG-17F	2877	?		Last noted 1973
MiG-17F	2884	?		Last noted 9-1967
MiG-17F	2961 White	?		Camouflaged, post-UAR markings; four rocket launch rails and bomb racks under fuselage. Preserved Military Museum, Saladin Citadel, Cairo
MiG-17F	2975 Black	?		Camouflaged, post-UAR markings; four rocket launch rails and bomb racks under fuselage. Sold to the USA for evaluation
MiG-17F	3147 Black	?		Camouflaged, post-UAR markings; possible confusion with 2147
MiG-17F	4021 Black	?		Camouflaged, post-UAR markings
MiG-17F	?	0228		Ex-East German Air Force 308 Red. Also reported for Syria (possibly taken over by Syria after dissolution of the UAR)
MiG-17F	?	0432		Ex-East German Air Force 653 Red
MiG-17F	?	0467		Ex-East German Air Force 784 Red
MiG-17F	?	0537		Ex-East German Air Force 593 Red
MiG-17F	?	0585		Ex-East German Air Force 599 Red
MiG-17F	?	0659		Ex-East German Air Force 667 Red
MiG-17F	?	0714		Ex-Soviet Air Force?
MiG-17F	?	0858		Ex-East German Air Force 565 Red. Also reported for Syria (possibly taken over by Syria after dissolution of the UAR)
MiG-17F	?	0937		Ex-East German Air Force 585 Red
MiG-17F	?	0993		Ex-East German Air Force 660 Red
MiG-17F	?	1080		Ex-East German Air Force 606 Red
MiG-17F	?	7122		Ex-East German Air Force 309 Red
MiG-17F	?	7129		Ex-East German Air Force 926 Red
MiG-17F	?	7151		Ex-Soviet Air Force?
MiG-17F	?	7250		Ex-Soviet Air Force?
MiG-17F	?	7422		Ex-Soviet Air Force?
MiG-17F	?	7424		Ex-East German Air Force 388 Red
MiG-17F	?	7432		Ex-East German Air Force 392 Red
MiG-17F	?	7443		Ex-East German Air Force 383 Red
MiG-17F	?	7502		Ex-East German Air Force 310 Red
MiG-17F	?	7503		Ex-East German Air Force 387 Red
MiG-17F	?	8044		D/D 11-1967; No.1 Sqn?
MiG-17F	?	8047		D/D 11-1967; No.1 Sqn?
MiG-17F	?	8432		D/D late 1967
MiG-17F	?	0115311		Ex-Soviet Air Force?
MiG-17F	?	0115326		Ex-Soviet Air Force?
MiG-17F	?	0415371		Ex-Soviet Air Force?
MiG-17F	?	05153314		Ex-Soviet Air Force?
MiG-17F	?	0515385		Ex-Soviet Air Force?
MiG-17F	?	0915346		Ex-Soviet Air Force?
PZL Lim-5 (MiG-17F)	?	1C 06-01		Ex-East German Air Force 201 Red
PZL Lim-5	?	1C 06-06		Ex-East German Air Force 475 Red
PZL Lim-5	?	1C 06-09		Ex-East German Air Force 752 Red
PZL Lim-5	?	1C 06-13		Ex-East German Air Force 303 Red
PZL Lim-5	?	1C 06-18		Ex-East German Air Force 318 Red
PZL Lim-5	?	1C 06-20		Ex-East German Air Force 500 Red
PZL Lim-5	?	1C 06-27		Ex-East German Air Force 527 Red
PZL Lim-5	?	1C 07-01		Ex-East German Air Force 301 Red
PZL Lim-5	?	1C 07-05		Ex-East German Air Force 214 Red
PZL Lim-5	?	1C 07-07		Ex-East German Air Force 925 Red

PZL Lim-5	?	1C 07-12		Ex-East German Air Force 773 Red
PZL Lim-5	?	1C 07-16		Ex-East German Air Force 799 Red
PZL Lim-5	?	1C 07-21		Ex-East German Air Force 731 Red
PZL Lim-5	?	1C 07-22		Ex-East German Air Force 735 Red
PZL Lim-5	?	1C 07-25		Ex-East German Air Force 539 Red
PZL Lim-5	?	1C 07-30		Ex-East German Air Force 850 Red
PZL Lim-5	?	1C 08-06		Ex-East German Air Force 658 Red
PZL Lim-5	?	1C 08-08		Ex-East German Air Force 800 Red
PZL Lim-5	?	1C 08-09		Ex-East German Air Force 695 Red
PZL Lim-5	?	1C 08-10		Ex-East German Air Force 815 Red
PZL Lim-5	?	1C 08-14		Ex-East German Air Force 845 Red
PZL Lim-5	?	1C 08-17		Ex-East German Air Force 941 Red
PZL Lim-5	?	1C 08-18		Ex-East German Air Force 900 Red
PZL Lim-5	?	1C 08-19		Ex-East German Air Force 902 Red
PZL Lim-5	?	1C 08-26		Ex-East German Air Force 974 Red
PZL Lim-5	?	1C 09-01		Ex-East German Air Force 912 Red
PZL Lim-5	?	1C 09-05		Ex-East German Air Force 916 Red
PZL Lim-5	?	1C 09-10		Ex-East German Air Force 946 Red
PZL Lim-5	?	1C 09-15		Ex-East German Air Force 960 Red
PZL Lim-5	?	1C 09-24		Ex-East German Air Force 973 Red
PZL Lim-5	?	1C 09-25		Ex-East German Air Force 855 Red
PZL Lim-5	?	1C 09-29		Ex-East German Air Force 879 Red
PZL Lim-5	?	1C 10-01		Ex-East German Air Force 601 Red
MiG-17PF	2802 Black	?		No.31 Sqn. UARAF insignia, 'crow-bat' unit badge; four rocket launch rails
MiG-17PF	2803 Black	?		No.31 Sqn. UARAF insignia, 'crow-bat' unit badge. Damaged 5-6-1967 but later repaired
MiG-19S	2041 Black	?		UARAF insignia
MiG-19S	2900	?		
MiG-19S	2901	?		
MiG-19S	2921	?		
MiG-19S	2965	?		
MiG-19S	3024 Black	?		No.20 Sqn. Preserved Egyptian Air Force Museum, Cairo-Almaza
MiG-19S	3101	?		
MiG-19S	3105	?		
MiG-19S	3220	?		
MiG-19S	3221 Black	?		No.20 Composite Sqn, UARAF insignia, 1967
MiG-19S	3501	?		
MiG-19S	3502	?		
MiG-19S	3503	?		
MiG-19S	3504	?		
MiG-19S	3505	?		
MiG-19S	3506	?		
MiG-19S	3507	?		
MiG-19S	3508	?		
MiG-19S	3509	?		
MiG-19S	3510	?		
MiG-19S	3511	?		
MiG-19S	3512	?		
MiG-19S	3513	?		
MiG-19S	3514	?		
MiG-19S	3515	?		
MiG-19S	3516	?		
MiG-19S	3517	?		
MiG-19S	3518	?		
MiG-19S	3519	?		
MiG-19S	3520	?		

MiG-19S	3521	?		
MiG-19S	3522	?		
MiG-19S	3523	?		
MiG-19S	3524	?		
MiG-19S	3525	?		
MiG-19S	3526	?		
MiG-19S	3527	?		
MiG-19S	3528	?		
MiG-19S	3529	?		
MiG-19S	3530	?		
MiG-19S	3531	?		
MiG-19S	3532	?		
MiG-19S	3533	?		
MiG-19S	3534	?		
MiG-19S	3535	?		
MiG-19S	3536	?		
MiG-19S	3537	?		
MiG-19S	3538	?		
MiG-19S	3539	?		
MiG-19S	3540	?		
MiG-19S	3541	?		
MiG-19S	3542	?		
MiG-19S	3543	?		
MiG-19S	3544	?		
MiG-19S	3545	?		
MiG-19S	3546	?		
MiG-19S	3547	?		
MiG-19S	3548	?		
MiG-19S	3549	?		
MiG-19S	3550	?		
MiG-19S	3551	?		
MiG-19S	3552	?		
MiG-19S	3553	?		
MiG-19S	3554	?		
MiG-19S	3555	?		
MiG-19S	3556	?		
MiG-19S	3557	?		
MiG-19S	3558	?		
MiG-19S	3559	?		
MiG-19S	3560	?		
MiG-19S	3561	?		
MiG-19S	3562	?		
MiG-19S	3563	?		
MiG-19S	3564	?		
MiG-19S	3565	?		
MiG-19S	3566	?		
MiG-19S	3567	?		
MiG-19S	3568	?		
MiG-19S	3569	?		
MiG-19S	3570	?		
MiG-19S	3571 Black	?		UARAF insignia
MiG-19S	3572	?		
MiG-19S	3573	?		
MiG-19S	3574	?		
MiG-19S	3575	?		
MiG-19S	3576	?		
MiG-19S	3577	?		

MiG-19S	3578	?		
MiG-19S	3579	?		
MiG-19S	3580	?		
MiG-19S	3581	?		
MiG-19S	3582	?		
MiG-19S	3583	?		
MiG-19S	3584	?		
MiG-19S	3585	?		
MiG-19S	3586	?		
MiG-19S	3587	?		
MiG-19S	3588	?		
MiG-19S	3589	?		
MiG-19S	3590	?		
MiG-19S	3591	?		
MiG-19S	3592	?		
MiG-19S	3593	?		
MiG-19S	3594	?		
MiG-19S	3595	?		
MiG-19S	3596	?		
MiG-19S	3597	?		
MiG-19S	3598	?		
MiG-19S	3599	?		
Shenyang F-6	2808 Black	46-****		Two-tone grey camouflage, post-UAR insignia
Shenyang F-6	2824	46-****		
Shenyang F-6	2851	46-****		
Shenyang F-6	2872	46-****		
Shenyang F-6	2965 Black	46-****		Two-tone grey camouflage, post-UAR insignia
Shenyang F-6C	3802	46-****		Used as decoy at Helwan AB
Shenyang F-6C	3803	46-****		
Shenyang F-6C	3808	46-****		
Shenyang F-6C	3824	46-****		
Shenyang F-6C	3825	46-****		Stored Bilbeis
Shenyang F-6C	3836	46-****		Stored Bilbeis
Shenyang F-6C	3840	46-****		
Shenyang F-6C	3851	46-****		
Shenyang F-6C	3860	46-****		Preserved Cairo (?)
Shenyang F-6C	3872 Black	46-****		Two-tone grey camouflage post-UAR insignia
Shenyang F-6C	3876	46-****		Stored Bilbeis
Shenyang F-6C	3877	46-****		
Shenyang F-6C	3878 Black	46-****		Two-tone grey camouflage, post-UAR insignia
Shenyang FT-6	3952	48-*****		
Shenyang FT-6	3953 Black	48-*****		All-white c/s, post-UAR insignia
Shenyang FT-6	3954	48-10102		
Shenyang FT-6	3956	48-*****		
Shenyang FT-6	3957	48-*****		Transferred to the USA for trials
MiG-21F-13	5001 Black	?		D/D 6-1962; natural metal finish, UARAF insignia
MiG-21F-13	5002	?		
MiG-21F-13	5006	?		
MiG-21F-13	5010	?		
MiG-21F-13	5011	?		
MiG-21F-13	5020	?		
MiG-21F-13	5068	?		To the USA; became N4318W, c/n in FAA register as 5068 which is obviously wrong
MiG-21F-13	5071	?		
MiG-21F-13	5108	?		
MiG-21F-13	5119	?		

MiG-21F-13	5172 Black	?		Natural metal finish, UARAF insignia. Seen in 1965
MiG-21F-13	5201	?		
MiG-21F-13	5202 Black	?		Natural metal finish, UARAF insignia
MiG-21F-13	5204	?		
MiG-21F-13	5205	?		
MiG-21F-13	5206	?		
MiG-21F-13	5208	?		
MiG-21F-13	5209	?		
MiG-21F-13	5210	?		
MiG-21F-13	5211 Black	?		Flight Training Unit, Cairo-West AB. Natural metal finish, UARAF insignia
MiG-21F-13	5225	?		
MiG-21F-13	5240	?		
MiG-21F-13	5279 Black	?		Seen in 1965; natural metal finish
MiG-21F-13	5341 Black	?		Sand/green camouflage, UARAF insignia
MiG-21F-13	5358	?		
MiG-21F-13	5401	?		
MiG-21F-13	5402	?		Seen in 1973; serial also reported as MiG-21PF!
MiG-21F-13	5403	?		102 Air Brigade, seen 1973; serial also reported as MiG-21PFM!
MiG-21F-13	5463	?		Preserved Inshas
MiG-21F-13	5528	?		
MiG-21F-13	5617	?		Preserved Helwan
MiG-21F-13	5701	860801		Czechoslovak-built (Aero S-106). Ex-Czechoslovak Air Force 0801 Black, D/D 14-4-1969
MiG-21F-13	5702	860802		Czechoslovak-built (Aero S-106). Ex-Czechoslovak Air Force 0802 Black, D/D 14-4-1969
MiG-21F-13	5703	860803		Czechoslovak-built (Aero S-106). Ex-Czechoslovak Air Force 0803 Black, D/D 14-4-1969
MiG-21F-13	5704	860804		Czechoslovak-built (Aero S-106). Ex-Czechoslovak Air Force 0804 Black, D/D 14-4-1969
MiG-21F-13	5705	860805		Czechoslovak-built (Aero S-106). Ex-Czechoslovak Air Force 0805 Black, D/D 14-4-1969
MiG-21F-13	5706	860806		Czechoslovak-built (Aero S-106). Ex-Czechoslovak Air Force 0806 Black, D/D 3-6-1969
MiG-21F-13	5707	860807		Czechoslovak-built (Aero S-106). Ex-Czechoslovak Air Force 0807 Black, D/D 3-6-1969
MiG-21F-13	5708	860808		Czechoslovak-built (Aero S-106). Ex-Czechoslovak Air Force 0808 Black, D/D 3-6-1969
MiG-21F-13	5709	860809		Czechoslovak-built (Aero S-106). Ex-Czechoslovak Air Force 0809 Black, D/D 3-6-1969
MiG-21F-13	5710	860810		Czechoslovak-built (Aero S-106). Ex-Czechoslovak Air Force 0810 Black, D/D 3-6-1969
MiG-21F-13	5711	860811		Czechoslovak-built (Aero S-106). Ex-Czechoslovak Air Force 0811 Black, D/D 3-6-1969
MiG-21F-13	5712	860812		Czechoslovak-built (Aero S-106). Ex-Czechoslovak Air Force 0812 Black, D/D 3-6-1969
MiG-21F-13	5713	860813		Czechoslovak-built (Aero S-106). Ex-Czechoslovak Air Force 0813 Black, D/D 3-6-1969
MiG-21F-13	5714	860814		Czechoslovak-built (Aero S-106). Ex-Czechoslovak Air Force 0814 Black, D/D 3-6-1969
MiG-21F-13	5715	860815		Czechoslovak-built (Aero S-106). Ex-Czechoslovak Air Force 0815 Black, D/D 3-6-1969
MiG-21F-13	5716	960901		Czechoslovak-built (Aero S-106). Ex-Czechoslovak Air Force 0901 Black, D/D 31-7-1969
MiG-21F-13	5717	960902		Czechoslovak-built (Aero S-106). Ex-Czechoslovak Air Force 0902 Black, D/D 4-12-1969
MiG-21F-13	5718	960907		Czechoslovak-built (Aero S-106). Ex-Czechoslovak Air Force 0907 Black, D/D 4-12-1969

MiG-21F-13	5719	960908		Czechoslovak-built (Aero S-106). Ex-Czechoslovak Air Force 0908 Black, D/D 4-12-1969
MiG-21F-13	5720	960909		Czechoslovak-built (Aero S-106). Ex-Czechoslovak Air Force 0909 Black, D/D 4-12-1969
MiG-21F-13	5721	960910		Czechoslovak-built (Aero S-106). Ex-Czechoslovak Air Force 0910 Black, D/D 4-12-1969
MiG-21F-13	5722	960911		Czechoslovak-built (Aero S-106). Ex-Czechoslovak Air Force 0911 Black, D/D 4-12-1969
MiG-21F-13	5723	960912		Czechoslovak-built (Aero S-106). Ex-Czechoslovak Air Force 0912 Black, D/D 4-12-1969
MiG-21F-13	5724	960913		Czechoslovak-built (Aero S-106). Ex-Czechoslovak Air Force 0913 Black, D/D 4-12-1969
MiG-21F-13	5755	960914		Czechoslovak-built (Aero S-106). Ex-Czechoslovak Air Force 0914 Black, D/D 4-12-1969
MiG-21F-13	5726	960915		Czechoslovak-built (Aero S-106). Ex-Czechoslovak Air Force 0915 Black, D/D 4-12-1969
MiG-21F-13	5843 Black	?		D/D 1963-64, No.26 Sqn. Tan/green camouflage, unit badge on nose
MiG-21F-13	5844	?		D/D 1963-64
MiG-21F-13	5846	?		D/D 1963-64
MiG-21F-13	5902	?		
MiG-21F-13	5903	?		D/D 1963-64
MiG-21F-13	5908 Black	?		D/D 1963-64. Preserved Cairo Military Museum, Saladin Citadel; now no serial
MiG-21F-13	5913	?		
MiG-21F-13	5914	?		
MiG-21FL	5072	?		Natural metal finish, UARAF insignia
MiG-21FL	5203	?		
MiG-21FL	5207 Black	?		Natural metal finish, UARAF insignia
MiG-21FL	5212	?		
MiG-21FL	5213	?		
MiG-21FL	5214	?		
MiG-21FL	5215	?		
MiG-21FL	5216	?		
MiG-21FL	5218	?		
MiG-21FL	5219	?		
MiG-21FL	5220	?		
MiG-21FL	5221	?		
MiG-21FL	5222	?		
MiG-21FL	5223	?		
MiG-21FL	5224	?		
MiG-21FL	5250	?		
MiG-21FL	5251	?		
MiG-21FL	5254	?		
MiG-21FL	5258	?		
MiG-21FL	5259	?		
MiG-21FL	5264	?		
MiG-21FL	5401	?		D/D 1964
MiG-21FL	5402	?		D/D 1964
MiG-21FL	5403 Black	?		D/D 1964; serial also reported as MiG-21PFM! Natural metal finish, UARAF insignia
MiG-21FL	5404	?		D/D 1964
MiG-21FL	5405	?		D/D 1964
MiG-21FL	5406	?		D/D 1964
MiG-21FL	5407	?		D/D 1964
MiG-21FL	5408	?		D/D 1964
MiG-21FL	5409	?		D/D 1964
MiG-21FL	5410	?		D/D 1964
MiG-21FL	5411	?		D/D 1964

MiG-21FL	5412	?		D/D 1964
MiG-21FL	5413	?		D/D 1964
MiG-21FL	5414	?		D/D 1964
MiG-21FL	5415	?		D/D 1964
MiG-21FL	5416	?		D/D 1964
MiG-21FL	5417	?		D/D 1964
MiG-21FL	5418	?		D/D 1964
MiG-21FL	5419	?		D/D 1964
MiG-21FL	5420	?		D/D 1964
MiG-21FL	5421	?		D/D 1964
MiG-21FL	5422	?		D/D 1964
MiG-21FL	5423	?		D/D 1964
MiG-21FL	5424	?		D/D 1964
MiG-21FL	5425	?		D/D 1964
MiG-21FL	5426	?		D/D 1964
MiG-21FL	5427	?		D/D 1964
MiG-21FL	5428	?		D/D 1964
MiG-21FL	5429	?		D/D 1964
MiG-21FL	5430	?		D/D 1964
MiG-21FL	5431	?		D/D 1964
MiG-21FL	5432	?		D/D 1964
MiG-21FL	5433	?		D/D 1964
MiG-21FL	5434	?		D/D 1964
MiG-21FL	5435	?		D/D 1964
MiG-21FL	5436	?		D/D 1964
MiG-21FL	5437	?		D/D 1964
MiG-21FL	5438	?		D/D 1964
MiG-21FL	5439	?		D/D 1964
MiG-21FL	5440	?		D/D 1964
MiG-21PFM	1072	?		D/D circa 1970
MiG-21PFM	'2358 Black'	?		D/D circa 1970. Silver overall. Spurious serial; preserved Luxor
MiG-21PFM	5201	?		D/D 1966
MiG-21PFM	5202	?		D/D 1966
MiG-21PFM	5203	?		D/D 1966
MiG-21PFM	5204	?		D/D 1966
MiG-21PFM	5205	?		D/D 1966
MiG-21PFM	5206	?		D/D 1966
MiG-21PFM	5207	?		D/D 1966
MiG-21PFM	5208	?		D/D 1966
MiG-21PFM	5209	?		D/D 1966
MiG-21PFM	5210	?		D/D 1966
MiG-21PFM	5211	?		D/D 1966
MiG-21PFM	5212	?		D/D 1966
MiG-21PFM	5213	?		D/D 1966
MiG-21PFM	5214	?		D/D 1966
MiG-21PFM	5215	?		D/D 1966
MiG-21PFM	5216	?		D/D 1966
MiG-21PFM	5217	?		D/D 1966
MiG-21PFM	5218	?		D/D 1966
MiG-21PFM	5219	?		D/D 1966
MiG-21PFM	5220	?		D/D 1966
MiG-21PFM	5221	?		D/D 1966
MiG-21PFM	5222	?		D/D 1966
MiG-21PFM	5223	?		D/D 1966
MiG-21PFM	5224	?		D/D 1966
MiG-21PFM	5225	?		D/D 1966
MiG-21PFM	5226	?		D/D 1966

MiG-21PFM	5227	?		D/D 1966
MiG-21PFM	5228	?		D/D 1966
MiG-21PFM	5229	?		D/D 1966
MiG-21PFM	5230	?		D/D 1966
MiG-21PFM	5231	?		D/D 1966
MiG-21PFM	5232	?		D/D 1966
MiG-21PFM	5233	?		D/D 1966
MiG-21PFM	5234	?		D/D 1966
MiG-21PFM	5235	?		D/D 1966
MiG-21PFM	5236	?		D/D 1966
MiG-21PFM	5237	?		D/D 1966
MiG-21PFM	5238	?		D/D 1966
MiG-21PFM	5239	?		D/D 1966
MiG-21PFM	5240	?		D/D 1966
MiG-21PFM	5241	?		D/D 1966
MiG-21PFM	5242	?		D/D 1966
MiG-21PFM	5243	?		D/D 1966
MiG-21PFM	5244	?		D/D 1966
MiG-21PFM	5245	?		D/D 1966
MiG-21PFM	5246	?		D/D 1966
MiG-21PFM	5247	?		D/D 1966
MiG-21PFM	5248	?		D/D 1966
MiG-21PFM	5249	?		D/D 1966
MiG-21PFM	5250	?		D/D 1966. Sold to the USA for trials in the early 1980s
MiG-21PFM	5251	?		D/D 1966
MiG-21PFM	5252	?		D/D 1966
MiG-21PFM	5253	?		D/D 1966
MiG-21PFM	5254	?		D/D 1966
MiG-21PFM	5255	?		D/D 1966
MiG-21PFM	5256	?		D/D 1966
MiG-21PFM	5257	?		D/D 1966
MiG-21PFM	5258	?		D/D 1966
MiG-21PFM	5259	?		D/D 1966
MiG-21PFM	5260	?		D/D 1966
MiG-21PFM	5261	?		D/D 1966
MiG-21PFM	5262	?		D/D 1966
MiG-21PFM	5263	?		D/D 1966
MiG-21PFM	5264	?		D/D 1966
MiG-21PFM	5265	?		D/D 1966
MiG-21PFM	5266	?		D/D 1966
MiG-21PFM	5267	?		D/D 1966
MiG-21PFM	5268	?		D/D 1966
MiG-21PFM	5269	?		D/D 1966
MiG-21PFM	5270	?		D/D 1966
MiG-21PFM	5271	?		D/D 1966
MiG-21PFM	5272	?		D/D 1966
MiG-21PFM	5273	?		D/D 1966
MiG-21PFM	5274	?		D/D 1966
MiG-21PFM	5275	?		D/D 1966
MiG-21PFM	5364?	?		D/D c.1970? Possible misread for 5264!
MiG-21PFM	5463	?		D/D c.1970
MiG-21PFM	5620	?		D/D c.1970. Sold to the USA for trials in the early 1980s
MiG-21PFM	5634	?		D/D c.1970
MiG-21PFM	5654	?		D/D c.1970
MiG-21PFM	8312	?		D/D c.1970
MiG-21PFM	8501	?		D/D c.1970
MiG-21PFS	8001	?		

MiG-21PFS	8002	?		
MiG-21PFS	8003	?		
MiG-21PFS	8004	?		
MiG-21PFS	8005	?		
MiG-21PFS	8006	?		
MiG-21PFS	8007	?		
MiG-21PFS	8008	?		
MiG-21PFS	8009	?		
MiG-21PFS	8010	?		
MiG-21PFS	8011	?		
MiG-21PFS	8012	?		
MiG-21PFS	8013	?		
MiG-21PFS	8014	?		
MiG-21PFS	8015	?		
MiG-21PFS	8016	?		
MiG-21PFS	8017	?		
MiG-21PFS	8018	?		
MiG-21PFS	8019	?		
MiG-21PFS	8020	?		
MiG-21PFS	8021	?		
MiG-21PFS	8022	?		
MiG-21PFS	8023	?		
MiG-21PFS	8024	?		
MiG-21PFS	8025 Black	?		Tan/green camouflage
MiG-21PFS	8026	?		
MiG-21PFS	8027	?		
MiG-21PFS	8028	?		
MiG-21PFS	8029	?		
MiG-21PFS	8030	?		
MiG-21PFS	8031	?		
MiG-21PFS	8032	?		
MiG-21PFS	8033	?		
MiG-21PFS	8034	?		
MiG-21PFS	8035	?		
MiG-21PFS	8036	?		
MiG-21PFS	8037	?		
MiG-21PFS	8038	?		
MiG-21PFS	8039	?		
MiG-21PFS	8040 Black	?		Preserved 1973 October War Panorama near Cairo as 8040 White, spurious brown/yellow camouflage
MiG-21PFS	8041	?		
MiG-21PFS	8042	?		
MiG-21PFS	8043	?		
MiG-21PFS	8044	?		
MiG-21PFS	8045	?		
MiG-21PFS	8046	?		
MiG-21PFS	8047	?		
MiG-21PFS	8048	?		
MiG-21PFS	8049	?		
MiG-21PFS	8050	?		
MiG-21PFS	8051	?		
MiG-21PFS	8052	?		
MiG-21PFS	8053	?		
MiG-21PFS	8054	?		
MiG-21PFS	8055	?		
MiG-21PFS	8056	?		
MiG-21PFS	8057	?		

MiG-21PFS	8058	?		
MiG-21PFS	8059	?		
MiG-21PFS	8060	?		
MiG-21PFS	8061	?		
MiG-21PFS	8062	?		
MiG-21PFS	8063	?		
MiG-21PFS	8064	?		
MiG-21PFS	8065 Black	?		Tan/green camouflage
MiG-21PFS	8066	?		
MiG-21PFS	8067 Black	?		Silver overall. Preserved at an Egyptian airbase
MiG-21PFS	8068	?		
MiG-21PFS	8069	?		
MiG-21PFS	8070 Black	?		Tan/green/brown camouflage
MiG-21PFS	8071	?		
MiG-21PFS	8072	?		Preserved 1973 October War Panorama near Cairo
MiG-21PFS	8073	?		
MiG-21PFS	8074	?		
MiG-21PFS	8075 Black	?		Tan/green/brown camouflage
MiG-21R	4799 Black	?		
MiG-21RF	1501	?		
MiG-21RF	8501 Black	?		No.21 Sqn. Tan/green/brown camouflage
MiG-21RF	8502 Black	?		No.26 Sqn. Tan/green/brown camouflage
MiG-21RF	8503	?		No.26 Sqn
MiG-21RF	8504	?		No.26 Sqn
MiG-21RF	8505	?		No.26 Sqn
MiG-21RF	8506 Black	?		No.26 Sqn. Tan/green/brown camouflage
MiG-21M	8301	?		
MiG-21M	8302	?		
MiG-21M	8303	?		
MiG-21M	8304	?		
MiG-21M	8305	?		
MiG-21M	8306	?		
MiG-21M	8307	?		
MiG-21M	8308	?		
MiG-21M	8309	?		
MiG-21M	8310	?		
MiG-21M	8311	?		
MiG-21M	8312	?		
MiG-21MF	8116	?	?	Noted 2005
MiG-21MF	8212 Black	?	?	Green/tan camouflage
MiG-21MF	8226 White	?	?	Noted 2005, tan/green/brown camouflage, orange fin, wingtips and fuselage spine
MiG-21M	8360 White	?		Grey/green/black camouflage, orange markings
MiG-21MF	8410	?	?	
MiG-21MF	8424 Black	?	?	Tan/green/brown camouflage
MiG-21MF	8427	?	?	
MiG-21MF	8451	?	?	Noted 2005
MiG-21MF	8454 Black	?	?	Tan/green camouflage plus orange fin, wingtips and fuselage spine
MiG-21MF	8457	?	?	Sent to USA for testing in early 1980s
MiG-21MF	8460 Black	?	?	Tan/green/brown camouflage
MiG-21MF	8468 White	?	?	Grey/green/black camouflage, orange fin, wingtips and fuselage spine
MiG-21MF	8501	?	?	
MiG-21MF	8502	?	?	
MiG-21MF	8522	?	?	
MiG-21MF	8610	?	?	
MiG-21MF	8611	?	?	
MiG-21MF	8618 White	?	?	Noted 2005, tan/green/brown camouflage, orange fin, wingtips and fuselage spine

MiG-21MF	8627	?	?	
MiG-21MF	8632	?	?	
MiG-21MF	8652	?	?	
MiG-21MF	8654	?	?	
MiG-21MF	8661	?	?	Noted 2004
MiG-21MF	8666	?	?	
MiG-21MF	8668	?	?	Noted 2005
MiG-21MF	8676 White	?	?	Grey/green/black camouflage, orange fin, wingtips and fuselage spine
MiG-21MF	8678	?	?	Noted 2006
MiG-21MF	8686	?	?	
MiG-21MF	8688	?	?	
MiG-21MF	8691 Black	?	?	26 Air Brigade. Tan/green camouflage
MiG-21MF	8692 Black	?	?	22 Air Brigade. Tan/green camouflage
MiG-21MF	8697 Black	?	?	Tan/green camouflage
MiG-21US	5610 White	**6851**		Grey/green/black camouflage, orange fin, wingtips and fuselage spine
MiG-21US	5611 White	**6851**		Grey/green/black camouflage, orange fin, wingtips and fuselage spine
MiG-21US	5612 White	**6851**		Grey/green/black camouflage, orange fin, wingtips and fuselage spine
MiG-21US	5617 White	**6851**		Grey/green/black camouflage, orange fin, wingtips and fuselage spine
MiG-21US	5632 Black	**6851**		Sand/green/dark green camouflage
MiG-21US	5640 White	**6851**		Grey/green/black camouflage, orange fin, wingtips and fuselage spine
MiG-21US	5641	**6851**		
MiG-21US	5642 Black	**6851**		Tan/green camouflage
MiG-21US	5643 White	**6851**		Grey/green/black camouflage, orange fin, wingtips and fuselage spine
MiG-21US	5644	07685154		
MiG-21US	5645	**6851**		
MiG-21US	5646	**6851**		
MiG-21US	5647	**6851**		
MiG-21US	5648	**6851**		
MiG-21US	5649	**6851**		
MiG-21US	5650	**6851**		
MiG-21US	5651	**6851**		
MiG-21US	5652	**6851**		
MiG-21US	5653	**6851**		
MiG-21US	5654 Black	**6851**		Tan/green/brown camouflage
MiG-21US	5655	**6851**		
MiG-21US	5656	**6851**		
MiG-21US	5657	**6851**		
MiG-21US	5658 White	**6851**		Grey/green/black camouflage, orange fin, wingtips and fuselage spine
MiG-21US	5659	**6851**		
MiG-21US	5660	**6851**		
MiG-21US	5661	**6851**		
MiG-21US	5662	**6851**		
MiG-21US	5663	**6851**		
MiG-21US	5664	**6851**		
MiG-21UM	0642	?	?	
MiG-21UM	4640	?	?	
Chengdu F-7B	4501	?		
Chengdu F-7B	4502 Black	?		
Chengdu F-7B	4503	?		
Chengdu F-7B	4504 Black	?		Early-style canopy. Last seen 11-2008
Chengdu F-7B	4505 Black	?		Early-style canopy. No.104 Sqn. Last seen 11-2007
Chengdu F-7B	4506 Black	?		Early-style canopy. No.104 Sqn. Last seen 11-2007
Chengdu F-7B	4507	?		No.104 Sqn. Last seen 11-2007
Chengdu F-7B	4508	?		
Chengdu F-7B	4509 Black	?		No.104 Sqn. Last seen 11-2007
Chengdu F-7B	4510 Black	?		Early-style canopy. No.104 Sqn. Last seen 11-2008
Chengdu F-7B	4511 Black	?		

Chengdu F-7B	4512 Black	?		Early-style canopy
Chengdu F-7B	4513	?		
Chengdu F-7B	4514 Black	?		Early-style canopy
Chengdu F-7B	4515 Black	?		Early-style canopy. No.104 Sqn. Last seen 11-2008
Chengdu F-7B	4516 Black	?		
Chengdu F-7B	4517	?		No.104 Sqn. Last seen 11-2007
Chengdu F-7B	4518 Black	?		No.104 Sqn. Last seen 11-2007
Chengdu F-7B	4519	?		No.104 Sqn. Last seen 11-2007
Chengdu F-7B	4520	?		
Chengdu F-7B	4521	?		
Chengdu F-7B	4522	?		
Chengdu F-7B	4523	?		
Chengdu F-7B	4524	?		
Chengdu F-7B	4525	?		No.104 Sqn. Last seen 11-2007
Chengdu F-7B	4526	?		
Chengdu F-7B	4527	?		
Chengdu F-7B	4528	?		
Chengdu F-7B	4529	?		
Chengdu F-7B	4530	?		
Chengdu F-7B	4531	?		
Chengdu F-7B	4532	?		
Chengdu F-7B	4533 Black	?		Late-style canopy
Chengdu F-7B	4534	?		
Chengdu F-7B	4535	?		No.104 Sqn. Last seen 11-2007
Chengdu F-7B	4536	?		
Chengdu F-7B	4537	?		
Chengdu F-7B	4538	?		
Chengdu F-7B	4539	?		
Chengdu F-7B	4540	?		
Chengdu F-7B	4541	?		
Chengdu F-7B	4542	?		
Chengdu F-7B	4543	?		
Chengdu F-7B	4544	?		
Chengdu F-7B	4545	?		
Chengdu F-7B	4546	?		
Chengdu F-7B	4547 Black	?		Late-style canopy. No.104 Sqn. Two-tone grey camouflage
Chengdu F-7B	4548	?		
Chengdu F-7B	4549	?		
Chengdu F-7B	4550	?		
Chengdu F-7B	4551	?		
Chengdu F-7B	4552	?		
Chengdu F-7B	4553	?		
Chengdu F-7B	4554	?		
Chengdu F-7B	4555	?		
Chengdu F-7B	4556	?		No.104 Sqn
Chengdu F-7B	4557	?		
Chengdu F-7B	4558	?		
Chengdu F-7B	4559	?		
Chengdu F-7B	4560	?		
Chengdu F-7B	4561	?		
Chengdu F-7B	4562	?		
Chengdu F-7B	4563	?		
Chengdu F-7B	4564	?		
Chengdu F-7B	4565	?		
Chengdu F-7B	4566	?		
Chengdu F-7B	4567	?		
Chengdu F-7B	4568	?		

Chengdu F-7B	4569	?		
Chengdu F-7B	4570	?		
Chengdu F-7B	4571	?		
Chengdu F-7B	4572	?		
Chengdu F-7B	4573	?		
Chengdu F-7B	4574	?		
Chengdu F-7B	4575	?		
Chengdu F-7B	4576	?		
Chengdu F-7B	4577	?		
Chengdu F-7B	4578	?		
Chengdu F-7B	4579	?		
Chengdu F-7B	4580	?		
MiG-23MS	9101	12400****		
MiG-23MS	9501 Black	124004215		Sold to China; tested as '18 Grey'. Preserved People's Liberation Army Air Force Museum, Datangshan
MiG-23MF?	6840	03902*****		Sold to the USA for trials
MiG-23MF?	6842	03902*****		Sold to the USA for trials
MiG-23BN	2017	32400****		
MiG-23BN	4421???	324004421		Also reported as c/n 0393204421 under the post-1974 system! Preserved Royal Army Museum, Brussels, as 'Soviet Air Force 23 Red'
MiG-23UB	7721	?		Sold to the USA for trials
MiG-23UB	7805	?		Sold to the USA for trials
MiG-23UB	9091 Black	?		
Mi-1	41	?		
Mi-1	42	?		
Mi-1	43	?		
Mi-1	44	?		
Mi-1	45	?		
Mi-1	46	?		
Mi-1	47	?		
Mi-1	48	?		
Mi-1	49	?		
Mi-1	50	?		
Mi-1	51	?		
Mi-1	52	?		
Mi-1	53	?		
Mi-1	54	?		
Mi-1	55	?		
Mi-1	56	?		
Mi-1	57	?		
Mi-1	58	?		
Mi-4	31	?		
Mi-4	32	?		
Mi-4	33	?		
Mi-4	34	?		
Mi-4	35	?		
Mi-4	36	?		
Mi-4	37	?		
Mi-4	38	?		
Mi-4	39	?		
Mi-4	40	?		
Mi-4	61	?		
Mi-4	62	?		
Mi-4	63	?		

Mi-4	64	?		
Mi-4	65	?		
Mi-4	66	?		
Mi-4	67	?		
Mi-4	68	?		
Mi-4	69	?		
Mi-4	70	?		
Mi-4	71	?		
Mi-4	72	?		
Mi-4	73	?		
Mi-4	74	?		
Mi-4	75	?		
Mi-4	76	?		
Mi-4	77	?		
Mi-4	78	?		
Mi-4	79	?		
Mi-4	80	?		
Mi-4	81	?		
Mi-4	82	?		
Mi-4	83	?		
Mi-4	84	?		
Mi-4	85	?		
Mi-4	86	?		
Mi-4	87	?		
Mi-4	88	?		
Mi-4	89	?		
Mi-4	90	?		
Mi-6	173	?		
Mi-6	174	?		
Mi-6	190	?		
Mi-6	417	?		
Mi-6	460	?		
Mi-6	718	?		
Mi-6	801	?		Preserved Cairo-Almaza
Mi-6	802	?		Wfu Cairo-Embada
Mi-6	806	?		Wfu Cairo-Embada
Mi-6	807	?		
Mi-6	817 White		?	Camouflaged, UARAF insignia
Mi-6	820 White	?		Camouflaged, UARAF insignia
Mi-6	824 White	?		Camouflaged, UARAF insignia. Sold to the USA for trials
Mi-6	826	?		Wfu Cairo-Embada
Mi-6	882 Black	?		Sand camouflage, post-UAR insignia
Mi-6	883 (1)	?		Serial later reused for a Mi-8T, see below!
Mi-6	885 Black	?		Sand camouflage, post-UAR insignia
Mi-6	887	?		
Mi-6	1124 (1)	?		Serial later reused for a Mi-8T, see below!
Mi-8TV	822 White	?	?	Sand/brown camouflage, western-made intake filter
Mi-8T	880	?	?	
Mi-8T	881	?	?	
Mi-8T	883 (2)	?	?	Serial previously on a Mi-6, see above!
Mi-8T	884	?	?	
Mi-8T	886	?	?	
Mi-8T	887	?	?	
Mi-8T	988	?	?	
Mi-8T	989	?	?	Scrapped 1989

Mi-8T	998	?	?	
Mi-8T	999	?	?	
Mi-8T	1004	?	?	
Mi-8T	1010	?	?	
Mi-8T	1012	?	?	Scrapped 1989
Mi-8T	1025	?	?	
Mi-8T	1026	?	?	
Mi-8T	1029	?	?	
Mi-8T	1036	?	?	
Mi-8TV	1037	?	?	Sand/brown camouflage, 1971
Mi-8TV	1038	?	?	
Mi-8T	1046	?	?	
Mi-8TV	1048	?	?	Sand c/s
Mi-8T	1051	?	?	
Mi-8T	1124 (2)	?	?	Serial previously on a Mi-6, see above!
Mi-8T	1208 Black	?	?	Sand c/s. Crash-landed near Abu Rudeis and captured by Israelis 16-10-1973
Mi-8T	1217	?	?	
Mi-8TV	1219?	?	?	Sand c/s
Mi-8T	1256	?	?	
Mi-8T	1283	?	?	533 Helicopter Brigade
Mi-8TV	1311 Black	?	?	Sand c/s
Mi-8T	1320	?	?	
Mi-8T	1330	?	?	
Mi-8T	1382	?	?	
Mi-8TV	1404	?	?	Sand c/s
Mi-8T	1405	?	?	
Mi-8T	1406	?	?	
Mi-8T	1411	?	?	
Mi-8T	1416	?	?	
Mi-8T	1419	?	?	
Mi-8TV	1425	?	?	Sand c/s
Mi-8TV	1427	?	?	
Mi-8TV	1429	?	?	Sand c/s
Mi-8TV	1441	?	?	Sand c/s
Mi-8T	1455	?	?	
Mi-8TV	1461	?	?	Sand c/s
Mi-8T	1465 Black	?	?	Sand c/s, Mi-8MT-style intake filters
Mi-8T	1467	?	?	
Mi-8T	1468	?	?	
Mi-8T	1469	?	?	
Mi-8T	1476	?	?	
Mi-8T	1483	?	?	
Mi-8T	1486	?	?	
Mi-8T	2255	?	?	533 Helicopter Brigade
Mi-8T	2265	?	?	533 Helicopter Brigade
Mi-8T	2268	?	?	
Mi-8PS	2276	?	?	533 Helicopter Brigade. Sand c/s
Mi-8T	2285	?	?	533 Helicopter Brigade
Mi-8T	?	?	?	Sold to the USA, to USAF 90-00528
Mi-17?	3213	?	?	
Mi-17?	3231	?	?	
Mi-17	3251	?	?	
Mi-17?	3253	?	?	
Mi-17?	3254	?	?	
Mi-17-1V	3255	?	?	
Mi-17?	3256	?	?	
Mi-17?	3257	?	?	
Mi-17?	3258	?	?	
Mi-17?	3260	?	?	
Mi-17-1V	3261 Black	?	?	Operated by Egyptian Police, fitted with optronic surveillance system

Mi-17?	3266	?	?	
Mi-17-1V	3270 Black	?	?	Sand c/s
Mi-17-1V	3271	?	?	Sand c/s
Mi-17-1V	3272	?	?	Sand c/s
Mi-17?	3273	?	?	
Mi-17?	3275	?	?	
Mi-17?	3278	?	?	
Mi-17-1V?	3281	?	?	
Mi-17-1V	3282	?	?	Sand c/s
Mi-172	3286 Black	?	?	Sand c/s
Mi-17?	3288	?	?	
Mi-172	3276	?	?	
Su-7BMK	'2356'			Preserved Luxor, fake serial
Su-7BMK	7001			Preserved Egyptian Air Force Museum, Cairo-Almaza AB
Su-7BMK	7023	?		
Su-7BMK	7025 Black	?		Three-tone camouflage, post-UAR insignia
Su-7BMK	7035	?		
Su-7BMK	7047	?		
Su-7BMK	7107	?		Sold to the USA for evaluation; preserved Dugway, Utah
Su-7BMK	7108	?		
Su-7BMK	7121	?		
Su-7BMK	7166 Black	?		Three-tone camouflage, post-UAR insignia
Su-7BMK	7185 Black	?		Natural metal finish, UARAF insignia
Su-7BMK	7201	?		
Su-7BMK	7206	?		
Su-7BMK	7208 Black	?		Natural metal finish, UARAF insignia
Su-7BMK	7220	?		
Su-7BMK	7224	?		
Su-7BMK	7242	?		
Su-7BMK	7253	?		
Su-7BMK	7265	?		
Su-7BMK	7270	?		
Su-7BMK	7271 Black	?		Two-tone camouflage, post-UAR insignia
Su-7BMK	7275	?		
Su-7BMK	7276	?		
Su-7BMK	7320 Black	?		Preserved Military Museum, Saladin Citadel, Cairo
Su-7BMK	7343	?		
Su-7BMK	7545	?		
Su-7BMK	7604	?		
Su-7BMK	7643	7607		Sold to the USA for evaluation; preserved Nellis AFB as 'Iraqi Air Force 547'
Su-7BMK	7645	?		Sold to the USA for evaluation
Su-7BMK	7649 Black	?		Three-tone camouflage, post-UAR insignia
Su-7BMK	7664	?		
Su-7BMK	7671 Black	?		Two-tone camouflage, post-UAR insignia
Su-7BMK	7681	?		
Su-7BMK	7706 Black	?		Three-tone camouflage, post-UAR insignia
Su-7BMK	7721 Black	?		Two-tone camouflage, post-UAR insignia
Su-7BMK	7722	?		
Su-7BMK	7732 Black	?		Three-tone camouflage, post-UAR insignia
Su-7BMK	7904 Black	?		Two-tone camouflage, post-UAR insignia
Su-7BMK	7912 Black	?		Three-tone camouflage, post-UAR insignia
Su-7UMK	6900	?		
Su-7UMK	7904	?		
Su-7UMK	7907	?		
Su-7UMK	7912	?		
Su-17K	1256 Black			Silver overall, probably fake serial; preserved in Egypt
Su-20	7771 Black	?		Two-tone camouflage. Preserved Sinai War Memorial as '7771 White'
Su-20	7780 Black	?		Three-tone camouflage, post-UAR insignia

Su-20	7781	?		
Su-20	7789 Black	?		Two-tone camouflage, post-UAR insignia
Su-20	7794	?		Preserved at Kom Ashwin AB
Su-20	?	72410		To West German Air Force for evaluation as 98+62
Su-20	?	72412		To West German Air Force for evaluation as 98+61
Tu-16	4005 Black/05	?		No.34 Sqn. Destroyed 5-6-1967
Tu-16	4009 Black	?		No.34 Sqn. Destroyed 5-6-1967
Tu-16	4012 Black	?		Preserved Cairo-Almaza
Tu-16	4027 Black	?		No.34 Sqn. Destroyed 5-6-1967
Tu-16	4030 Black	?		No.34 Sqn. Destroyed 5-6-1967
Tu-16	4035 Black/35	?		
Tu-16	4047 Black/47	***0402		No.34 Sqn. Destroyed 5-6-1967
Tu-16	4055 Black/55	?		No.34 Sqn. Destroyed 5-6-1967
Tu-16	4065 Black	?		No.34 Sqn. Destroyed 5-6-1967
Tu-16	4074 Black	?		No.34 Sqn. Destroyed 5-6-1967
Tu-16	4087 Black	?		No.34 Sqn. Destroyed 5-6-1967
Tu-16	4092 Black	?		No.34 Sqn. Destroyed 5-6-1967
Tu-16KS	4106 Black	?		No.95 Sqn. Destroyed 5-6-1967
Tu-16KS	4108 Black/08	?		Natural metal finish. No.95 Sqn. Destroyed 5-6-1967
Tu-16KS	4114 Black	?		No.95 Sqn. Destroyed 5-6-1967
Tu-16KS	4117 Black	6203220		Natural metal finish. No.95 Sqn. Destroyed 5-6-1967
Tu-16	4301 Black/01	?		Tan/green/grey camouflage
Tu-16R	4376 Black	?		*Badger-E*, 90th ODRAE ON
Tu-16R	4378 Black	?		*Badger-E*, 90th ODRAE ON
Tu-16R	4380 Black	?		*Badger-F*, 90th ODRAE ON
Tu-16R	4381 Black	?		*Badger-E*, 90th ODRAE ON
Tu-16	4383 Black	?		
Tu-16R	4384 Black	?		*Badger-F*, 90th ODRAE ON
Tu-16	4386 Black	?		Sold to the USA for evaluation
Tu-16P	4387 Black	?		90th ODRAE ON
Tu-16R	4392 Black	?		*Badger-E*, 90th ODRAE ON
Tu-16R	4393 Black	?		*Badger-E*, 90th ODRAE ON
Tu-16	4402 Black	?		
Tu-16	4403 Black	?		
Tu-16KSR-2A	4404 Black	?		Tan/green/grey camouflage
Tu-16KSR-2-11	4406 Black/06	?		Tan/green/grey camouflage
Tu-16KSR-2-11	4407 Black/07	?		Tan/green/grey camouflage
Tu-16KS	4408 Black	?		
Tu-16	4409 Black	?		
Tu-16	4416 Black	?		
Yak-11	511 Black	17****		Czechoslovak-built (Let C-11). To France 1984
Yak-11	529 Black	17****		Czechoslovak-built (Let C-11). To France 1984
Yak-11	532 Black	17****		Czechoslovak-built (Let C-11). To France 1984
Yak-11	533 Black	170101		Czechoslovak-built (Let C-11). To France 1984; later to UK as G-BTHD
Yak-11	536 Black	17****		Czechoslovak-built (Let C-11). To France 1984
Yak-11	539 Black	17****		Czechoslovak-built (Let C-11). To France 1984, became F-AZJB; c/n reported in error as 25III03
Yak-11	540 Black	17****		Czechoslovak-built (Let C-11). To France 1984
Yak-11	542 Black	17****		Czechoslovak-built (Let C-11). To France 1984
Yak-11	543 Black	172623		Czechoslovak-built (Let C-11). To France 1984
Yak-11	563 Black	17****		Czechoslovak-built (Let C-11). To France 1984
Yak-11	564 Black	17****		Czechoslovak-built (Let C-11). To France 1984
Yak-11	565 Black	17****		Czechoslovak-built (Let C-11). To France 1984
Yak-11	570 Black	17****		Czechoslovak-built (Let C-11). To France 1984
Yak-11	579 Black	17****		Czechoslovak-built (Let C-11). To France 1984
Yak-11	580 Black	17****		Czechoslovak-built (Let C-11). To France 1984
Yak-11	581 Black	17****		Czechoslovak-built (Let C-11). To France 1984

Yak-11	588 Black	17****	Czechoslovak-built (Let C-11). To France 1984
Yak-11	589 Black	17****	Czechoslovak-built (Let C-11). To France 1984
Yak-11	590 Black	171101	Czechoslovak-built (Let C-11). To Israel ?-1964; later to France as F-AZHQ
Yak-11	593 Black	17****	Czechoslovak-built (Let C-11). To France 1984
Yak-11	621 Black	17****	Czechoslovak-built (Let C-11). To France 1984
Yak-11	667 Black	17****	Czechoslovak-built (Let C-11). To France 1984
Yak-11	704 Black	17****	Czechoslovak-built (Let C-11). To France 1984
Yak-11	705 Black	171139?	Czechoslovak-built (Let C-11). C/n reported in error as 1701139 (one digit too many) but Batch 01 seems unlikely; also reported as 171205. To France 1984, later to UK as G-BTUB
Yak-11	706 Black	17****	Czechoslovak-built (Let C-11). To France 1984
Yak-11	707 Black	17****	Czechoslovak-built (Let C-11). To France 1984
Yak-11	708 Black	17****	Czechoslovak-built (Let C-11). To France 1984
Yak-11	709 Black	17****	Czechoslovak-built (Let C-11). To France 1984
Yak-11	710 Black	17****	Czechoslovak-built (Let C-11). To France 1984
Yak-11	790 Black	172624	Czechoslovak-built (Let C-11). To France 1984, became F-AZYA
Yak-11	?	170406	Czechoslovak-built (Let C-11). To France 1984, to USA 1986 as N33UA
Yak-11	?	171103	Czechoslovak-built (Let C-11). To France 1984, later to UK as G-IYAK
Yak-11	?	171231?	Czechoslovak-built (Let C-11). C/n reported in error as 1701231 (one digit too many) but Batch 01 seems unlikely. To France 1984, later to USA as N11SN
Yak-11	?	171304	Czechoslovak-built (Let C-11). To France 1984, later to USA
Yak-11	?	171306	Czechoslovak-built (Let C-11). To France 1984, later to USA
Yak-11	?	171315	Czechoslovak-built (Let C-11). To France 1984
Yak-11	?	171521	Czechoslovak-built (Let C-11). To France 1984, later to USA as N134JK
Yak-11	?	171529	Czechoslovak-built (Let C-11). To France 1984, later to USA as N21241
Yak-11	?	171729	Czechoslovak-built (Let C-11). To France 1984
Yak-11	?	172503	Czechoslovak-built (Let C-11). To France 1984, became F-AZOK
Yak-11	?	172612	Czechoslovak-built (Let C-11). To France 1984, later to USA as N9YK
Yak-11	?	172701	Czechoslovak-built (Let C-11). Impounded Cyprus on delivery; to UK as G-AYAK
Yak-11	?	172809	Czechoslovak-built (Let C-11). To France 1984, later to USA as N3UA
Yak-11	?	17****	Czechoslovak-built (Let C-11). To France 1984, became F-AZIM; c/n reported in error as 904623
Yak-11	?	17****	Czechoslovak-built (Let C-11). To France 1984, became F-AZFJ; c/n reported in error as 25III02
Yak-11	?	17****	Czechoslovak-built (Let C-11). To France 1984, became F-AZNN; c/n reported in error as 25III05
Yak-11	?	17****	Czechoslovak-built (Let C-11). To France 1984, became F-AZFB; c/n reported in error as 25III06
Yak-11	?	17****	Czechoslovak-built (Let C-11). To France 1984, became F-AZPA; c/n reported in error as 25III07
Yak-11	?	17****	Czechoslovak-built (Let C-11). To France 1984, later to USA as N18AW; c/n reported in error as 25III20
Yak-11	?	17****	Czechoslovak-built (Let C-11). To France 1984, became F-AZIR; c/n reported in error as 25III21
Yak-11	?	17****	Czechoslovak-built (Let C-11). To France 1984, later to USA as N25YK; c/n reported in error as 25III25
Yak-18A	607	116****	To France 1984, became F-AZFK
Yak-18A	627	116****	Reported in error as C-11. To France 1984, later to UK as G-BMJY/'Soviet Air Force 07 Yellow'
Yak-18A	640	1161609	To France 1984, became F-AZFG
Yak-18A	710	116****	C/n reported as '710', which cannot be correct. To France 1984, later to Switzerland as HB-RBD

Additionally, the following surplus Czechoslovak Air Force CS-102s were listed in Czech sources as sold to Egypt and Iraq: c/ns 142634, 622043, 622044, 722465 (sold on 3rd September 1969), 722506, 722466, 722612, 722627 (sold on 24th April 1970), 522548 (sold on 24th July 1970), 722469 (sold on 24th October 1971), 722601, 722605 (sold on 25th November 1971), 512117 (sold on 7th April 1972), 722632 (sold on 10th April 1972), 722503, 822209 (sold on 22nd May 1972), 722611 (sold on 7th June 1972) and 722609 (sold on 24th October 1972). Unfortunately it is not known which of these aircraft are the Egyptian ones.

Bearing no national insignia or serial, an F-7N awaits delivery to the IRIAF.

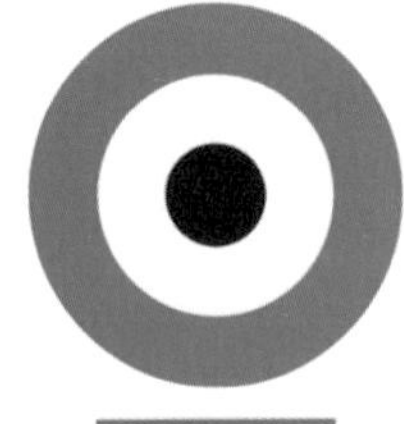

Soon-to-be-Iranian F-7Ns on the factory apron at Chengdu.

Iran

On 11th February 1979 a revolution took place in the Kingdom of Iran, ousting Shah Mohammed Reza Pahlavi and ending the rule of the Pahlavi dynasty that had run the country since 1921. The Shi'a Muslim clergy led by Ayatollah Ruhollah M. Khomeini took over, and the Islamic Republic of Iran was proclaimed on 1st April 1979. Accordingly the former Imperial Iranian Air Force (IIAF, or *Nirou Havai Shahanshahiye Iran*) was transformed into the Islamic Republic of Iran Air Force (IRIAF). Another Iranian armed service with a strong aviation component is the Islamic Revolution Guards Corps (IRGC), or *Pasdaran*, established in 1980 by Khomeini; this is a sort of National Guard or interior troops whose function is to enforce Islamic law and suppress internal unrest.

From the outset the new Iranian government took a strongly anti-American and anti-Israeli stand, and all further deliveries of American military hardware to Iran were promptly stopped. It should be noted that the

Islamic Republic of Iran Air Force Chengdu F-7N 3-7510

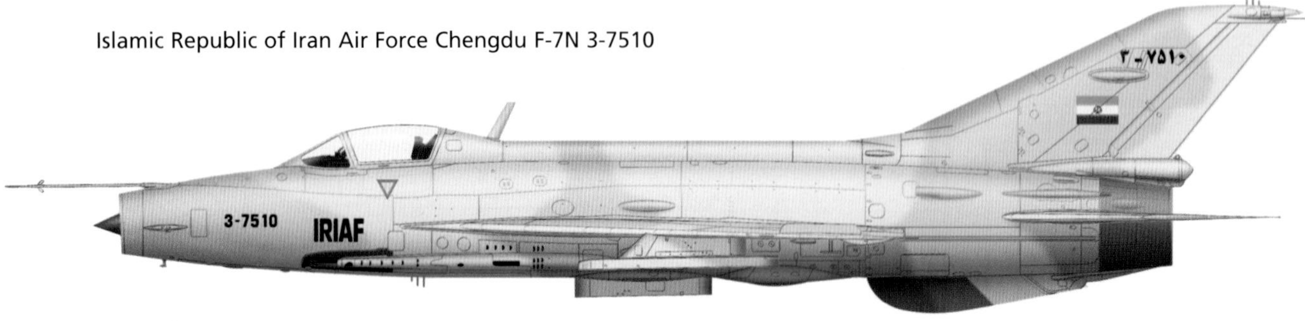

Above: An F-7N serialled 3-7510 at an airshow in Tehran.

Above left: An IRIAF FT-7N in sand/grey camouflage stripped down for maintenance. Unfortunately the serial is not legible. Note the position of the roundel.

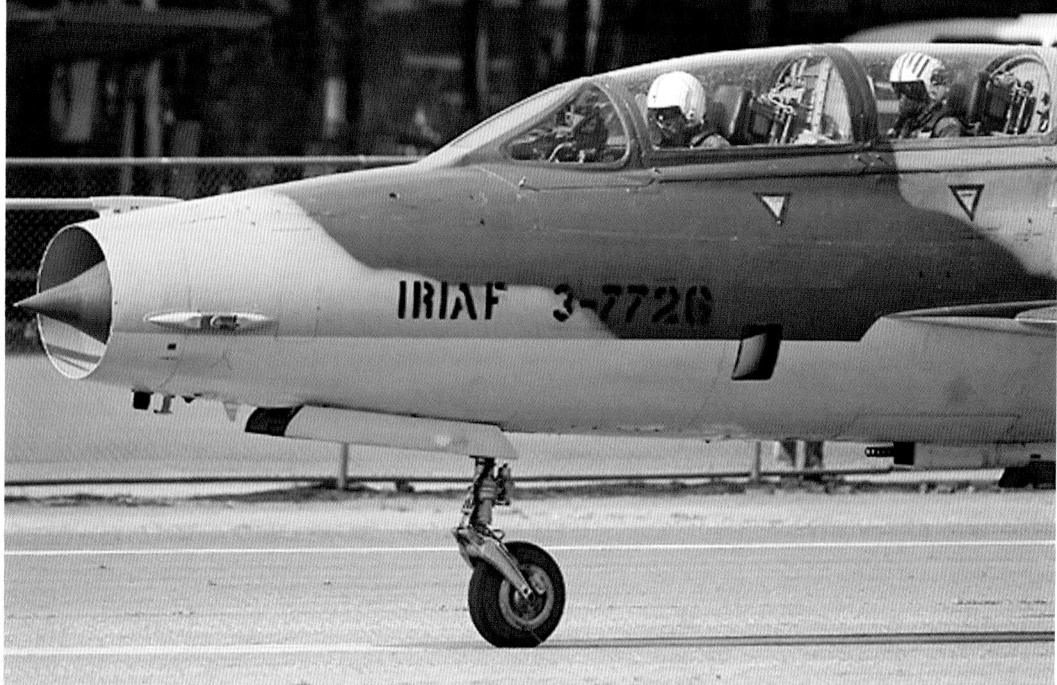

In contrast, FT-7N 3-7726 wears a sand/green camouflage scheme.

Four F-7Ns (the one nearest to camera is 3-7509) over the Persian Gulf coast.

This FT-7N serialled 3-7718 is one of several painted in this striking red/white livery. Note the Chinese-designed drop tank which differs from the Soviet PTB-490.

3-7703, another FT-7N wearing the red/white colour scheme.

An official publicity shot of F-7Ns in three-tone camouflage with an array of weapons. The last digits of the serials have been retouched by Iranian censors.

West apparently underestimated the Iranians' ability to make do and mend, which allowed them to maintain the existing US-built IRIAF aircraft in operational condition and even clone some of them. However, fully realising that these aircraft would not last indefinitely, Iran also sought alternative suppliers as early as the mid-1980s, turning to China and the Soviet Union (and subsequently Russia).

In 1983 the IRIAF acquired 24 Shenyang F-6 fighter-bombers (a Chinese version of the

Mikoyan MiG-19S *Farmer-C*) from North Korea; the jets arrived aboard a North Korean ship in April 1983. They were mostly used in the counter-air role, with Syria, Pakistan and China providing spares and maintenance support. According to *Flight International*, 16 F-6s were still operational in late 1991.

During and after the Iran-Iraq War, which raged from 22nd September 1980 to August 1988, Iran tried to rebuild its stock of aircraft. In 1989 the IRIAF purchased nine Mikoyan MiG-21PF (*izdeliye* 76) *Fishbed-D* fighters and four MiG-21U (*izdeliye* 66-600) *Mongol-A* trainers which had been phased out by the East German Air Force; however, they were impounded in Dresden after German reunification in 1990 and none were delivered (some sources suggest two aircraft whose fate is not 100% known did arrive in Iran but this is doubtful).

The MiG-21 did reach Iran in its 'Chinese copy' form – the Chengdu F-7N fighter (a derivative of the MiG-21F-13 *Fishbed-C*). Derived from the old F-7M Airguard export model with single-delta wings but with four wing pylons, the F-7N was a simplified version developed for Iran (hence the N). Since Iran had long been branded as a 'rogue state' because of its anti-Western and anti-Israeli rhetoric and its alleged aspirations to create nuclear weapons, western military equipment supplies had been embargoed and using western avionics was impossible. Therefore the F-7N was fitted with Chinese avionics, reportedly including an SY-80 pulse-Doppler radar instead of the F-7M's GEC-Marconi Skyranger radar.

This ex-East German Air Force MiG-21PF was earmarked for export to Iran but impounded at Dresden after German reunification.

This MiG-21UM is another ex-EGAF aircraft which was meant for sale to Iran but not delivered. Note the decidedly 'non-German' camouflage.

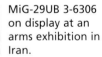

MiG-29UB 3-6306 on display at an arms exhibition in Iran.

Two IRIAF MiG-29s (3-6111 and 3-6115) pass over an ancient fortress in Iran. 3-6111 apparently carries live R-27R1 and R-60MK missiles, while the other aircraft has the zebra-striped dummy versions.

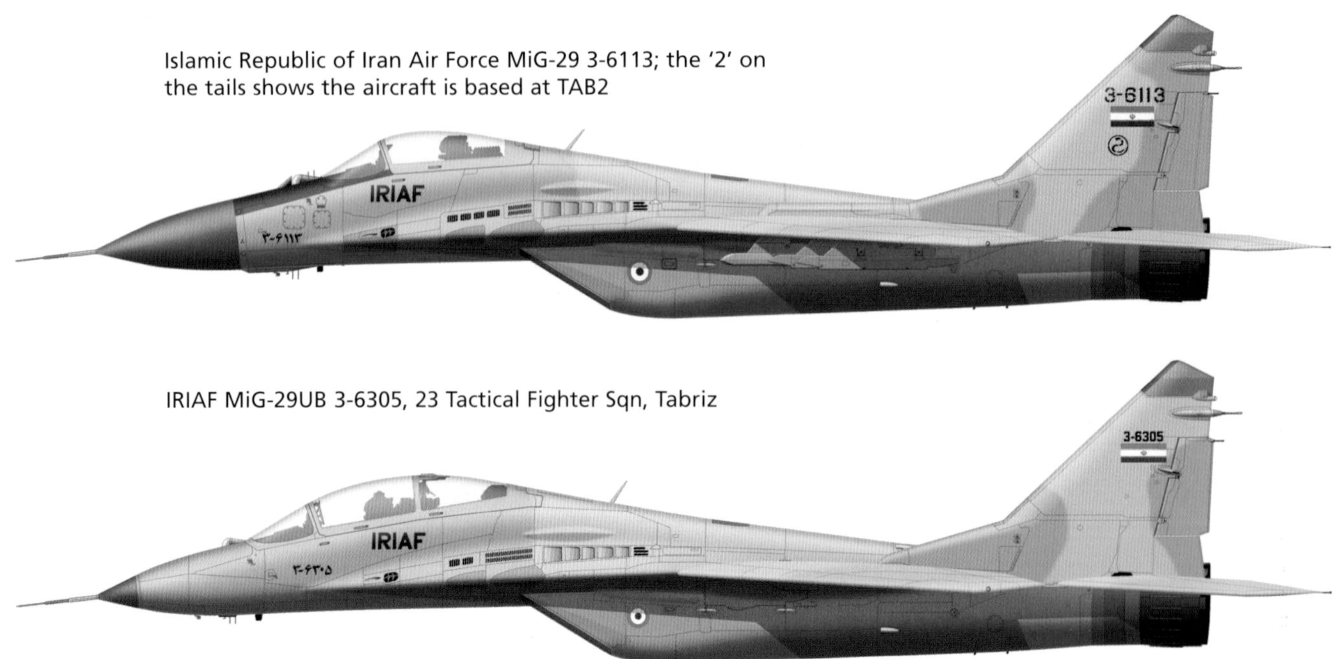

Islamic Republic of Iran Air Force MiG-29 3-6113; the '2' on the tails shows the aircraft is based at TAB2

IRIAF MiG-29UB 3-6305, 23 Tactical Fighter Sqn, Tabriz

18 (some sources suggest 15 or 21) F-7Ns were ordered in 1985 and delivered in 1986; they were reportedly originally operated by the IRGC but later transferred to the Air Force. Four or five Guizhou FT-7N trainers derived from the MiG-21UM *Mongol-B* were procured at the same time. Understandably there was great secrecy about this order, since China was already supplying F-7s/FT-7s to Iraq.

No confirmation has been found for a story suggesting that 12 F-7Ns were successfully used in the Iran-Iraq War thanks to their similarity to the Iraqi MiG-21s. However, the delivery in 1993 of 18 F-7Ns and seven FT-7 trainers, and five more in 1996 have been recorded (other reports say 40 F-7Ns/FT-7Ns were delivered in 1990). The aircraft are concentrated at Ardestani AB (aka TAB5 – Tactical

A tow tractor (probably locally built) tows a single-seat Iranian MiG-29 serialled 3-6105.

MiG-29s 3-6111 and 3-6115 show the efficacy of their blue/grey camouflage over the mountains of northern Iran. This camouflage scheme is unique to the IRIAF *Fulcrums*.

MiG-29 3-6114 forming part of a military hardware display appears to have a three-tone camouflage (sand and two shades of grey). 'P.27' on the placard beside the inert missiles is actually R-27 in Cyrillic (copied by the Iranians)!

Opposite: MiG-29UB 3-6307 seen immediately after becoming airborne.

Above: Four IRIAF MiG-29UBs on the flight line; note the variance in camouflage colours.

Right: An Iranian MiG-29 belches flames as it fires a volley from its GSh-301 cannon.

Below: MiG-29s 3-6111 and 3-6115 bank away from the camera ship, showing a full load of two R-27R medium-range AAMs, two R-60M short-range AAMs and the MiG-29's distinctive centreline drop tank with a vertical duct through it for the APU exhaust.

Opposite page: Two views of MiG-29 3-6118 on final approach. The fighter carries four R-73 short-range AAMs for dogfight training.

Islamic Republic of Iran Air Force Su-22M4 3-6971

The IRIAF obtained a number of Su-22M4s in January 1991 when Iraqi jets were flown to Iran en masse. They include this camouflaged example which appears to be serialled 3-6971.

3-6910, another ex-Iraqi Su-22M4, wears this striking 'Great White shark' colour scheme with a mischievous grin.

Islamic Republic of Iran Air Force Su-22M4 3-6910 in special colours, Shiraz International airport, 2009

A pair of IRIAF Su-24MK (3-6807 and 3-6811) cruise over the snow-covered mountains of northern Iran. This photo illustrates the camouflage unique to the Iranian *Fencers*, the tan and brown colours continuing all the way down the fuselage sides (unlike Algerian, Libyan or Syrian examples).

Air Base 5) in Omidiyeh, serving with the 51st, 52nd and 53rd Tactical Fighter Squadrons. The F-7Ns/FT-7Ns wear a distinctive tan/bluish grey camouflage and serials in Farsi and European characters (often applied differently on different sides, or on the nose and tail).

When the eight-year war with Iraq ended, Iran decided to follow the example of its warlike neighbour and order the Mikoyan MiG-29. In the late 1980s there was a rapprochement between the Soviet Union and Iran; in June 1989 the then President Ali Akbar Hashemi Rafsanjani paid a visit to Moscow, signing a number of important contracts, including an order for an arms package worth US$ 1.9 billion. (Some sources, though, say that a contract for the delivery of 20 MiG-29 (*izdeliye* 9.12B) *Fulcrum-A* fighters and four MiG-29UB *Fulcrum-B* combat trainers was signed on 25th November 1989.) The IRIAF took delivery of the first batch of *Fulcrums* in late 1989; the aircraft were declared operational with the 11th Tactical Fighter Squadron at Tehran-Mehrabad International airport, which is also a major air force base (TAB1), on 7th October 1990. The type is also operated by the 23rd TFS at Tabriz (TAB2).

One aircraft crashed on the delivery flight when the Soviet pilot lost his way, ejecting when the aircraft ran out of fuel. Another Iranian *Fulcrum* crashed fatally when the pilot became disoriented at low altitude. The IRIAF

3-6843, a Su-24MK of the 13th TFS, lines up for take-off from runway 29R at Tehran-Mehrabad. The aircraft carries an UPAZ-1A 'buddy' refuelling pod. Note the '1' on the tail signifying TAB1 (Tehran).

Here, Su-24MK 3-6810 is seen at a military hardware exhibition at Tehran-Mehrabad International airport in company with F-7N 3-7521. The aircraft is fitted with PTB-3000 drop tanks. Note the grubby paint on the radome.

Here, sister ship 3-6853 is seen during a similar display.

Su-24MK 3-6843 'burns rubber' at the moment of touchdown.

This view of Su-24MK 3-6807 leading sister ship 3-6852 during a formation approach provides an interesting comparison of old and new camouflage schemes (three-tone vs. two-tone) and radome colours. 3-6807 was delivered from Russia, while 3-6852 is an ex-Iraqi machine.

tried to blame the crash on a mechanical failure but the manufacturer's experts proved the aircraft was OK; the cause was obviously controlled flight into terrain (CFIT) – in other words, pilot error.

According to RSK MiG (the MiG Russian Aircraft Corporation), nine Iraqi Air Force MiG-29s were flown to neutral Iran in January 1991 at the close of the First Gulf War (Operation *Desert Storm*) to escape destruction by the anti-Iraqi coalition forces. The fighters were promptly interned and subsequently transferred to the IRIAF by way of reparations for damage done during the Iran-Iraq War. In 1992 Iran placed another order with Russia for 48 MiG-29s (40 single-seaters and eight trainers) but the then Russian President Boris N. Yeltsin vetoed the deal when the USA put pressure on Russia, threatening to impose sanctions. Yet a single MiG-29 was delivered after all as an attrition replacement.

On 1st-10th February 1996 the IRIAF staged an aviation displayed at Tehran-Mehrabad airport. The static park included one of the single-seat MiG-29s. Another *Fulcrum-A* (3-6114) was on display at a similar event in 2003.

In the mid-1990s the Iranians started upgrading the MiG-29 on their own. Project *Talle* added fixed IFR probes, allowing the fighters to refuel from Boeing 707-3J9C airliners converted locally into three-point tankers with Beech 1800 podded hose drum units, and new retractable probes are to be fitted eventually.

Overleaf: IRIAF Su-24MKs supplied by Russia, including 3-6809, have overwing strakes incorporating flare dispensers; the ex-Iraqi ones lack them.

An excellent landing study of 3-6809 equipped with an UPAZ-1A pod.

Islamic Republic of Iran Air Force Su-24MK 3-6853, TAB7, Shiraz; the serial is in European characters on the nose and in Farsi on the tail

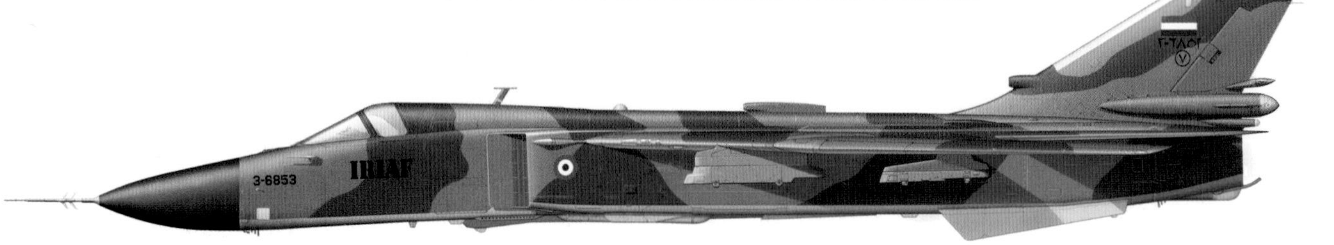

IRIAF Su-24MK 3-6810 in early tan/green/brown camouflage; the aircraft carries PTB-3000 drop tanks

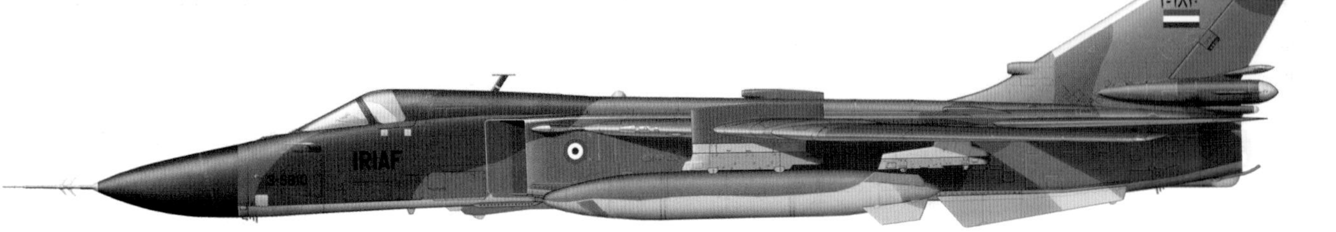

IRIAF Su-24MK 3-6856 still in the basic colours of its ex-owner, the Iraqi AIr Force; note the different placement of serials (in Farsi on the nose and in European characters on the tail)

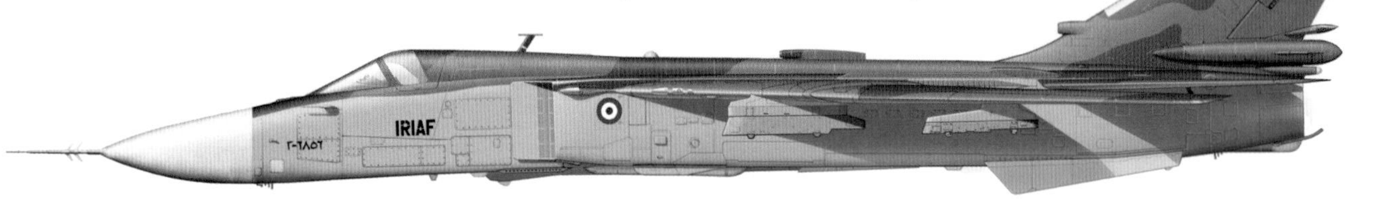

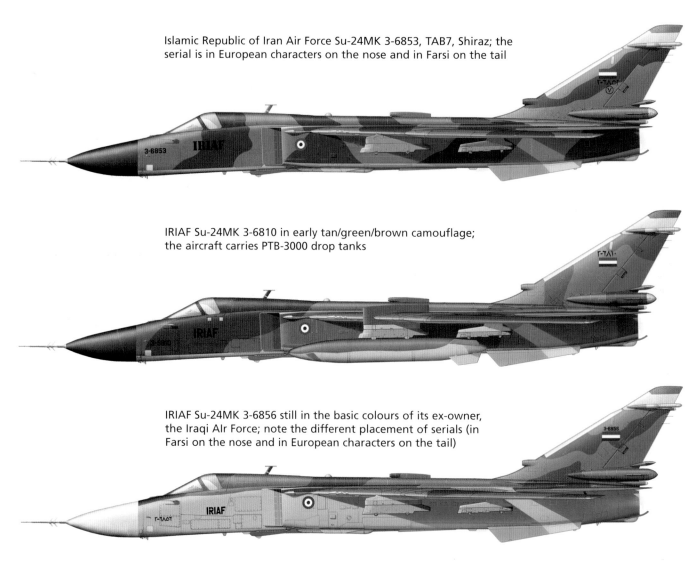

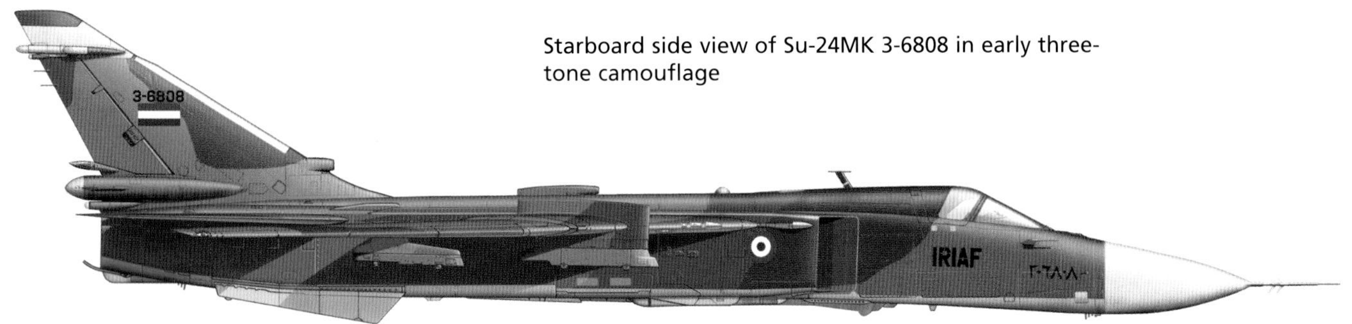

Starboard side view of Su-24MK 3-6808 in early three-tone camouflage

Project *Khorsheed* saw the development of indigenous 1,000- and 1,200-litre (220 and 264 Imp gal) drop tanks for the MiG-29.

In the aftermath of the First Gulf War, when Iraqi aircraft were ferried *en masse* to Iran to escape destruction, four Iraqi Air Force Sukhoi Su-20 *Fitter-D* fighter-bombers and 40 Su-22 *Fitter-F* and Su-22M4 *Fitter-K* fighter-bombers landed at Noujeh AB (formerly Shahrokhi AB), Hamedan, in western Iran. A few *Fitters*, which were in better shape than the rest, were taken on charge by the Islamic Revolutionary Guards Corps; however, neither the IRGC nor the IRIAF found it expedient to use them operationally. Most of them were either scrapped or passed on to Sudan.

Islamic Revolution Guards Corps Su-25K 15-2456 loaded with two B-8M1 FFAR pods, two inert R-60M AAMs and two PTB-800 drop tanks.

A fine shot of sister ship 15-2454. Note the IRGC emblem on the tail.

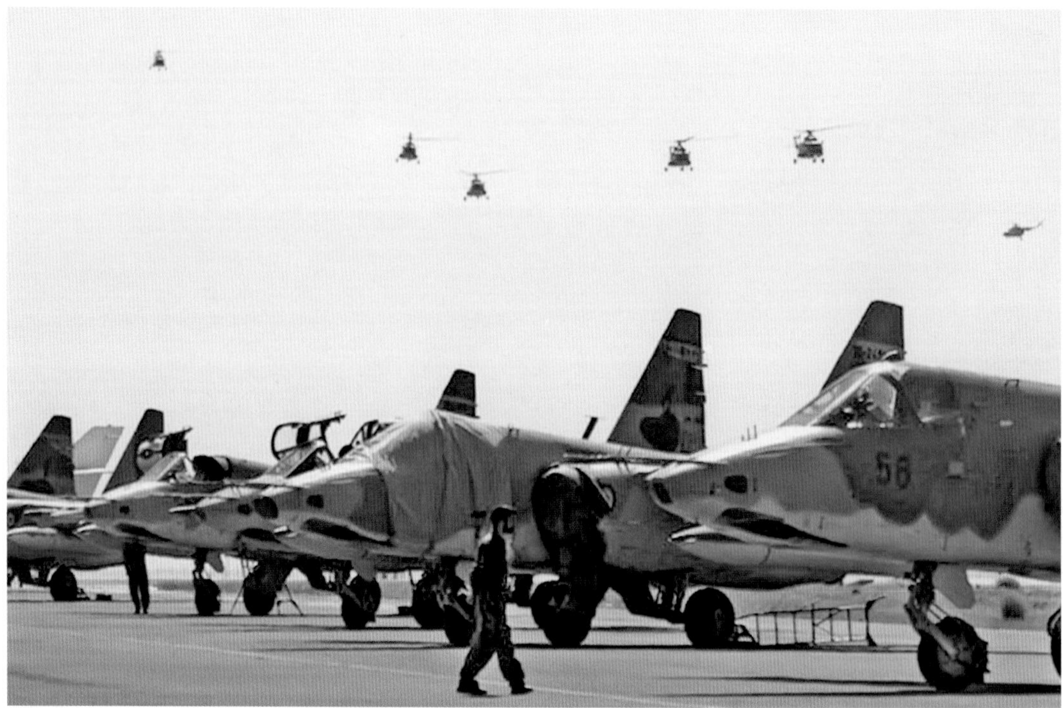

IRGC Su-25s on the flight line, with Mi-17 helicopters of the same outfit flying above. The third aircraft from camera is a Su-25UBK trainer.

IRGC Su-25UBK 15-2459 seen on final approach with the flaps and slats fully deployed.

Another view of the same aircraft. Note the gunpowder stains on the underside of the nose caused by firing the GSh-2-30 cannon.

IRGC Su-25K 15-2451 in flight, showing considerable signs of operational wear and tear.

On 21st January 1991 seven Iraqi Air Force Sukhoi Su-25K *Frogfoot-A* attack aircraft were flown to Iran, seeking a temporary 'safe haven' from Coalition force attacks. The Iranians interned the aircraft and subsequently appropriated them. The Su-25s were initially taken on charge by the IRIAF but never flown by it due to the lack of spares, operating manuals and pilot training, appearing only on publicity photos. However, in 2003 the Islamic Revolutionary Guards Corps took delivery of three Su-25UBK *Frogfoot-B* trainers built in Ulan-Ude, Russia; the original intention had been to order a dozen Su-25s, but the contract eventually signed was for only three aircraft. Apparently the single-seaters were transferred to the IRGC at this point, receiving appropriate serials prefixed 15-. In 2005, citing a source in Russia's defence industry, Middle East News Line reported that the IRIAF had

Islamic Revolution Guards Corps An-74T-200 15-2253 seen prior to 2010 in its original camouflage colours. Note the lack of the IRGC badge.

Some IRGC An-74T-200s, including 15-2257, had an anonymous all-white colour scheme.

The IRGC emblem features a hand clutching a Kalashnikov assault rifle and the numerals 1357.

15-2250, the first IRGC An-74T-200, on short finals; note the appropriate badge on the tail.

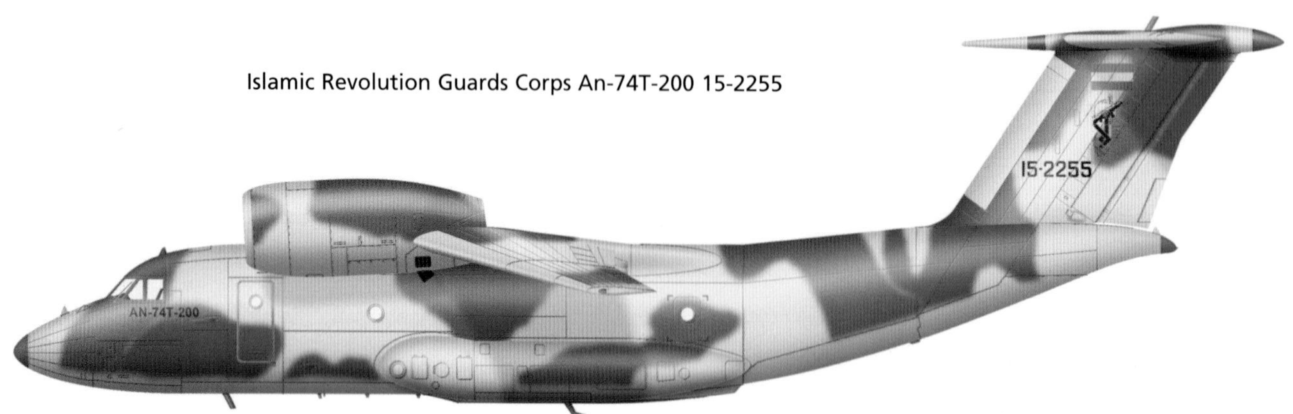

Islamic Revolution Guards Corps An-74T-200 15-2255

Starboard side view of 15-2250, showing that the camouflage colours were distributed irregularly.

placed an order for three 'Su-25UBT' (*sic*) trainers which were due for delivery in 2006.

In 1990 Iran placed an order with the Soviet Union for 14 Sukhoi Su-24MK *Fencer-D* tactical bombers. The IRIAF was long in need of a capable tactical strike aircraft because the McDonnell Douglas F-4 Phantom II fighter-bombers were becoming increasingly difficult to maintain, with less than 20% of the fleet remaining serviceable. The IRIAF wanted 28 Su-24MKs – enough to equip two squadrons, but financial constraints forced it to reduce the initial order to 12 aircraft (plus spares).

Before delivery could take place, the First Gulf War flared up. Barely a few months after the first of the Su-24MKs had arrived, 24 (some sources suggest 18) Iraqi Air Force *Fencer-Ds* fled to Iran in January 1991, seeking shelter from Operation *Desert Storm*. Of course, the Iranian government made good use of this windfall, impounding the Iraqi aircraft and adding them to the IRIAF inventory as reparations for damages sustained in the previous war with Iraq. The completion of the original order in 1992 gave Iran a total of 36 *Fencer-Ds*. The entire fleet was declared operational in 1994, and the service introduction was relatively smooth.

Originally the type was operated by two units – the 13th TFS at Tehran-Mehrabad International airport (TAB1) and the 72nd TFS at Shiraz-Shahid Dastghaib International airport (TAB7). Yes, Tactical Fighter Squadrons, even though the *Fencers* do not qualify as fighters; the IRIAF has no bomber squadrons. Two aircraft were in flyable storage at Isfahan-Shahid Beheshti International airport (alias Shahid Babai'e AB, or TAB8). However, since 1996 all IRIAF Su-24MKs are concentrated at Shiraz and operated by the 71st and 72nd TFS. Also, pairs of Su-24MKs are forward deployed on a three-month rotational basis at Bandar Abbas (TAB9) and Konarak AB (TAB10) at Chabahar, which has extensive underground hangars. The detachment at TAB10 is tasked with an anti-shipping role in times of war.

15-2260 is a convertible An-74TK-200 and wears a civil-style green/ white livery (but has the IRGC badge nevertheless).

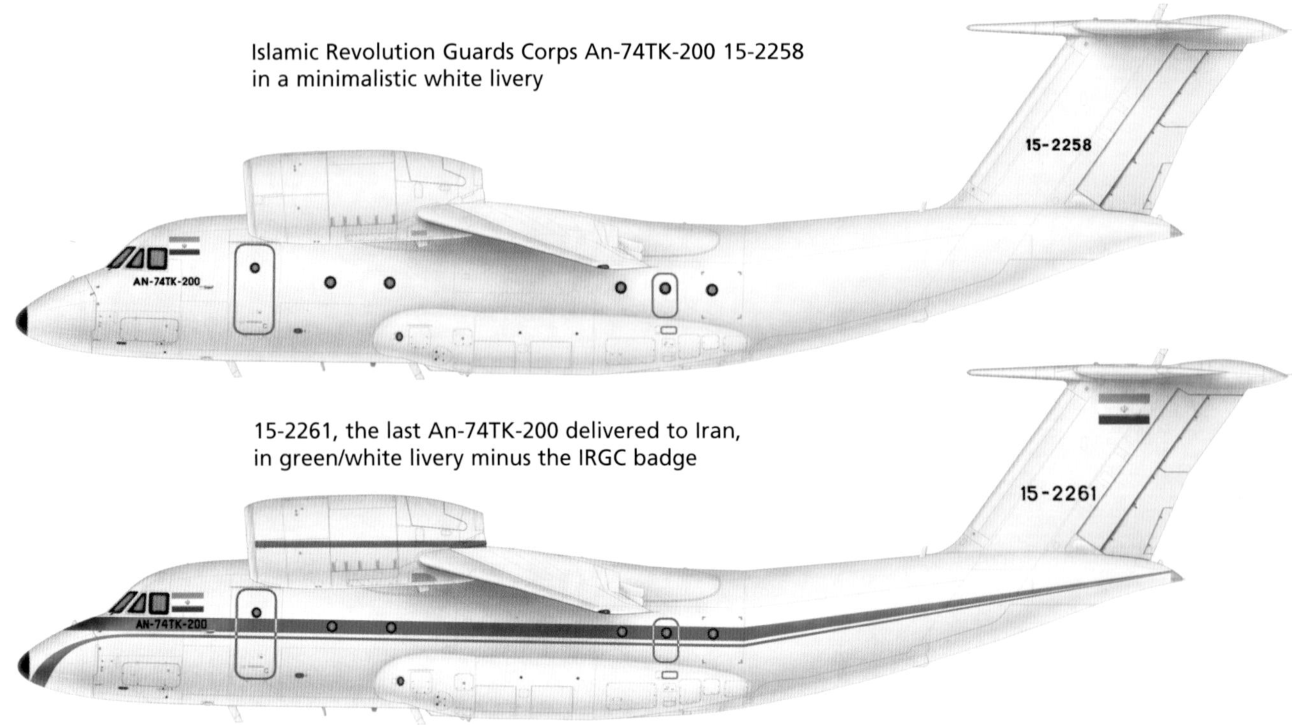

Islamic Revolution Guards Corps An-74TK-200 15-2258 in a minimalistic white livery

15-2261, the last An-74TK-200 delivered to Iran, in green/white livery minus the IRGC badge

The Iranian flag is worn as a fin flash by all IRIAF, IRINA and IRGC aircraft.

Camouflaged (and very weathered) IRIAF IL-76TD 5-8209 on final approach.

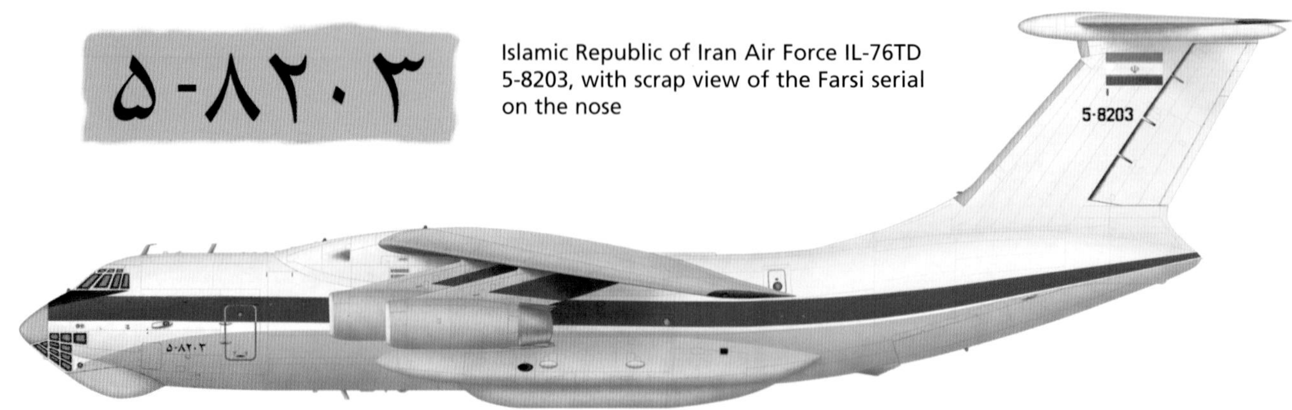

Islamic Republic of Iran Air Force IL-76TD 5-8203, with scrap view of the Farsi serial on the nose

Unlike the Su-24MKs supplied to Iraq, Libya and Syria, which have a two-tone brown camouflage on the upper surfaces, white radomes and the pale blue colour of the undersurfaces extending all the way to the top of the fuselage sides, the Iranian *Fencer-Ds* had a dark green/dark earth scheme, the blue colour on the fuselage being limited to the belly. Later this gave place to a lighter tan/brown camouflage scheme with a black radome. The bombers wear bold 'IRIAF' titles; the serials are in European characters on the nose and in Farsi on the tail to port and vice versa to starboard. The ex-Iraqi machines initially retained their factory finish but were repainted in due course.

In-flight refuelling is done using either Boeing 707-3J9C and Boeing 747-131F tankers fitted with Beech 1800 HDUs or other Su-24MKs fitted with the type's own UPAZ-1A 'buddy' refuelling pods, 12 of which were supplied to Iran. The *Fencers* use an interesting mix of Russian, Chinese and Iranian ordnance, including Russian S-24 heavy unguided rockets, Kh-25L and Kh-29L laser-guided air-to-surface missiles, Kh-28 and Kh-58U anti-radar missiles, KAB-500L laser-guided bombs and R-60M air-to-air missiles for self-defence. The indigenous category embraces Sattar-1/-2/-3 LGBs, GBU-78 Qassed TV-guided bombs, Fajr-e-Darya (Sea Dawn) anti-shipping missiles – a copy of the Italian Sistel Sea Killer Mk 2 – and Kite stand-off submunitions dispensers. The Chinese weapons are C-801K and C-802 anti-shipping missiles (the latter model was also manufactured in Iran).

A few IRIAF IL-76TDs, including 5-8203, had a green cheatline reminiscent of the Algerian IL-76s and IL-78s.

On 1st-10th February 1996 the IRIAF held an air display at Tehran-Mehrabad International airport. The static park included a Su-24MK; this was the first occasion when the Iranian *Fencers* could be examined at close range.

The Iranian Su-24MKs have fired in anger in 1997 when they were used against the Iraqi-based Mojahedin-e-Khalq dissident movement. On 29th September and 4th October, acting in concert with IRIAF F-4Es, the *Fencers* delivered strikes against the Mojahedin-e-Khalq headquarters in Iraq with precision-guided munitions.

Four IRIAF Su-24MK have been lost in accidents. The first one occurred on 8th February

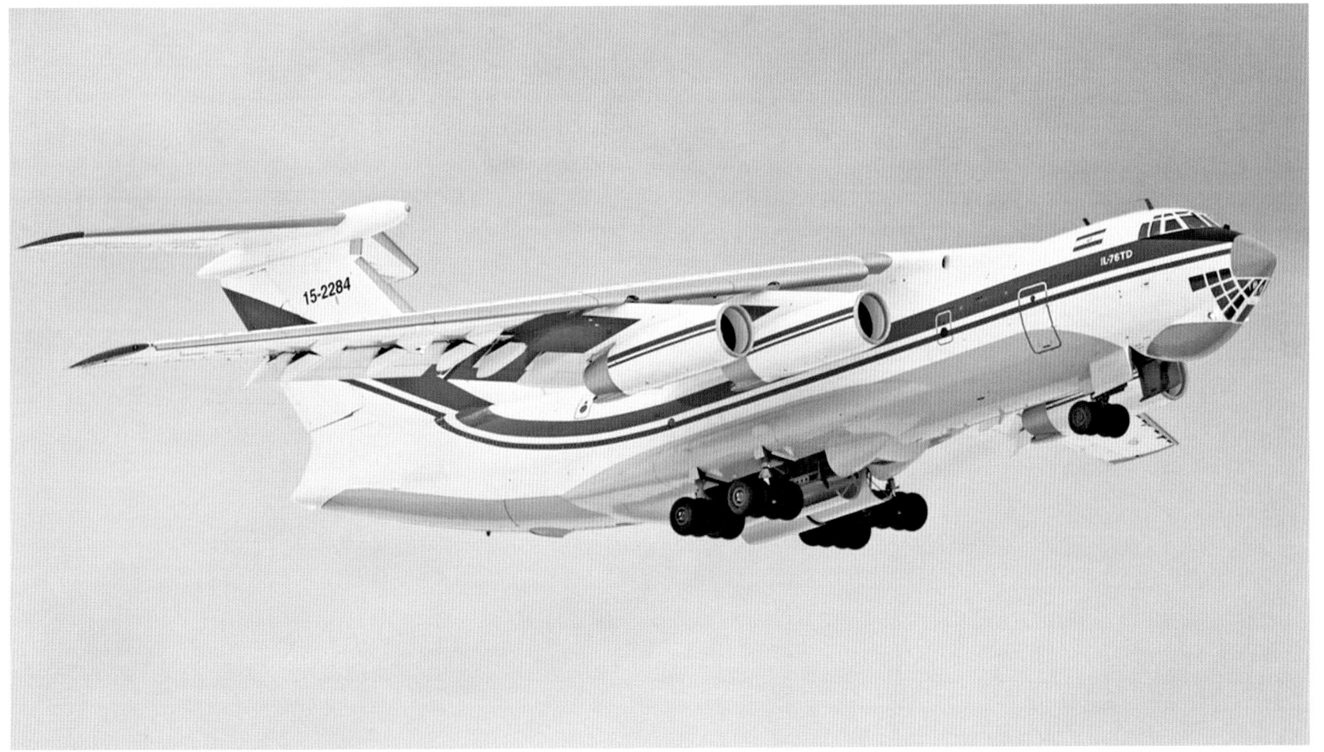

Resplendent in its new colours, Islamic Revolution Guards Corps IL-76TD 15-2284 is seen during a pre-delivery check flight after an overhaul.

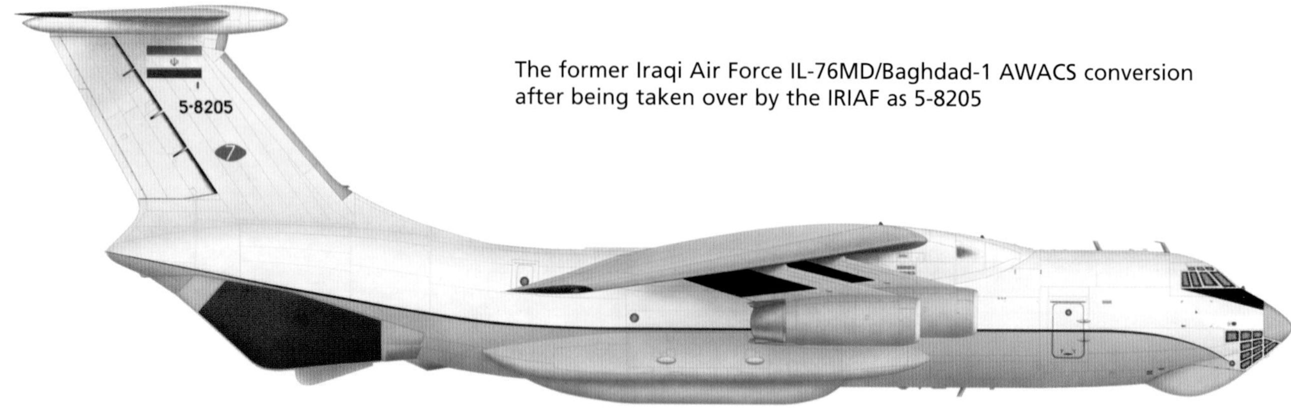

The former Iraqi Air Force IL-76MD/Baghdad-1 AWACS conversion after being taken over by the IRIAF as 5-8205

Looking rather neglected, 5-8205 (the Baghdad-1 AWACS) sits at Tehran-Mehrabad airport in 2009 in company with a Boeing 747-200B. Note the emblem of TAB7 on the fin.

1993. A pair of *Fencer-Ds* was coming in to land at Tehran-Mehrabad International airport after participating in the Air Force Day flypast. As they made a left turn in the approach pattern to runway 29L, they crossed the flight path of an Iran Air Tours Tu-154M airliner (EP-ITD, c/n 91A903) which had just taken off from runway 29R, bound for Mashhad. The bombers were flying in close formation; the flight leader barely managed to take evasive action and had a near-miss with the airliner, but his wingman collided with it, ripping away the tail section. Both aircraft crashed in flames; the 12 crew and 199 passengers of the Tu-154M were killed, as was the crew of the bomber.

In December 1995 a Su-24MK crashed into Lake Maharloo 27 km (16¾ miles) south-east of Shiraz during a low-level practice flight, killing the crew; the lake was habitually used for training Su-24M crews in anti-shipping strike missions. One more *Fencer* crashed near Shiraz on 29th July 2000 after suffering technical problems during a training sortie; this

5-8208, the ill-fated Simorgh AWACS (formerly Adnan-1) based on the IL-76MD, which crashed in 2009.

The former Iraqi Air Force IL-76MD/Adnan-1 AWACS conversion after being taken over by the IRIAF as 5-8208

time the crew ejected safely. In 2008 another Su-24MK made a hard landing at Tehran-Mehrabad International airport after an excessively fast approach; the aircraft bounced several times and apparently a leak developed in the fuel system, causing a massive fire. Yet, the crew managed to eject safely from ground level before the jet was completely engulfed by the flames and destroyed.

Starting in 1997, the Islamic Revolutionary Guards Corps took delivery of 12 brand-new Antonov An-74 *Coaler-B* STOL tactical transports built in Khar'kov. The first eight of these are An-74T-200 pure freighters; the other four are convertible An-74TK-200s. The aircraft were delivered in a sand/brown/green camouflage scheme, although some were later painted white overall – with or without a green cheatline. Several An-74s sported the IRGC emblem on the fin, though some of them later had its removed. The *Coalers* operate mainly from Tehran-Mehrabad airport, with a second base at Mashhad (though it may have been abandoned by now).

Another Antonov type that has made its way to Iran is the An-140-100 twin-turboprop

Escorted by two IRIAF MiG-29s, the Simorgh makes a flypast during a military parade.

A fine shot of the Simorgh on short finals to Tehran-Mehrabad.

An Islamic Revolution Guards Corps Mi-171, 15-1240, disgorges troopers at the hover by means of rappelling lines. The helicopter has a late-model one-piece cargo ramp but no weather radar.

regional airliner. Although designed in the Ukraine after the demise of the Soviet Union, it still merits inclusion here 'by fact of pedigree'. In fact, it has much closer associations with Iran than any other aircraft of Soviet/CIS origin. In 1995, barely two years after the programme had been launched, the Antonov Design Bureau and the Iranian Aircraft Manufacturing Industry Co. (IAMI, better known by the Farsi acronym HESA) signed a deal envisaging licence production of the An-140 in Iran. No fewer than 105 examples were to be assembled at the HESA facility in Shahinshahr near Isfahan as the IrAn-140 'Faraz' – initially from semi-knocked-down (SKD) kits supplied by the Khar'kov State Aircraft Production Enterprise, although the percentage of locally manufactured components was to increase gradually. (Later the plan was scaled down to 80 aircraft.) Safiran Airlines was the launch customer, followed by Iran Air Tour, Kish Air, Caspian Airlines and Iran Aseman Airlines. However, the programme has been making slow progress. In 2008 the Iranian Police briefly operated the fourth Iranian-built An-140. More recently two former Safiran Airlines IrAn-140s have been transferred to the Iranian Police Aviation. At least one of them has been converted for patrol duties by HESA; this includes installation of a gyrostabilised optoelectronic surveillance system 'turret' under the fuselage (aft of the nose gear unit).

On 16th-23rd January 1991 Iran came into possession of 17 former Iraqi Air Force Il'yushin IL-76MDs which were flown to Iran at the end of the First Gulf War and impounded. Ten of them were subsequently included into

IRGC Mi-171s showed considerable variations in structural design and equipment, 15-1236 seen here has the old-model clamshell cargo doors; on the other hand, it is equipped with a Kontur weather radar and emergency flotation gear.

A line-up of seven IRGC Mi-171s. The nearest one is a late example with a cargo ramp. Note the position of the IRGC badge.

Featuring clamshell doors but also a radar, 15-1223 carries the IRGC badge on the engine cowling. Note the black-tipped radome and the serial presentation with an 'underline' instead of a hyphen (15_1223).

IRGC personnel (some of them in full kit) line up for an exercise in which the Guards will make use of Mi-171 helicopters and Fath Vehicle Industries Safir jeeps armed with 106-mm M40 recoilless guns.

Here Mi-171 15_1223 is seen in an altogether different civil-style colour scheme.

the IRIAF inventory, receiving serials prefixed 5; they are operated by the 72nd Transport Air Squadron at Shahid Abbas Dowran AB (TAB7) in Shiraz, aka Shahid Dastghaib International airport. They wear 'IL-76TD' nose titles and a variety of colour schemes (an Iraqi-style simple grey/white scheme, a two-tone grey wrap-around camouflage scheme and two civilian-style liveries, including one whose wide green cheatline resembles that of the Algerian Air Force IL-76s/IL-78s). On the IRIAF *Candids* the serials can be applied in Farsi or European characters, or both.

Eight of the IRIAF IL-76s were regular transports; the other two were the Baghdad-1 and Adnan-1 AWACS conversions (with a ventral radome and a conventional rotodome respectively – see Iraqi section). The former of these was grounded at Tehran-Mehrabad airport not later than April 2009 in rather tatty condition, the green/black Iraqi Airways livery bleeding through the locally applied white paint; it was probably never used operationally. The other AWACS, which was renamed 'Simorgh' (a benevolent flying creature with magical properties from Persian mythology), remained

Islamic Republic of Iran Naval Aviation Mi-171 SN-2105 inspects a tugboat in the Persian Gulf. Note the open emergency exit allowing the personnel inside to use their firearms if necessary.

Sister ship SN-2102 illustrates the blue camouflage worn by Iranian naval Mi-171s. Note the non-standard radar of western origin in a smaller thimble radome positioned higher up.

operational. According to some sources, the original Thomson-CSF TRS-2105/06 Tigre G surveillance radar installed in Iraq was replaced with a newer Iranian-made radar, which could trace aerial targets within a 1,000-km (621-mile) range, and the upgrade was performed with Russian assistance. The aircraft entered IRIAF service in April 2008; however, its career proved to be brief. On 22nd September 2009 a military parade was held in Tehran to mark the anniversary of the start of the Iran-Iraq War; it featured a flypast of several IRIAF aircraft, including the Simorgh AWACS escorted by Northrop F-5E/F Tiger II fighters. There are differing accounts of what happened next. Some sources claim that a fire broke out in one of the IL-76MD's engines; the crew attempted an emergency landing on runway 29L at Mehrabad International airport but the rotodome broke away (possibly as a result of the pylons being overstressed in an excessively vigorous manoeuvre) and struck the tail unit, severing it from the airframe. Other sources suggest that there was a mid-air collision with an F-5F serialled 3-7167 (c/n Z1014) whose crew of two ejected and survived, albeit with injuries. Whatever the cause, the tailless IL-76MD became uncontrollable and spiralled earthwards, crashing 15 km (9.3 miles) northwest of the city of Varamin (a county centre in Tehran Province) and exploding in a huge fireball; the crew of seven was killed. The crash was caught on video by a cameraman who was filming an IRIAF F-4E Phantom II from the back of a transport aircraft (variously reported as a Lockheed C-130 Hercules or a Boeing 707-3J9C tanker).

A further five *Candids* – again marked as IL-76TDs – were operated by the Islamic Revolutionary Guards Corps, wearing serials prefixed 15-; they are based at Tehran (Mehrabad International airport) and possibly at Mashhad (Shahid Hashemi Nejad International airport). These wore either an all-white or a white/green/red colour scheme with the serial in European characters. Two IRGC IL-76s were lost in accidents. On 24th February 2002 IL-76TD 15-2281 had just departed Mashhad with a full load of Pasdaran troopers when the No.3 engine caught fire. The crew managed a safe emergency landing at Mashhad, all 230 occupants escaping unhurt, but the fire damage was so severe that the aircraft was a write-off (the starboard wing spars failed and the wing collapsed).

A little less than a year later, on 19th February 2003, IL-76TD 15-2280 crashed into Mt. Sirch 35 km (21.74 miles) south-east of Kerman in bad weather en route from Zahedan to Kerman, killing all on board. Different sources give conflicting reports on the number of occupants – 275 (eight crewmembers and 267 passengers) or 302 (18 crewmembers and 284 passengers), but all sources agree that it was the deadliest aircraft accident in Iran. The 'passengers' were troopers from the IRGC's 'Sarallah' 41st Army Division. The most likely cause was pilot error (controlled flight into terrain in poor visibility); however, there was also conjecture that the aircraft had been shot down, the Abu-Bakr Brigades terrorist organisation claiming responsibility for this.

The fate of the remaining two ex-Iraqi IL-76MDs is unknown, as no Iranian identities have been reported for them; quite possibly they have been cannibalised for spares. In 1993 four IL-76TDs were reportedly delivered to Iran from Russia as part of a military equipment package, but none have been identified.

The latest Iranian military aircraft of Soviet origin – and the most exotic one as well – is a heavily modified Tupolev Tu-154M *Careless* medium-haul airliner. The type has seen extensive service in Iran since 1992; over the years, more than 90 of these trijets have been operated by ten Iranian air carriers (mostly charter airliners), which usually leased them from Russian, Tajik and Uzbek airlines, albeit several Tu-154Ms were actually bought. However, the type's service record had been marred by five crashes with a large loss of life. In most cases the aircraft was not to blame – three out of five crashes were caused by human error (leading to a mid-air collision, controlled flight into terrain and a hard landing respectively), one by uncontained engine failure/fire and one by a tyre burst on landing (arguably because a worn-out tyre was not replaced in time). Nevertheless, after the crash of Tu-154M RA-85787 operated by Taban Air on 24th January 2010 the Iranian Civil Aviation Authority ran out of patience and ordered the airlines to withdraw all Russian-made aircraft. Thus, on 20th February 2011 commercial operations of Iranian Tu-154Ms were discontinued and the 26 examples then in Iran were placed in storage.

In 2012, however, one of the Tu-154Ms formerly owned by Iran Air Tours (the largest Iranian operator of the type) found further use. The aircraft was transferred to HESA, which converted it into a multi-mission flying testbed. The entire forward fuselage of a Northrop RF-5A Freedom Fighter reconnaissance aircraft (including the cockpit) was grafted onto the fin leading edge, supplanting the standard bullet-shaped fairing incorporating a communications antenna. The aircraft, which retains the basic dark blue/white Iran Air Tours livery, wears 'Hesa Testbed Aircraft' titles in English and Persian but no registration or serial; the RF-5A nose is painted Dayglo orange. In this guise the testbed, which has been referred to as 'Armita' (possibly standing for 'AiRcraft Manufacturing Industry Test Aircraft'), was first noted at Mehrabad airport in August 2012. Initially it will be used for testing Iranian-made ejection seats fired from the RF-5A cockpit. Later, a pylon will be mounted under the fuselage to enable captive-carry aerodynamic tests of future Iranian unmanned aerial vehicles.

The only Iranian helicopters of Russian origin are the Kazan'-built Mil' Mi-17V-5 *Hip-H* and its Ulan-Ude-built equivalent, the Mi-171E (likewise with a stepped nose and full-width cargo ramp). 38 such helicopters have been delivered between 1998 and 2004. The three Mi-17V-5s and five of the Mi-171Es were delivered to the Iranian Red Crescent relief organisation founded in 1979 as a successor to Imperial Iran's Red Lion and Sun Society. Though nominally owned by the Air Force, they wear a striking red/white livery with 'I.R. Iranian Red Crescent Air Rescue' titles; some of them are additionally fitted with external long-range tanks or with flotation gear for overwater operations. The helicopters are maintained by Pars Air, a civilian contractor. Ten more were on order in 2010 but no information on further deliveries to IRC is available.

Additionally, at least 21 Mi-171s have been delivered to the Islamic Revolutionary Guards Corps. They are based at Shiraz (TAB7) and Fajr, and most of them wear tan/brown camouflage. These helicopters have the old-style rounded fully glazed nose, two entry doors, and most have the old clamshell cargo doors, although the newest ones feature the late-style one-piece cargo ramp; some are fitted with the Russian Kontur (Contour) weather radar while others have none. Available photos show that the IRGC Mi-171s are operated both with and without weapons pylons as required.

The Iranian Navy, too, operates the Mi-171. Five such helicopters in the 'glass-nosed' version with clamshell cargo doors and only one port side entry door (suggesting they are earlier-production machines) were delivered to the Islamic Republic of Iran Naval Aviation (IRINA) unit at Bandar Abbas in 2000. They wear a two-tone blue naval camouflage and have been retrofitted with a non-standard radar in a thimble radome smaller than that of the Kontur.

The fourth (para)military operator of the type is the Iranian Police Aviation, which has at least two Mi-171Sh assault helicopters. Again, these combine the old 'glass nose' plus Kontur radar with the late-model cargo ramp; they wear a two-tone green camouflage scheme.

Known Islamic Republic of Iran Air Force and Islamic Revolution Guards Corps aircraft of Soviet/Russian/Ukrainian origin.				
Type	**Serial**	**C/n**	**F/n**	**Notes**
An-74T-200	15-2250	365.470.99.1021	2004	Sand/tan/green camouflage, IRGC badge on tail; repainted in green/white livery with IRGC badge by 2008, badge removed by 2010
An-74T-200	15-2251	365.470.99.1028	2005	Sand/tan/green camouflage, IRGC badge on tail
An-74T-200	15-2252	365.470.99.1032	2006	Green/white livery, no badge. Transferred (leased?) to Yas Air in the same c/s as EP-GOQ by 5-2009
An-74T-200	15-2253	365.470.99.1038	2008	Sand/tan/green camouflage, no badge; repainted in green/white livery by 2010
An-74T-200	15-2254	365.470.99.1040	2009	Sand/tan/green camouflage, no badge
An-74T-200	15-2255	365.470.99.1045	2010	Sand/tan/green camouflage, IRGC badge on tail. Crashed Tehran 27-11-2006
An-74T-200	15-2256	365.470.121.1048	2101	All-white c/s, no titles. Leased to Yas Air 2009 as EP-GOX
An-74T-200	15-2257	365.470.121.1050	2102	All-white c/s, IRGC badge on tail; repainted in green/white livery with no badge after 2007
An-74TK-200	15-2258	365.470.121.1053	2103	All-white c/s, no titles
An-74TK-200	15-2259	365.470.121.1055	2104	All-white c/s, no titles
An-74TK-200	15-2260	365.470.121.1058	2105	Green/white livery; IRGC badge on tail in 2004-09. Leased to Yas Air as EP-GOY in the same c/s, badge not restored after return from lease in 2010
An-74TK-200	15-2261	365.470.121.1059	2106	Green/white livery, no badge
An-140-100 (IrAn-140)	HESA 90-02	90-02		Police Aviation; Khar'kov c/n 365.253.02.009 and f/n 0203. Ex-Safiran Airlines EP-SFE, D/D 9-2007; became, see next line
	2201			Reserialled 11-2008
An-140-100 (IrAn-140)	HESA 90-03	90-03		Police Aviation; Khar'kov c/n 365.253.02.015 and f/n 0205. Ex-Safiran Airlines EP-SFF, D/D 2007; returned to HESA 2008 and redelivered 7-10-2008; became, see next line
	2202			Reserialled 12-2008
An-140-100 (IrAn-140)	HESA 90-04	90-04		Police Aviation; Khar'kov c/n 365.253.05.016 and f/n 0301. Leased from HESA for one month in 2008
IL-76MD	5-8201	0043449455	3704	Ex-Iraqi Air Force YI-ALX, flown to Iran 16-1-1991; IRIAF. White/grey c/s with dark green cheatline and white tail, serial probably in Farsi on nose and European characters on tail
IL-76TD	5-8202	0073474224	5606	Ex-Iraqi Air Force IL-76MD 'Falsie' YI-ANE, flown to Iran 18-1-1991; IRIAF. White/grey c/s with dark blue tail and dark blue cheatline with red pinstripe, serial in European characters on tail, huge 'IL-76TD' titles
IL-76TD	5-8203	0073476288	5802	Ex-Iraqi Air Force IL-76MD 'Falsie' YI-ANG, flown to Iran 16-1-1991; IRIAF. White/grey c/s with dark green cheatline and white tail, no titles, serial in Farsi on nose and European characters on tail
IL-76TD	5-8204	0083482495	6304	Ex-Iraqi Air Force IL-76MD 'Falsie' YI-ANK, flown to Iran 18-1-1991; IRIAF. Same c/s as above but with 'IL-76TD' nose titles
IL-76MD (AWACS)	5-8205	?	?	Ex-Iraqi Air Force 'Baghdad-1' (no serial); IRIAF. Chipped grey/white c/s with thin black cheatline, '7' on tail to denote TAB7, serial in European characters on tail, no titles. Wfu Tehran-Mehrabad by 4-2009
IL-76TD	5-8206	?	?	Ex-Iraqi Air Force IL-76MD 'Falsie', previous identity unknown, probably ex-YI-ANC or YI-ANN; IRIAF. Two-tone grey camouflage, 'IL-76TD' nose titles, serial in Farsi on nose and European characters on tail (2008); repainted in the same blue/white c/s as 5-8202 by 12-2011
IL-76MD	5-8207	0033448416	3604	Ex-Iraqi Air Force YI-ALW, flown to Iran 16-1-1991; IRIAF
IL-76MD/Simorgh	5-8208	0083484542	6406	Ex-Iraqi Air Force 'Adnan-1' (no serial), ex-IL-76MD 'Falsie' YI-ANL, flown to Iran ?-1-1991; IRIAF. Grey/white c/s with thin black cheatline, no titles, serial in Farsi on nose only, no titles. Crashed near Varamin 22-9-2009
IL-76TD	5-8209	1003403087	7802	Ex-Iraqi Air Force IL-76MD 'Falsie' YI-ANO, flown to Iran 18-1-1991; IRIAF. Two-tone grey camouflage (same as 5-8206) in 2008; repainted in the same blue/white c/s as 5-8202 by 2-2011
IL-76TD	5-8210	0063469055	5204	Ex-Iraqi Air Force IL-76MD 'Falsie' YI-ANA, flown to Iran 19-1-1991; IRIAF. Grey/white c/s without cheatline, serial in European characters on nose and tail, no titles
IL-76TD	15-2280	0073481442	6201	Ex-Iraqi Air Force IL-76MD 'Falsie' IL-76MD 'Falsie' YI-ANI, flown to Iran 16-1-1991; IRGC. Green/white c/s. Crashed near Kerman 19-2-2003
IL-76TD	15-2281	0073475236	5609	Ex-Iraqi Air Force IL-76MD 'Falsie' YI-ANF, flown to Iran 16-1-1991; IRGC. Damaged beyond repair Mashhad 24-2-2002
IL-76TD	15-2282	0063471155	5409	Ex-Iraqi Air Force IL-76MD 'Falsie' YI-AND, flown to Iran 16-1-1991; IRGC. White/grey with green/gold cheatline, green tail with IRGC badge and serial, 'IL-76TD' nose titles
IL-76TD	15-2283	0063469071	5208	Ex-Iraqi Air Force IL-76MD 'Falsie' YI-ANB. Flown to Iran 18-1-1991; IRGC. All-white c/s, IRGC badge on tail, 'IL-76TD' nose titles

IL-76MD	15-2284	0033448393	3509	Ex-Iraqi Air Force YI-ALT, flown to Iran 16-1-1991; IRGC. All-white c/s, serial in European characters on tail, 'IL-76TD' nose titles (2009); repainted by 2010 to feature grey belly and heavy green cheatline with red pinstripe curving upwards onto tail
IL-76MD 'Falsie'	?	0063470102	5306	Ex-Iraqi Air Force YI-ANC, flown to Iran 23-1-1991; fate unknown
IL-76MD 'Falsie'	?	0093496894	7304	Ex-Iraqi Air Force YI-ANN, flown to Iran 23-1-1991; fate unknown
MiG-21PF	'3-0914'	760914		Ex-East German Air Force 870 Red; grey camouflage, serial (fake) in European characters, IRIAF titles; not delivered, preserved Rimini, Italy
MiG-21PF	?	760602		Ex-East German Air Force 816 Red; earmarked for Iran, not delivered, scrapped 1991
MiG-21PF	?	760609		Ex-East German Air Force 828 Red; earmarked for Iran, not delivered, scrapped 1991
MiG-21PF	?	761005		Ex-East German Air Force 843 Red; earmarked for Iran, not delivered, scrapped 1994
MiG-21PF	?	761008		Ex-East German Air Force 851 Red; earmarked for Iran, not delivered, scrapped 1991
MiG-21PF	?	761010		Ex-East German Air Force 858 Red; earmarked for Iran, not delivered, scrapped 1991
MiG-21PF	?	761105		Ex-East German Air Force 883 Red; earmarked for Iran, not delivered, scrapped 1990
MiG-21PF	?	761106		Ex-East German Air Force 885 Red; earmarked for Iran, not delivered, scrapped 1994
MiG-21PF	?	761108		Ex-East German Air Force 890 Red; earmarked for Iran, not delivered, scrapped 1991
MiG-21U	?	663316		Ex-East German Air Force 278 Black; earmarked for Iran, not delivered, scrapped 1991
MiG-21U	?	664617		Ex-East German Air Force 288 Black; earmarked for Iran, not delivered
MiG-21U	?	664716		Ex-East German Air Force 290 Black; earmarked for Iran, not delivered
MiG-21U	?	664718		Ex-East German Air Force 291 Black; earmarked for Iran, not delivered, sold to the USA/private owner as N121TJ
F-7N	3-7501	?		Grey/tan camouflage, Arabic numerals to starboard
F-7N	3-7502	?		Sand/green/brown camouflage, serial in Farsi
F-7N	3-7503	?		Reported as 3-7603 but may be a mis-sighting
F-7N	3-7504	?		Sand/green/brown camouflage, serial in Farsi
F-7N	3-7507	?		Grey/tan camouflage, Arabic numerals to starboard. Reported as 3-7607 but may be a mis-sighting
F-7N	3-7510	?		Grey/tan camouflage, serial in Farsi to port
F-7N	3-7512	?		Grey/tan camouflage, serial in European characters to port
F-7N	3-7514	?		Grey/tan camouflage, serial in Farsi to port
F-7N	3-7515	?		
F-7N	3-7518	?		
F-7N	3-7521	?		Sand/green/brown camouflage, serial in Farsi
F-7N	3-7524	?		Grey/tan camouflage, Arabic numerals
F-7N	3-7527	?		Grey/tan camouflage, Arabic numerals
FT-7N	3-7702	?		Red/white c/s
FT-7N	3-7703	?		
FT-7N	3-7705	?		Grey/tan camouflage, serial in European characters
FT-7N	3-7706	?		Sand/green camouflage, serial in European characters, '5' on tail to denote TAB5
FT-7N	3-7708	?		Sand/green/brown camouflage, serial in European characters, '5' on tail
FT-7N	3-7709	?		
FT-7N	3-7712	?		
FT-7N	3-7714	?		
FT-7N	3-7716	?		Grey/tan camouflage, serial in Farsi
FT-7N	3-7718	?		Red/white c/s
FT-7N	3-7720	?		Grey/tan camouflage, serial in European characters
FT-7N	3-7721	?		Sand/green camouflage, serial in European characters
FT-7N	3-7722	?		Grey/tan camouflage, Arabic numerals
FT-7N	3-7724	?		Grey/tan camouflage, Arabic numerals
FT-7N	3-7726	?		Sand/green/brown camouflage, serial in Farsi
MiG-29	3-6102	29605*****	?	Grey/blue camouflage
MiG-29	3-6103	29605*****	?	Grey/blue camouflage. 23 TFS
MiG-29	3-6104	29605*****	?	Ex-Iraqi Air Force 29044, taken over in 1991. Grey/blue camouflage
MiG-29	3-6105	29605*****	?	Grey/blue camouflage
MiG-29	3-6106	29605*****	?	Grey/blue camouflage
MiG-29	3-6107	29605*****	?	Grey/blue camouflage

MiG-29	3-6109	29605*****	?	Grey/blue camouflage
MiG-29	3-6110	29605*****	?	Grey/blue camouflage
MiG-29	3-6111	29605*****	?	Grey/blue camouflage
MiG-29	3-6112	29605*****	?	Grey/blue camouflage
MiG-29	3-6113	29605*****	?	Grey/tan camouflage. 23 TFS, '2' on tail to denote TAB2
MiG-29	3-6114	29605*****	?	Grey/tan camouflage
MiG-29	3-6115	29605*****	?	Grey/blue camouflage
MiG-29	3-6116	29605*****	?	Grey/blue camouflage
MiG-29	3-6117	29605*****	?	Grey/blue camouflage
MiG-29	3-6118	29605*****	?	Grey/blue camouflage
MiG-29	3-6132	29605*****	?	Ex-Iraqi Air Force 29032, taken over in 1991. Grey/blue camouflage
MiG-29	3-6133	29605*****	?	Ex-Iraqi Air Force 29038, taken over in 1991. Grey/blue camo, red eagle's head artwork on port fin
MiG-29UB	3-6301	N509030*****	?	Grey/blue camouflage. 23 TFS, '2' on tail
MiG-29UB	3-6302	N509030*****	?	Grey/tan camouflage
MiG-29UB	3-6303	N509030*****	?	Grey/blue camouflage
MiG-29UB	3-6305	N509030*****	?	Grey/tan camouflage. 23 TFS
MiG-29UB	3-6306	N509030*****	?	Grey/blue camouflage
MiG-29UB	3-6307	N509030*****	?	Ex-Iraqi Air Force 29004, taken over in 1991. Grey/tan camouflage
Mi-17V-5	6-9506/IRC.1	?	?	Iranian Red Cross. D/D 12-2006; red/white/green livery
Mi-17V-5	6-9507/IRC.2	?	?	Iranian Red Cross. D/D 12-2006; red/white/green livery
Mi-17V-5	6-9508/IRC.3	?	?	Iranian Red Cross. D/D 12-2006; red/white/green livery. Crashed 18-1-2007
Mi-171E	6-9509/IRC.4	171E.00.364.07.3501.U		Iranian Red Cross. D/D 28-1-2009; red/white/black livery
Mi-171E	6-9510/IRC.5	171E.00.364.07.3502.U		Iranian Red Cross. D/D 28-1-2009; red/white/black livery, equipped with external tanks
Mi-171E	6-9511/IRC.6	171E.00.364.07.3503.U		Iranian Red Cross. D/D 1-3-2009; red/white/black livery
Mi-171E	6-9512/IRC.7	171E.00.364.07.3504.U		Iranian Red Cross. D/D 1-3-2009; red/white/black livery, equipped with flotation gear
Mi-171E	6-9513/IRC.8	171E.00.364.07.3505.U		Iranian Red Cross. D/D 1-3-2009; red/white/black livery
Mi-171	15-1221	?	?	IRGC, based Shiraz; brown camouflage
Mi-171	15-1222	?	?	IRGC
Mi-171	15-1223	?	?	IRGC, based Fajr; clamshell doors, Kontur radar, tan/brown camouflage. Repainted in white/green/red c/s by 12-2010
Mi-171	15-1224	?	?	IRGC, based Fajr; tan/brown camouflage
Mi-171	15-1225	?	?	IRGC, based Fajr; clamshell doors, Kontur radar, tan/brown camouflage
Mi-171	15-1226	?	?	IRGC, based Shiraz; tan/brown camouflage
Mi-171	15-1227	?	?	IRGC, based Shiraz; clamshell doors, tan/brown camouflage
Mi-171	15-1228	?	?	IRGC, based Fajr; tan/brown camouflage
Mi-171	15-1229	?	?	IRGC, based Fajr; tan/brown camouflage
Mi-171	15-1230	?	?	IRGC, based Fajr; tan/brown camouflage, later green/white c/s
Mi-171	15-1231	?	?	IRGC, based Fajr; clamshell doors, Kontur radar, tan/brown camouflage
Mi-171	15-1232	?	?	IRGC, based Fajr; tan/brown camouflage
Mi-171	15-1233	?	?	IRGC, based Fajr. Clamshell doors, tan/brown camouflage
Mi-171	15-1234	?	?	IRGC, based Shiraz; tan/brown camouflage
Mi-171	15-1235	?	?	IRGC, based Shiraz; tan/brown camouflage
Mi-171	15-1236	?	?	IRGC, based Shiraz; clamshell doors, Kontur radar, tan/brown camouflage, equipped with flotation gear
Mi-171	15-1237	?	?	IRGC, based Shiraz; full-width cargo ramp, Kontur radar, tan/brown camouflage, IRGC badge
Mi-171	15-1238	?	?	IRGC, based Shiraz; tan/brown camouflage
Mi-171	15-1239	?	?	IRGC, based Fajr; green/white c/s
Mi-171	15-1240	?	?	IRGC, based Fajr; full-width cargo ramp, tan/brown camouflage
Mi-171	15-1241	?	?	IRGC, based Fajr; dark green c/s
Mi-171	SN-2101	?	?	Naval Aviation, two-tone blue camouflage
Mi-171	SN-2102	?	?	Naval Aviation, two-tone blue camouflage
Mi-171	SN-2103	?	?	Naval Aviation, two-tone blue camouflage
Mi-171	SN-2104	?	?	Naval Aviation, two-tone blue camouflage
Mi-171	SN-2105	?	?	Naval Aviation, two-tone blue camouflage
Mi-171Sh	1502	?	?	Police Aviation, two-tone green camouflage

Su-22M4	3-6901	?		Green/brown camouflage
Su-22M4	3-6910	?		'Great White shark' special colour scheme. Preserved at Shiraz (Shahid Abbas Dowran AB)
Su-24MK	3-6801	416045*******?		D/D 1990. Sand/tan/green camouflage, wing strakes, white radome, white serial. Reported in error as c/n 0715331, which was Russian Air Force Su-24M '01 White' until 1993
Su-24MK	3-6802	416045*******?		D/D 1990. Sand/tan/green camouflage, wing strakes
Su-24MK	3-6803	416045*******?		D/D 1990. Sand/tan camouflage, wing strakes, '7' on tail to denote TAB7. Reported in error as c/n 0715327, which was Russian Air Force Su-24M '07 White' until 1993
Su-24MK	3-6804	416045*******?		D/D 1990. Reported in error as c/n 0715330, which was Russian Air Force Su-24M '10 White' until 1993
Su-24MK	3-6805	416045*******?		D/D 1990. Reported in error as c/n 0715306, which was Russian Air Force Su-24M '22 White' until 1993
Su-24MK	3-6806	416045*******?		D/D 1990. C/n reported as 0815340 (ex-Russian Air Force Su-24M '40 White'?) but doubtful!
Su-24MK	3-6807	416045*******?		D/D 1990. Sand/tan camouflage, wing strakes, white radome, '7' on tail. C/n reported as 0815329 (ex-Russian Air Force Su-24M '43 White'?) but doubtful!
Su-24MK	3-6808	416045*******?		D/D 1990. C/n reported as 0815306 (ex-Russian Air Force Su-24M '74 White'?) but doubtful!
Su-24MK	3-6809	416045*******?		D/D 1990. Sand/tan camouflage, wing strakes, '7' on tail. C/n reported as 0815310 (ex-Russian Air Force Su-24M '30 White'?) but doubtful!
Su-24MK	3-6810	416045*******?		D/D 1990. Sand/tan camouflage, wing strakes. C/n reported as 0815314 (ex-Russian Air Force Su-24M '34 White'?) but doubtful!
Su-24MK	3-6811	416045*******?		D/D 1990. Sand/tan camouflage, wing strakes. C/n reported as 0815312 (ex-Russian Air Force Su-24M '32 White'?) but doubtful!
Su-24MK	3-6812	416045*******?		D/D 1990. Sand/tan camouflage. C/n again reported as 0815329 – see comment for 3-6807!
Su-24MK	3-6818	416045*******?		D/D 1990
Su-24MK	3-6843	416045*******?		Ex-Iraqi Air Force 24***, D/D 1991. Sand/tan camouflage, '7' on tail. C/n reported as 1041626, which was Russian Air Force Su-24M '12 White'
Su-24MK	3-6844	416045*******?		Ex-Iraqi Air Force 24***, D/D 1991. C/n reported as 1041635, which was Russian Air Force Su-24M '15 White', but doubtful!
Su-24MK	3-6845	416045*******?		Ex-Iraqi Air Force 24***, D/D 1991. C/n reported as 1041627, which was Russian Air Force Su-24M '14 White', but doubtful!
Su-24MK	3-6846	416045*******?		Ex-Iraqi Air Force 24***, D/D 1991. C/n reported as 1041631, which was Russian Air Force Su-24M '81 White', but doubtful!
Su-24MK	3-6847	416045*******?		Ex-Iraqi Air Force 24***, D/D 1991. Sand/tan camouflage, '7' on tail. Reported in error as c/n 0415301, which was Russian Air Force Su-24M '44 White' until 1993
Su-24MK	3-6848	416045*******?		Ex-Iraqi Air Force 24***, D/D 1991. Sand/tan camouflage. C/n reported as 0415317 but doubtful!
Su-24MK	3-6849	416045*******?		Ex-Iraqi Air Force 24***, D/D 1991. Reported in error as c/n 1141616, which was Russian Air Force Su-24M '41 White' until 1993
Su-24MK	3-6850	416045*******?		Ex-Iraqi Air Force 24***, D/D 1991. C/n reported as 1615304 but doubtful!
Su-24MK	3-6851	416045*******?		Ex-Iraqi Air Force 24***, D/D 1991. C/n reported as 1615318 but doubtful!
Su-24MK	3-6852	416045*******?		Ex-Iraqi Air Force 24***, D/D 1991. Sand/tan camouflage, '7' on tail. C/n reported as 1815307 but doubtful!
Su-24MK	3-6853	416045*******?		Ex-Iraqi Air Force 24***, D/D 1991. C/n reported as 1815308 but doubtful!
Su-24MK	3-6856	416045*******?		Ex-Iraqi Air Force 24***, D/D 1991. Standard Su-24MK camouflage with pale blue sides and white radome; later IRIAF-style sand/tan camouflage, '7' on tail. C/n reported as 2515307 but doubtful!
Su-24MK	3-6857	416045*******?		Ex-Iraqi Air Force 24***, D/D 1991. Sand/tan camouflage. C/n reported as 2515315 but doubtful!
Su-24MK	3-6859	416045*******?		Ex-Iraqi Air Force 24***, D/D 1991. Standard Su-24MK camouflage with pale blue sides and white radome
Su-24MK	3-6860	416045*******?		Ex-Iraqi Air Force 24***, D/D 1991. Sand/tan/green camouflage, white radome, white serial
Su-25K	15-2451	255081*****	?	Sand/tan/green camouflage, IRGC badge on tail
Su-25K	15-2454	255081*****	?	Sand/tan/green camouflage, IRGC badge on tail
Su-25K	15-2455	255081*****	?	Sand/tan/green camouflage, IRGC badge on tail
Su-25K	15-2456	255081*****	?	Sand/tan/green camouflage, IRGC badge on tail
Su-25UBK	15-2457	382201*****	?	Sand/tan/green camouflage, IRGC badge on tail
Su-25UBK	15-2458	382201*****	?	Sand/tan/green camouflage, IRGC badge on tail
Su-25UBK	15-2459	382201*****	?	Sand/tan/green camouflage, IRGC badge on tail
Tu-154M 'Armita'	no serial	88A795		Ex-Iran Air Tour EP-MCS, multi-purpose testbed

Iraq

The Iraqi Air Force (IrAF, or *al Quwwat al-Jawwiya al-Iraqiya*) originated as the Royal Iraqi Air Force in 1931, changing its name after the revolution on 14th July 1958 in which King Faisal II was assassinated, along with the greater part of his family and the Minister of Defence, and the Republic of Iraq was established. After the revolution, the Soviet Union and its Warsaw Pact allies (notably Czechoslovakia) established ties with the new republic and started supplying armaments right away; these included aircraft for the IrAF. Shortly after the revolution the new Commander-in-Chief of the IrAF, Brig. Gen. J. Awqati, arranged a large order for MiG-15 and MiG-17 fighters, IL-28 bombers and other military hardware.

In 1960 the 'extremely progressive' regime of Gen. Abd al-Karim Qasim degenerated into a military dictatorship. Actually Qasim was communist-minded and pro-Soviet. In 1960 he made the fatal mistake of nationalising the Iraqi Petroleum Company – a step which the IPC's Anglo-American owners would not tolerate. On 8th-9th February 1963 Qasim was unseated and executed in a coup led by the Ba'ath Party (the Arab Socialist Renaissance Party), reportedly with backing from the British government and the CIA. The Ba'ath Party was ousted from government just seven months

An Iraqi Air Force UTI-MiG-15 (Aero CS-102) serialled 546 Black in natural metal finish with post-1963 insignia.

The Iraqi flag of 1958-63, which was used as the Iraqi Air Force fin flash in those years.

Iraqi pilots pose with one of the Air Academy's CS-102s (529 Black or 539 Black).

Four rather grubby Iraqi CS-102s (including 541 Black, 542 Black and 544 Black) in diamond formation.

later. However, relations with the Soviet Union improved again when the Ba'ath Party returned to power after the 17th July 1968 coup and Saddam Hussein became head of state. Deliveries of Soviet military hardware continued until 1990 when Saddam Hussein made the fatal mistake of invading Kuwait; consequently further arms supplies to Iraq were embargoed in accordance with the sanctions imposed by the United Nations.

Up to 1967 the IrAF fighters and bombers retained the natural metal finish in which they had been delivered, but camouflage patterns were hastily introduced after the Six-Day War. The three- or four-digit serials (applied in Arab characters) were initially allocated in blocks to batches of aircraft as they were ordered. Later, in 1988, the IrAF introduced a new five-digit serial system, the first two digits denoting the aircraft type; for instance, the MiG-21s' serials were in the 21xxx range, Su-25s were serialled in the 25xxx block and so on.

Mikoyan/Gurevich MiG-15*bis* *Fagot-B* fighters (including Czechoslovak-built Aero S-103s) and UTI-MiG-15 *Midget* trainers (including Aero CS-102s) were the first to arrive. Deliveries began in 1958; in the 1960s, a squadron of MiG-15*bis* fighter-bombers was formed. There are indications that ten to 13 of the single-seaters were former Czechoslovak Air Force aircraft converted to MiG-15*bis*SB fighter-bombers; additionally, at least seven Czechoslovak-built MiG-15*bis*R reconnaissance aircraft were supplied. (However, the recent book *Iraqi Fighters, 1953-2003* by Tom Cooper claims that no single-seat MiG-15s were ever operated by the IrAF and that their pre-assigned serials were transferred to IL-28 bombers.) There was also a training squadron equipped with *Midgets* at the Flying School (later restyled as Air Academy); interestingly, at least some of the CS-102s were likewise surplus aircraft sold from CzAF stocks in 1969-72 as attrition replacements. 30 UTI-MiG-15s were reportedly still operational in early 1987.

The Iraqi Air Force triangle insignia (one would hardly call it a roundel) and the 'pan-Arabic' fin flash used in 1963-2003.

One of the UTI-MiG-15s crashed at Habbaniya on 22nd November 1960, killing trainee pilot 1st Lt. Jamal Jamil and the Soviet instructor pilot. Another *Midget* was lost in a fatal crash at al-Rashid AB near Baghdad on 3rd June 1961 during a night training sortie, 1st Lt. Sohail Ibrahim losing his life.

According to available sources, the Iraqi Air Force took delivery of 20 Mikoyan/Gurevich MiG-17F *Fresco-C* day fighters (in two batches of ten) in 1959, followed by ten MiG-17PF *Fresco-D* all-weather interceptors in 1962. The *Frescos* saw service with the No.5 Sqn at al-Rashid AB (previously equipped with de Havilland Vampire FB.52 fighter-bombers) and No.7 Sqn at Kirkuk (previously equipped with Hawker Fury FB.10 fighter-bombers). Later, after an unsuccessful mutiny by No.5 Sqn officers, the unit was disbanded on 20th December 1963 and the MiG-17s were pooled in the No.7 Sqn. Two Iraqi MiG-17s have been lost in action against Kurdish separatists in 1963 (see below); a further seven were destroyed in accidents on 21st May 1961, 26th July 1962, 16th March 1963, 28th October 1963, 5th January 1964, 12th October 1966 and an unknown date in 1961.

There have been extremely contradictory reports concerning deliveries of the Mikoyan/Gurevich MiG-19 to Iraq. Some sources claim that 15 Soviet-built MiG-19S *Farmer-C* day fighters were delivered to the Iraqi Air Force (the No.9 Sqn at al-Rashid AB) in 1960, supplemented by 40 ex-Egyptian Air Force Shenyang F-6C 'Chinese copies' in 1983.

However, the abovementioned book by Tom Cooper says no more than 15 MiG-19s were delivered from the Soviet Union and, in addition to *Farmer-Cs*, they included a number of MiG-19PM *Farmer-D* missile-armed all-weather interceptors! The latter bit appears highly unlikely, since the MiG-19PM (which was the most sophisticated variant) would sooner be supplied to the Warsaw Pact nations which were at the forefront of the Cold War, not to a third-world country! Yet, the book says (with reference to Iraqi sources) the interceptors had cannons, whereas the *Farmer-D* had none; this suggests the interceptors might in fact have been MiG-19P *Farmer-Bs* – a version which was exported in sizeable numbers. On 8th February 1963, the day of the aforementioned coup, a No.6 Sqn Hawker Hunter F.59 piloted by one of the Ba'athist rebels (1st Lt. Munthir al-Windawi) strafed the flight line at al-Rashid AB, destroying six MiG-19s and damaging others. In 1964, following the arrival of the first MiG-21s, the surviving MiG-19s were phased out and sold to Egypt. Only a single example remained; it is now on display at the IrAF Museum in Baghdad.

Still other sources say Iraq received 30 MiG-19s of unspecified origin from North Korea in 1983. The *Farmers* were based at al-Rashid, Amarah, Karbalah and Jalibah. According to *Interavia*, the Iraqi Air Force still had 40 F-6s in early 1987; more than 30 of them were reportedly operational in late 1991. However, this again seems highly improbable.

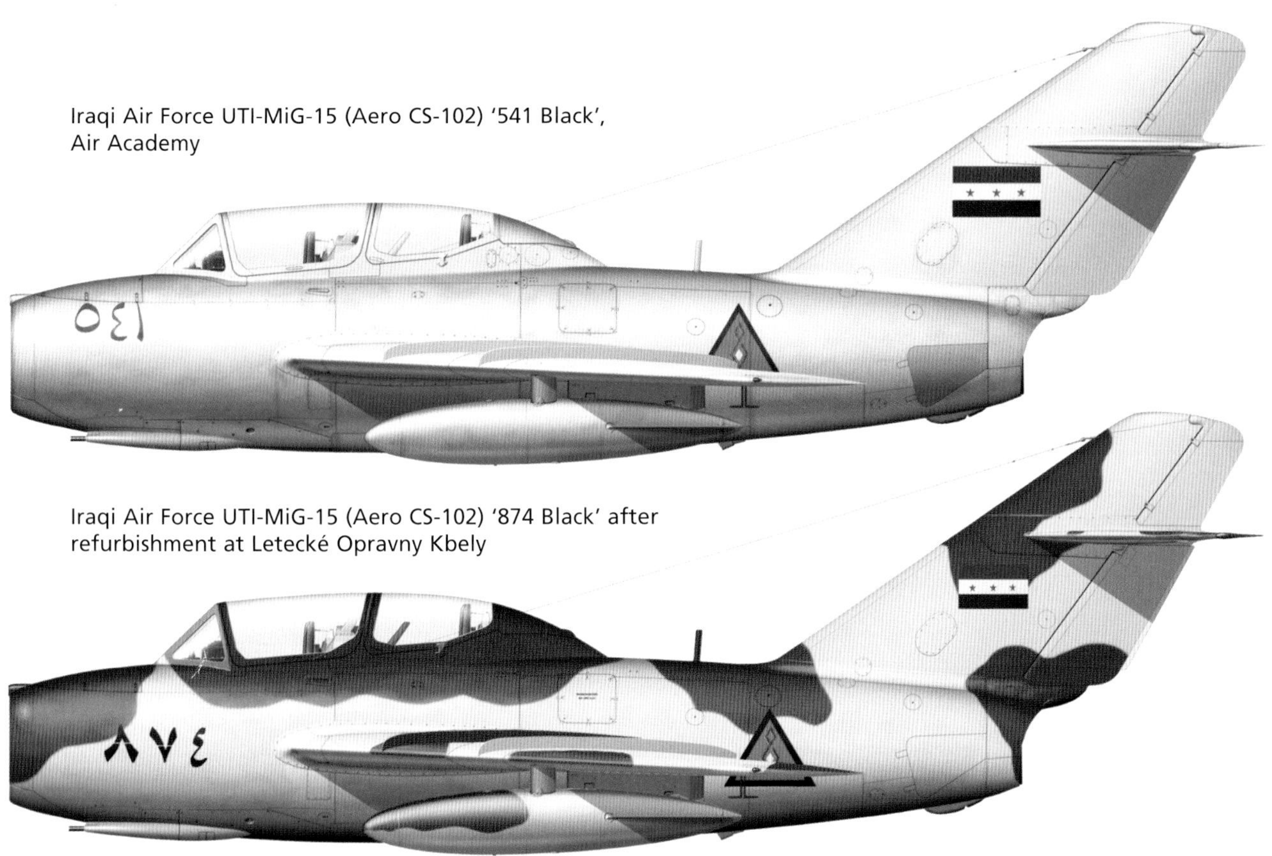

Iraqi Air Force UTI-MiG-15 (Aero CS-102) '541 Black', Air Academy

Iraqi Air Force UTI-MiG-15 (Aero CS-102) '874 Black' after refurbishment at Letecké Opravny Kbely

A number of Iraqi MiG-19s were destroyed on the ground during the First Gulf War of 1990-91 (Operation *Desert Storm*) when Saddam Hussein strategically used them as decoys at his airbases in an attempt to save his real combat aircraft. Others have been reportedly sold to Uganda (?), Afghanistan and... North Korea (!?).

The first Mikoyan MiG-21F-13 (*izdeliye* 74) *Fishbed-C* fighters arrived in Iraq in 1963 and ultimately 35 were delivered to No.11 Sqn at al-Rashid AB. One of these aircraft serialled 534 became famous when Capt. Munir Habib Jamil Redfa, who had been bought off by Israeli secret agents, defected on 16th August 1966 from El Arish AB in Egypt, where he was posted at the time, landing at Hatzor AB in Israel. It is known that the MiG-21F-13 equipped No.11 Sqn and No.17 Sqn. Five MiG-21F-13s from the former unit were destroyed on the ground in the abovementioned strafing attack by al-Windawi's Hunter

Gleaming with fresh paint, camouflaged Iraqi Air Force CS-102 '874 Black' awaits redelivery after an overhaul at Prague-Kbely, with Czechoslovak Air Force Avia-14T transports in the background.

Top: 'Kilroy was here'. MiG-15*bis* '1021 Black' derelict at Kirkuk bears a 'pawmark' painted on by the Allied troops participating in Operation *Desert Storm*.

Above: Despite being non-airworthy already, this camouflaged Iraqi MiG-15*bis* has been viciously dismembered.

on 8th February 1963; the survivors were used in punitive actions against the coup plotters, taking out several rebel strongholds with S-5 unguided rockets. The last Iraqi *Fishbed-Cs* were withdrawn from service around 1988, by which time their natural metal finish had given place to sand/green camouflage.

The first batch of 16 MiG-21FL (*izdeliye* 77) *Fishbed-D* all-weather interceptors with Tumanskiy R11F2S-300 engines and R-2L radars was supplied to the IrAF in 1966; they entered service with the No.17 Sqn at al-Rashid AB which was commissioned on 8th January that year. A second delivery took place in 1967; a total of 37 are known to have been delivered but some sources suggest the figure is close to 90. It appears that several MiG-21PF (*izdeliye* 76) *Fishbed-D* fighters from East German Air Force stocks were earmarked for sale to Iraq in 1989 but not delivered.

55 MiG-21PFM (*izdeliye* 94A) *Fishbed-Fs* featuring a new two-piece canopy and a new ejection seat, an RP-21 radar and provisions for a centreline cannon pod were reportedly purchased in 1970. Some sources say only 36 were delivered in 1967-68, the first of these entering service with the No.9 Sqn, which had been reactivated; the other unit flying the type was the No.11 Sqn. However, many MiG-21PFMs were transferred to Egypt and Syria (before or after delivery) to compensate for their losses in the Six-Day War, which explains why so few Iraqi MiG-21s have been identified by their serials. Some sources state the total number involved was over 100, but this may be a case of MiG-21PFs being confused with MiG-21PFMs. It has been reported that some of the *Fishbed-Fs* served with No.17 Sqn stationed in Syria in 1973 and also with No.11 Sqn in 1980, seeing action against Iran. Also, at least one East German Air Force MiG-21PFMA was earmarked for sale to Iraq in 1989 but not delivered.

Approximately 15 MiG-21R (*izdeliye* 94RA) *Fishbed-H* reconnaissance aircraft were reported purchased in 1979. They served with the elite No.1 FRS (Fighter/Reconnaissance Squadron) but no further details are available.

40 MiG-21MF (*izdeliye* 96F) *Fishbed-J* fighters featuring a new Tumanskiy R13-300 engine, a new RP-22 radar, increased fuel capacity and a built-in cannon arrived in 1973; additionally, from 1974 onwards the unreliable R-3S air-to-air missiles of previous MiG-21 versions were gradually supplanted by the much-improved R-13M1. The MiG-21MFs were serialled 657 through 696, the earlier fighters with these serials having been sent to Egypt or Syria. Another batch was purchased in 1979. The MiG-21MFs equipped the No.9 Sqn at Firnas AB near Mosul and No.11 Sqn, which transferred their previous aircraft to the No.17 Sqn, now an operational conversion unit.

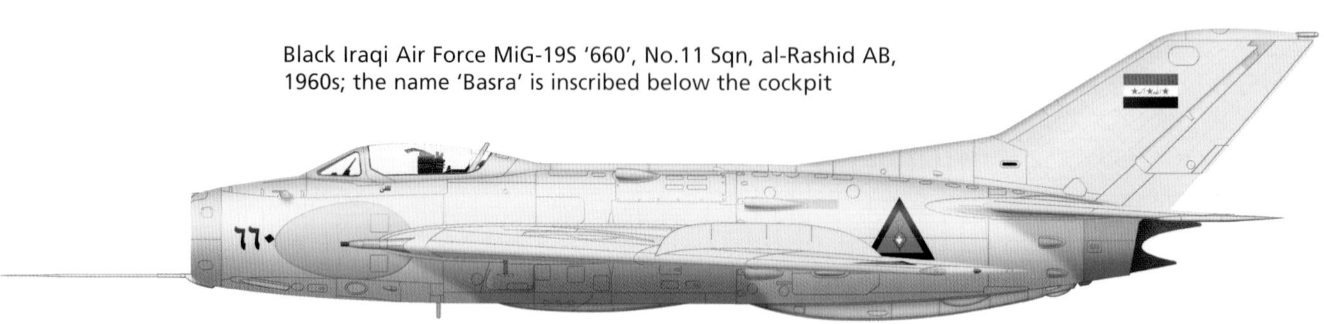

Black Iraqi Air Force MiG-19S '660', No.11 Sqn, al-Rashid AB, 1960s; the name 'Basra' is inscribed below the cockpit

A fine shot of an Iraqi Air Force MiG-17F in post-1963 markings serialled 444 Black.

In contrast, MiG-17F '441 Black' wears an ex-Royal Iraqi Air Force fin flash modified by adding a yellow disc in the centre.

The MiG-21*bis* (*izdeliye* 75A) *Fishbed-L* was the last of the fighter variants, 61 aircraft being delivered from February 1983; first deliveries went to No.11 Sqn. Other MiG-21*bis* units were the No.9 Sqn (which re-equipped in the 1980s), No.47 Sqn at al-Hurrya AB near Tikrit, and No.70 Sqn at al-Rashid AB. It appears that the *Fishbed-Ls* were serialled in the 211xx and 212xx series. In 1990 it was dis-

A poor but interesting picture of an Iraqi MiG-17PF serialled 458 Black.

A trio of IrAF MiG-19Ss wearing interim (1958-63) fin flashes.

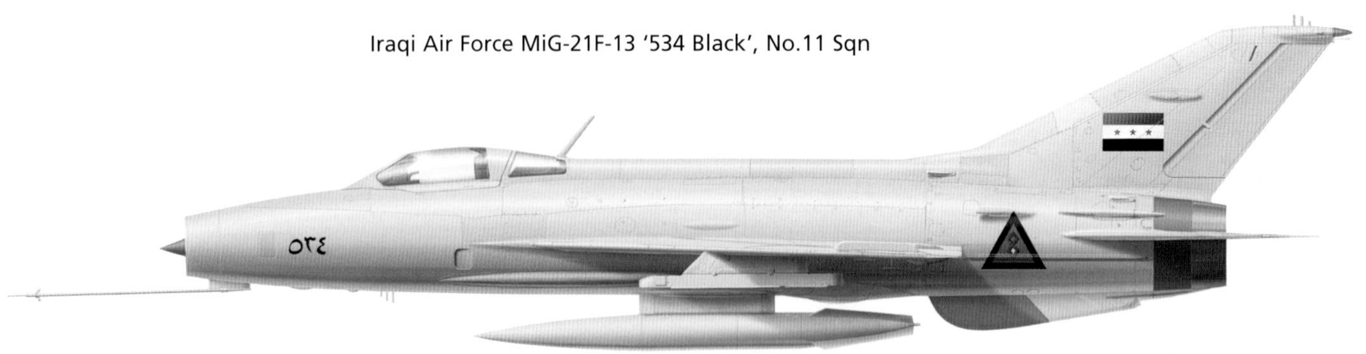

Iraqi Air Force MiG-21F-13 '534 Black', No.11 Sqn

covered that some Iraqi aircraft were being refurbished by the FWD (*Flugzeugwerft Dresden*) facility in East Germany but had been impounded due to the UN sanctions; four more were found under similar circumstances at the Moma Stanojlovic aircraft repair plant in Batajnica, Yugoslavia (Serbia).

At least ten MiG-21U (*izdeliye* 66-400 and/or *izdeliye* 66-600) *Mongol-A* trainers were delivered from 1968. At least eight MiG-21US (*izdeliye* 68A) *Mongol-B* trainers were reported to have arrived in Iraq in 1974, and MiG-21UM (*izdeliye* 69) *Mongol-Bs* followed; they were operated by the No.17 (OCU) Sqn of the IrAF Academy based at Tikrit. The East German Air Force (and, after German reunification on 3rd October 1990, the *Luftwaffe*) intended to sell surplus MiG-21 trainers to Iraq but the sales fell through, probably as a result of Iraq's invasion of Kuwait. One had earlier been allocated an Iraqi serial number. In the table below it is assumed that other aircraft seen at Dresden were Iraqi aircraft sent there for an overhaul.

The genuine Soviet-built *Fishbeds* and *Mongols* were not the only ones supplied to the Iraqi Air Force. In 1982 Iraq received, courtesy of the Egyptian government, 70 Chengdu F-7B (Chinese-built MiG-21F-13 derivative) fighters; these were initially serialled in the 15xx range but subsequently reserialled in the 215xx and 216xx batches. By the time the squadrons became operational it was too late for them to take on the role of interceptors in the Iran-Iraq War on 1980-88 and the F-7Bs were used instead for ground attacks. They

Four views of the Iraqi Air Force MiG-21F-13 '534 Black' which was flown to Israel by a defector on 19th August 1966. Interestingly, the aircraft lacks the wing pylons which were used to carry the missiles.

were augmented by up to 20 Guizhou FT-7B trainers delivered around 1982. Unfortunately, some of the latter have been misidentified as MiG-21UMs, which is very confusing, as both types appear to be intermingled in the same serial blocks. (Here the book *Iraqi Fighters, 1953-2003* again gives conflicting evidence, stating that no more than 30 F-7Bs/FT-7Bs were ever delivered and that they were never used operationally due to their obsolescence, serving for flight and weapons training.)

In 1974 the Iraqi Air Force started taking delivery of an initial order for 18 Mikoyan MiG-23MS *Flogger-E* fighters, accompanied by two MiG-23UB *Flogger-C* trainers. MiG-23 deliveries to the IrAF totalled at least 90. Deliveries of fighter variants included at least 20 MiG-23MSs operated by the No.23 and No.39 Sqns; later the survivors were transferred to the new No.59 (OCU) Sqn at Tammuz AB near Habbaniya. Quite apart from the flight mode limitations and the spate of accidents that accompanied the service introduction period, the Iraqis were displeased with the *Flogger-E*'s avionics (especially the S-21 radar) and the R-3S missiles that were supplied with the fighters; however, after 1978 the surviving MiG-23Ss were modified to carry the more advanced R-13M1 AAMs. In 1979 the No.39 Sqn moved from al-Rashid AB to al-Walid AB and then, in 1980, to Tammuz AB.

In the early 1980s the IrAF received 18 MiG-23MF *Flogger-Bs* equipped with the more capable S-23 radar and armed with better R-23 and R-60 AAMs, which saw service with the No.26, No.81 and No.84 Sqns (according to other sources, No.39 Sqn). In 1984 they were followed by at least 20 MiG-23MLA *Flogger-Gs* powered by a new R35-300 engine, fitted with an even better N003 radar and armed with R-24 and R-60M AAMs. Some of the MiG-23MLAs were upgraded locally, enabling them to carry French-made AM-39 Exocet anti-shipping missiles. The MiG-23UB trainers were distributed between squadrons operating the fighter and strike versions. At least half of the fleet appears to have been lost during the Iran-Iraq War, and most of the survivors were ultimately knocked out by the anti-Iraqi Coalition's air strikes during the First Gulf War. Interestingly, the Iraqis upgraded some of their MiG-23MLAs *in situ* by fitting French-made Thomson-CSF TMV-002 Remora ECM pods carried on the port wing glove pylon and Soviet ASO-2 chaff/flare dispensers (sourced from grounded Su-22M4 fighter-bombers) for self-protection. The dispensers were installed on top of the wing glove fairings in the same fashion as the BVP-30-26M flare dispensers on Soviet Air Force MiG-23MLD *Flogger-Ks*. This arrangement proved quite effective during the First Gulf War.

Left and below left: An Iraqi Air Force pilot climbs into his MiG-21MF serialled 1190 Black and receives last-minute instructions before a sortie.

The wreckage of an Iraqi MiG-21 shot down by the Iranians, with the charred body of an R-13 AAM alongside.

An Iraqi Air Force MiG-21*bis* armed with four R-13M1 AAMs. Oddly, the fighter has no serial.

A camouflaged Iraqi MiG-21F-13 captured by Allied troops in the Second Gulf War.

MiG-21F-13 '709 Black' served as a gate guard at Shaibah airbase.

This strangely painted MiG-21F-13 is preserved at Baghdad airport.

Starting in 1980, the Iraqi Air Force purchased at least 18 Mikoyan MiG-25s. The majority of these were MiG-25P *Foxbat-A* interceptors operated by No.96 Sqn at al-Taqaddum AB near Qadisiyah; they became operational in May 1981. According to the book *Iraqi Fighters, 1953-2003*, at the insistence of the Iraqis they were upgraded in situ to MiG-25PDS *Foxbat-D* standard by installing new Smerch-2A radars and other new avionics. Some sources say the interceptors belonged to the No.1 FRS; Flight A was manned by Iraqi personnel while the aircraft of Flight B were allegedly operated by Soviet pilots. The reconnaissance/strike versions – initially MiG-25RB *Foxbat-Bs*, augmented in 1985 or 1986 by MiG-25RBT *Foxbat-Bs* with the SRS-16 *Tan**gazh*** (Pitch) signals intelligence suite – were concentrated in the No.96 Sqn (some sources say No.17 FRS) since 1983. (According to Tom Cooper, the first reconnaissance *Foxbats* delivered to Iraq were MiG-25Rs with no strike capability, and the MiG-25RBTs were only delivered after the Iraqis decided to modify the MiG-25Rs for carrying Spanish-

A very weathered (and damaged) MiG-21FL serialled 21112 Black seen after being captured by US troops.

This MiG-21FL served as a gate guard at an Iraqi airbase. However, it did not actually carry R-60M missiles when it was active.

made bombs in order to make attacks on Tehran.) A pair of MiG-25PU *Foxbat-C* trainers (some sources say six) were also delivered. Later, in mid-1986, an additional batch of ten MiG-25PDs and six MiG-25RBTs was delivered to reinforce the IrAF during the Iran-Iraq War. Some of the Iraqi *Foxbats* were retrofitted with overwing BVP-30-26M flare dispensers replacing the inboard boundary layer fences. There was also an abortive attempt to modify one MiG-25 as a suppression of enemy air defences (SEAD) aircraft armed with French anti-radar missiles known locally as Baz-AR (*baz* is Arabic for falcon) – the would-have-been Iraqi equivalent of the MiG-25BM *Foxbat-F*.

Three MiG-25RBs were lost in the Iran-Iraq War, though only one was a combat loss. 20 of the remaining *Foxbats* were destroyed or captured by Coalition forces during the First Gulf War. However, this was not the end of the MiG-25's Iraqi career; the MiG-25RBTs flew reconnaissance missions over Jordan and Saudi Arabia until the Second Gulf War began in 2003. The efforts of the Royal Jordanian Air Force Lockheed Martin F-16As and the USAF McDonnell Douglas F-15s stationed in Saudi Arabia to intercept them proved futile – the *Foxbat* would be gone by the time the interceptor had reached its flight level.

Iraq was the second Middle Eastern state to express an interest in the Mikoyan MiG-29, ordering 42 of the type – 36 single-seat MiG-29 (*izdeliye* 9.12B) *Fulcrum-As* and six MiG-29UB *Fulcrum-B* combat trainers – in 1987. The first 18 (some sources say 25) aircraft were delivered towards the end of the year. The Iraqi MiG-29s were used in the air defence role, serving with the No.6 Sqn based at Tammuz AB; there were plans to establish a second MiG-29 squadron but they were never implemented. Unconfirmed reports state that 35 *Fulcrum-As* and six *Fulcrum-Bs* were on strength in August 1990, one aircraft having been written off. The existence of the type in the IrAF was officially revealed when a single-seater serialled 29060 Black was shown at a military hardware display at Baghdad's Saddam Hussein International airport in early 1990. The first 18 aircraft reportedly wore a desert camouflage scheme; the rest, including 29060 Black, were delivered in the MiG-29's standard Soviet two-tone grey camouflage.

Combat losses in the First Gulf War (and the ensuing exodus to Iran), coupled with accident attrition, reduced the Iraqi MiG-29 fleet to 18 by the end of 1991. Due to the lack of spares eight of the *Fulcrums* (including one MiG-29UB) were mothballed; the other ten continued in service until 1999 or 2000. More recent information, however, suggests that only 37 of the 42 aircraft ordered were actually delivered; of these, 17 were destroyed and four others damaged during the First Gulf War, four more were flown to Iran, and 12 remained in service after 1991.

In May 1966 the Iraqi Air Force placed an initial order for 34 Sukhoi Su-7BMK *Fitter-A* fighter-bombers. A second order for 20 followed in July 1967, which gives a total of 54. (Actually these orders did not consist solely of

Iraqi Air Force MiG-21UM '21038 Black' abandoned intact at al-Taqaddum AB.

Covered with sand, this Iraqi MiG-21R reconnaissance aircraft serialled 21302 Black was captured intact during the Second Gulf War.

An Iraqi Air Force pilot poses with his MiG-21MF. Note the BAC Jet Provosts in the background.

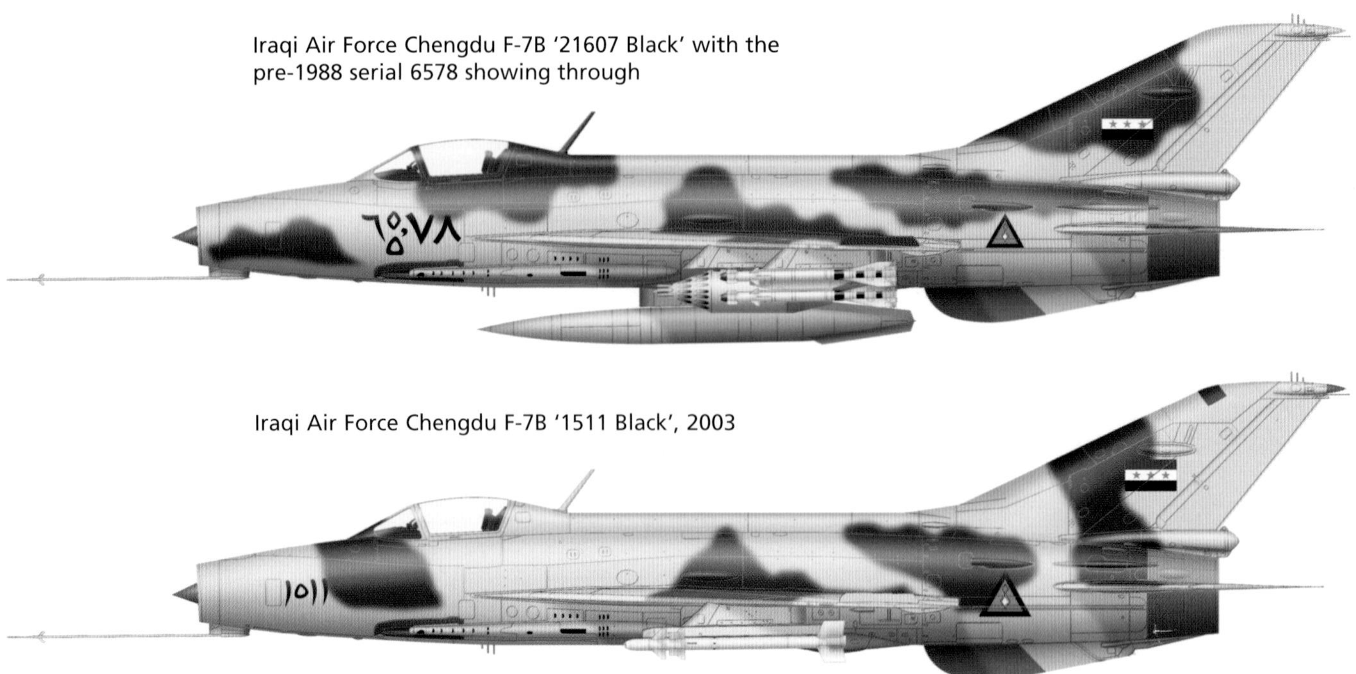

Iraqi Air Force Chengdu F-7B '21607 Black' with the pre-1988 serial 6578 showing through

Iraqi Air Force Chengdu F-7B '1511 Black', 2003

single-seaters but included Su-7UMK *Moujik* trainers as well. Some sources say the IrAF received 42 aircraft (36 Su-7BMKs and six Su-7UMKs) – or even as many as 83 Su-7s!

The first group of Iraqi pilots arrived in the Soviet Union to take conversion training for the Su-7 at the Krasnodar Military Pilot College in the spring of 1967. Subsequently Iraqi Su-7 pilots trained in Czechoslovakia as well; in the autumn of 1970 a special course was set up at the CzAF's Training Centre at Přerov AB, using aircraft on loan from the CzAF. This training did not go without incident and two CzAF Su-7s – a single-seater and a trainer – were lost when Iraqi trainees were at the controls (fortunately with no loss of life).

The No.1 Sqn based at Kirkuk in north-eastern Iraq received the first 18 Su-7BMKs in October 1967 and was commissioned on 3rd December. In October 1968 the No.5 Sqn, likewise based at Kirkuk, received ten *Fitter-As* and four more shortly afterwards, becoming operational on 1st February 1969. A third unit, the No.8 Sqn at Wahda AB near Basra, re-equipped from Il'yushin IL-28 *Beagle* tactical bombers to the Su-7 in 1969, receiving the 20 aircraft delivered under the second contract.

The remains of several scrapped IrAF aircraft on the dump of an Iraqi airbase, with a Chengdu F-7B in the foreground.

In 1974 the No.1 Sqn converted to the Su-20 (see below), ceding its remaining Su-7s to the other two units. The No.5 Sqn followed suit in 1977, re-equipping with Su-22s, and the surviving *Fitter-As* were concentrated in the No.8 Sqn, which had moved to Abu Ubaida AB near al-Kut in south-eastern Iraq. This squadron became an operational conversion unit for pilots transitioning to the 'swing-wing' Sukhois. However, in 1984 this squadron disbanded, putting an end to the Su-7's career in Iraq; the No.44 Sqn that took over as the OCU was equipped with Su-22s.

The first batch of Iraqi Su-7s was delivered in natural metal finish. After the Six-Day War, however, the aircraft received an olive drab/tan camouflage with pale blue undersurfaces; two different camouflage schemes were used.

In 1986 Egypt donated about 30 Su-7BMKs to Iraq; however, these were in such poor condition that they were unfit for service and were used only as decoys. This explains why Western intelligence agencies overestimated the number of Iraqi *Fitter-As*; Western aviation magazines wrote that 50 Su-7BMKs were in service at the end of 1986, this number dwindling to 30 by 1990 and to 20 by 1995. No Su-7s remained in service by 2000.

The Iraqi Air Force also operated the variable-geometry versions of the *Fitter*. The Sukhoi Su-20 *Fitter-D* (the export version of the Su-17) came first; the initial lot of 18 aircraft was ordered in 1972 (though the book *Iraqi Fighters, 1953-2003* says that the Iraqis actually *did not* order the type and the delivery came as a complete surprise for them). The first ten aircraft were airlifted to al-Rashid AB near Baghdad by Soviet Air Force An-12 transports in October 1973, in the middle of the Yom Kippur War, the remainder arriving by sea via Basra in 1974. These aircraft entered service with the No.1 Sqn at Hurriya AB near Kirkuk in northern Iraq. In all, at least 35 Su-20s were delivered, remaining in service until 2003.

The IrAF also operated Guizhou FT-7s, including 21079 Black abandoned at al-Taqaddum AB.

The Su-22 *Fitter-F* (the export version of the Su-17M) followed in 1975, equipping the newly established No.44 Sqn (also at Hurriya AB; other sources say Habbaniya) and No.109 Sqn at Wahda AB in southern Iraq; at least 36 were delivered to these two units. The aircraft came together with Kh-23E air-to-surface mis-

This F-7B is seen derelict at al-Taqaddum in 2003 with the new serial 21607 Black hand-written over the original serial 6578 White.

To the victor belong the spoils: A US Marine Corps Sikorsky MH-53E Super Sea Stallion of HMH-465 'War Horses' prepares to lift Iraqi Air Force F-7B '6578 White' which was captured by the Marines.

Right: An Iraqi pilot poses with his black-nosed MiG-23MS.

Far right: A white-nosed IrAF MiG-23MS returns from a sortie with four R-13M1s. Note the odd position of the wing insignia.

This dumped and gutted MiG-23MS (23105 Black) wears the badge the No.59 Sqn on the port air intake trunk.

siles, and a few were Su-22R reconnaissance aircraft equipped with KKR-1 camera pods.

The next version delivered to Iraq was the Su-22M *Fitter-H* (equivalent to the Su-17M2). The first 18 arriving in 1978, entering service with No.5 Sqn at al-Bakr AB near Tikrit. They were upgraded *in situ* at Hurriya AB in 1981 to give them SEAD capability by carrying Kh-28 anti-radar missiles. Later deliveries of Su-22Ms had this capability from the start; these aircraft re-equipped the No.109 Sqn which turned over its older Su-22s to the No.44 Sqn, the latter becoming an operational conversion unit.

Freshly refurbished by the Russian Air Force's 121st Aircraft Repair Pant, Iraqi Air Force MiG-23MLA '23255 Black' awaits redelivery at Kubinka AB. The placard next to it reads 'Finished products' (that is, delivery line).

Another view of 23255 Black – this time amid deep snowdrifts; the aircraft was undeliverable due to UN sanctions.

'Everything OK – ready to go.' IrAF MiG-23MLA '23266 Black' is 'waved off' by the crew chief before a sortie.

An Iraqi pilot climbs out of the same aircraft.

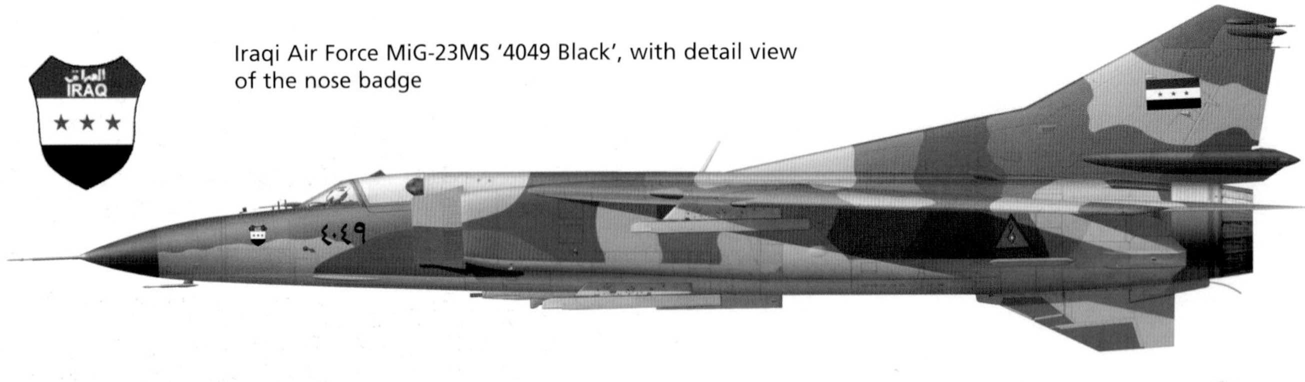

Iraqi Air Force MiG-23MS '4049 Black', with detail view of the nose badge

Iraqi Air Force MiG-23ML '23270 Black' carrying R-24R AAMs and a PTB-800 drop tank

Iraqi Air Force MiG-23UB '23033 Black' armed with four R-3S AAMs

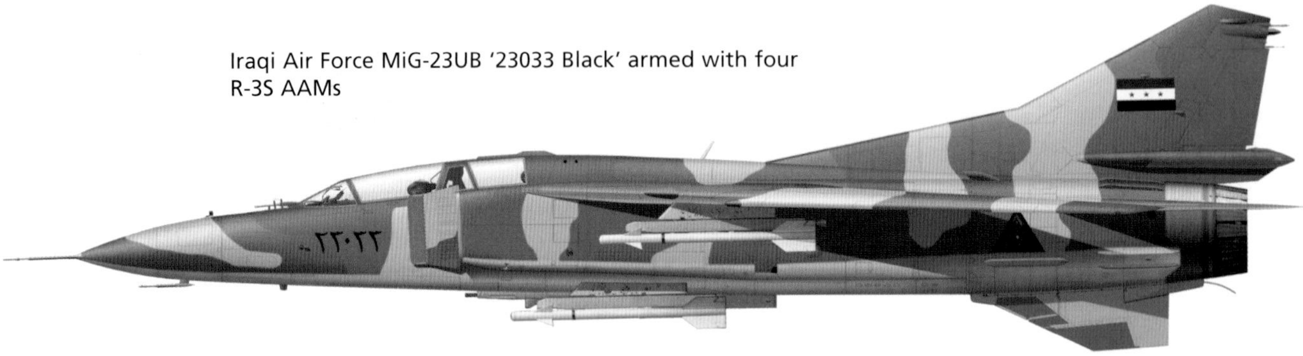

The Su-20s, Su-22s and the first Su-22Ms wore a sand/olive drab desert camouflage; subsequent aircraft received a dark earth/olive drab scheme. A curious feature of the Su-22s and Su-22Ms was that, unlike the Su-20s, the Iraqi triangle national insignia was carried on both the forward fuselage and the rear fuselage until the mid-1980s when the additional insignia on the nose were dispensed with.

In early 1984 the IrAF introduced the Su-22M3 *Fitter-J* 9 equivalent to the Su-17M3) able to carry Kh-25 laser-guided air-to-surface missiles and Kh-25MP ARMs. The first 18 aircraft equipped the newly established No.69

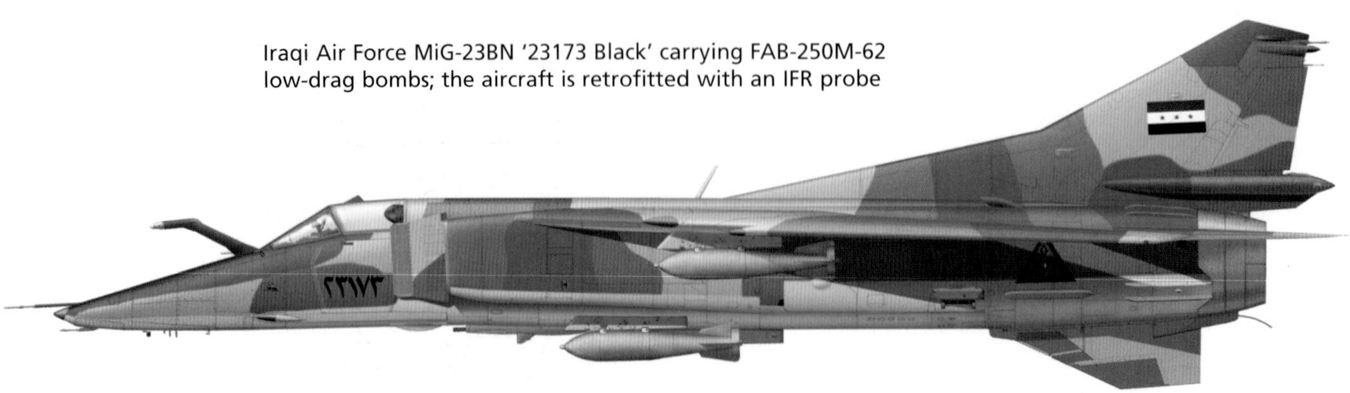

Iraqi Air Force MiG-23BN '23173 Black' carrying FAB-250M-62 low-drag bombs; the aircraft is retrofitted with an IFR probe

Several Iraqi Air Force MiG-23BNs, including 23173 Black, were retrofitted with IFR probes borrowed from the Dassault Mirage F.1EQ. The aircraft was seen at a military airshow at Baghdad-Saddam Hussein International airport in 1990.

This photo of the same aircraft provides details of the camouflage colours and pattern.

Three-quarters rear view of MiG-23BN '23173 Black'.

Above and above right: Saddam's ploy to bury his combat jets in the sand in order to save them from destruction failed. Here, US troops have unearthed a couple of MiG-25s, including MiG-25RBT '25107 Black'.

Below: Sister ship '25106 Black' captured during Operation *Desert Storm* looks somewhat the worse for wear.

Bottom: Captured almost intact, MiG-25RBT '25105 Black' was shipped to the USA to become an exhibit of the USAF Museum.

Sqn, also based at al-Bakr AB. Finally, in 1986-87 the Iraqis took delivery of 36 Su-22M4 *Fitter-Ks* (equivalent to the Su-17M4) which were operated by the No.5 and No.109 Sqns. A number of Su-22UM3 *Fitter-E* trainers were also supplied.

The Su-20s and Su-22s were actively used in the Iran-Iraq war of 1980-88; among other things, they staged chemical attacks against Iranian troops, using bombs filled with nerve agents. Combat attrition was high, a total of 64 being lost to the Iranian air defences.

Figures on the number of Iraqi *Fitters* and their attrition vary widely. One source states that 119 Su-7/17/22s were in service as of 12th January 1991; of these, five aircraft were shot down and another 14 destroyed on the ground during Operation *Desert Storm*, and 34 fled to nearby Iran (where they were seized), leaving an estimated 66 on strength after the war. Other sources claim that 70 Su-20/-22s were operational in 1990, the number declining to 45 in 1995 and just fifteen in 2000-02. Four Su-20s and 40 Su-22s

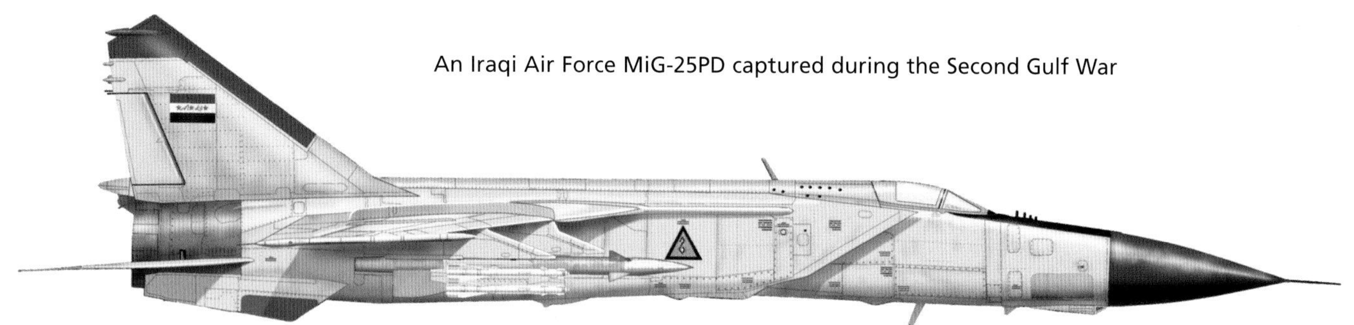

An Iraqi Air Force MiG-25PD captured during the Second Gulf War

escaped to Iran and another two Su-22s were shot down.

In the early 1970s Iraq placed another large order for Soviet military aircraft, including a substantial number of MiG-23BN *Flogger-H* fighter-bombers. The first 18 aircraft were delivered in 1974, entering service with the reborn No.29 Sqn at Ali Ibn Abu Talib AB (aka Tallil AB); the second MiG-23BN unit was the newly established No.49 Sqn at Abu Ubaida AB, which likewise received 18 aircraft. To make up for combat losses and accident attrition in 1974-75 (at least four and two MiG-23BNs respectively) an additional lot of 15 was purchased in 1974-75, and further additions of 60 more MiG-23BNs took place in 1976-77; in all, about 100 *Flogger-Hs* were delivered to the Iraqi Air Force, serving with the Nos. 77 and 78 Sqns. The Iraqi MiG-23BNs were later modified to fire AM-39 Exocet and other non-Soviet missiles. Moreover, at least one was fitted with a fixed L-shaped in-flight refuelling probe (borrowed from the Dassault Mirage F.1) on the starboard side of the nose just ahead of the canopy. It is assumed that the latter modification was at least approved by the Mikoyan OKB, as it was included in an official history of the OKB published in 2000.

Iraqi MiG-23s suffered heavy losses during the Iran-Iraq War. By the end of January 1981, only 40 MiG-23s of any type were in flying condition. There was no record of MiG-23BNs in action in the 1991 Gulf War; although many were probably destroyed on the ground, four managed to escape to Iran where they were interned.

During the early phase of the Iran-Iraq War, when the IrAF realised that it would need a more appropriate attack aircraft for close air support, Iraq approached the Soviet Union with a request to purchase a wide variety of military equipment. As a result, Iraq became the first non-Warsaw Pact country to obtain the Sukhoi Su-25K *Frogfoot-A* attack aircraft and its Su-25UBK *Frogfoot-B* trainer version. Russian press reports claim that the Iraqi Air Force received a total of 73 Su-25s, of which four were Su-25UBK combat trainers. The aircraft were delivered to Iraq by sea in crates and reassembled by Soviet technicians; the first batch of 18 began arriving in late 1985, followed by the second in 1986. Pilot training was carried out by Soviet instructors in parallel with the deliveries.

The first IrAF unit operating the type – No.115 Sqn – was formed in early 1986, followed by a second (No.116 Sqn) in 1987.

MiG-25PD '25211' did not require exhumation because the Iraqis had not had time to bury it.

Above: The badly damaged hulk of MiG-25RU '25002 Black' at al-Taqaddum AB.

Left: A US soldier poses with the wreckage of an Iraqi MiG-25PD shot down by a USAF fighter.

Iraqi Air Force MiG-25RBT '25106 Black' with the huge PTB-5000 drop tank fitted

During the Iran-Iraq War, the Su-25s represented the main Iraqi strike force and were deployed according to a mobile basing philosophy, which involved operating from the many airfields around the country on an irregular rotation cycle.

The First Gulf War took its toll on the Su-25 fleet. Seven *Frogfeet* were flown to Iran in January 1991 to escape destruction and were never returned. On 6th February 1991, two Su-25Ks were shot down by USAF F-15 Eagles. Others were destroyed on the ground or captured by Coalition forces. According to press information in January 1998, Iraq still had 12 Su-25s, and at least three Su-25Ks were seen in a flypast over Baghdad in December 2002.

Prior to the Six-Day War the Iraqi Air Force operated a single light bomber squadron – the No.8 Sqn established at al-Rashid AB on 10th February 1960 – equipped with ten Il'yushin IL-28 *Beagle* tactical bombers and two IL-28U *Mascot* trainers. The aircraft were supplied via Egypt in 1958, replacing the de Havilland Venom FB.50 fighter-bombers operated earlier. One unit known to have operated the IL-28 is the No.8 Sqn at Wahda AB.

Later, the Iraqi Air Force received 24 Sukhoi Su-24MK *Fencer-D* tactical bombers. It has been reported that the type was offered to Iraq as early as 1986 but the IrAF did not place an order for an initial 18 aircraft (it's really funny how this quantity keeps repeating itself time and time again!) until 1988. There is some controversy over when the first deliveries took place. Russian sources with strong ties to the Sukhoi OKB stated that the first bomber was airlifted to al-Bakr AB by a Soviet Air Force Antonov An-22 Antey (*Cock*) transport in early June 1988; Israeli sources suggest that all 24 Su-24MKs were delivered in 1990 (14 in the first quarter of the year and a further ten by the end of the year). A possible explanation that one aircraft was delivered in 1988 for familiarisation, the rest following in 1990.

Two Su-24MK squadrons – the re-established No.8 Fighter-Bomber Squadron at al-Bakr AB and the No.18 FBS at as-Sahra AB – were formed but did not become operational, and the intended third squadron – the No.28 FBS at Kirkuk – was never formed. The Iraqis did not use Su-24MKs against the Coalition forces during the 1991 Gulf War – allegedly because only 20 pilots had received partial training and only one crew was combat-ready. Reports that the 130-strong Soviet team supporting the type's service introduction was withdrawn in 1990 (due to UN sanctions imposed after the Iraqi invasion of Kuwait) explain this.

In January 1991 all 24 *Fencers* were flown to what was misguidedly seen as a safe haven in Iran (where the Su-24MKs were promptly impounded along with the other Iraqi aircraft and eventually appropriated by the Iranians). This was made possible by the fact that three Soviet flying instructors remained in Iraq and were able to give the local pilots just enough training to allow them to make the ferry flights. In spite of being flown by inexperienced pilots, all the *Fencers* reached Iran safely without being intercepted by Coalition fighters. Two aircraft were repeatedly attacked by a pair of USAF F-15Cs which fired AIM-7M Sparrow medium-range AAMs and then AIM-9 Sidewinder short-range AAMs, but the bombers' ECM/IRCM suite managed to decoy all the missiles. (Interestingly, some sources claim that 25 Su-24MKs were actually delivered to Iraq and 24 of them were flown to Iran, the 25th bomber remaining at al-Bakr AB; this aircraft, dubbed 'Waheeda' ('The loner' in Arabic), allegedly remained in service until 2003, operating from Tammuz AB where it was eventually captured by US troops and taken to the USA for evaluation.)

After the 1991 war the USA successfully foiled any Iraqi moves to replace the bombers. True, some sources have suggested that Iran

Iraqi Air Force MiG-25BM '25201 Black'

returned six Su-24MKs to Iraq or that six never left Iraq, but neither story has been confirmed. One certainty is that there were no Su-24s airworthy in Iraq in 2004.

In the 1960s, the Iraqi Air Force acquired eight Tupolev Tu-16KSR-2-11 *Badger-G* missile strike aircraft, which were operated by the No.10 Sqn at Habbaniya. These aircraft were used during the Iran-Iraq War to attack Iranian Army positions, as well as military and civilian objectives in Iran. In particular, the Tu-16s bombed Tehran-Mehrabad airport and carried out several missile launches. Subsequently, Iraq purchased four examples of the *Badger-G*'s Chinese-built equivalent – the Xian H-6D (B-6D), together with a large number of C-601 Silkworm and C-611 anti-shipping missiles; these were operated by the No.10 Sqn. After the disintegration of the Soviet Union, China supplied Iraq with spares for its Tu-16/H-6 fleet. By 1991 virtually all Iraqi Tu-16s had run out of service life. Some were damaged or destroyed in Coalition air strikes during the First Gulf War.

In 1973, shortly after the Yom Kippur War, the Iraqi Air Force ordered the Tupolev Tu-22 bomber. The Iraqi pilots took their training at the 47th Aircrew Training Centre at Zyabrovka AB, Belorussia, in 1973-74. Upon completion of the training the Iraqis were allowed to pick the best of the resident 290th Independent Long-Range Reconnaissance Regiment's Tu-22Rs which were then converted to Tu-22B *Blinder-A* standard by the Kazan' aircraft factory that had built them.

The training didn't always run smoothly. One trainee pilot was killed in the crash of a Tu-22U *Blinder-D* trainer; the Russian instructor and navigator ejected safely but for some reason the Iraqi trainee never tried to eject. Iraqi crews continued proficiency training at Zyabrovka even after delivery of the aircraft.

According to various reports, in 1975 the IrAF took delivery of 12 Tu-22B bombers and two Tu-22UD trainers with the IFR probes removed. (Some sources claim that *'from 1981 the IrAF received four Tu-22Ks and between 200 and 300 Kh-22M and Kh-22MP (AS-4) missiles'*, but this is pure fantasy – the *Blinder-B* and the Kh-22 were never exported. The Tu-22K/KD/KPDs were few, and the Soviet Air

An Iraqi Air Force MiG-25PD awaiting redelivery at a Soviet aircraft repair plant.

Force would not part with any of these aircraft, which were one of its most potent strike assets!)

The Tu-22s were in service with the 7th Bomber Squadron of the 4th Composite Bomber Wing, operating from al-Taqaddum AB in central Iraq approximately 74 km (436 miles) west of Baghdad and al-Walid AB 435 km (270 miles) west of Baghdad in the so-called H-3 base cluster (hence it is also known as 'H-3 Main'). The aircraft wore a typical Middle Eastern two-tone camouflage and were reportedly serialled consecutively from 1101 Black to 1114 Black; it is not known which ones were the trainers.

Iraqi pilots were quick to master the low-level flying technique and put it to good use during the Iran-Iraq War. After delivery, Iraqi Tu-22Bs had the bomb release button moved from the navigator's station to the pilot's control wheel and special reference lines applied to the port half of the windscreen to make them better suited for ultra-low-level sorties. Several *Blinders* were lost during the Iran-Iraq War; the survivors remained at al-Taqaddum, where the non-airworthy bombers were destroyed by US air strikes on 17th January 1991 during the First Gulf War.

The Iraqi Air Force took delivery of an unknown number of Antonov An-2 *Colt* utility biplanes built by PZL in Poland. Only two have been identified so far.

In 1961 the Iraqi Air Force purchased its first three Antonov An-12 *Cub* transports, namely Irkutsk-built An-12As. These were followed by three Voronezh-built An-12Bs in 1965 and by five Tashkent-built An-12BPs in 1966 and 1968 to give a total of 11 – enough to equip a squadron (the No.3 Sqn at Rashid AB). Unlike the An-12As, which had an overall grey colour scheme, the others had a white upper fuselage and vertical tail, with a thin black cheatline separating them from the grey belly; another difference was that the serial

Iraqi Air Force MiG-29 (*izdeliye* 9.12B) '29060 Black'; note the absence of wing pylons.

Here the same aircraft is seen at the military hardware display staged at Baghdad airport in 1990.

'29060 Black' takes off, the landing gear just beginning to retract. Some Iraqi MiG-29s wore desert camouflage; others, including this one, were delivered in the type's standard two-tone grey scheme.

was applied not only in Arab characters but also in European characters (the latter version was prefixed 'I.A.F.'). In the early 1970s the five An-12BPs were transferred to the civil register, ostensibly being operated by Iraqi Airways and wearing a civil-style colour scheme with a green cheatline and Iraqi Airways titles. This move was meant to facilitate flights abroad (typically to pick up spares for IrAF combat aircraft).

One of the *Cubs* was converted locally into a single-point flight refuelling tanker, using the probe-and-drogue system with a western-made hose drum unit (HDU). Thus was born a version which had no Soviet equivalent.

Tactical transport duties were performed by six Antonov An-24T *Coke* twin-turboprop transports delivered in 1968. Initially they wore full Iraqi Air Force markings but were placed on the civil register in 1982-84, gaining Iraqi Airways livery. Additionally, an unknown quantity of Antonov An-26 *Curl* tactical transports was delivered; only a single civil-registered example in known, but that was in all probability an IrAF aircraft as well.

Iraq became the first (and largest) foreign customer for the Il'yushin IL-76 heavy transport, the Iraqi Air Force taking delivery of 41 examples between September 1977 and June 1990. The first six aircraft represented the initial IL-76 *sans suffixe* version in its *Candid-B* military variety with a gunner's station; the next 12 were IL-76Ms with a higher gross weight and the rest were even heavier IL-76MDs. The last 15 aircraft were built with no gunner's station (that is with the same type of tailcone as the commercial IL-76T/TD *Candid-A*), despite the 'IL-76MD' nose titles, and may thus be called IL-76MD 'Falsie'. All the *Candids* were quasi-civil, being nominally operated by Iraqi Airways. At least five examples from early deliveries and one of the IL-76MDs had a grey/white colour scheme, but most wore full Iraqi Airways livery, albeit the emerald green colour of the fuselage top and vertical tail was replaced by black.

The Iraqis developed indigenous special-mission versions of the *Candid* in the late 1980s, using western equipment. In 1988 one 'true' IL-76MD was converted into a single-point refuelling tanker for the IrAF's Dassault Mirage F.1EQ fighter-bombers, as well as MiG-23BN and Su-22M4 fighter-bombers retrofitted locally with IFR probes. In contrast to the IL-78 *Midas* tanker, the podded HDU (probably a Douglas D-704 'buddy' refuelling pack, a number of which had been supplied for the Mirages) was carried on the centreline on a pylon fitted to the cargo ramp (!). This obviously required extreme caution on take-off and landing so as to avoid scraping the runway. The aircraft wore a grey/white IrAF colour scheme but no insignia or civil registration.

Also in 1988, an unidentified IL-76MD 'Falsie' was converted into the Baghdad-1 AWACS aircraft. A Thomson-CSF TRS-2100 Tigre S surveillance radar manufactured locally under French licence was installed under the rear fuselage in a huge glassfibre blister fairing supplanting the cargo doors, with a strake below it to improve directional stability. The aircraft wore basic Iraqi Airways colours but the airline logos and registration were painted out. Iraqi specialists claimed that the radar, which was manned by four operators, had a scan 'substantially in excess of 180°' and could detect, identify and track targets at up to 350 km (217 miles) range. Since in its basic form the Tigre is ground-based, changes were made to the radar set in order to reduce susceptibility to ground clutter. Tactical information was transmitted in real time by data link or voice link; the aircraft also featured indigenous radio and radar ESM equipment.

Later, two more IL-76MD 'Falsies' were converted for the AWACS role as the Adnan-1 and Adnan-2 (named after former Iraqi Defence Minister Gen. Adnan Khajrallah Talfah killed in a helicopter crash in May 1988). These had the TRS-2105/06 Tigre G radar installed in a conventional rotodome of 9 m (29 ft 6 in) diameter mounted on twin pylons immediately aft of the wings; two canted trapezoidal strakes were fitted to the rear fuselage sides to ensure directional stability. The first aircraft had a grey/white colour scheme but no insignia other than an Iraqi flag and 'Adnan-1' titles in Arabic, whereas the Adnan-2 wore a two-tone grey wraparound camouflage scheme with full Iraqi Air Force insignia.

Nearly half the Iraqi IL-76 fleet (20 aircraft) was returned to the Soviet Union; presumably they were traded-in for newer IL-76MDs. One IL-76MD was written off in a landing accident; three other *Candids* were lost to enemy action (one during the Iran-Iraq War and two during the First Gulf War). The other 17 were flown to Iran at the closing stage of the latter war to escape destruction. Again, Iran kept these aircraft, 15 of which eventually entered service with the Islamic Republic of Iran Air Force and the Islamic Revolution Guards Corps. On 5th November 2000 IL-76MD YI-ALV, the sole example remaining in Iraq, began scheduled domestic passenger services (!) between Baghdad and Basra (in company with an An-26 serving the Baghdad-Mosul route). These aircraft had to be used because almost the entire Iraqi Airways airliner fleet was stored outside Iraq.

In 1965 the Iraqi Air Force took delivery of two Tupolev Tu-124 *Cookpot* short-haul airliners, becoming one of the three foreign operators of the type. The aircraft were in 36-seat or 22-seat VIP configuration and the exact version was thus Tu-124K-36 or Tu-124K2-22 respectively. For several years the jets wore a red cheatline and overt military markings, with the serials applied in both European and Arab characters. In the 1970s they were transferred to the civil register, gaining the green/white livery of Iraqi Airways. Both Tu-124Ks were eventually destroyed on the ground by Allied air strikes during the First Gulf War (Operation *Desert Storm*), but they were obviously long since out of service by then.

In 1970 a single Tupolev Tu-134 *Crusty* short-haul airliner (the original short-fuselage variety with no thrust reversers) was delivered to Iraq. The aircraft was completed in Tu-134K

Iraqi Air Force Su-7BMK '755' as delivered in natural metal finish

Iraqi Air Force Su-7BMK '946' in desert camouflage

VIP configuration and used for government transportation; hence, though civil-registered and painted in old Iraqi Airways colours, it was almost certainly operated by the Iraqi Air Force. Its Iraqi career proved to be brief; after a minor accident at Jeddah in June 1971 the Tu-134K was returned to the Soviet Union, serving first with the Air Force and then with an aviation industry enterprise.

The Mil' Mi-2 *Hoplite* light helicopter made its way to Iraq in 1977. The primary operator of the type was the Ministry of Agriculture, but from 1984 onwards a total of 15 Mi-2s were delivered to the Iraqi Air Force. Oddly, six of them had construction numbers commencing 52, which identifies them as the Mi-2R agricultural version; the others represented the Mi-2T utility version and the Mi-2P passenger version.

The first medium helicopter type in service with the Iraqi Air Force (or rather the Iraqi Army Aviation) was the Mil' Mi-4 *Hound*, of which an unknown quantity was purchased in the early 1960s, serving with the No.4 Sqn at al-Rashid AB. Subsequently the Iraqi Army Aviation became by far the largest foreign customer for the ubiquitous Mil' Mi-8 medium helicopter, ordering more than 220 'first-generation' Mi-8s – chiefly Mi-8TV *Hip-C* transport/assault helicopters but also a few Mi-8PPA *Hip-J* ECM helicopters – and more than 200 Mi-17 *Hip-Hs*. There is no reliable information as to how many were actually delivered before the arms embargo took effect (several Mi-8/Mi-17s built for Iraq were diverted to other customers when UN sanctions were imposed). Additionally, it appears that several Iraqi Mi-8s were impounded in Hungary and subsequently pressed into service with the Hungarian Air Force (a good thing should not be wasted!). A few Mi-8s wore the livery of Iraqi Airways but, again, it is not certain if they were really civilian; one example registered YI-ACS is known.

Heavy-lift helicopters were represented by the Mil' Mi-6 *Hook*. The Iraqi Air Force was one of the relatively few foreign customers for the type, receiving 14 by September 1980. Six Mil' Mi-26 *Halo* heavy-lift helicopters were also ordered but none were delivered to the IrAF due to the UN sanctions.

The Iraqi Army Aviation operated the Mil' Mi-24A *Hind-A* and Mi-25 *Hind-D* attack helicopters since the late 1970s. There is no reliable information as to how many were actually delivered. Russian sources state that 30 remained in service by early 1995, discounting at least seven aircraft lost in the Iran-Iraq War and five more destroyed or captured by the US Army during the First Gulf War.

Photos of Iraqi Air Force Su-7BMKs are scarce. This one wears a typical 'Middle Eastern' camouflage.

The Iraqi Air Force in action

The Iraqi Air Force has been perpetually at war ever since the 1958 revolution – both on the home front and abroad. They first fired in anger in 1959, when pan-Arabist officers opposed to the Communist leadership in the Ministry of Defence raised mutiny on 8th March. The following day four MiG-17Fs of No.5 Sqn destroyed the dissenters' makeshift radio station in Mosul with 57-mm S-5 unguided rockets, depriving the rebels of their mouthpiece; this was a key factor in quelling the mutiny. Almost exactly four years later, on 8th February 1963, the MiG-17Fs of No.5 Sqn were involved in another coup – this time on the rebels' side. They flew 60 sorties against

A US Army serviceman poses in front of the vanquished enemy – an Iraqi Air Force Su-7BMK serialled 7042 Black under the post-1988 serial system – at Habbaniya during the 2003 invasion of Iraq.

An IrAF Su-20 serialled 1202 Black under the pre-1988 system.

This Iraqi Su-22M (the serial is illegible) is interesting in that it wears the IrAF triangle insignia both on the rear fuselage and on the nose.

The tail of an Iraqi Su-22M shot down by an Iranian Hawk missile fired by the Tabuk SAM site during Operation Beit al-Moghadass on 11th May 1982.

An Iranian soldier inspects the wreck of another downed Iraqi Su-22M. Note that the fin flash is weathered away almost completely.

the Ministry of Defence building in Baghdad, attacking it with rockets and cannon fire.

Concurrently, in February 1963, the government troops were in action against the Kurdish ethnic minority in northern Iraq during the First Kurdish-Iraqi War (1961-70). The Kurds were a people forcibly torn apart, the state borders having been drawn so that the area populated by Kurds was divided between Iraq, Syria and Turkey, thus leading to Kurdish separatism (supported by Iran). Thus in February 1963 the Iraqi Air Force MiG-17Fs were first put into action against the Kurdish separatists – a mission they would perform throughout the war. In so doing two *Fresco-Cs* were shot down by the rebels' ground fire in 1963. One, a No.5 Sqn aircraft flown by Capt. Khalil Abdel Rahman, was downed on 15th February and the other, a No.7 Sqn aircraft flown by 1st Lt. Zohair Abdel Wahid, on 6th October; both pilots lost their lives.

On the morning of 5th June 1967 – the opening day of the third Arab-Israeli war, or Six-Day War – several Iraqi Air Force aircraft were destroyed on the ground at the so-called H-3 base cluster west of Baghdad by an Israeli strike. In retaliation, the Tu-16 bombers from al-Walid AB delivered a strike against Israeli airbases, one of the bombers (captained by

Sqn Ldr Hussein Mohammad Hussein) being shot down by Mirage IIICJs over Ramat David AB on 6th June. Further Israeli raids against bases in western Iraq were foiled by IrAF MiG-21PFMs and Hawker Hunters. That same day there was a skirmish between Israeli fighters and Iraqi MiG-21FLs over H-3 airbase.

Also in 1967, the freshly delivered Iraqi Su-7BMKs drew first blood when the No.1 Sqn was put into action against the Kurdish separatists in northern Iraq. Kurdish targets were attacked with unguided rockets and cannon fire.

The Iraqi Air Force was heavily involved in the Yom Kippur War (6th-26th October 1973). A strong Iraqi contingent was temporarily deployed to Syria, extending help. It included all operational MiG-17PFs of No.7 Sqn, 18 MiG-21FLs of No.9 Squadron deployed to al-Mezzeh AB, the No.17 Sqn equipped with MiG-21MFs and two fighter-bomber squadrons with Su-7BMKs (some sources say 18 aircraft); No.1 Sqn operated from Blei AB while No.5 Sqn was stationed at Damascus airport. Their first sortie was on 7th October when the Iraqi pilots claimed two Israeli Douglas A-4E Skyhawk attack aircraft, but a MiG-21FL and a single Su-7BMK were shot down by IDF/AF fighters. In addition to attacking the tanks of the Israeli 7th Armoured Brigade on the Golan Heights and making deep penetration raids into Israeli territory, the Iraqi jets flew reconnaissance missions. The Israeli air defences took a heavy toll – 12 of the Iraqi *Fitters* involved were shot down. The MiG-17PFs flew not only combat air patrol but also strike missions. Only one Iraqi MiG-17 was shot down during this war, crashing near el-Qunaitra on the Golan Heights; interestingly, it was flown by a Syrian pilot on that occasion.

Shortly afterwards, the Second Kurdish-Iraqi War (1974-75) broke out; the Kurdish *peshmerga* rebels were supported not only by substantial arms deliveries from Iran but also by Iranian troops making incursions into Iraq. Hence IrAF units were flung into the fray again. These included a squadron of MiG-19Ss (for which this was their combat debut in Iraq), the abovementioned No.17 Sqn with MiG-21MFs, another fighter squadron with MiG-21PFMs, the No.1 Sqn with Su-20s, a unit of MiG-23BNs and even the newly delivered Tu-22B bombers. The latter had to operate from high altitude, delivering 3,000-kg (6,610-lb) bombs, because the separatists and the Iranian intervention troops were protected by Raytheon MIM-23 Hawk SAM batteries set up on the Iranian side of the border. Hence the losses of Iraqi aircraft were far greater than anticipated; in particular, at least four MiG-23BNs fell prey to Iranian missiles, with another two lost in accidents. However, in late 1974 Saddam Hussein began negotiations with the Iranian Shah Mohammed Reza Pahlavi, reaching an agreement that Iran would stop its support of the rebels in exchange for a demarcation of the border on terms which were more favourable for Iran. After that, the rebellion was crushed at the end of March 1975, the Kurdish leaders fleeing abroad.

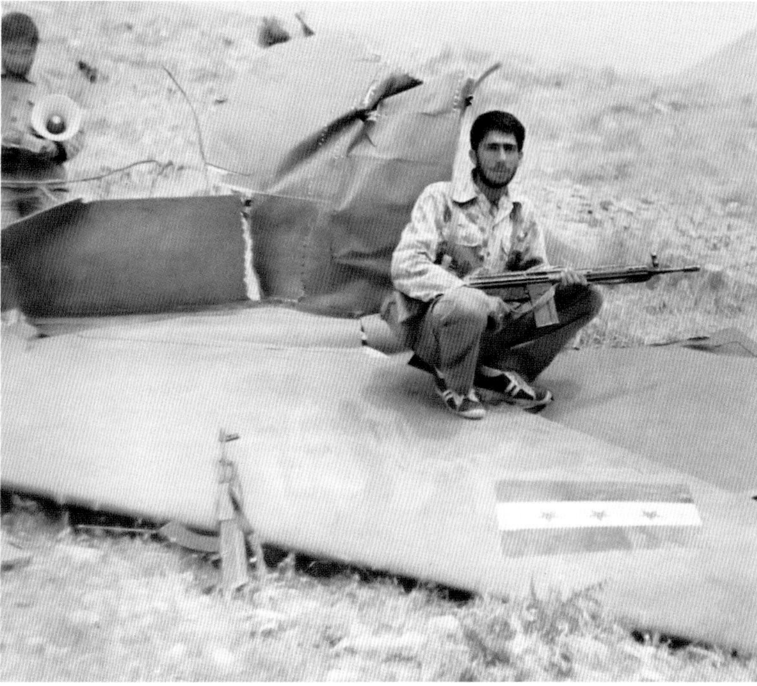

Sit on the fallen enemy? A member of the Iranian Baseej militia (note the civilian clothing) poses with the wreckage of an Iraqi Su-22M. It appears that the Iranians used whatever firearms were available, including Belgian-made FN FAL assault rifles and locally made KLT-7.62 collapsible-stock assault rifles – a 'Chinese copy' of a Chinese copy of the Kalashnikov AKM.

Iran-Iraq War

In January 1979 the Shah of Iran was overthrown during the Islamic Revolution led by Ayatollah Ruhollah M. Khomeini, Iran becoming a republic run according to strict Islamic laws. The new government purged the armed forces of officers thought to have royalist ideas, with the result that the armed forces were considerably weakened. Now, Iraq had a long history of border disputes with Iran; also, the Iranians are Shi'a Muslims, whereas the power in Iraq was concentrated in the hands of a Sunni Muslim minority, and the Iraqi government feared that the Iranian revolution might encourage insurgency among Iraq's long-suppressed Shi'a majority. Hence, deciding to take advantage of Iran's perceived temporary weakness, Iraq launched Operation *Qadisiya* (named after the

These incomplete Su-20s (including 20501 Black) abandoned by the Iraqis at Habbaniya AB were captured by US troops in 2003. Note the graffiti on the nose.

Here, 20501 Black is seen as found by the Americans inside the skeleton of a tent.

A horde of US servicemen pose for a photo with the war booty. Note the shattered canopy.

Top: Iraqi Air Force Su-22M4 '22564 Black' was part of the military hardware display at Baghdad-Saddam Hussein International airport in 1991.

Above and left: More aspects of '22564 Black' at the show in company with a MiG-29, a Su-25K and a Pilatus PC-6 Turbo Porter.

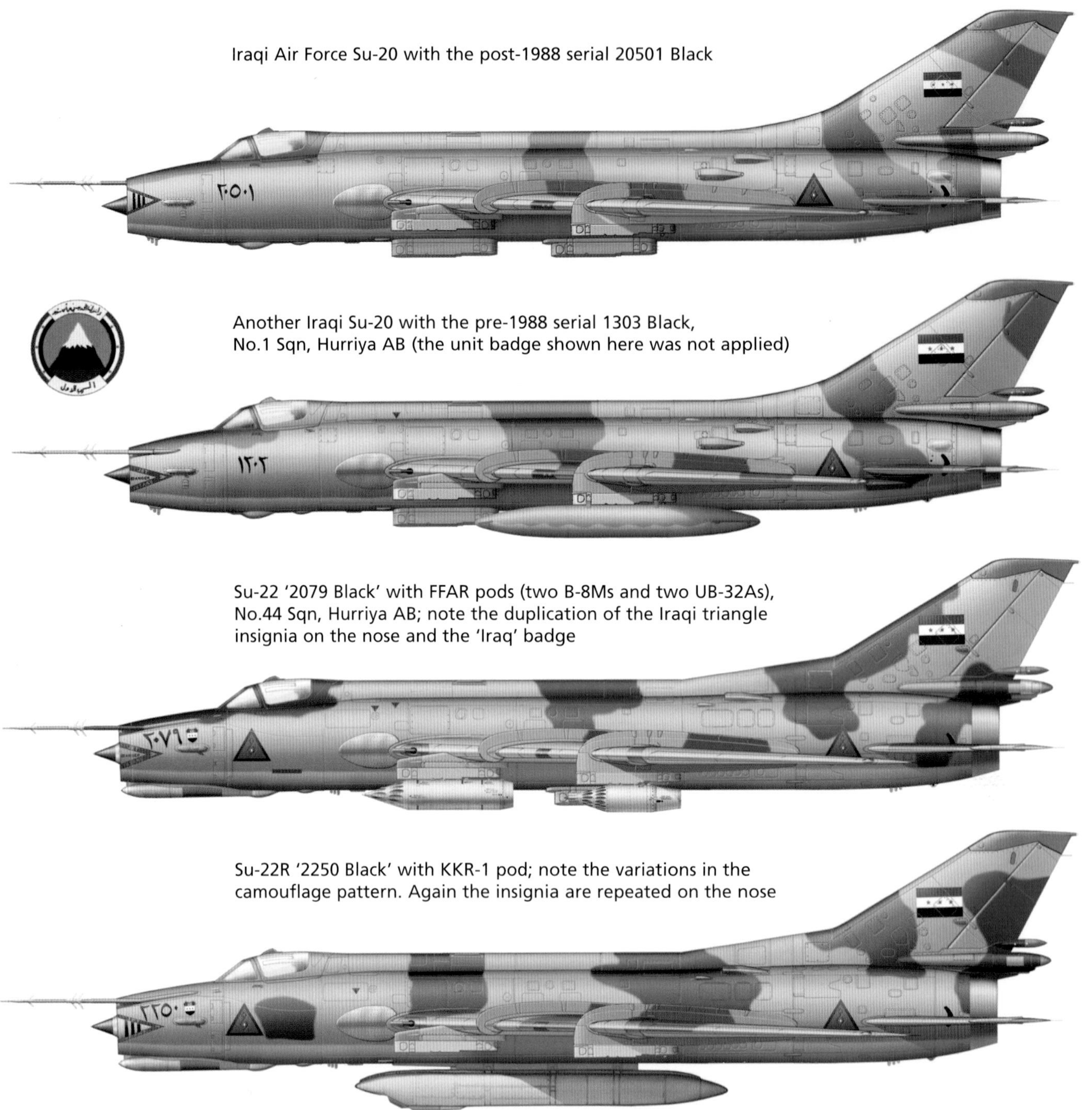

Iraqi Air Force Su-20 with the post-1988 serial 20501 Black

Another Iraqi Su-20 with the pre-1988 serial 1303 Black, No.1 Sqn, Hurriya AB (the unit badge shown here was not applied)

Su-22 '2079 Black' with FFAR pods (two B-8Ms and two UB-32As), No.44 Sqn, Hurriya AB; note the duplication of the Iraqi triangle insignia on the nose and the 'Iraq' badge

Su-22R '2250 Black' with KKR-1 pod; note the variations in the camouflage pattern. Again the insignia are repeated on the nose

Battle of al-Qadisiya – the decisive engagement between the Arab Muslim army and the Sassanid Persian army in November 636 A.D. that resulted in the Islamic conquest of Persia and was the key to the conquest of Iraq). On 22nd September 1980 a simultaneous invasion of Iran by air and land began without warning, starting a bloody eight-year war. This is known as the Iran-Iraq War but is occasionally referred to as the First Gulf War – a name more commonly applied to the 1990-91 war.

By end of 1980, the Iraqis were at the gates of Abadan but fanatical Iranian resistance prevented further significant advances. In 1981 Iranian counterattacks were unsuccessful in regaining much ground but in 1982 the Iranians started to push back the aggressors (this counteroffensive is known as Operation *Undeniable Victory*). Saddam Hussein's offer to negotiate withdrawal in May 1982 was rejected, and by using 'human wave' attacks in 1983 the Iranians forced the Iraqi army back into their own territory and prepared for the assault on the al-Faw oil port near Basra in 1984. This launched the southern front into a war of attrition. In 1985, having received fresh

The hulk of a captured Iraqi Su-22UM3 trainer serialled 22533 Black at a military hardware display in Iran.

supplies of aircraft from France and the Soviet Union, the Iraqis pushed on with a major air offensive. In response, the Iranians stepped up the bombing of Iraqi cities, and on 9th February 1986 an Iranian amphibious assault captured the port and peninsula of al-Faw, which were not recaptured until April 1988.

In the meantime, the Iraqis, supplied with French AM-39 Exocet missiles, stepped up the attacks on shipping in the Persian Gulf which became known as the Tanker War. As a result of shipping losses and sustained massive attacks on the Kharq Island oil terminal, Iran's oil exports were halved. This reduction in oil supply, combined with Syria's blocking of the Banias pipeline, predictably caused oil prices to skyrocket, which affected not only the belligerents but most of the world. On 20th July 1988 the United Nations Security Council passed Resolution 598 calling for an immediate ceasefire, which Iran chose to ignore for the time being. However, the Iraqis, having recaptured the Majnoun Islands, went on to mount an armoured strike penetrating deep into northern Iran. These setbacks, combined with superpower pressure, finally forced the Iranians to accept the UN Resolution, the end result being *status quo ante bellum*. Successes in the final months of the war enabled the Iraqis to claim a military victory, but to the rest of the world it was a pyrrhic victory.

Iraqi MiG-19s saw action in this war only briefly. Since the IrAF had sufficient numbers of more modern interceptors, the *Farmers* were assigned to the close air support role. However, it soon became apparent that attack helicopters were better suited for this, and the MiG-19s were relegated to the training role.

The bulk of the Iraqi Air Force's fighter force in the war comprised about 90 MiG-21MFs, a few dozen MiG-21PFMs and the surviving MiG-21FLs and MiG-21F-13s from the Arab-Israeli wars of 1967 and 1973. They equipped Nos. 5, 9, 12, 17 and 18 Fighter Squadrons, augmented by the No.1 FRS flying MiG-21Rs. (Some sources paint a different picture: No.9 Sqn at Firnas AB, with a forward operating location at Abu Ubaida AB; No.11 Sqn at al-Rashid AB, with a FOL at Wahda AB (both flying MiG-21MFs); No.17 (OCU) Sqn with MiG-21FLs and MiG-21Us at Tikrit; No.47 Sqn with MiG-21*bis* at al-Hurrya AB near Kirkuk; and No.70 Sqn at al-Rashid AB and Wahda AB, with MiG-21MFs and MiG-21Rs.) They were up

This unserviceable Su-22M and the Kh-28M anti-radar missile on a ground handling dolly were captured by US forces in an HAS in Iraq during the Second Gulf War (Operation *Iraqi Freedom*) in 2003.

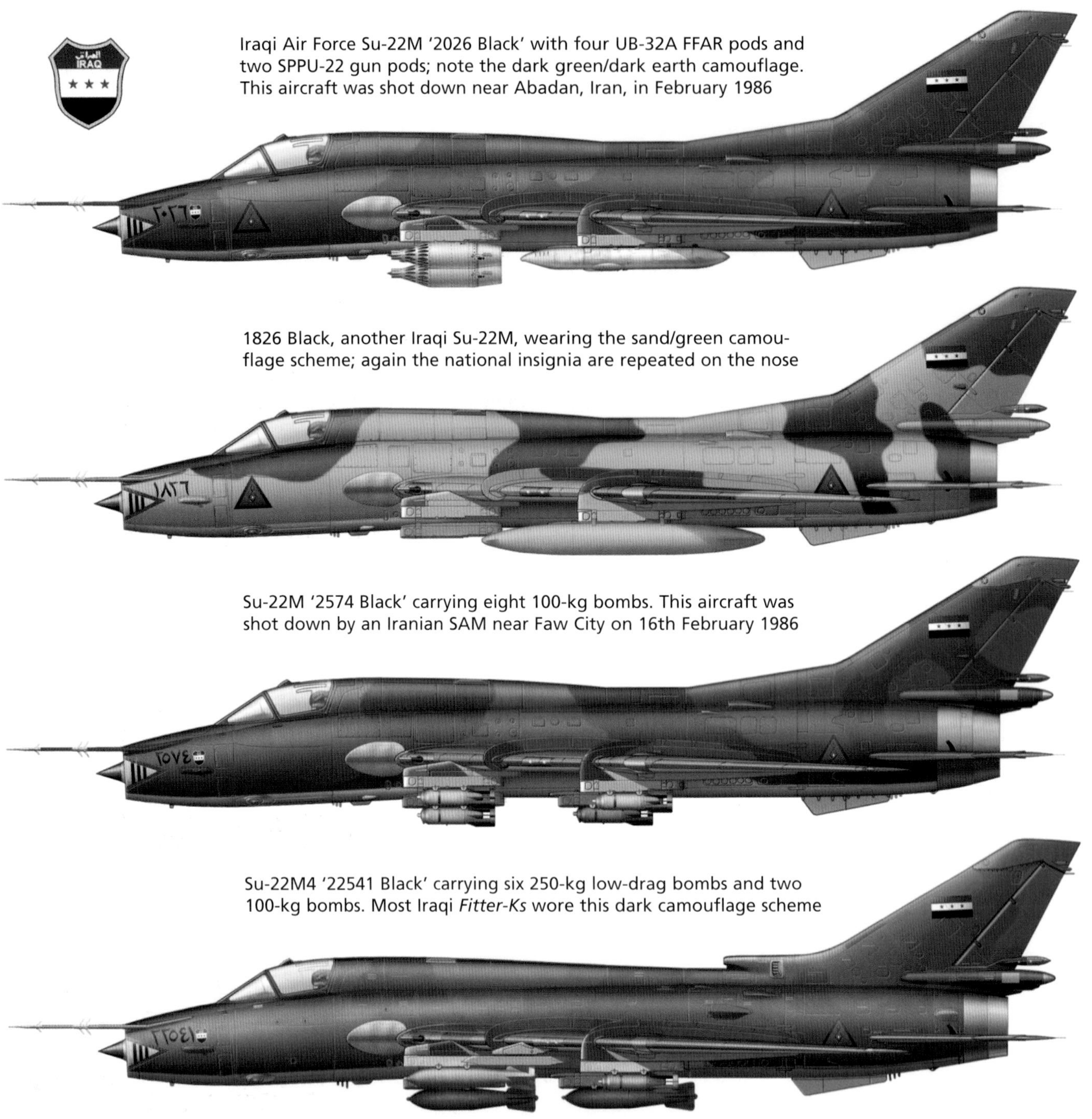

Iraqi Air Force Su-22M '2026 Black' with four UB-32A FFAR pods and two SPPU-22 gun pods; note the dark green/dark earth camouflage. This aircraft was shot down near Abadan, Iran, in February 1986

1826 Black, another Iraqi Su-22M, wearing the sand/green camouflage scheme; again the national insignia are repeated on the nose

Su-22M '2574 Black' carrying eight 100-kg bombs. This aircraft was shot down by an Iranian SAM near Faw City on 16th February 1986

Su-22M4 '22541 Black' carrying six 250-kg low-drag bombs and two 100-kg bombs. Most Iraqi *Fitter-Ks* wore this dark camouflage scheme

against IRIAF Grumman F-14A Tomcats, which were far superior, and McDonnell Douglas F-4E Phantom IIs, against which the MiG-21MF could hold its own; the Iranians' second line of defence was the Northrop F-5E Freedom Fighter. At the beginning of the war the Iraqis were handicapped by the unreliable R-13 missiles, but in April 1981 the first MiG-21MFs were modified (with French assistance) to fire Matra R.550 Magic Mk 1 missiles. The result was felt immediately; within a week the MiG-21MFs had shot down two F-4Es, two F-5Es and a helicopter for the loss of only one of their own. However, the F-14A armed with AIM-7E Sparrow medium-range AAMs and AIM-54A Phoenix beyond-visual-range AAMs was so superior to the MiG-21 that Iraqi pilots were instructed not to tangle with the Tomcat. Also, the Magic missiles were difficult to obtain and in 1983, to tide them over until more arrived from France, the Iraqis negotiated a deal with Jordan for 200 AIM-9B Sidewinder missiles in return for two captured IRIAF F-5E fighters and supplies of crude oil.

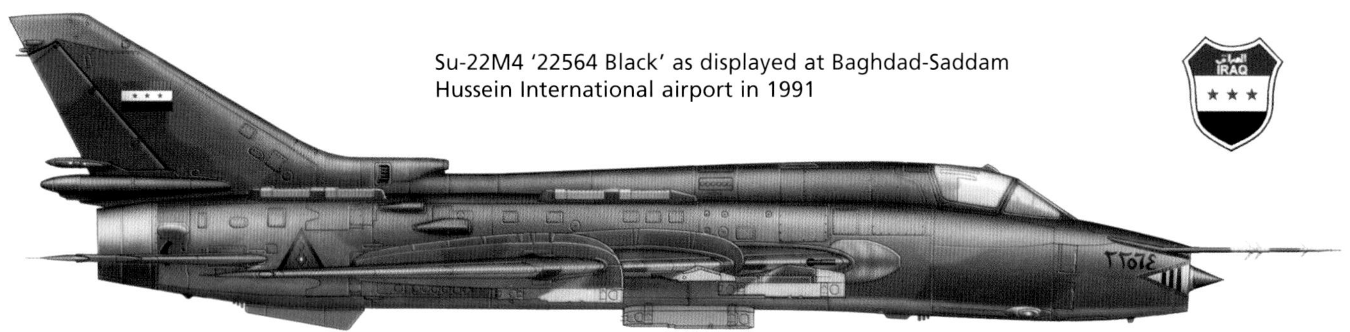

Su-22M4 '22564 Black' as displayed at Baghdad-Saddam Hussein International airport in 1991

In 1983 several No.9 Sqn MiG-21*bis* fighters deployed to Wahda AB were used in an anti-shipping strike role. Painted in a three-tone blue/white camouflage and armed with four UB-32-57 rocket pods each, they attacked Iranian gunboats in the northern part of the Persian Gulf. The missions were discontinued in 1987 when the gunboat threat disappeared.

It may be mentioned that the MiG-21MFs claimed 43 'kills' in aerial battles against 49 alleged losses. One interesting fact is the 1986 Iranian victory claim for a MiG-21 brought down by cannon fire from a Bell AH-1J Sea Cobra helicopter. The *Fishbeds* that scored 'kills' include MiG-21MF '1019 Black' (No.11 Sqn) in which Lt. Sadiq shot down an F-4E Phantom II on 8th September 1980, and MiG-21*bis* '21178 Black'. The former aircraft had also shot down an Israeli Dassault Mirage IIICJ in October 1973 during the Yom Kippur War.

The Iraqi MiG-23s actually entered the fray before the start of the invasion. A pair of MiG-23MS fighters were escorting MiG-21R reconnaissance aircraft flying over the border region when Iranian F-14A Tomcats summoned by ground control attacked them, destroying one of the *Floggers* with a missile.

In a surprise attack on the opening day of the war, three MiG-23BNs hit Tehran-Mehrabad airfield 520 km (323 miles) inside the Iranian border, causing substantial damage before one (or possibly two) of them was shot down by the F-4Es scrambled to intercept. The damage done would have been greater, had the attackers realised exactly where they were and set up their weapons earlier. About half the sorties that day were flown by MiG-23BNs. (It should be noted that such interdiction raids by small groups of MiG-23BNs were successful in the opening phases of the war, but as the Iranian air defences became more effective, Iraqi losses mounted because IrAF aircraft lacked adequate radar warning receivers. For example, all three *Flogger-Hs* attacking the oil terminals on Kharq Island were destroyed by IRIAF F-14As, and between 3rd and 19th October 1980 eleven more MiG-23BNs were shot down.)

The *Floggers'* main role in the war was air defence. To counter Iranian air raids, pairs of No.39 Sqn MiG-23MSs were deployed from Tammuz AB, which was too far away from the action, to forward operating locations along the border in the autumn of 1980. Within a

Below: An Iraqi Air Force Su-25K.

Centre and bottom: Su-25K '25590 Black' on display at Baghdad-Saddam Hussein International airport in 1991.

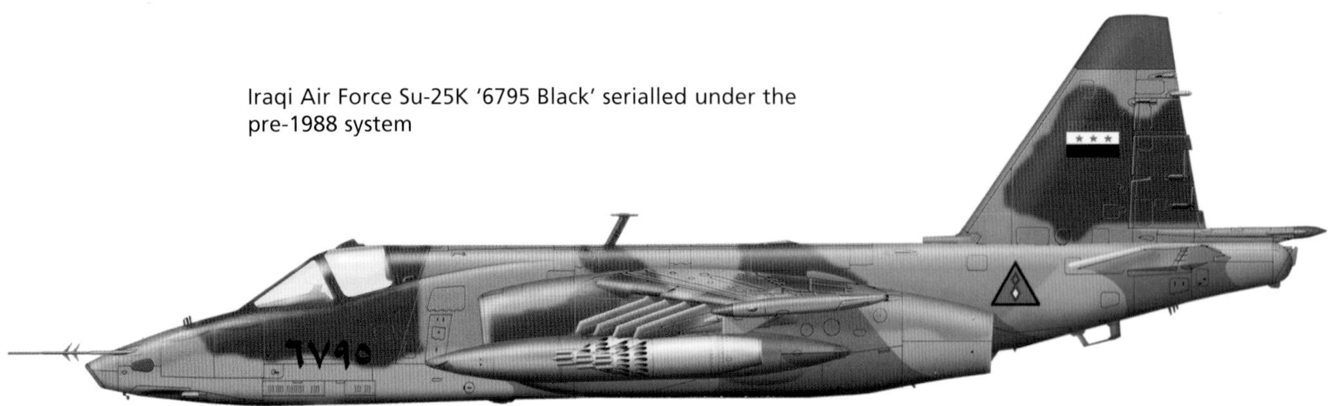

Iraqi Air Force Su-25K '6795 Black' serialled under the pre-1988 system

year the unit's CO had claimed five 'kills' against Iranian helicopters. A squadron of MiG-23MSs was moved in to reinforce the defences of Baghdad in 1981. Six *Flogger-Es* were taking off to intercept a large Iranian assault when they were bounced by two F-14As that shot down two of them and dispersed the others.

By the end of January 1981, only 40 MiG-23s of any version were serviceable; the

Two more views of Su-25K '25590 Black' at the 1991 display in Baghdad.

MiG-23BN fighter-bombers were the hardest hit, since they operated at low altitude and the Iranian air defences took a heavy toll. The MiG-23 pilots had achieved scant success, claiming only two F-5Es, two F-4Es and one F-4D. Changing their tactics, the Iraqis resorted to using two MiG-23BNs as bait; the pair lingered at low altitude after a bombing raid, luring the Iranian fighters into pursuit (to be immediately pounced upon by a lurking group of fighters) or over a nest of Iraqi SAM sites. At first the tactic was so successful that the Iranians deployed a squadron of F-14As onto a nearby airfield, even though it was within Iraqi Army artillery range.

For the rest of 1981 and 1982 the MiG-23MS squadrons became less involved in the main fighting on the southern front but were instead deployed to defend Iraqi oil rigs in the north and cities in the centre of the country. In 1982 large numbers of MiG-23MFs were ordered; deliveries began in 1983 and MiG-23MFs took over as the Iraqi Air Force's primary interceptor type, to be joined later by twenty MiG-23MLs; the latter scored the first confirmed 'kill' on 11th August 1984, shooting down an Iranian F-14A, and also succeeded in destroying IRIAF F-4Es, a Fokker F.27M Troopship transport and even an Israeli reconnaissance UAV. In the war, both sides modified their aircraft to use whatever missiles and other weapons could be obtained.

In the war of attrition on the southern sector that lasted until late 1987, Iraqi MiG-23BNs were constantly deployed to wear down the Iranian attacks. In 1985 the Iranians bombed Baghdad and other Iranian cities defended at that time by MiG-23MFs.

WIth a piece of skin carrying the IrAF fin flash chopped out by vandals... oh, sorry – *tourists*, this derelict Su-25K does a rather undignified tail-sit.

From February 1984, the Iraqis resorted to chemical warfare and the toxic agents were often delivered in bombs dropped by MiG-23BNs. Until the arrival of five Dassault Super Etendards leased from the French Navy in 1983-85, the *Flogger-Hs* played a major role in attacks against shipping in the Persian Gulf. Some credit for the success of the final Iraqi offensives in 1988 goes to the more effective use of strike aircraft – notably MiG-23BNs – in close support of the army.

The MiG-25 was used on the Iranian front from the spring of 1981 onwards. Capt. Mohommed Rayyan, nicknamed 'Sky Falcon',

A pair of Iraqi Air Force Su-24MK bombers in cruise flight, probably photographed from a sister ship.

This IrAF Su-24MK carries what looks like a KMGU-1 submunitions dispenser on the centreline, an MBD3-U6-68 multiple ejector rack with small bombs under the starboard wing glove and an unidentified equipment pod (probably of western origin) on the swivelling outer wing pylon.

Iraqi Air Force Su-24MK '24210 Black'

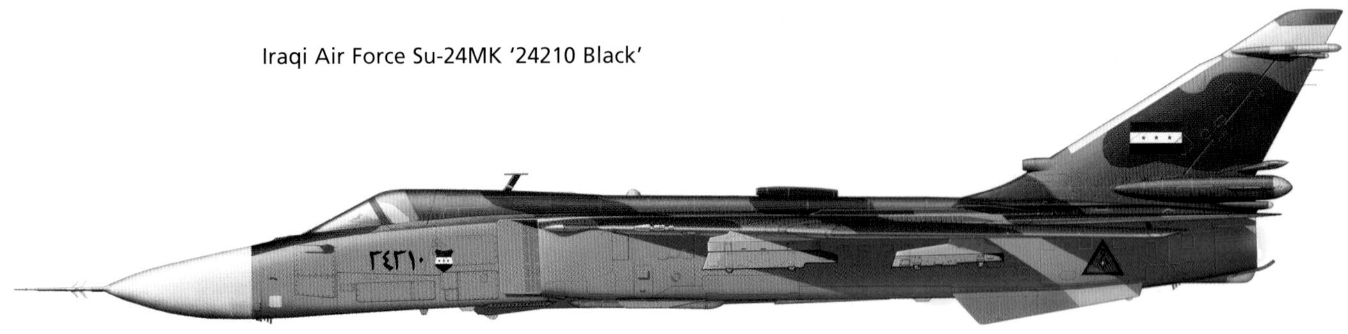

A pair of Iraqi Su-24MKs in low-speed flight with the wings at 16° sweep.

scored eight 'kills' in the MiG-25PDS (in addition to the two scored earlier in the MiG-21MF), making him the top-scoring Iraqi ace of the war and the most successful MiG-25 fighter pilot ever. However, in 1986, having attained the rank of Colonel, Rayyan was shot down and killed by AIM-54 missiles fired by Iranian F-14As; this was the only MiG-25PDS loss in the Iran-Iraq War. (*Iraqi Fighters, 1953-2003* gives a different story, stating that the only MiG-25PDS loss in the war was an aircraft that had taken gunfire hits from an IRIAF F-5E and was written off in the ensuing crash landing in June 1986.) In addition to Iranian F-4E and F-5E fighters, RF-4E reconnaissance aircraft and a Lockheed C-130 Hercules transport, the Iraqi MiG-25PDSs scored one 'kill' that was denounced as a criminal action. On 3rd May 1982 an Algerian Government Gulfstream Aerospace G-1159 Gulfstream II business jet (7T-VHB, c/n 230) was en route from Algiers to Tehran via Larnaca, carrying the Algerian Foreign Minister Mohammed Seddik Ben Yahia on a secret peace mediation mission when it was shot down at 11,280 m (37,000 ft) by a missile fired by a MiG-25PDS. Shortly before an air defence radar operator had demanded that the pilots turn back, but the pilots had chosen to press on. The aircraft crashed near Qotur in northern Iran, killing the crew of four and ten passengers; neither Iran nor Iraq accepted responsibility for the shootdown.

Iraqi MiG-25RBTs made bombing raids on Tehran and the Iranian oil rigs in the Persian Gulf, delivering four to eight FAB-500M-62T heat-insulated low-drag bombs in level flight at 20,000 m (65,600 ft) and Mach 2.5 or higher. The first mission against Tehran was flown by the CO of the No.84 Sqn on 13th

Iraqi Air Force IL-28 '427 Black'

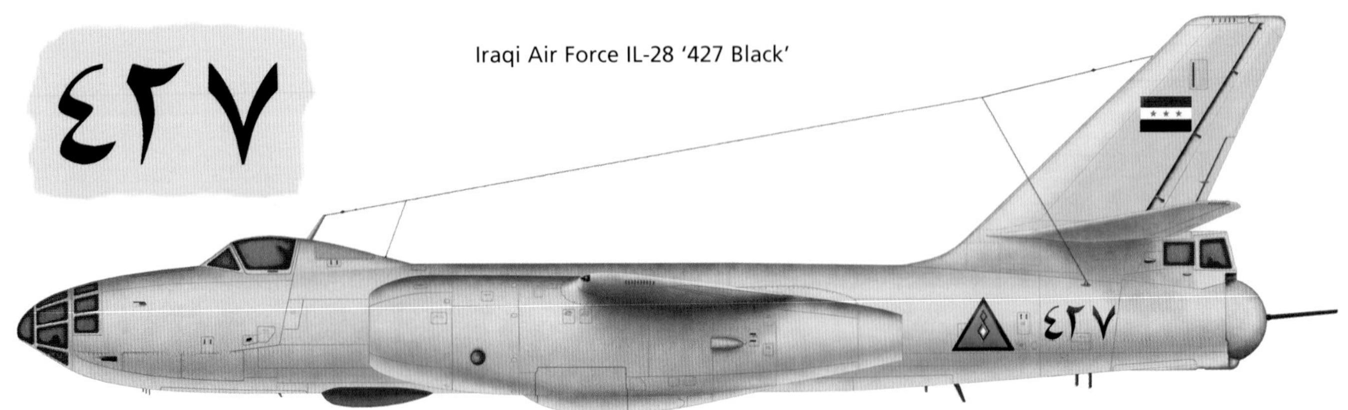

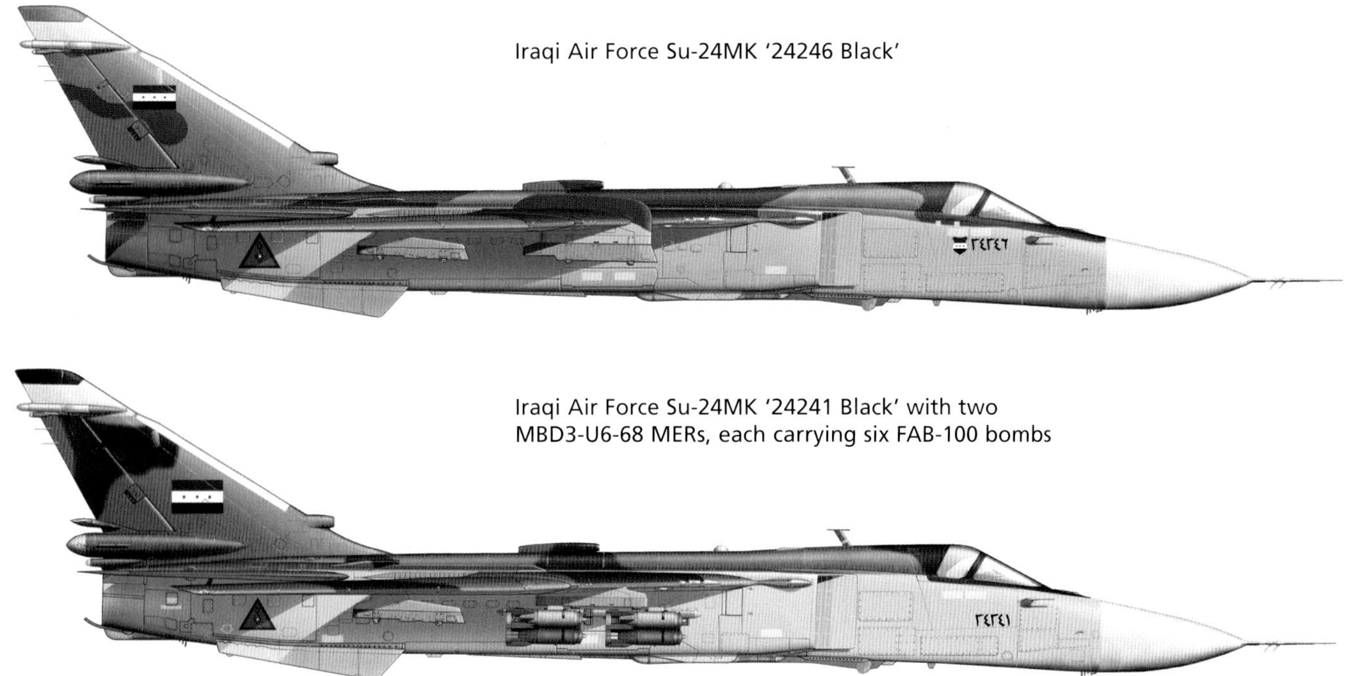

Iraqi Air Force Su-24MK '24246 Black'

Iraqi Air Force Su-24MK '24241 Black' with two MBD3-U6-68 MERs, each carrying six FAB-100 bombs

March 1985. Operating from a FOL at Hurrya AB, the *Foxbat-Bs* raided Tabriz, Qazvin, Karaj, Rasht and Hamedan; another FOL was at Abu Ubaida AB from where raids were staged against Isfahan, Bushehr, Shiraz and the oil terminals on Kharq Island. Later the reconnaissance/strike *Foxbats* operated from Ali Ibn Abu Talib AB (Tallil AB). One aircraft was downed by an Iranian Hawk SAM; another was lost when an engine failure forced the pilot to eject. One more newly refurbished aircraft crashed on landing after a checkout flight in December 1987.

Although the Iraqi Air Force's No.8 Sqn was an operational conversion unit, its Su-7BMKs took part in the opening stage of the Iran-Iraq War, despite their obsolescence; three of the unit's aircraft fell to the Iranian air defences. However, it was mostly the 'swing-wing' *Fitters* that were involved in the war from the outset of Operation *Qadisiya*. In the winter of 1980-81 the type was grounded by engine problems, but once these had been addressed the Su-20s were back in business. The *Fitter-Cs* mostly flew CAS missions, armed with bombs of up to 500 kg (1,102 lb) calibre, including parachute-retarded bombs for low-level attacks. Some examples, however, flew counter-air missions with four R-3S AAMs and two drop tanks under the fuselage.

The newly acquired Su-22s *sans suffixe* could carry Kh-23E air-to-surface missiles but the Iraqis proved unable to master this weapon's command line-of-sight guidance system. The only case when the Kh-23E was used operationally was in 1982 when a Su-22 attacked a bridge over the Karoun River in the south of Iran's south-western Khuzestan Province – and missed. Almost the entire fleet of Su-22s *sans suffixe* was lost in the Iran-Iraq War.

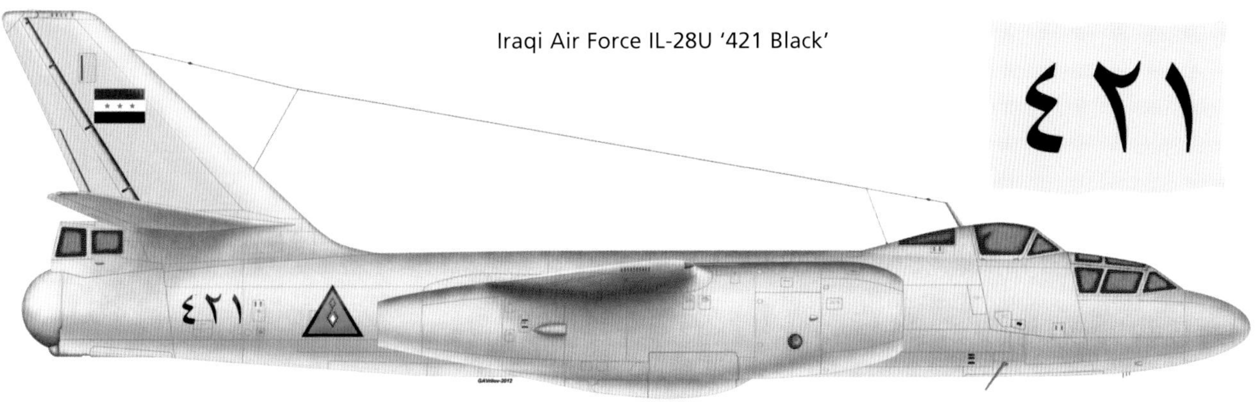

Iraqi Air Force IL-28U '421 Black'

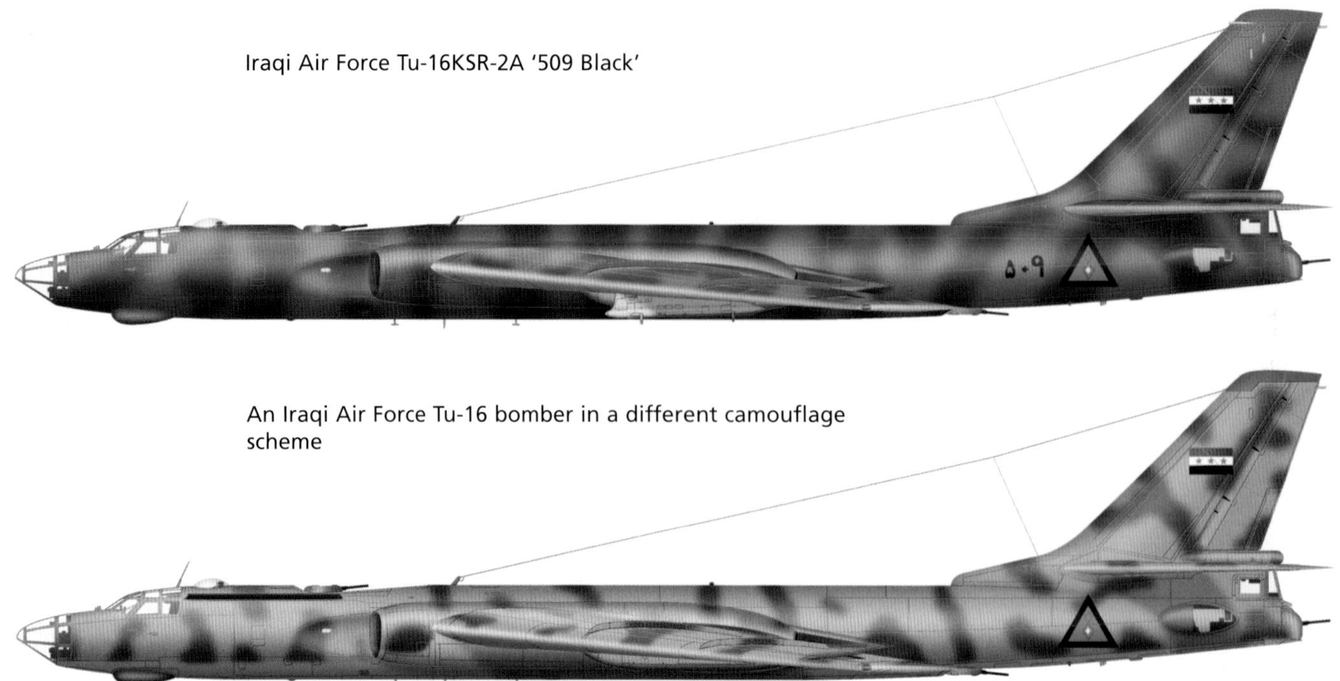

Iraqi Air Force Tu-16KSR-2A '509 Black'

An Iraqi Air Force Tu-16 bomber in a different camouflage scheme

The Su-22M3s of the newly established No.69 Sqn joined the action in 1985. The unit flew its first combat sortie on 15th August that year, attacking targets in Iran with FAB-500ShN retarded bombs; the unit CO led the mission personally. Some of the aircraft carried SPS-141MVGE jammer pods to facilitate air defence penetration. The Iraqi Su-22M4s arrived in 1986 and got only a small piece of the action. Among other things, they carried Kh-25MP anti-radar missiles for SEAD missions; these weapons were used for the first time on 17th April 1986 when a Su-22M4 took out the radar of an Iranian Hawk SAM site. Generally, however, these missiles were little used in the war.

The Iraqis also had trouble with the Kh-29L missiles supplied together with the Su-22M3s, finding it hard to fly the aircraft and aim the missile at the same time (thereby prolonging the exposure to the enemy air defences). By September 1987 they found a solution, managing to integrate the missile with the French Thomson-CSF ATLIS (Automatic Tracking and Laser Integration System) laser/electro-optical targeting pod carried by the Iraqi Air Force's Dassault Mirage F.1EQ fighters. Thus, the aircraft could work as a pair, the Mirage designating targets for the Su-22. Several dozen such sorties were flown between 17th April and 23rd July 1988.

In the course of the war the Iraqi Air Force lost a total of 64 Su-20/Su-22s of all versions to enemy action. Still, the *Fitter* was able to absorb quite a lot of battle damage and bring the pilot home, and the Iraqis appreciated this, as well as the aircraft's sizeable ordnance load. Therefore Iraq kept buying more Su-22M3/

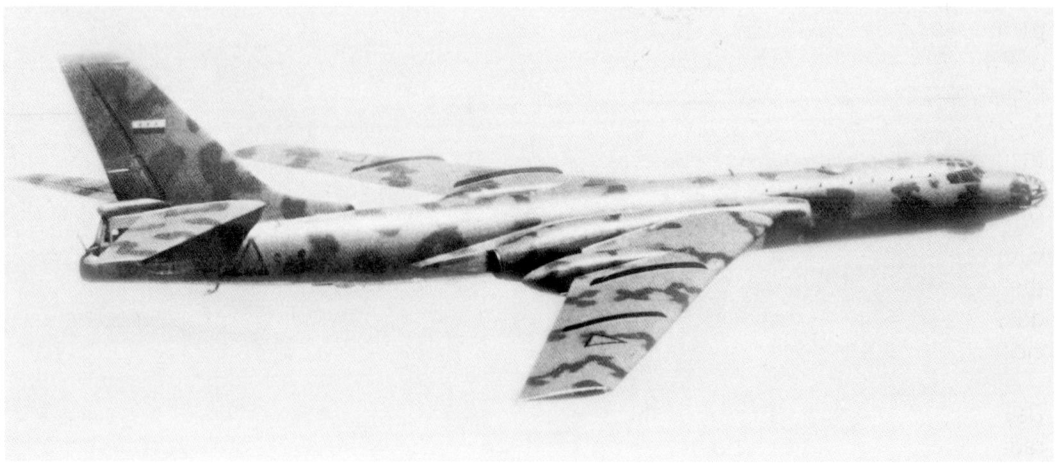

An air-to-air of an Iraqi Air Force Tu-16, apparently serialled 509 Black.

This series of photos shows the wreckage of an Iraqi Tu-16 shot down during a raid against Iran on 23rd September 1980. The local residents have gathered to take a look at the fallen aggressor.

Su-22M4s – both as attrition replacements and to expand the fleet, and the type saw increasing use on the Iranian front, eventually taking the Iranian air defences out of the picture.

The Su-25K also participated in the Iran-Iraq War, joining the action in 1987. The *Frogfeet* operated from a variety of locations, including Ali Ibn Abu Talib AB, Abu Ubaida AB, Jalibah AB, Artawi AB and Wahda AB. There are reports of the Iraqi Air Force frequently achieving up to 1,200 combat sorties per day during the war, of which around 900 were performed by the Su-25K carrying out the bulk of the strike missions. At the peak of the fighting each *Frogfoot* flew as many as 15 sorties per day; though this might sound improbable, these are official Sukhoi OKB statistics, not Iraqi Air Force reports. President Saddam Hussein decorated all of the Iraqi Su-25 pilots with the country's highest military award at the end of the war. One Su-25K was shot down by an Iranian Hawk SAM, but the pilot ejected safely.

Iraqi Air Force Tu-22Bs were in action from Day One of the war. The aircraft's combat radius was big enough to hit any target in Iran, and sorties were flown day and night. The bombers operated both from their main base at Habbaniya and from Balad AB about 70 km (44 miles) north of Baghdad. Soviet military advisors tried suggesting the most rational ways of using the Tu-22 in combat but the Iraqis, who were noted for their arrogance, ignored those recommendations. Pride goeth before the fall: the first Iraqi Tu-22 was shot down as early as 23rd September 1980.

Soviet military advisors in Iraq recalled that the discipline of Saddam Hussein's airmen was unyielding. One of 'our men in Baghdad' once witnessed the methods used to keep up the fighting spirit. As the first targets in Iran were designated during a mission briefing, one of the pilots protested, saying he was not about to go killing brother Moslems. Secret service officers immediately took the dissenter to the back of the aircraft parking ramp and shot him there and then. Nobody questioned the rightness of the war anymore.

Military and industrial installations in Tehran and Isfahan were the Tu-22s' prime targets. For example, on 23rd September 1980 the *Blinders* bombed Tehran-Mehrabad International airport; the Iranians claimed one

Iraqi Air Force Tu-22B '4501 Black'

An Iraqi Air Force Tu-22UD trainer

A freshly refurbished Tu-22B destined for Iraq sits parked at Dyagilevo AB, Ryazan', in company with a Soviet Air Force Myasishchev 3M bomber.

An Iraqi Air Force Tu-22UD awaiting delivery. The IFR probe has been removed. Oddly, the aircraft still carries its former Soviet tactical code '16 Red'.

bomber shot down in this raid. About a week later, a large group of Tu-22Bs escorted by fighters knocked out two major car assembly plants near the airport.

For a short while in the opening stages of the war, IrAF Tu-22Bs also operated from bases in Saudi Arabia and North Yemen (in the latter case, Sana'a). This arrangement, which Saddam Hussein had negotiated with the two countries, kept the valuable (and costly) bombers safe from being destroyed on the ground by Iranian air raids. From early 1981 onwards the Tu-22Bs were used only sporadically to minimise wear and tear on them, since the Soviet Union had

An IrAF Tu-22B undergoes pre-flight checks.

The wreckage of an Iraqi Tu-22UD destroyed by an American cruise missile in its revetment at al-Taqaddum AB in 2003. Note that a section of the radome has been cut out by souvenir hunters.

Another view of the same Tu-22UD. The IrAF triangle insignia are discernible on the rear fuselage.

The remains of an IrAF Tu-22B bomber at al-Taqaddum AB.

Iraqi Air Force An-12B I.A.F. 805 in grey/white livery rests between missions; note the exhaust stains on the rear fuselage.

embargoed all further arms supplies to Iraq. The embargo remained in force, even though Saddam Hussein repeatedly asked the Soviet government for more Tu-22s.

In 1982 Iraqi Tu-22Bs hit several major targets deep within Iran, primarily large concentrations of troops and oil refineries. Iran claimed the destruction of two bombers that year, but this should be taken with a grain of salt. Official kill statistics in any war are notoriously optimistic, and if Iraqi and Iranian reports were to be believed it appeared that the entire air forces of both nations had been destroyed several times over!

War or no war, the bombers had to be refurbished; one by one they were flown back to the Soviet Union and worked on by Aircraft Repair Plant No.360 at Dyagilevo AB, Ryazan'. The aircraft were redelivered in late 1984; unlike the delivery flights, which had originated from Zyabrovka AB, this time they were ferried by 290th ODRAP crews to Simferopol' in the Crimea, where Iraqi pilots accepted the aircraft and flew them back home.

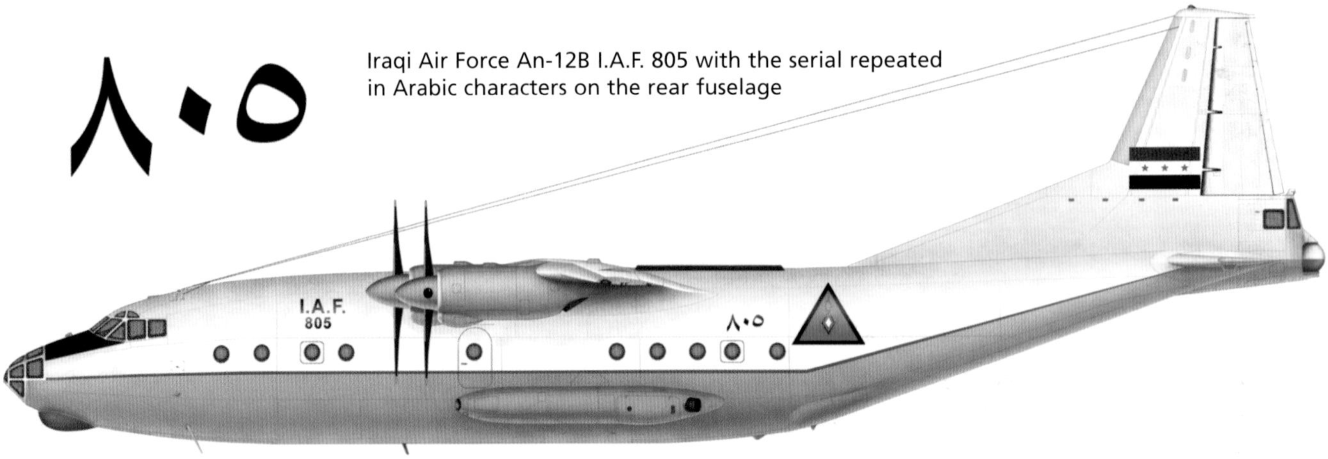

٨٠٥

Iraqi Air Force An-12B I.A.F. 805 with the serial repeated in Arabic characters on the rear fuselage

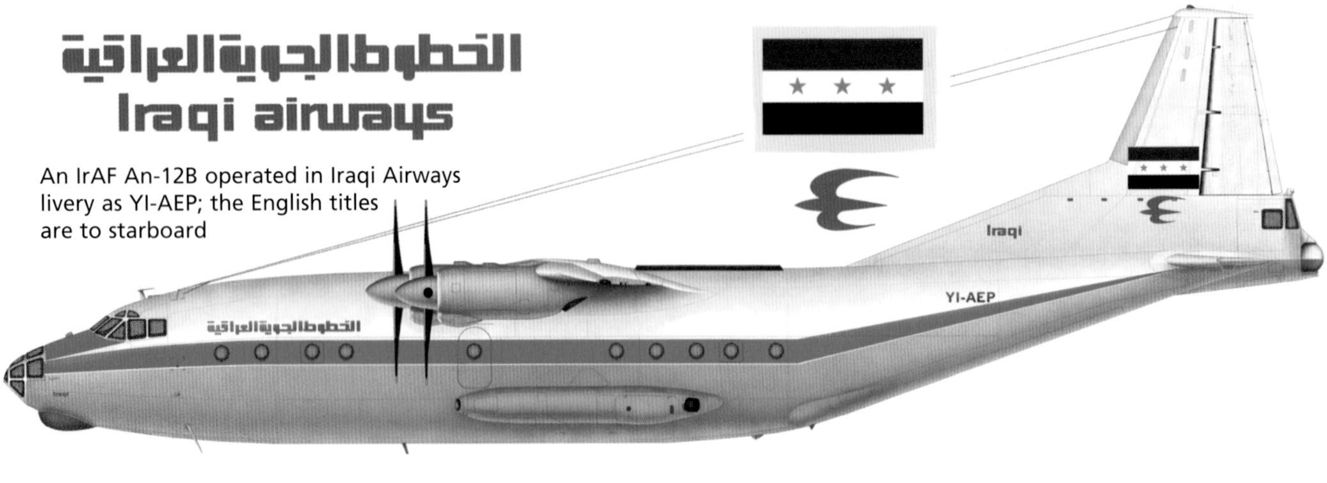

الخطوط الجوية العراقية

Iraqi airways

An IrAF An-12B operated in Iraqi Airways livery as YI-AEP; the English titles are to starboard

In May 1985 the IrAF *Blinders* resumed strikes against Tehran, Isfahan, Shiraz and other Iranian cities. They also began attacking Iranian tankers and the oil terminal on Kharq Island; the latter attacks, which commenced in 1984 and continued until the end of hostilities, were known as the Tanker War. In 16 days of late May/early June alone, 23 raids against Tehran were carried out. In retaliation, Iran bombarded Baghdad with intermediate-range ballistic missiles and made several air raids against the city. This was the beginning of the War of the Cities, as the methodical flattening of each other's cities came to be known; it continued on and off until hostilities ceased in 1988.

As Iran beefed up its air defences, Iraqi pilots discovered that the Tu-22 could absorb a lot of battle damage. On one occasion a missile fired by an Iranian F-4D took off half the horizontal tail. The pilot felt a jolt and noted a deterioration in pitch control but managed to

Top: Identically painted An-12B I.A.F. 807, with a support placed under the tail to stop the aircraft from tipping over accidentally.

Above: An-12B I.A.F. 805 is caught by the camera seconds before touch-down.

Below: Despite the Iraqi Airways livery, An-12BP YI-AFJ was an Iraqi Air Force aircraft, just like the rest of the Iraqi *Cubs*.

Right: An-12BP YI-AEP seen visiting Berlin. The registration and Iraqi Airways titles are barely legible.

Below: A quasi-civil Iraqi Air Force An-12BP about to touch down.

Bottom: An-12BP YI-AER visiting Paris, probably to pick up spares for IrAF Mirages.

Left: An-12BP YI-AFJ, again with barely readable registration and titles.

Below: An-12BP I.A.F.806 taxies in after landing.

Bottom: Here, YI-AEP is seen after a repaint with bolder titles and registration.

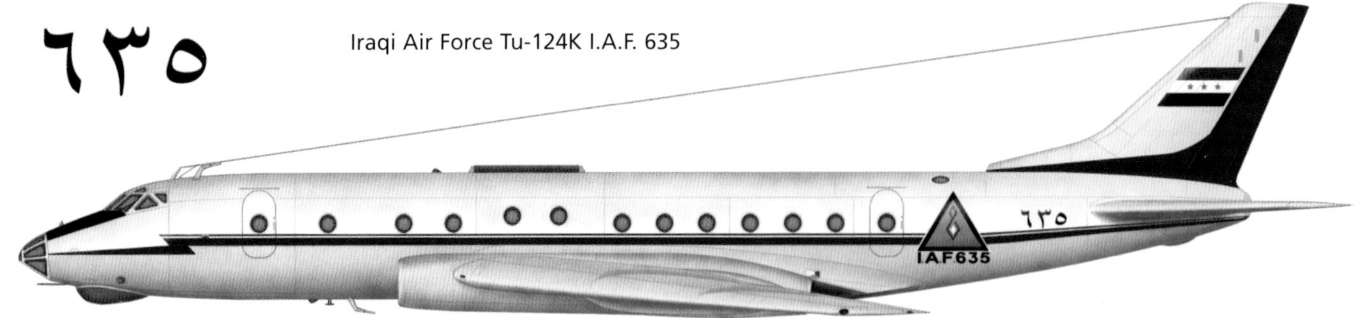

Iraqi Air Force Tu-124K I.A.F. 635

make it home and land safely. In another case a Hawk SAM detonated under the bomber, causing severe shrapnel damage to the lower fuselage, but again the aircraft made it back to base. (The MIM-23 has a proximity fuse and doesn't need to score a bull's eye to do the job.)

On 19th May 1988 the *Blinders* scored a major success in the Tanker War, sending two Iranian supertankers up in flames at Kharq Island. These were the M/V *Awaj* displacing 316,379 tons and M/V *Sanandaj* (the first tanker thus named) displacing 253,837 tons; both ships were totalled, and more than 50 crewmen on the two tankers died.

In the course of the Iran-Iraq War the Iraqi Mi-6 helicopters were used both for landing tactical assault groups and for transport missions. Several machines were reportedly lost to enemy action, including attacks by IRIAF Bell AH-1J Sea Cobra helicopters. Iraqi Mi-8TVs were used for a variety of tasks, including vertical envelopment, destruction of soft-skinned vehicles, personnel, artillery, emplacements and bridges, providing close air support for armoured groups and commandos, mine-laying, reconnaissance and artillery spotting. Iraqi Mi-24As and Mi-25s were used for a variety of tasks, including destruction of soft-skinned and armoured vehicles, personnel, artillery, emplacements and bridges, escorting heliborne assaults, providing close air support for armoured groups and commandos, mine-laying, reconnaissance, artillery spotting and even chemical warfare.

In the course of the war there were 118 aircraft-versus-helicopter engagements and 56 helicopter-versus-helicopter engagements, including ten between Iraqi Mi-24s and Iranian Sea Cobras. The outcome of such engagements depended mainly on the situation and crew skill. If the Sea Cobra pilots were lucky enough to spot the enemy first they tried to take him out with TOW anti-tank missiles at long range. If they missed, the AH-1J had no chances of outrunning the Mi-24 and would

Below: A still from a video showing the Adnan-1 AWACS (formerly Baghdad-2); note how wide the centre section of the rotodome is.

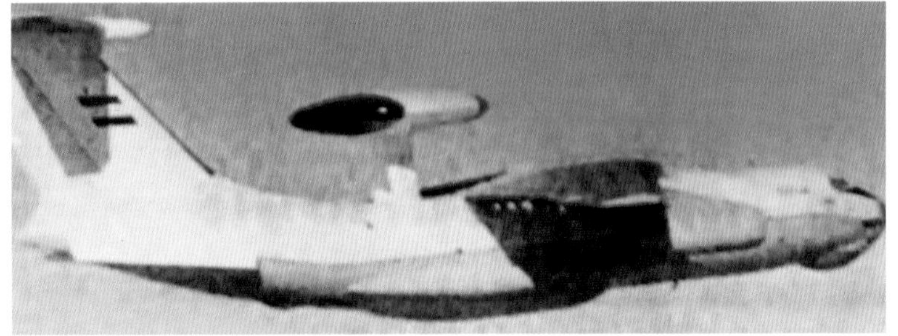

Bottom: The Baghdad-1 AWACS converted from an IL-76MD 'Falsie', showing the huge rear radome. The colour scheme is the basic livery of Iraqi Airways.

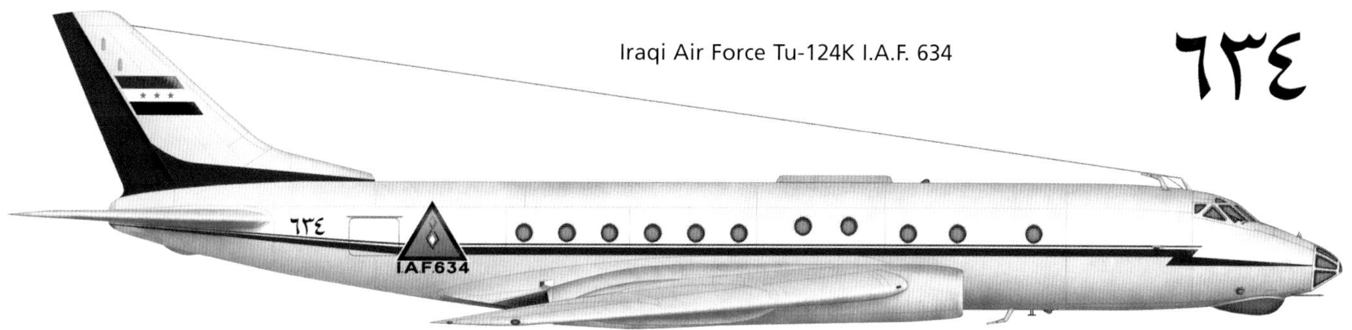

Iraqi Air Force Tu-124K I.A.F. 634

start making evasive manoeuvres to prevent the *Hind's* crew from taking accurate aim. In so doing the Iranians would try to lure the pursuer within range of their air defences or call in fighters by radio for help. If the Iraqis managed to catch the enemy off guard they would climb to 1,000 m (3,280 ft) and dive at the Cobra, trying to get it from behind.

The first air-to-air engagement involving a *Hind* actually happened a few days before the Iran-Iraq war 'officially' began. On 7th September 1980 five Mi-24s crossed the border, attacking an Iranian border post; IRIAF fighters scrambled to intercept, shooting down one of the attackers. The first helicopter duel in world history took place shortly after the outbreak of the war, in November 1980, near Dezfûl in south-western Iran. Sneaking up unnoticed to a pair of Mi-24s, two Sea Cobras attacked with TOW missiles. One *Hind* went down immediately, the other was damaged and crashed about 10 km (6.2 miles) away; the Iranians landed at the crash site and captured a surviving Iraqi major. A second clash between Mi-24s and AH-1Js happened on 24th April 1981 near Panjevin; again, the Iranians shot down both *Hinds* with no losses for themselves.

It was not until 14th September 1983 that the tables were turned when a Mi-24 shot

Iraqi Air Force IL-76MD 'Falsie' YI-ANJ in grey/white colours similar to those of the IrAF An-12s

Iraqi Air Force IL-76M YI-AKU; note that the Arabic titles are not repeated on the nose

Iraqi Air Force IL-76MD 'Falsie' YI-ANH in full Iraqi Airways livery.

Another Iraqi IL-76MD 'Falsie' visiting Prague-Ruzyne.

IL-76M YI-AIN in the same livery, except for a subtly different presentation of the Iraqi Airways titles (in bolder type).

IL-76M YI-AKO in the grey/white colour scheme.

Grey/white IL-76M YI-AKQ visiting a European airport. Here the Arabic titles are not repeated on the nose.

IL-76M YI-AKW at Prague-Ruzyne. Like YI-AIN, these three aircraft were returned to the Soviet Union under a trade-in arrangement.

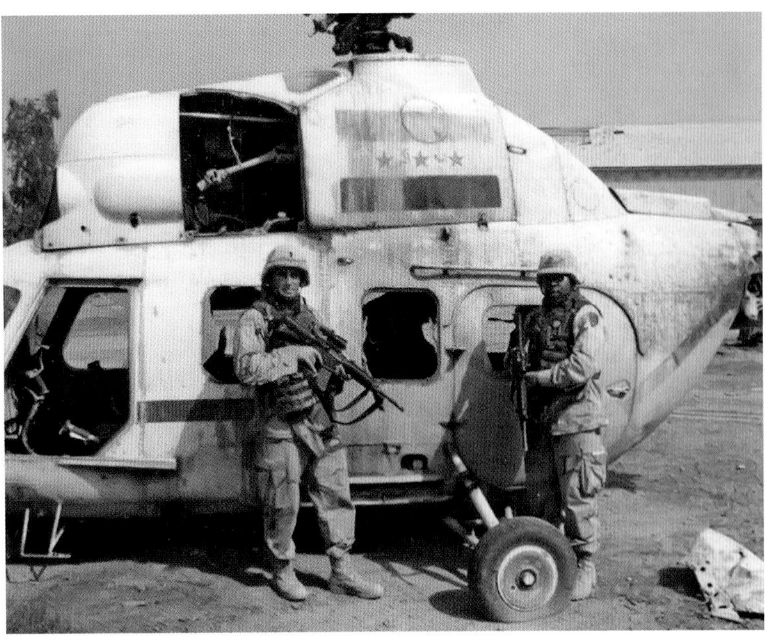

US Army servicemen pose with a very dead Iraqi Air Force Mi-2 helicopter, which is missing at least one engine and the tailboom.

down a Sea Cobra near Basra. On 5th February Iraq claimed the destruction of three more Sea Cobras by Mi-24s. On 25th February 1984 a group of *Hinds* attacked a group of AH-1Js, destroying three of them. Another Sea Cobra fell victim to a Mi-24 on 13th February 1986, the Iranians also claiming one 'kill'. Three days later 'Khomeini's falcons' lost another AH-1J but took their revenge five days later, shooting down a Mi-24.

The last engagement between the two types was recorded on 22nd May 1986 when Mi-24s attacked a pair of Sea Cobras, destroying one of them. Thus, the overall 'kill' ratio is 10:6 in favour of the *Hind*; some Western experts, though, claim the opposite. Iraqi Mi-24s had encounters with other Iranian helicopters as well; in May and June 1988 alone they shot down six Agusta-Bell AB.214 utility helicopters and one AB.212. By the end of the war Iraqi pilots flying Mi-8TVs, Mi-24As/ Mi-25s and Aérospatiale SA 342L Gazelles had destroyed 53 Iranian choppers.

However, the most remarkable 'kill' scored by a *Hind* took place on 27th October 1982 when an Iraqi Mi-25 shot down an IRIAF F-4D Phantom II near Aïn Hoshah. This was probably the only occasion when a helicopter succeeded in shooting down a fast jet. Most sources describing the incident state the Phantom was destroyed head-on by anti-tank missiles but a Polish author claims it was shot down by machine-gun fire.

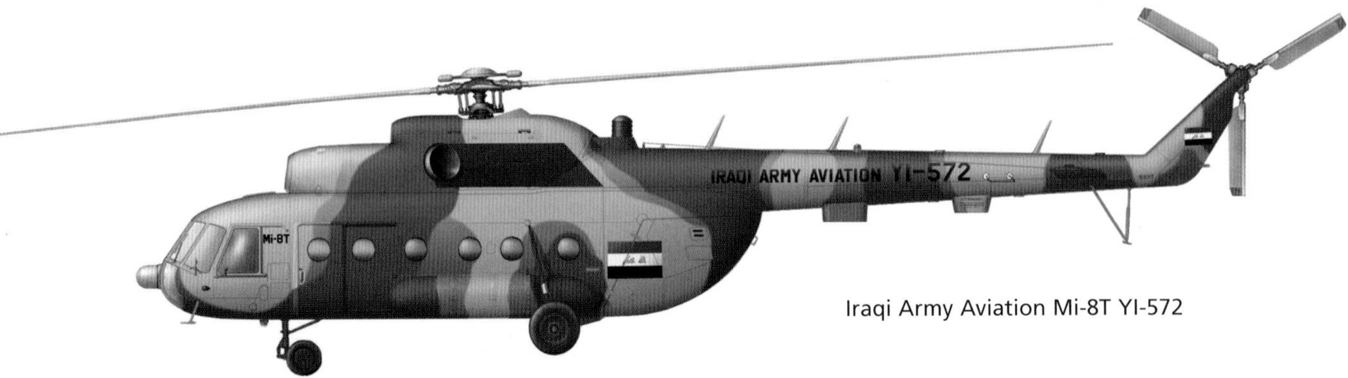

Iraqi Army Aviation Mi-8T YI-572

In parallel with the action in Iran, the Iraqi MiG-21s, MiG-23BNs, Su-20s and Mi-25s were used for suppressing the new Kurdish uprising which began in 1983. The Kurdish leaders saw this as an opportune time, believing that the Baghdad regime would be unable to wage war on two fronts and would agree to give the Kurds the coveted autonomy. They counted wrong; Saddam Hussein was determined not to back down in the face of separatism. The most violent phase of the conflict was the al-Anfal campaign of 1986-89, which is widely regarded as genocide against the Kurdish people and culminated in the infamous Halabja massacre, or Bloody Friday. On 16th March 1988 Iraqi combat jets attacked the town of Halabja in Iraqi Kurdistan with bombs filled with chemical agents, including mustard gas and VX nerve agent. The attack killed between 3,200 and 5,000 people and injured around 7,000 to 10,000 more, most of them civilians. The rebellion ended in 1988 with an agreement of amnesty between the Iraqi government and the Kurdish rebels, who thus failed to achieve their goals.

First Gulf War (Operation *Desert Storm*)

On 2nd August 1990 the Iraqi Army invaded Kuwait. There were several reasons for this aggression. Firstly, there were territorial claims – Iraq had long considered Kuwait to be part of its territory that had been wrongfully occupied by Great Britain, as Kuwait had been associated with Basra in the days of the Ottoman Empire. Secondly, both nations were OPEC members, and Iraq accused Kuwait of not observing the oil production quota, which led to a slump in oil prices, and of slant-drilling across the border into the Rumaila Oil Field, which is in Iraqi territory. Thirdly, Iraq had incurred a large debt to Kuwait and Saudi Arabia in the course of the war with Iran; Iraq pressured both nations to forgive the debt, but they refused.

In July 1990 Iraq complained about Kuwaiti policies and posed an ultimatum, demanding US$ 10 billion in compensation for the use of the Rumaila Oil Field and openly threatening to take military action. Nobody, including the Kuwaitis, seriously believed that Iraq would invade; yet, invade it did, mounting a two-pronged assault on Kuwait City. The ground offensive was supported by Iraqi aircraft and helicopters, including two Su-22 squadrons at Wahda AB in southern Iraq, Mi-6, Mi-8TV and Mi-17-1V helicopters carrying commando teams. The Baghdad-1 and Adnan-1/-2 AWACS aircraft monitored the war zone – as they would also do later in the war.

Caught off guard, the Kuwaiti military nevertheless offered some resistance. 15 Iraqi choppers, including Mi-8s and Mi-25s, were lost to Kuwaiti ground fire. So was a MiG-23BN and one of the Su-22s, which were shot down

Opposite page, below: A recent addition to the 'New Iraqi' Army Aviation fleet is this Mi-8T serialled YI-572. Note the non-standard radar in a thimble radome and the new Iraqi flag featuring the legend 'Allah akbar' instead of the three green stars.

Below: A ramp-equipped Mi-171E with exhaust/air mixers awaits delivery to post-Saddam Iraq. Note the addition of an optoelectronic surveillance system under the nose, western ESM equipment with aerials on the nose and tailboom, the western IRCM flare launchers and the spent case chutes for the machine-guns in the doorways.

An Iraqi Army Aviation Mi-17 with a strange serial in European characters

by a MIM-23B I-Hawk SAM battery on Bubiyan Island, the Su-22 pilot losing his life. However, the battery was promptly silenced by another Su-22 which fired a Kh-25MP anti-radar missile. The Iraqi Mi-25s also participated in the invasion, escorting the troopship helicopters, suppressing pockets of resistance and destroying a few Kuwaiti tanks. Within 12 hours most of the resistance had ended and the Kuwaiti royal family had fled; soon the entire country was occupied and a pro-Iraqi provisional administration had been installed, later succeeded by Saddam Hussein's cousin Ali Hassan al-Majid as the governor of Kuwait on 8th August.

The Iraqi aggression caused worldwide condemnation and led first to immediate economic sanctions against Iraq by the UN and then to military action by the USA, who launched Operation *Desert Shield* on 7th August 1990. When the US-led coalition started building up troops in Saudi Arabia in the autumn of 1990, the Iraqi Air Force in turn began preparing for a pre-emptive strike against them. In particular, the ground-based early warning radar sites in Saudi Arabia were targeted, and on one occasion a Su-22M4 carrying a Kh-28S ARM got a lock-on against a USAF Boeing E-3A Sentry AWACS monitoring the area from Saudi airspace 250 km (155 miles) away.

On 29th November 1990 the UN Security Council passed Resolution 678 which gave Iraq until 15th January 1991 to withdraw from Kuwait and empowered states to use 'all necessary means' to force Iraq out of Kuwait after the deadline. Iraq ignored the ultimatum, and on 17th January 1991 the anti-Iraqi coalition launched Operation *Desert Storm* to expel Iraqi troops from Kuwait. This began with an aerial bombardment, followed by a ground campaign from 23rd February.

On the night of 18th January an IrAF MiG-25PD scored the first Iraqi aerial victory in the war, downing a US Navy McDonnell Douglas F/A-18C Hornet strike aircraft over Anbar Province. The pilot was killed; it was not until 2009 that he was identified as Capt. Michael 'Scott' Speicher. That same night MiG-23MLAs launching from al-Bakr AB attacked two USAF General Dynamics F-111F Aardvark tactical bombers with missiles, albeit no confirmed 'kills' were scored. One more *Flogger-G* almost collided with an unseen USAF Lockheed F-117A 'stealth' fighter-bomber over Baghdad, a crash being avoided only because the crew of an E-3A AWACS monitoring the battle area hastily ordered the F-117 pilot to descend. On 19th January a MiG-29 flown by Jameel Sayhood shot down a Royal Air Force Panavia Tornado GR.1A strike aircraft piloted by Flt Lt Gary Lennox and Flt Lt Adrian Weeks. On another occasion a MiG-25PD eluded eight USAF McDonnell Douglas F-15C Eagles and fired three missiles at a USAF EF-111 Raven ECM aircraft, missing it but forcing the Raven to abort the mission. In yet another incident, two MiG-25PDs attacked a pair of F-15s (which evaded the missiles) and outran the American fighters when counterattacked. Two more F-15s joined the pursuit; the Eagles fired a total of ten missiles at the retreating *Foxbats* but they were out of reach.

Yet, that was all the good luck the Iraqi pilots had. On 17th January 1991, two US Navy Hornets of VFA-81 shot down two MiG-21*bis*, the first with AIM-7M Sparrows and the second with AIM-9M Sidewinders. These were two of the only six MiG-21s/F-7 (among the 100-plus available) that flew a combat sortie in that war. That same day two USAF (33rd TFW/58th TFS) Eagles each destroyed one MiG-25PD with Sparrow missiles. Additionally, several MiG-25s were damaged while taxying when they hit mines strewn by Royal Air Force Panavia Tornado

GR.4s by means of JP233 submunitions dispensers; a total of 18 *Foxbats* were destroyed or disabled on the ground.

According to the US Department of Defense, three Iraqi MiG-29s were shot down on 17th January 1991 and two more on 19th January. On 24th January the Iraqis attempted a strike against the Saudi oil refinery in Abqaiq. However, the strike package of two Mirage F.1EQs escorted by two MiG-23s was detected by a USAF E-3 AWACS aircraft, which vectored two Royal Saudi Air Force F-15s towards them. When the Eagles appeared the MiGs turned tail, but the Mirages pressed on and were promptly shot down.

On the evening of 6th February 1991 two USAF F-15Cs (79-0078 and 84-0019) of the 36th TFW/53rd TFS on temporary deployment to al-Kharj AB, Saudi Arabia, intercepted a pair of Iraqi MiG-21s and a pair of Su-25s. All four Iraqi aircraft were shot down, both Su-25s coming down in the desert not far from the Iranian border.

The air superiority of the coalition forces was so overwhelming that the majority of the Iraqi Air Force's Su-25Ks did not manage to launch from their own bases. In fact, the Iraqi basing philosophy for all of its combat aircraft meant that the Su-25s were deployed to various locations throughout the country's vast complex of airfields and reserve landing strips, some in shelters, but many were parked out in the open. At least one *Frogfoot-A* was destroyed by an air strike, while others were captured more or less intact by the coalition's ground forces.

Below: A Mi-171 in the stepped nose/'flatass' version wearing the distinctive 'chevron' camouflage scheme of the 'New Iraqi' Army Aviation but as yet no national insignia or serial.

Bottom: An Iraqi Army Aviation Mi-171 hangared at Taji AB.

A partly dismantled Iraqi Army Aviation Mi-25.

This Iraqi Mi-25 serialled 4493 was captured by US forces in not-airworthy condition. The large flag on the fuselage was a feature of Army Aviation helicopters.

Many Iraqi aircraft were destroyed on the ground by Coalition force air strikes or ground troops. These included two standard IL-76MD 'Falsies' and the Adnan-2 AWACS, numerous MiG-23BNs destroyed at Ali Ibn Abu Talib AB, and many other fighters and fighter-bombers.

In January 1991, when Saddam Hussein realised he was losing the war, he ordered the greater part of the surviving IrAF aircraft to be flown to neighbouring Iran (which maintained a neutral stance in the war) to save them from destruction by the Coalition force. The 115 'refugees' included 17 IL-76s (including the Baghdad-1 and Adnan-1 AWACS), four Su-20s, 40 Su-22s of various sub-types, seven Su-25Ks, 12 MiG-23BNs, four MiG-25s, seven MiG-29s (some sources say only four reached their destination, the other three crashing en route), all 24 Su-24MKs and 24 Dassault Mirage F.1EQ fighters; additionally, 17 airliners belonging to Iraqi Airways were flown out. However, Iran impounded the Iraqi aircraft and never returned them, presumably regarding them to be fitting compensation for the damages sustained in the 1980-88 war.

The Mi-25s were not used against the Coalition during Operation *Desert Storm*; Saddam Hussein obviously wanted to save them for use against 'the enemy within', that is, the Kurds. Yet, losses were not altogether avoided. One Mi-25 was knocked out by a 'smart bomb' dropped by a USAF F-15C, three more were blown up on their hardstand by the vanguard of the US Army's 24th Infantry Division and a fifth was captured almost intact

Iraqi Army Aviation Mi-25 '4493'

by the vanguard of the US Army's 28th Airborne Division at Basra.

Seeing that his troops were being overwhelmed by the coalition forces, on 27th February 1991 Saddam Hussein ordered a retreat from Kuwait. Four days later the last Iraqi units had been expelled, but not before they had set fire to nearly 700 Kuwaiti oil wells and mined the approaches to them, foiling any attempts to extinguish the fires. Not content with the liberation of Kuwait, the coalition forces pursued the enemy 150 km (93 miles) into Iraqi territory, inflicting heavy losses, before returning to the border.

Operation *Desert Storm* ended on 16th April 1991. After this, so-called 'no-fly zones' were established in northern and southern Iraq in connection with Kurdish and Shi'a uprisings (and Iraqi action against these). Yet Iraqi Air Force aircraft regularly violated these zones, especially in the south where they were in action against Shiite rebels. *Hinds* were also used in these operations, which were finally terminated on 22nd August 1992 when the USA threatened with renewed strikes against Iraq. On 20th and 22nd March 1992, two unarmed Su-22s were intercepted and shot down by USAF F-15Cs during Operation *Provide Comfort* while on a positioning flight from al-Hurriya to Tikrit (which was in the northern no-fly zone); the Americans had decided another attack against the Kurds might be in progress.

On 25th December 1992, two USAF Lockheed Martin F-16 Fighting Falcons used AIM-120 AMRAAM missiles in anger for the first time ever, shooting down an Iraqi MiG-25. Two hours later an F-15E had a brush with a MiG-25, neither side scoring a 'kill'. On 2nd January 1993 a MiG-25 trying to intercept a Lockheed U-2R high-altitude reconnaissance aircraft was attacked by an F-15C, again with no losses on either side. One of the MiG-29s that had survived the First Gulf War was shot down by a USAF F-15C in 1993; another *Fulcrum* was lost under unknown circumstances in 1995.

An Iraqi 'helicopter gunship' – almost certainly a Mi-25 – was destroyed along with several other military aircraft and an ammunition dump at Tikrit on the night of 26th May 1995. It is certain that the aircraft were sabotaged by Iraqi National Congress insurgent forces. More losses came on 17th December 1998 when several Mi-25s were destroyed on the ground by US cruise missiles during Operation *Desert Fox*. The last recorded Iraqi 'kill' was on 23rd December 2002, when a MiG-25PD shot down a USAF General Atomics RQ-1 Predator unmanned combat aerial vehicle.

Second Gulf War (Operation *Iraqi Freedom*)

In the late 1980s Saddam Hussein had declared that 'binary chemical weapons' would be used on Israel if it used military force against Iraq. This was his fatal mistake that was ultimately his undoing. The then US President George W. Bush and the then British Prime Minister Tony Blair accused Iraq of possessing weapons of mass destruction and having ties to the al-Qaeda terrorist network. (Afterwards, it was revealed that the intelligence reports of alleged Iraqi WMD had been falsified in order to justify a military intervention and the removal of Saddam Hussein – in fact, Iraq had no such weapons at this stage.)

On 20th March 2003 a broad coalition led by the USA and the UK invaded Iraq, launching the active phase of Operation *Iraqi Freedom*. This was known as the Second Gulf War (or third, if you count the Iran-Iraq War as the first one) – or simply as the Iraq War.

The war itself was brief, the invasion encountering little opposition. Baghdad fell on 9th April and major military operations were completed by 1st May 2003. Surprisingly, this time the Iraqi Air Force offered no resistance at all to the invasion – perhaps because, thanks to an arms embargo imposed in 1991, it had been desperately short of spares to keep its aircraft flying. True, in late 2000 the Iraqis did succeed in obtaining spares stocks illegally from Belarus – a source that, unfortunately for them, dried up just one year later. The Bosnian company Orao stepped into the breach until mid-March 2003, when Saddam Hussein personally ordered the disassembling and hiding of all combat aircraft In an attempt to save at least some of them, as it was clear they would not stand a chance against the US forces. Officers were 'discouraged', to put it mildly, from acting at their own initiative and therefore, the inaction of the IrAF is understandable. Several MiG-25s were buried in the sand (!) – a gesture of despair, since apparently no attempt had been made to seal them against ingress of sand. This did not stop the machines from being – literally – unearthed by Allied ground forces that overran their hiding places.

Once Iraq had been completely occupied (and it would remain under US occupation until 2011), the ruling Ba'ath party was banned and an Iraqi interim government was formed. Yet Saddam Hussein managed to evade capture until 13 December 2003, when he was hunted down and captured near his home town of Tikrit in Operation *Red Dawn*. Almost three years later, after a year-long trial, he was sentenced to death on 5th November 2006 and executed on 30th December 2006. The bottom line was a new 'democratic Iraq' – and an ongoing insurgency, with terrorist attacks occurring on a daily basis.

New Iraqi Air Force: from the ground up

The 2003 invasion and American occupation of Iraq had destroyed whatever assets the Iraqi Air Force had left by then, so for all practical purposes the IrAF ceased to exist. However, once the USA had achieved its goal of eliminating Saddam Hussein and installing a pro-American regime, the government of 'New Iraq' set about rebuilding the armed forces, including the air force (now referred to as IQAF). Predictably, the new regime was obliged to equip the IQAF with western types (though, in fairness, the old IrAF had operated French combat aircraft as well).

There are two notable exceptions, however. Rather than choose a western tactical transport, such as the Alenia C-27J Spartan or CASA C-295, the IQAF placed an order for six Antonov An-32B *Cline* transports in 2009. Perhaps the price was the decisive factor, or the fact that several 85% complete An-32 airframes were sitting at the Antonov Aircraft Factory in Kiev for want of a customer and could be completed quickly – much quicker than if western aircraft were ordered. Five of the six aircraft had been delivered by July 2012. The An-32Bs are most likely operated by the 23rd Sqn based at New al-Muthana AB near Baghdad which also operates ex-USAF Lockheed C-130Hs. Like all other IQAF aircraft, they have three-digit serials with the Iraqi national prefix YI-.

The other exception is the Mi-8 helicopter. In December 2004 the Iraqi Ministry of Defence signed a US$ 105 million contract with the Polish defence consortium BUMAR for the refurbishment and delivery of 24 second-hand Mi-17s. Specifically, these were Kazan'-built Mi-17V-5s with the stepped nose and one-piece cargo ramp. Reports on actual deliveries (dates and in-service numbers) are rather contradictory; one source says only eight helicopters had been delivered and two more are on their way, while another source maintains that 16 Mi-17V-5s had been delivered between February 2005 and November 2008. These helicopters are in service with the 15th SOF Sqn formed specifically for the Iraqi Special Operations Forces. Additionally, in 2007 Iraq placed an order with the Ulan-Ude Aircraft Factory for 28 or 30 Mi-171E helicopters (broadly similar to the Mi-17V-5). These were manufactured in 2007-08 and are operated by the 4th Sqn at Taji AB. The IQAF Mi-17V-5s and Mi-171Es wear a rather odd camouflage scheme of gloss chocolate brown, sand and olive green applied in a distinctive 'go faster' chevron pattern. Additionally, at least two Mi-8Ts (reportedly refurbished in the Ukraine) have been delivered in a totally different three-tone desert camouflage with 'Iraqi Army Aviation' titles; they sport a non-standard weather radar in a thimble radome and an IRCM jammer aft of the main rotor head of the sort usually fitted to military Mi-8MT/MTV *Hip-Hs*.

Known Iraqi Air Force aircraft of Soviet/Russian origin.
1. 'Old' Iraqi Air Force

Type	Serial/ registration	C/n	F/n	Notes
An-2	2142	1G 174-20		
An-2	2143	1G 178-49		
An-12A (+)	505 Black	024010		Irkutsk-built. Overall grey c/s
An-12A (+)	506 Black	024011		Overall grey c/s. Derelict Baghdad
An-12A (+)	507 Black	024012		Overall grey c/s. Derelict Baghdad
An-12B (+)	I.A.F. 636?	402709		Voronezh-built. Reported as 636 (exact serial presentation and c/s not known)
An-12B (+)	I.A.F. 637	402710		Grey/white c/s
An-12B (+)	I.A.F. 638	402711		Grey/white c/s
An-12BP (+)	I.A.F. 685	6344305		Tashkent-built. Grey/white c/s. Became, see next line
	YI-AES			Registered by 1974. Returned to the USSR by 2-81 as CCCP-11650 No.2

An-12BP (+)	I.A.F. 686	6344306		Grey/white c/s; serial previously applied simply as 686 in Arabic characters. Became, see next line
	YI-AGD			Registered by 1976; to Royal Jordanian Air Force as 352?
An-12BP (+)	805 Black	8345909		Grey/white c/s, no cheatline. Became, see next line
	YI-AEP			Registered by 1970; sold to the Sudan Air Force 1992 as ST-ALV No.1
An-12BP (+)	I.A.F. 806	8345910		Grey/white c/s. Became, see next line
	YI-AFJ			Registered by 1973
An-12BP (+)	I.A.F. 807	8345908		Grey/white c/s. Became, see next line
	YI-AER			Registered by 1973; sold to the Sudan Air Force as 988
An-24T	?	1022805?		Serial unknown. Became, see next line
	YI-AEM			Crashed near Kirkuk 24-9-1980
An-24T	?	1022806?		
	YI-AEN			Serial unknown. Became, see next line
An-24T	?	1022807?		
	YI-AFG			Serial unknown. Became, see next line
An-24T	?	1022808?		
	YI-ALY			Serial unknown. Became, see next line
An-24T	?	1022809?		
	YI-AMB			Serial unknown. Became, see next line
An-24T	?	1022810?		
	YI-ALN			Damaged Nasiriya 28-8-1980 but repaired; derelict Talil by 2003
An-24T	769	?		Became one of the above
An-24T	797	?		Became one of the above
An-24T	799	?		Became one of the above
An-24T	803	?		Became one of the above
An-24T	804	?		Became one of the above
An-26	YI-ALA	3810		
IL-28	423 Black	?		No.8 Sqn. Wfu al-Hurrya AB by 9-1980
IL-28	424 Black	?		No.8 Sqn
IL-28	425 Black	56605703		Omsk-built. No.8 Sqn. Wfu al-Taqaddum
IL-28	426 Black	56605704		No.8 Sqn. Wfu al-Taqaddum
IL-28	427 Black	56605717		No.8 Sqn. Wfu al-Taqaddum
IL-28	428 Black	?		No.8 Sqn
IL-28	429 Black	?		No.8 Sqn. Wfu al-Bakr AB
IL-28	430 Black	?		No.8 Sqn. Wfu al-Taqaddum
IL-28	431 Black	?		No.8 Sqn
IL-28	432 Black	56606540		No.8 Sqn. Shot down by Turkish Air Force Republic F-84Fs 16-8-1962
IL-28	433 Black	?		No.8 Sqn, old (second type) fin flash
IL-28	434 Black	56606207		No.8 Sqn. Wfu al-Taqaddum
IL-28	437 Black	?		No.8 Sqn. Wfu al-Taqaddum
IL-28BM	564 Black	5901703		Irkutsk-built. No.8 Sqn. Wfu al-Taqaddum
IL-28BM	565 Black	5901801		No.8 Sqn. Wfu al-Taqaddum
IL-28U	421 Black	69808		Moscow-built. No.8 Sqn. Wfu al-Taqaddum
IL-28U	422 Black	69520		No.8 Sqn. Wfu al-Taqaddum
IL-76 (military)	YI-AIK	073410292	0803	D/D 27-9-1977. Returned 1984, to Soviet Ministry of Aircraft Industry (MAP) as CCCP-76495
IL-76 (military)	YI-AIL	073410293	0804	D/D 13-9-1977. Returned 1986, to Gromov Flight Research Institute (LII) as CCCP-76528
IL-76 (military)	YI-AIM	073410320	0810	D/D 1-10-1977. Returned by 1980, to MAP as CCCP-76497
IL-76 (military)	YI-AIN	073410301	0806	D/D 31-10-1977. Returned 1984, to MAP as IL-76T 'Falsie' CCCP-76496
IL-76 (military)	YI-AIO	073410315	0809	Shot down by Iranian fighter near Baghdad-Saddam Hussein International airport 23-9-1980
IL-76 (military)	YI-AIP	073410308	0807	D/D 18-8-1978. Returned 1984, to LII as CCCP-76529, converted to IL-76LL engine testbed
IL-76M	YI-AKO	093416506	1307	Reported as ex-Iraqi AF 2803. Grey/white c/s. Returned 1988, to IL-76T 'Falsie' CCCP-76490, converted to IL-76-11 avionics testbed
IL-76M	YI-AKP	093421630	1608	D/D 11-3-1980, grey/white c/s. Returned 1987, to MAP as IL-76T 'Falsie' CCCP-76491
IL-76M	YI-AKQ	093421635	1609	D/D 19-2-1980, grey/white c/s. Returned by 1988, to LII as IL-76T 'Falsie' CCCP-06188, converted to IL-76LL engine testbed

IL-76M	YI-AKS	093418543	1406	Reported as ex-Iraqi AF 2068. D/D 1-8-1979. Returned 9-1-1987, to Sukhoi OKB as IL-76T 'Falsie' CCCP-76759
IL-76M	YI-AKT	093418548	1407	D/D 28-7-1979. Returned 1987, to MAP as IL-76T 'Falsie' CCCP-76492 (second use of registration)
IL-76M	YI-AKU	093421637	1610	D/D 14-3-1980, grey/white c/s. Returned 1987, to MAP as IL-76T 'Falsie' CCCP-76754
IL-76M	YI-AKV	0013428831	2108	D/D 18-5-1981. Returned 1987, to TransSuper as IL-76T 'Falsie' CCCP-78731
IL-76M	YI-AKW	0013428839	2110	D/D 1-7-1981, grey/white c/s. Returned by 1989, to LII as IL-76T 'Falsie' CCCP-76756
IL-76M	YI-AKX	0013433990	2508	D/D 11-12-1981. Returned 1988, to MAP as IL-76T 'Falsie' CCCP-76757
IL-76M	YI-ALL	0013433984	2506	Reported as ex-Iraqi AF 4600. D/D 28-2-1982. Returned 1988, to MAP as IL-76T 'Falsie' CCCP-76755
IL-76M	YI-ALO	0013433996	2509	Reported as ex-Iraqi AF 4660 (or 4214). D/D 17-2-1982. Returned 1988, to MAP as IL-76T 'Falsie' CCCP-76788
IL-76M	YI-ALP	0013433999	2510	Reported as ex-Iraqi AF 4601. D/D 17-2-1982. Returned 1988, to MAP as IL-76T 'Falsie' CCCP-76789
IL-76MD	YI-ALQ	0023441189	3008	D/D 4-12-1989. Returned 1992, to IL-76TD 'Falsie' CCCP-76823
IL-76MD	YI-ALR	0023441200	3010	D/D 4-12-1989. Returned by 2-92, to MAP as IL-76TD 'Falsie' CCCP-76821
IL-76MD	YI-ALS	0033442247	3202	D/D 2-2-1983. Returned by 9-91, to LII as IL-76TD 'Falsie' CCCP-78738
IL-76MD	YI-ALT	0033448393	3509	D/D 30-9-1983. Flown to Iran 16-1-1991; to IRGC as 15-2284
IL-76MD	YI-ALU	0033448398	3510	D/D 31-10-1983. Destroyed by Allied bombing at al-Tooz 18-1-1991 or shot down 27-1-1991
IL-76MD	YI-ALV	0033448409	3603	D/D 31-10-1983. Wfu Baghdad-Saddam International airport by 2003
IL-76MD	YI-ALW	0033448416	3604	D/D 5-11-1983. Flown to Iran 16-1-1991; to IRIAF as 5-8207
IL-76MD	YI-ALX	0043449455	3704	D/D 7-2-1984. Flown to Iran 16-1-1991; to IRIAF as 5-8201
IL-76MD 'Falsie'	YI-ANA	0063469055	5204	D/D 31-5-1986. Flown to Iran 19-1-1991; to IRIAF as 5-8210
IL-76MD 'Falsie'	YI-ANB	0063469071	5208	D/D 28-6-1986. Flown to Iran 18-1-1991; to IRGC as 15-2283
IL-76MD 'Falsie'	YI-ANC	0063470102	5306	D/D 18-6-1986. Flown to Iran 23-1-1991; fate unknown
IL-76MD 'Falsie'	YI-AND	0063471155	5409	D/D 14-10-1986. Flown to Iran 16-1-1991; to IRGC as 15-2282
IL-76MD 'Falsie'	YI-ANE	0073474224	5606	D/D 23-3-1987. Flown to Iran 18-1-1991; to IRIAF as 5-8202
IL-76MD 'Falsie'	YI-ANF	0073475236	5609	D/D 30-5-1987. Flown to Iran 16-1-1991; to IRGC as 15-2281
IL-76MD 'Falsie'	YI-ANG	0073476288	5802	D/D 26-6-1987. Flown to Iran 16-1-1991; to IRIAF as 5-8203
IL-76MD 'Falsie'	YI-ANH	0073476307	5807	D/D 30-6-1987. Destroyed by Allied bombing at al-Taqaddum AB 18-1-1991
IL-76MD 'Falsie'	YI-ANI	0073481442	6201	D/D 30-12-1987. Flown to Iran 16-1-1991; to IRGC as 15-2280
IL-76MD 'Falsie'	YI-ANJ	0083482481	6301	D/D 31-1-1988, grey/white c/s! Crashed Baghdad 12-1-1989
IL-76MD 'Falsie'	YI-ANK	0083482495	6304	D/D 17-5-1988. Flown to Iran 18-1-1991; to IRIAF as 5-8204
IL-76MD 'Falsie'	YI-ANL	0083484542	6406	D/D 21-6-1988. Converted to, see next line
Adnan-1	no serial?			Flown to Iran ?-1-1991; to IRIAF as 5-8208
IL-76MD 'Falsie'	YI-ANM	0093495886	7302	D/D 26-2-1990. Fate unknown; possibly converted to Adnan-2 AWACS
IL-76MD 'Falsie'	YI-ANN	0093496894	7304	D/D 2-3-1990. Flown to Iran 23-1-1991; fate unknown
IL-76MD 'Falsie'	YI-ANO	1003403087	7802	D/D 28-6-1990. Flown to Iran 18-1-1991; to IRIAF as 5-8209
Baghdad-1	no serial	***34*****	?	Converted IL-76MD 'Falsie'. Flown to Iran ?-1-1991; to IRIAF as 5-8205
Adnan-2	no serial	***34*****	?	Converted IL-76MD 'Falsie'. Destroyed by Allied bombing ?-1990
MiG-15*bis*	415 Black	?		
MiG-15*bis*	416 Black	?		
MiG-15*bis*	417 Black	?		
MiG-15*bis*	418 Black	?		
MiG-15*bis*	419 Black	?		
MiG-15*bis*	420 Black	?		
MiG-15*bis*	423 Black	?		
MiG-15*bis*	429 Black	?		
MiG-15*bis*	431 Black	?		
MiG-15*bis*	432 Black	?		
MiG-15*bis*	906 Black	?		
MiG-15*bis*	909 Black	?		
MiG-15*bis*	911 Black	?		
MiG-15bis	913 Black	?		
MiG-15*bis*	1021 Black	?		Dumped at Kirkuk AB
MiG-15*bis*R	?	623923		Czechoslovak-built (Aero S-103); ex-Czechoslovak Air Force 3923 Black
MiG-15*bis*R	?	713019		Czechoslovak-built (Aero S-103); ex-Czechoslovak Air Force 3019 Black
MiG-15*bis*R	?	713025		Czechoslovak-built (Aero S-103); ex-Czechoslovak Air Force 3025 Black
MiG-15*bis*R	?	713027		Czechoslovak-built (Aero S-103); ex-Czechoslovak Air Force 3027 Black
MiG-15*bis*R	?	713107		Czechoslovak-built (Aero S-103); ex-Czechoslovak Air Force 3107 Black

MiG-15*bis*R	?	713115		Czechoslovak-built (Aero S-103); ex-Czechoslovak Air Force 3115 Black
MiG-15*bis*R	?	713116		Czechoslovak-built (Aero S-103); ex-Czechoslovak Air Force 3116 Black
UTI-MiG-15	539 Black	?		Flying School (Air Academy), natural metal finish; D/D 1962, first aircraft of the fourth batch delivered
UTI-MiG-15	541 Black	?		Flying School (Air Academy), natural metal finish
UTI-MiG-15	542 Black	?		Flying School (Air Academy), natural metal finish; preserved Iraqi Air Force Museum, Baghdad
UTI-MiG-15	543 Black	?		Flying School (Air Academy)
UTI-MiG-15	544 Black	?		Flying School (Air Academy), natural metal finish
UTI-MiG-15	545 Black	?		Flying School (Air Academy)
UTI-MiG-15	546 Black	?		Flying School (Air Academy)
UTI-MiG-15	547 Black	?		Flying School (Air Academy)
UTI-MiG-15	548 Black	?		Flying School (Air Academy)
UTI-MiG-15	549 Black	?		Flying School (Air Academy), natural metal finish
UTI-MiG-15	874 Black	?		Czechoslovak-built (Aero CS-102). Two-tone camouflage. Still operational in early 1987
UTI-MiG-15	878 Black	?		Czechoslovak-built (Aero CS-102)?
UTI-MiG-15	966 Black	?		Two-tone camouflage. Destroyed during the First Gulf War
MiG-17F	440 Black	?		D/D 1-1959, No.5 Sqn; first aircraft of the first batch delivered
MiG-17F	441 Black	?		D/D 1-1959, No.5 Sqn; first type (Royal Iraqi Air Force style) fin flash
MiG-17F	442 Black	?		D/D 1-1959, No.5 Sqn
MiG-17F	443 Black	?		D/D 1-1959, No.5 Sqn; first type (Royal Iraqi Air Force style) fin flash
MiG-17F	444 Black	?		D/D 1-1959, No.5 Sqn
MiG-17F	445 Black	?		D/D 1-1959, No.5 Sqn
MiG-17F	446 Black	?		D/D 1-1959, No.5 Sqn
MiG-17F	447 Black	?		D/D 1-1959, No.5 Sqn
MiG-17F	448 Black	?		D/D 1-1959, No.5 Sqn
MiG-17F	449 Black	?		D/D 1-1959, No.5 Sqn
MiG-17F	450 Black	?		D/D 1959, No.5 Sqn; first aircraft of the second batch delivered
MiG-17F	451 Black	?		D/D 1959, No.5 Sqn
MiG-17F	452 Black	?		D/D 1959, No.7 Sqn; second type (1959-63) green/white fin flash
MiG-17F	453 Black	?		D/D 1959, No.7 Sqn
MiG-17F	454 Black	?		D/D 1959, No.7 Sqn
MiG-17F	455 Black	?		D/D 1959, No.7 Sqn
MiG-17F	456 Black	?		D/D 1959, No.7 Sqn
MiG-17F	457 Black	?		D/D 1959, No.7 Sqn
MiG-17F	459 Black	?		D/D 1959, No.7 Sqn
MiG-17F	460 Black	?		D/D 1959, No.7 Sqn
MiG-17F	461 Black	?		D/D 1959, No.7 Sqn
MiG-17F	462 Black	?		D/D 1959, No.7 Sqn
MiG-17F	463 Black	?		D/D 1959, No.7 Sqn
MiG-17F	464 Black	?		D/D 1959, No.7 Sqn
MiG-17F	465 Black	?		D/D 1959, No.7 Sqn
MiG-17F	466 Black	?		D/D 1959, No.7 Sqn
MiG-17F	467 Black			D/D 1959, No.7 Sqn
MiG-17F	468 Black			D/D 1959, No.7 Sqn
MiG-17F	469 Black			D/D 1959, No.7 Sqn
MiG-17PF	458 Black			No.7 Sqn. Preserved Iraqi AF Museum, Baghdad; fake serial?
MiG-17PF	508 Black			D/D 1962, No.7 Sqn; first aircraft of the third batch delivered
MiG-17PF	509 Black			D/D 1962, No.7 Sqn
MiG-17PF	510 Black			D/D 1962, No.7 Sqn
MiG-17PF	511 Black			D/D 1962, No.7 Sqn
MiG-17PF	512 Black			D/D 1962, No.7 Sqn
MiG-17PF	513 Black			D/D 1962, No.7 Sqn; captured by Israel
MiG-17PF	514 Black			D/D 1962, No.7 Sqn; third type (pan-Arabic) fin flash
MiG-17PF	515 Black			D/D 1962, No.7 Sqn
MiG-17PF	516 Black			D/D 1962, No.7 Sqn
MiG-17PF	517 Black			D/D 1962, No.7 Sqn

MiG-19S	489 Black	?		Natural metal finish, second type (1959-63) green/white/black fin flash
MiG-19S	498 Black	?		Seen 1961
MiG-19S	499 Black	?		Seen 1961
MiG-19S	500 Black	?		Natural metal finish, second type (1959-63) green/white/black fin flash
MiG-19S	501 Black	?		No.9 Sqn
MiG-19S	502 Black	?		No.9 Sqn
MiG-19S	503 Black	?		No.9 Sqn
MiG-19S	504 Black	?		No.9 Sqn
MiG-19S	518 Black	?		No.9 Sqn
MiG-19S	519 Black	?		No.9 Sqn
MiG-19S	520 Black	?		No.9 Sqn
MiG-19S	521 Black	?		No.9 Sqn
MiG-19S	660 Black	?		Possibly F-6. Natural metal finish, third type (pan-Arabic) fin flash, named 'Basra'
MiG-21F-13	522 Black	74****		Derelict al-Taqaddum AB 2005
MiG-21F-13	523 Black	74****		No.11 Sqn
MiG-21F-13	524 Black	74****		
MiG-21F-13	525 Black	74****		No.11 Sqn
MiG-21F-13	526 Black	74****		
MiG-21F-13	527 Black	74****		
MiG-21F-13	528 Black	74****		No.11 Sqn
MiG-21F-13	529 Black	74****		No.11 Sqn
MiG-21F-13	530 Black	74****		No.11 Sqn
MiG-21F-13	531 Black	74****		No.11 Sqn
MiG-21F-13	532 Black	74****		No.11 Sqn
MiG-21F-13	533 Black	74****		No.11 Sqn
MiG-21F-13	533 Black	74****		
MiG-21F-13	534 Black	74****		No.11 Sqn. Hijacked to Israel 16-8-1966; tested by IDF/AF as '007' then despatched to the USA
MiG-21F-13	535 Black	74****		No.11 Sqn
MiG-21F-13	536 Black	74****		No.11 Sqn
MiG-21F-13	537 Black	74****		No.11 Sqn
MiG-21F-13	538 Black	74****		No.11 Sqn
MiG-21F-13	'706 Black'	74****		Preserved Iraqi Air Force Museum; probably fake serial as 706 belongs to the MiG-21PF serial block
MiG-21F-13	'709 Black'	74****		Gate guard at Shaibah AB with dummy installation of four AAMs; fake serial as 709 belongs to the MiG-21PF serial block
MiG-21F-13	21137 Black	74****		Derelict Tammuz 2003
MiG-21PF	...005 Black	?		Ex-East German Air Force? Noted 1990 impounded Dresden
MiG-21PF	...091 Black	?		Ex-East German Air Force? Noted 1990 impounded Dresden
MiG-21PF	...961 Black	?		Ex-East German Air Force? Noted 1990 impounded Dresden
MiG-21PF	?	760811		Ex-East German Air Force 862 Red. Noted 1990 impounded Dresden
MiG-21PF	?	760914		Ex-East German Air Force 870 Red. Noted 1990 impounded Dresden
MiG-21FL	539 Black	77****		D/D 1966
MiG-21FL	540 Black	77****		D/D 1966
MiG-21FL	541 Black	77****		D/D 1966
MiG-21FL	542 Black	77****		D/D 1966
MiG-21FL	543 Black	77****		D/D 1966
MiG-21FL	544 Black	77****		D/D 1966
MiG-21FL	545 Black	77****		D/D 1966
MiG-21FL	546 Black	77****		D/D 1966
MiG-21FL	547 Black	77****		D/D 1966
MiG-21FL	548 Black	77****		D/D 1966
MiG-21FL	549 Black	77****		D/D 1966
MiG-21FL	550 Black	77****		D/D 1966
MiG-21FL	551 Black	77****		D/D 1966
MiG-21FL	552 Black	77****		D/D 1966
MiG-21FL	553 Black	77****		D/D 1966
MiG-21FL	554 Black	77****		D/D 1966
MiG-21FL	555 Black	77****		D/D 1966

MiG-21FL	556 Black	77****		D/D 1966
MiG-21FL	557 Black	77****		D/D 1966
MiG-21FL	558 Black	77****		D/D 1966
MiG-21FL	559 Black	77****		D/D 1966
MiG-21FL	560 Black	77****		D/D 1966
MiG-21FL	561 Black	77****		D/D 1966
MiG-21FL	562 Black	77****		D/D 1966
MiG-21FL	563 Black	77****		D/D 1966
MiG-21FL	564 Black	77****		D/D 1966
MiG-21FL	565 Black	77****		D/D 1966
MiG-21FL	566 Black	77****		D/D 1966
MiG-21FL	665 Black	77****		D/D 1966; No.17 Sqn
MiG-21FL	666 Black	77****		D/D 1966
MiG-21FL	667 Black	77****		D/D 1966
MiG-21FL	668 Black	77****		D/D 1966; No.17 Sqn
MiG-21FL	669 Black	77****		D/D 1966
MiG-21FL	670 Black	77****		D/D 1966
MiG-21FL	671 Black	77****		D/D 1966
MiG-21FL	672 Black	77****		D/D 1966
MiG-21FL	673 Black	77****		D/D 1966
MiG-21FL	674 Black	77****		D/D 1966
MiG-21FL	675 Black	77****		D/D 1966
MiG-21FL	676 Black	77****		D/D 1966
MiG-21FL	677 Black	77****		D/D 1966
MiG-21FL	678 Black	77****		D/D 1966
MiG-21FL	679 Black	77****		D/D 1966
MiG-21FL	680 Black	77****		D/D 1966
MiG-21FL	681 Black	77****		D/D 1966
MiG-21FL	682 Black	77****		D/D 1966
MiG-21FL	683 Black	77****		D/D 1966
MiG-21FL	684 Black	77****		D/D 1966
MiG-21FL	703 Black	77****		D/D 1967. Also reported as a MiG-21PFM!
MiG-21FL	704 Black	77****		D/D 1967. Also reported as a MiG-21PFM!
MiG-21FL	705 Black	77****		D/D 1967. Also reported as a MiG-21PFM!
MiG-21FL	706 Black	77****		D/D 1967. Also reported as a MiG-21PFM!
MiG-21FL	707 Black	77****		D/D 1967. Also reported as a MiG-21PFM!
MiG-21FL	708 Black	77****		D/D 1967. Also reported as a MiG-21PFM!
MiG-21FL	709 Black	77****		D/D 1967. Also reported as a MiG-21PFM!
MiG-21FL	710 Black	77****		D/D 1967. Also reported as a MiG-21PFM!
MiG-21FL	711 Black	77****		D/D 1967. Also reported as a MiG-21PFM!
MiG-21FL	712 Black	77****		D/D 1967. Also reported as a MiG-21PFM!
MiG-21FL	713 Black	77****		D/D 1967. Also reported as a MiG-21PFM!
MiG-21FL	714 Black	77****		D/D 1967. Also reported as a MiG-21PFM!
MiG-21FL	715 Black	77****		D/D 1967. Also reported as a MiG-21PFM!
MiG-21FL	716 Black	77****		D/D 1967. Also reported as a MiG-21PFM!
MiG-21FL	717 Black	77****		D/D 1967. Also reported as a MiG-21PFM!
MiG-21FL	718 Black	77****		D/D 1967. Also reported as a MiG-21PFM!
MiG-21FL	719 Black	77****		D/D 1967. Also reported as a MiG-21PFM!
MiG-21FL	720 Black	77****		D/D 1967. Also reported as a MiG-21PFM!
MiG-21FL	721 Black	77****		D/D 1967. Also reported as a MiG-21PFM!
MiG-21FL	722 Black	77****		D/D 1967. Also reported as a MiG-21PFM!
MiG-21FL	723 Black	77****		D/D 1967. Also reported as a MiG-21PFM!
MiG-21FL	724 Black	77****		D/D 1967. Also reported as a MiG-21PFM!
MiG-21FL	725 Black	77****		D/D 1967. Also reported as a MiG-21PFM!
MiG-21FL	726 Black	77****		D/D 1967. Also reported as a MiG-21PFM!
MiG-21FL	727 Black	77****		D/D 1967. Also reported as a MiG-21PFM!
MiG-21FL	728 Black	77****		D/D 1967. Also reported as a MiG-21PFM!
MiG-21FL	729 Black	77****		D/D 1967. Also reported as a MiG-21PFM!

MiG-21FL	730 Black	77****		D/D 1967. Also reported as a MiG-21PFM!
MiG-21FL	731 Black	77****		D/D 1967. Also reported as a MiG-21PFM!
MiG-21FL	732 Black	77****		D/D 1967. Also reported as a MiG-21PFM!
MiG-21FL	733 Black	77****		D/D 1967. Also reported as a MiG-21PFM!
MiG-21FL	734 Black	77****		D/D 1967. Also reported as a MiG-21PFM!
MiG-21FL	21111 Black	77****		Camouflaged. Seen derelict in Iraq
MiG-21FL	21112 Black	?		Serial obliterated. Captured in damaged condition by Allied forces during Operation *Desert Storm*
MiG-21FL	21113 Black	77****		Noted 2004 Mosul AB
MiG-21FL	21114 White	77****		Painted black overall, serial applied as 1114, '9705055' painted on tail. Noted 2006 derelict Mosul AB
MiG-21FL	21115 Black	77****		Gate guard at (former) Saddam AB, natural metal finish
MiG-21PFM	702 Black	?		No.9 Sqn
MiG-21PFM	735 Black	?		
MiG-21PFM	736 Black	?		
MiG-21PFM	737 Black	?		
MiG-21PFM	82... Black	?		
MiG-21PFM	681 Black	?		Also reported as a MiG-21FL!
MiG-21PFM	863 Black	?		No.17 Sqn, natural metal finish
MiG-21PFM	21097 Black	?		Seen derelict minus rear fuselage, location unknown
MiG-21PFM	21124 Black	?		Sand/tan camouflage
MiG-21PFM	21127 Black	?		Derelict 2003
MiG-21PFMA	?	947007		Ex-East German Air Force '8711 Red', actually 474 Red Earmarked for export to Iraq 1989 but not delivered, scrapped
MiG-21R	1827 Black	?		Natural metal finish
MiG-21R	21302 Black	?		Tan/green camouflage. Destroyed by US forces at Ali Ibn Abu Talib AB 1991
MiG-21MF	657 Black	?	?	
MiG-21MF	658 Black	?	?	
MiG-21MF	659 Black	?	?	
MiG-21MF	660 Black	?	?	
MiG-21MF	661 Black	?	?	
MiG-21MF	662 Black	?	?	
MiG-21MF	663 Black	?	?	
MiG-21MF	664 Black	?	?	
MiG-21MF	665 Black	?	?	Also reported as a MiG-21FL!
MiG-21MF	666 Black	?	?	Also reported as a MiG-21FL!
MiG-21MF	667 Black	?	?	Also reported as a MiG-21FL!
MiG-21MF	668 Black	?	?	Also reported as a MiG-21FL!
MiG-21MF	669 Black	?	?	Also reported as a MiG-21FL!
MiG-21MF	670 Black	?	?	Also reported as a MiG-21FL!
MiG-21MF	671 Black	?	?	Also reported as a MiG-21FL!
MiG-21MF	672 Black	?	?	Also reported as a MiG-21FL!
MiG-21MF	673 Black	?	?	Also reported as a MiG-21FL!
MiG-21MF	674 Black	?	?	Also reported as a MiG-21FL!
MiG-21MF	675 Black	?	?	Also reported as a MiG-21FL!
MiG-21MF	676 Black	?	?	Also reported as a MiG-21FL!
MiG-21MF	677 Black	?	?	Also reported as a MiG-21FL!
MiG-21MF	678 Black	?	?	Also reported as a MiG-21FL!
MiG-21MF	679 Black	?	?	Also reported as a MiG-21FL!
MiG-21MF	680 Black	?	?	Also reported as a MiG-21FL!
MiG-21MF	681 Black	?		Also reported as a MiG-21FL! No.17 Sqn. Fought in Syria 1973, noted at al-Hurryiah AB 1980
MiG-21MF	682 Black	?		Also reported as a MiG-21FL! No.17 Sqn. Fought in Syria 1973, noted at al-Hurryiah AB 1980
MiG-21MF	683 Black	?	?	Also reported as a MiG-21FL!
MiG-21MF	684 Black	?	?	Also reported as a MiG-21FL!
MiG-21MF	685 Black	?	?	
MiG-21MF	686 Black	?	?	
MiG-21MF	687 Black	?	?	
MiG-21MF	688 Black	?	?	
MiG-21MF	689 Black	?	?	
MiG-21MF	690 Black	?	?	

MiG-21MF	691 Black	?	?	
MiG-21MF	692 Black	?	?	
MiG-21MF	693 Black	?	?	
MiG-21MF	694 Black	?	?	
MiG-21MF	695 Black	?	?	
MiG-21MF	696 Black	?	?	
MiG-21MF	818 Black	?		D/D 1971
MiG-21MF	819 Black	?		D/D 1971
MiG-21MF	820 Black	?		D/D 1971
MiG-21MF	821 Black	?		D/D 1971
MiG-21MF	822 Black	?		D/D 1971
MiG-21MF	823 Black	?		D/D 1971
MiG-21MF	824 Black	?		D/D 1971
MiG-21MF	825 Black	?		D/D 1971
MiG-21MF	826 Black	?		D/D 1971
MiG-21MF	827 Black	?		D/D 1971
MiG-21MF	828 Black	?		D/D 1971
MiG-21MF	829 Black	?		D/D 1971
MiG-21MF	830 Black	?		D/D 1971
MiG-21MF	831 Black	?		D/D 1971
MiG-21MF	832 Black	?		D/D 1971
MiG-21MF	833 Black	?		D/D 1971
MiG-21MF	1019 Black	?		D/D 1971
MiG-21MF	1051 Black	?		D/D 1971
MiG-21MF	1099 Black	?		Tan/green camouflage
MiG-21MF	1181 Black	?		Tan/green camouflage
MiG-21MF	1184 Black	?		Tan/green camouflage
MiG-21MF	1190 Black	?		Tan/green camouflage
MiG-21MF	1195 Black	?		
MiG-21MF	1232 Black	?		Tan/green camouflage
MiG-21MF	4901 Black?	?	?	
MiG-21MF	4902 Black?	?	?	
MiG-21MF	4903 Black?	?	?	
MiG-21MF	4904 Black?	?	?	
MiG-21MF	4905 Black?	?	?	
MiG-21MF	4906 Black?	?	?	
MiG-21MF	4907 Black?	?	?	
MiG-21MF	4908 Black?	?	?	
MiG-21MF	4909 Black?	?	?	
MiG-21MF	4910 Black?	?	?	
MiG-21MF	21158 Black	?	?	Tan/green camouflage. Derelict Tammuz 2003
MiG-21MF	21178 Black	?	?	Tan/green camouflage. Destroyed 1991
MiG-21MF	21182 Black	?	?	Tan/green camouflage. Derelict Habbaniya AB
MiG-21MF	?	N96011507	96-09-**?	Impounded Dresden 11-1990, Works Job No.8715
MiG-21*bis*	4097 Black	N750*****	?	
MiG-21*bis*	21138 Black	N750*****	?	Impounded/stored Moma Stanojlović aircraft repair plant, Batajnica 1997
MiG-21*bis*	21158 Black	N750*****	?	Derelict Habbaniya in 2006
MiG-21*bis*	21168 Black	N750*****	?	Impounded/stored Batajnica 1997
MiG-21*bis*	21173 Black	N750*****	?	Noted 2003 al-Taqaddum AB (also reported as Tammuz)
MiG-21*bis*	21174 Black	N750*****	?	Impounded/stored Moma Stanojlović aircraft repair plant, Batajnica 1997
MiG-21*bis*	21177 Black	N750*****	?	Impounded/stored Moma Stanojlović aircraft repair plant, Batajnica 1997
MiG-21*bis*	21178 Black	N750*****	?	Tan/green camouflage. Captured by US forces at Ali Ibn Abu Talib AB 1991
MiG-21*bis*	21186 Black	N750*****	?	Impounded/stored Moma Stanojlović aircraft repair plant, Batajnica 1997
MiG-21*bis*	21190 Black	N750*****	?	Impounded/stored Moma Stanojlović aircraft repair plant, Batajnica 1997
MiG-21*bis*	21195 Black	N750*****	?	Seen wfu al-Taqaddum AB 2003
MiG-21*bis*	21196 Black	N750*****	?	Seen wfu al-Taqaddum AB 2003
MiG-21*bis*	21198 Black	N750*****	?	Impounded/stored Moma Stanojlović aircraft repair plant, Batajnica 1997
MiG-21*bis*	21202 Black	N750*****	?	Seen wfu al-Taqaddum AB 2003

MiG-21*bis*	21204 Black	N750*****	?	Impounded/stored Moma Stanojlović aircraft repair plant, Batajnica 1997
MiG-21*bis*	21206 Black	N750*****	?	Impounded/stored Moma Stanojlović aircraft repair plant, Batajnica 1997
MiG-21*bis*	21208 Black	N750*****	?	Derelict 2003
MiG-21*bis*	21216 Black	N750*****	?	Derelict 2003
MiG-21*bis*	21221 Black	N750*****	?	Derelict 2003
MiG-21*bis*	21230 Black	N75093445	75-66-**?	Noted Habbaniya 2005 derelict
MiG-21*bis*	21231 Black	N750*****	?	Noted Habbaniya 2005 derelict
MiG-21*bis*	21233 Black	N750*****	?	Noted Habbaniya 2004
MiG-21*bis*	21240 Black	N750*****	?	Noted Habbaniya 2005 derelict
MiG-21*bis*	21250 Black	N750*****	?	Noted Habbaniya 2005
MiG-21*bis*	21252 Black	N750*****	?	Noted wfu Tammuz 2005
MiG-21*bis*	21256 Black	N750*****	?	Noted Habbaniya 2005
MiG-21*bis*	21261 Black	N750*****	?	
MiG-21*bis*	21262 Black	N750*****	?	Seen wfu al-Taqaddum AB 2003
MiG-21*bis*	21285 Black	N750*****	?	Impounded/stored Moma Stanojlović aircraft repair plant, Batajnica 1998
MiG-21*bis*	21286 Black	N750*****	?	Impounded/stored Moma Stanojlović aircraft repair plant, Batajnica 1997
MiG-21*bis*	?	N75070101	?	Impounded Dresden 11-1990, Works Job No.8137
MiG-21*bis*	?	N75093067	75-66-**?	Impounded Dresden 11-1990, Works Job No.8136
MiG-21*bis*	?	N75093463	75-66-**?	Impounded Dresden 11-1990 with Works Job No.8138
MiG-21U	?	663316		Broad-chord fin (*izdeliye* 66-600). impounded Dresden 1991, ex-East German Air Force 278 Black; earmarked for sale to Iraq but cancelled
MiG-21U	?	664718		Broad-chord fin (*izdeliye* 66-600). impounded Dresden 1991, ex-East German Air Force 291 Black; earmarked for sale to Iraq but cancelled
MiG-21US	?	05685147		Impounded Dresden 11-1990, Works Job No.8708
MiG-21US	?	04685150		Impounded Dresden 11-1990, Works Job No.8807
MiG-21US	5844 Black	07685154		Impounded Dresden 11-1990, Works Job No.8806
MiG-21UM	21022 Black	?		
MiG-21UM	21023 Black	?		Destroyed 1991
MiG-21UM	21027 Black	?		Wfu al Qadisiyah
MiG-21UM	21038 Black	?		Tan/green camouflage. Wfu al Qadisiyah
MiG-21UM	21040 Black	?		Wfu al-Taqaddum AB
MiG-21UM	21045 Black	?		Seen in 2006
MiG-21UM	21054 Black	?		
MiG-21UM	21057 Black	?		Wfu al-Taqaddum AB
MiG-21UM	21062 Black	?		
MiG-21UM	21068 Black	516999436	?	Impounded Dresden 11-1990, Works Job No.8235
MiG-21UM	21069 Black	?		
MiG-21UM	21072 Black	?		
MiG-21UM	21073 Black	?		
MiG-21UM	21091 Black	?		Tan/brown camouflage. Wfu Habbaniya
MiG-21UM	?	05695155		Impounded Dresden 11-1990, Works Job No.8237
MiG-21UM	?	516969066	?	Impounded Dresden 11-1990, Works Job No.8236
MiG-21UM	?	516975046	?	Impounded Dresden 11-1990, Works Job No.8238
Chengdu F-7B	1511 Black	?		Found 2003 in the desert, 150 km south of Baghdad; sand/green camouflage
Chengdu F-7B	1598?	?		Possible confusion with 6578 due to faded paintwork
Chengdu F-7B	6574	?		Became, see next line
	21603 Black			Seen wfu al-Taqaddum AB 2003
Chengdu F-7B	6577	?		Became, see next line
	21606 Black			Seen wfu al-Taqaddum AB 2003
Chengdu F-7B	6578 White	?		Green/brown/tan camouflage. Became, see next line
	21607 Black			Derelict al-Taqaddum AB 2003 with the serial 21607 hand-written over the original serial
Chengdu F-7B	8574 Black	?		Shot down ?-2-1988
Chengdu F-7B	21507 Black	?		Green/brown/tan camouflage.
Chengdu F-7B	21511 Black	?		Seen wfu al-Taqaddum AB 2003
Chengdu F-7B	21539 Black	?		Seen wfu al-Taqaddum AB 2003
Chengdu F-7B	21561 Black	?		Seen wfu al-Taqaddum AB 2003
Chengdu F-7B	21566 Black	?		Seen wfu al-Taqaddum AB 2003
Chengdu F-7B	21589 Black	?		Green/brown/tan camouflage. Pre-1988 serial unknown; seen derelict

Guizhou FT-7B	21071 Black	?		Seen wfu al-Taqaddum AB 2003
Guizhou FT-7B	21074 Black	?		Seen wfu al-Taqaddum AB 2003, reported in error as MiG-21UM
Guizhou FT-7B	21078 Black	?		Seen wfu al-Taqaddum AB 2003
Guizhou FT-7B	21079 Black	?		Seen wfu al-Taqaddum AB 2004
Guizhou FT-7B	21088 Black	?		Seen wfu al-Taqaddum AB 2005
MiG-23MS	1041 Black	?		D/D 1974, first batch
MiG-23MS	1428 Black	?		D/D 1976, second batch
MiG-23MS	1449 Black	?		No.39 Sqn, unit CO's aircraft.
MiG-23MS	1618 Black	?		D/D 1976, second batch
MiG-23MS	2217 Black	?		
MiG-23MS	4012 Black	124004012		D/D 1974. No.39 Sqn. Tan/green/brown camouflage, serial in Arab characters on nose and European characters on tail. Became, see next line
	23103 Black			No.39 Sqn, later No.59 Sqn
MiG-23MS	4049 Black	0391204049	?	D/D 1975; No.23 Sqn, later No.84 Sqn, sand/green/brown camouflage
MiG-23MS	23018 Black	?		
MiG-23MS	23047 Black	?		
MiG-23MS	23049 Black	?		
MiG-23MS	23105 Black	?		No.59 Sqn. Derelict
MiG-23MF	23114 Black	03902*****	?	Captured by US forces at al-Bakr AB 2003
MiG-23MF	23117 Black	03902*****	?	Captured by US forces 2003
MiG-23MF	23121 Black	03902*****	?	Captured by US forces 2003
MiG-23MF	23124 Black	03902*****	?	Captured by US forces 2003
MiG-23MF	23126 Black	03902*****	?	Destroyed by US forces at al-Bakr AB 2003
MiG-23MF	23127 Black	03902*****	?	Captured by US forces 2003
MiG-23MF	23132 Black	03902*****	?	Captured by US forces at al-Bakr AB 2003
MiG-23MF	23134 Black	03902*****	?	Captured by US forces at al-Bakr AB 2003
MiG-23MF	23136 Black	03902*****	?	Captured by US forces at al-Bakr AB 2003
MiG-23MF	23167 Black	03902*****	?	No.39 Sqn
MiG-23MF?	23181 Black	?	?	Destroyed in 1992, version not 100% sure
MiG-23MF	?	0390220215	?	Based Balad
MiG-23MF	?	0390220222	?	Based Balad
MiG-23MF	?	0390220223	?	Based Balad
MiG-23MF	?	0390221055	?	
MiG-23MLA	23200 Black	29603*****	?	Captured by US forces 2003
MiG-23MLA	23252 Black	29603*****	?	Updated to carry AM39 Exocet missiles
MiG-23MLA	23254 Black	29603*****	?	
MiG-23MLA	23255 Black	29603*****	?	
MiG-23MLA	23269 Black	2960325056	17530	Preserved Belgrade Aviation Museum, Serbia
MiG-23MLA	23270 Black	29603*****	?	Sand/green/dark green camouflage. Captured by US forces 2003
MiG-23MLA	23272 Black	2960325305	17***	Captured by US forces 2003
MiG-23MLA	23273 Black	29603*****	?	Additional ASO-2 flare dispensers. Captured by US forces 2003
MiG-23MLA	23278 Black	29603*****	?	
MiG-23MLA	23281 Black	29603*****	?	Captured by US forces at Qadisiya 2003
MiG-23MLA	23282 Black	29603*****	?	
MiG-23MLA	23285 Black	29603*****	?	Flown to Iran 1-1991
MiG-23MLA	23286 Black	29603*****	?	Flown to Iran 1-1991
MiG-23MLA	23287 Black	29603*****	?	Captured by US forces 2003
MiG-23MLA	23294 Black	29603*****	?	Flown to Iran 1-1991
MiG-23MLA	23295 Black	29603*****	?	Flown to Iran 1-1991
MiG-23MLA	23299 Black	29603*****	?	Flown to Iran 1-1991
MiG-23MLA	23306 Black	29603*****	?	Flown to Iran 1-1991
MiG-23MLA	23307 Black	29603*****	?	Flown to Iran 1-1991
MiG-23MLA	23372 Black	29603*****	?	
MiG-23MLA	?	2960324884	174**	
MiG-23MLA	?	2960325061	1761*	
MiG-23MLA	?	2960325326	17***	
MiG-23MLA	?	2960325337	17***	

MiG-23BN	1427 Black	03932*****	?	
MiG-23BN	1428 Black	0393211428	67**	No.29 Sqn
MiG-23BN	23070 Black	03932*****	?	Destroyed Tallil AB
MiG-23BN	23072 Black	03932*****	?	Captured by US forces 2003
MiG-23BN	23081 Black	03932*****	?	Captured by US forces 2003
MiG-23BN	23086 Black	03932*****	?	Captured by US forces 2003
MiG-23BN	23104 Black	03932*****	?	Captured by US forces 2003
MiG-23BN	23151 Black	03932*****	?	Wreck at Balad AB
MiG-23BN	23160 Black	0393202545	?	Wreck at Tallil AB
MiG-23BN	23163 Black	03932*****	?	Flown to Iran 1-1991
MiG-23BN	23166 Black	03932*****	?	Derelict
MiG-23BN	23168 Black	03932*****	?	Wreck at Balad AB
MiG-23BN	23169 Black	03932*****	?	Flown to Iran 1-1991
MiG-23BN	23170 Black	03932*****	?	Flown to Iran 1-1991
MiG-23BN	23171 Black	03932*****	?	Destroyed on ground by Allied air strike
MiG-23BN	23172 Black	03932*****	?	Destroyed Tallil AB 1991
MiG-23BN	23173 Black	03932*****	?	Sand/green/brown camouflage, fitted with IFR probe
MiG-23BN	23176 Black	03932*****	?	Captured by US forces 2003
MiG-23BN	23178 Black	03932*****	?	Destroyed Tallil AB 1991
MiG-23BN	23179 Black	03932*****	?	
MiG-23BN	23181 Black	2963222369	9***	Destroyed 1991
MiG-23BN	23182 Black	03932*****	?	
MiG-23BN	23183 Black	03932*****	?	Flown to Iran 1-1991, damaged on landing
MiG-23BN	23185 Black	03932*****	?	Captured by US forces 2003
MiG-23BN	23186 Black	03932*****	?	Captured by US forces 2003
MiG-23BN	?	0393202525	?	
MiG-23UB	1674 Black	B103****	?	Derelict Tammuz, 2003
MiG-23UB	1675 Black	B1037408?	?	Derelict Tammuz, 2003
MiG-23UB	23000 Black	B103****	?	
MiG-23UB	23001 Black	B103****	?	
MiG-23UB	23002 Black	B103****	?	
MiG-23UB	23003 Black	B103****	?	
MiG-23UB	23004 Black	B103****	?	Destroyed on ground by Allied air strike
MiG-23UB	23019 Black	B103****	?	
MiG-23UB	23020 Black	B103****	?	
MiG-23UB	23021 Black	B103****	?	Wreck at Tallil AB
MiG-23UB	23022 Black	B103****	?	
MiG-23UB	23023 Black	B103****	?	
MiG-23UB?	23032 Black	B103****	?	
MiG-23UB	23033 Black	B103****	?	Sand/green/brown camouflage
MiG-23UB	23300 Black	B103****	?	
MiG-25PDS	25201 Black	N840*****	?	Destroyed by air raid at al-Taqaddum AB
MiG-25PDS	25202 Black	N840*****	?	Destroyed at Ali Ibn Abu Talib AB
MiG-25PDS	25203? Black	N840*****	?	Existence not confirmed but likely
MiG-25PDS	25204 Black	N840*****	?	Retrofitted with BVP-30-26M flare dispensers?
MiG-25PDS	25205 Black	N840*****	?	Destroyed at al-Taqaddum AB
MiG-25PDS	25206 Black?	N840*****	?	Existence not confirmed but likely
MiG-25PDS	25207 Black?	N840*****	?	Existence not confirmed but likely
MiG-25PDS	25208 Black?	N840*****	?	Existence not confirmed but likely
MiG-25PDS	25209 Black?	N840*****	?	Existence not confirmed but likely
MiG-25PDS	25210 Black?	N840*****	?	Existence not confirmed but likely
MiG-25PDS	25211 Black	N840*****	?	Wfu Balad; captured by US Army
MiG-25PDS	25212 Black	N840*****	?	Captured by US Army
MiG-25PDS	25213 Black?	N840*****	?	Existence not confirmed but likely
MiG-25PDS	25214 Black?	N840*****	?	Existence not confirmed but likely
MiG-25PDS	25215 Black?	N840*****	?	Existence not confirmed but likely
MiG-25PDS	25216 Black	N840*****	?	

MiG-25RB	25101 Black	N840*****	?	Retrofitted with BVP-30-26M flare dispensers?
MiG-25RB	25102 Black?	N840*****	?	Existence not confirmed but likely
MiG-25RB	25103 Black	N840*****	?	Wfu Tammuz; also reported as MiG-25RBT
MiG-25RB	25104 Black	N840*****	?	Wfu Tammuz; also reported as MiG-25RBT
MiG-25RBT	2125 Black	N020*****	?	Pre-1988 serial
MiG-25RBT	25105 Black	N02020687	?	Captured intact by US Army at al-Taqaddum AB; preserved USAF Museum
MiG-25RBT	25106 Black	N020*****	?	Wfu al-Taqaddum AB, captured by US forces
MiG-25RBT	25107 Black	N020*****	?	Wfu Tammuz, captured by US forces
MiG-25RBT	25108 Black	N020*****	?	
MiG-25RBT	25109 Black	N020*****	?	Wfu al-Taqaddum AB
MiG-25PU	25001 Black	N220*****	?	Derelict al-Taqaddum AB, damaged
MiG-25PU	25002 Black	N220*****	?	Derelict al-Taqaddum AB, damaged
MiG-25PU	25003 Black	N220*****	?	Derelict Hamedan, Iran
MiG-25PU	2500* Black	N220*****	?	Crashed 1-1991 while attempting to flee to Iran
MiG-25PU	2500* Black	N220*****	?	Crashed 2000 due to fuel starvation
MiG-29	29030 Black	29605*****	?	
MiG-29	29032 Black	29605*****	?	Flown to Iran 1-1991; to IRIAF 3-6132
MiG-29	29038 Black	29605*****	?	Flown to Iran 1-1991; to IRIAF 3-6133
MiG-29	29040 Black	2960521830	?	Wfu Tammuz
MiG-29	29044 Black	29605*****	?	Flown to Iran 1-1991; to IRIAF 3-6104
MiG-29	29050 Black	29605*****	?	
MiG-29	29056 Black	29605*****	?	
MiG-29	29059 Black	29605*****	?	
MiG-29	29060 Black	29605*****	?	
MiG-29	29061 Black	29605*****	?	
MiG-29	29062 Black	2960522994	?	
MiG-29	29063 Black	29605*****	?	Wfu Tammuz
MiG-29	29072 Black	29605*****	?	Wfu al-Taqaddum AB
MiG-29	290** Black	2960521843		
MiG-29	290** Black	2960521844		
MiG-29	290** Black	2960521845		
MiG-29	290** Black	2960522311		
MiG-29	290** Black	2960522312		
MiG-29UB	29004 Black	N509030*****	?	Flown to Iran 1-1991; to IRIAF 3-6307
Mi-2R	5600	529448115		
Mi-2R	5601	529449115		
Mi-2R	5602	529450115		
Mi-2T	5603	519501115		
Mi-2T	5604	519502115		
Mi-2T	5605	519503115		
Mi-2T	5606	519504115		
Mi-2T	5607	519505115		
Mi-2R	?	528920114		
Mi-2R	?	528921114		
Mi-2R	?	528922114		
Mi-2P	?	539521115		
Mi-2P	?	539522115		
Mi-2P	?	539523115		
Mi-2P	?	539524115		
Mi-4	478	?		Derelict Tallil
Mi-4	481	?		Derelict Tallil
Mi-6	1098	?		Derelict Shaibah
Mi-8T	200 Black	226200	?	To Hungarian Air Force 6200 Red in 1992

Mi-8T	204 Black	226204	?	To Hungarian Air Force 6204 Red in 1992
Mi-8T	206 Black	226206	?	To Hungarian Air Force 6206 Red in 1992
Mi-8T	207 Black	226207	?	To Hungarian Air Force 6207 Red in 1992
Mi-8T	212 Black	226212	?	To Hungarian Air Force 6212 Red in 1992
Mi-8T	215 Black	226215	?	To Hungarian Air Force 6215 Red in 1992
Mi-8T	220 Black	226220	?	To Hungarian Air Force 6220 Red in 1992
Mi-8T	223 Black	226223	?	To Hungarian Air Force 6223 Red in 1992
Mi-8T	641 Black	22641?	?	
Mi-8T	650 Black	22650?	?	
Mi-8T	651 Black	22651?	?	
Mi-8T	656 Black	22656?	?	
Mi-8T	687 Black	22687?	?	
Mi-8PPA	25 Black	?	?	
Mi-17	1435 Black	226M174	?	Captured by US forces in Kuwait, to the USA; serial may be fake
Mi-17	4433 Black	226M**	?	Wreck at Tallil
Mi-17	4435 Black	226M**	?	
Mi-17	4475 Black	226M**	?	
Mi-17	4480 Black	226M**	?	
Mi-17	5653 Black	226M**	?	
Mi-17	5659 Black	226M**	?	
Mi-17	5733 Black	226M**	?	
Mi-17	5789 Black	226M**	?	
Mi-17	5853 Black	226M**	?	
Mi-17	5858 Black	226M**	?	Wreck at Shaibah
Mi-17	5872 Black	226M**	?	
Mi-17	5874 Black	226M**	?	
Mi-17	5963 Black	226M**	?	
Mi-17	8324 Black	226M**	?	
Mi-17	?	226M160	?	Captured by US forces
Mi-25	2110 Black?	?	?	Also reported as 3110!
Mi-25	2119 Black	?	?	
Mi-25	3118 Black?	?	?	Also reported as 2118; derelict at Taji AB
Mi-25	3128 Black	...09560	?	Flown to Iran; preserved Saadabad
Mi-25	4424 Black?	?	?	
Mi-25	4493 Black	?	?	Captured by US Army and shipped to the USA
Mi-25	4496 Black	760332	?	Captured by US Army and shipped to the USA, later preserved at US Army Museum
Mi-25	?	...09562	?	Captured by US Army and shipped to the USA
Su-7BMK	755 Black	?		D/D 10-67, natural metal finish
Su-7BMK	756 Black	?		D/D 10-67
Su-7BMK	757 Black	?		D/D 10-67
Su-7BMK	758 Black	?		D/D 10-67
Su-7BMK	759 Black	?		D/D 10-67
Su-7BMK	760 Black	?		D/D 10-67
Su-7BMK	761 Black	?		D/D 10-67
Su-7BMK	762 Black	?		D/D 10-67
Su-7BMK	763 Black	?		D/D 10-67
Su-7BMK	764 Black	?		D/D 10-67
Su-7BMK	765 Black	?		D/D 10-67
Su-7BMK	766 Black	?		D/D 10-67
Su-7BMK	767 Black	?		D/D 10-67
Su-7BMK	768 Black	?		D/D 10-67
Su-7BMK	769 Black	?		D/D 10-67, camouflaged
Su-7BMK	770 Black	?		D/D 10-67
Su-7BMK	771 Black	?		D/D 10-67
Su-7BMK	772 Black	?		D/D 10-67
Su-7BMK	773 Black	?		D/D 10-67

Su-7BMK	774 Black	?		D/D 10-67
Su-7BMK	808 Black	?		D/D 10-68
Su-7BMK	809 Black	?		D/D 10-68
Su-7BMK	810 Black	?		D/D 10-68
Su-7BMK	811 Black	?		D/D 10-68
Su-7BMK	812 Black	?		D/D 10-68
Su-7BMK	813 Black	?		D/D 10-68
Su-7BMK	814 Black	?		D/D 10-68
Su-7BMK	813 Black	?		D/D 10-68
Su-7BMK	814 Black	?		D/D 10-68
Su-7BMK	815 Black	?		D/D 10-68
Su-7BMK	816 Black	?		D/D 10-68
Su-7BMK	817 Black	?		D/D 10-68
Su-7BMK	870 Black	?		D/D 1969
Su-7BMK	871 Black	?		D/D 1969
Su-7BMK	881 Black	?		D/D 1969
Su-7BMK	883 Black?	?		D/D 1969; existence not confirmed
Su-7BMK	884 Black	?		D/D 1969
Su-7BMK	885 Black	?		D/D 1969
Su-7BMK	886 Black	?		D/D 1969
Su-7BMK	887 Black	?		D/D 1969
Su-7BMK	888 Black	?		D/D 1969
Su-7BMK	889 Black	?		D/D 1969
Su-7BMK	890 Black	?		D/D 1969
Su-7BMK	891 Black	?		D/D 1969
Su-7BMK	892 Black	?		D/D 1969
Su-7BMK	893 Black	?		D/D 1969
Su-7BMK	894 Black	?		D/D 1969
Su-7BMK	895 Black	?		D/D 1969
Su-7BMK	896 Black	?		D/D 1969
Su-7BMK	897 Black	?		D/D 1969
Su-7BMK	898 Black	?		D/D 1969
Su-7BMK	977 Black?	?		Existence not confirmed
Su-7BMK	978 Black	?		Not delivered?
Su-7BMK	979 Black	?		Not delivered?
Su-7BMK	980 Black	?		Not delivered?
Su-7BMK	981 Black	?		Not delivered?
Su-7BMK	982 Black	?		Not delivered?
Su-7BMK	983 Black	?		Not delivered?
Su-7BMK	984 Black	?		Not delivered?
Su-7BMK	985 Black	?		Not delivered?
Su-7BMK	986 Black	?		Not delivered?
Su-7BMK	987 Black	?		Not delivered?
Su-7BMK	988 Black	?		Not delivered?
Su-7BMK	989 Black	?		Not delivered?
Su-7BMK	990 Black	?		Not delivered?
Su-7BMK	991 Black	?		Not delivered?
Su-7BMK	992 Black	?		Not delivered?
Su-7BMK	993 Black	?		Not delivered?
Su-7BMK	994 Black	?		Not delivered?
Su-7BMK	995 Black	?		Not delivered?
Su-7BMK	996 Black	?		Not delivered?
Su-7BMK	997 Black	?		Not delivered?
Su-7BMK	998 Black	?		Not delivered?
Su-7BMK	999 Black	?		Not delivered?
Su-7BMK	1000 Black	?		Not delivered?
Su-7BMK	1227 Black	?		Not delivered?
Su-7BMK	1228 Black	?		Not delivered?

Su-7BMK	1229 Black	?		Not delivered?
Su-7BMK	1230 Black	?		Not delivered?
Su-7BMK	7042 Black	?		Reserialled under 1988 serial system showing type
Su-20	1162 Black	?		D/D 1973
Su-20	1163 Black	?		D/D 1973
Su-20	1164 Black	?		D/D 1973
Su-20	1166 Black	?		D/D 1973
Su-20	1167 Black	?		D/D 1973
Su-20	1168 Black	?		D/D 1973
Su-20	1170 Black	?		D/D 1973
Su-20	1173 Black	?		D/D 1973
Su-20	1203 Black	?		No.1 Sqn. Sand/olive drab camouflage
Su-20	1295 Black	?		D/D 1973
Su-20	1297 Black	?		D/D 1973
Su-20	1298 Black	?		D/D 1973
Su-20	1300 Black	?		D/D 1973
Su-20	1303 Black	?		D/D 1973. No.1 Sqn. Sand/olive drab camouflage
Su-20	1315 Black	?		D/D 1973
Su-20	1356 Black	?		D/D 1973
Su-20	1374 Black?	?		Also reported as 1574; D/D 1976
Su-22	2050 Black	?		Became, see next line
	20503 Black	?		Captured by US forces 2003 during the Second Gulf War
Su-20	20501 Black	?		Captured by US forces 2003. Sand/olive drab camouflage
Su-20	20502 Black	?		Captured by US forces 2003
Su-20	20505 Black	?		Captured by US forces 2003
Su-20	20507 Black	?		Captured by US forces 2003
Su-20	20508 Black	?		Fled to Iran during the Gulf War, damaged on landing
Su-20	20511 Black	?		Ex-2051. Captured by US forces 2003
Su-20	20512 Black	?		Fled to Iran 1991, damaged on landing
Su-20	20513 Black	?		Fled to Iran 1991, damaged on landing
Su-20	20514 Black	?		Fled to Iran 1991, damaged on landing
Su-20	20520 Black	?		Derelict at Kirkuk 2003. Sand/olive drab camouflage
Su-20	20525 Black	?		Captured by US forces 2003 during the Second Gulf War
Su-22	1107 Black	?		
Su-22	1108 Black	?		
Su-22	1109 Black	?		
Su-22	1374 Black	?		
Su-22	2051 Black	?		Became, see next line
	22511 Black			Captured by US forces 2003 at Tammuz during the Second Gulf War
Su-22	2076 Black	?		Became, see next line
	22588 Black	?		Derelict at Habbaniya 2003
Su-22	2077 Black	?		No.44 Sqn. Sand/olive drab camouflage
Su-22	2079 Black	?		No.44 Sqn. Sand/olive drab camouflage
Su-22	2157 Black	?		Became, see next line
	22596 Black	?		Derelict at Habbaniya 2003
Su-22R	2250 Black	?		No.44 Sqn. Sand/olive drab camouflage
Su-22M	1584 Black	?		Shot down near Basra 2-84
Su-22M	1736 Black	?		Shot down over Khuzestan Province in the 1980s
Su-22M	1836 Black	?		No.5 or No.69 Sqn. Sand/olive drab camouflage
Su-22M	2021 Black	?		
Su-22M	2026 Black	?		Dark green/dark earth camouflage
Su-22M	2574 Black	?		Dark green/dark earth camouflage. Shot down over Iran ?-2-1986
Su-22M	22541 Black	?		Dark green/dark earth camouflage
Su-22M	22607 Black	?		Fled to Iran 1991
Su-22M	22615 Black	?		Destroyed by Allied troops 2003 at Tammuz during the Second Gulf War

Su-22M	22619 Black	?		Fled to Iran 1991
Su-22M	22620 Black	?		Fled to Iran 1991, damaged on landing
Su-22M	22634 Black	?		Fled to Iran 1991
Su-22M	22635 Black	?		Fled to Iran 1991, damaged on landing
Su-22M	22654 Black	?		Fled to Iran 1991
Su-22M	22658 Black	?		Fled to Iran 1991
Su-22M	22659 Black	?		Fled to Iran 1991
Su-22M	22660 Black	?		Fled to Iran 1991
Su-22M	22661 Black	?		Fled to Iran 1991
Su-22M	22663 Black	?		Fled to Iran 1991, damaged on landing
Su-22M	22670 Black	?		Fled to Iran 1991
Su-22M	22671 Black	?		Fled to Iran 1991
Su-22M	22672 Black	?		Fled to Iran 1991
Su-22M4	22540 Black	?		Fled to Iran 1991
Su-22M4	22541 Black	?		Fled to Iran 1991
Su-22M4	22545 Black	?		Fled to Iran 1991
Su-22M4	22546 Black	?		Fled to Iran 1991, damaged on landing
Su-22M4	22549 Black	?		Fled to Iran 1991
Su-22M4	22554 Black	?		Fled to Iran 1991, damaged on landing
Su-22M4	22555 Black	?		Fled to Iran 1991
Su-22M4	22557 Black	?		Fled to Iran 1991
Su-22M4	22558 Black	?		Fled to Iran 1991
Su-22M4	22560 Black	?		Fled to Iran 1991
Su-22M4	22561 Black	?		Fled to Iran 1991
Su-22M4	22564 Black	?		
Su-22M4	22566 Black	?		Fled to Iran 1991
Su-22M4	?	54911		Wfu Tallil AB
Su-22UM3	1702 Black	175323*****		
Su-22UM3	22501 Black	175323*****		Fled to Iran 1991
Su-22UM3	22504 Black	175323*****		
Su-22UM3	22505 Black	175323*****		Fled to Iran 1991
Su-22UM3	22506 Black	175323*****		Captured by US forces during the Gulf War
Su-22UM3	22507 Black	175323*****		Fled to Iran 1991
Su-22UM3	22509 Black	175323*****		Fled to Iran 1991
Su-22UM3	22513 Black	175323*****		Fled to Iran 1991
Su-22UM3	22515 Black	175323*****		Fled to Iran 1991
Su-22UM3	22521 Black	175323*****		Fled to Iran 1991
Su-22UM3	22530 Black	175323*****		Fled to Iran 1991
Su-22UM3	22531 Black	175323*****		Fled to Iran 1991
Su-22UM3	22532 Black	175323*7204?		Captured and displayed in Iran; c/n stated as 1753237204 but one digit missing
Su-22UM3	22533 Black	175323*****		Fled to Iran 1991; wreckage displayed in Iran
Su-22UM3	22539 Black	175323*****		Fled to Iran 1991
Su-24MK	24624 Black	416045*****	?	
Su-24MK	24625 Black	416045*****	?	
Su-24MK	24626 Black	416045*****	?	
Su-24MK	24627 Black	416045*****	?	
Su-24MK	24628 Black	416045*****	?	
Su-24MK	24629 Black	416045*****	?	
Su-24MK	24630 Black	416045*****	?	
Su-24MK	24631 Black	416045*****	?	
Su-24MK	24632 Black	416045*****	?	
Su-24MK	24633 Black	416045*****	?	
Su-24MK	24634 Black	416045*****	?	
Su-24MK	24635 Black	416045*****	?	Captured by US troops at al-Bakr AB in 2003?
Su-24MK	24636 Black	416045*****	?	

Su-24MK	24639 Black	416045*****	?	
Su-24MK	24640 Black	416045*****	?	
Su-24MK	24641 Black	416045*****	?	
Su-24MK	24642 Black	416045*****	?	
Su-24MK	24644 Black	416045*****	?	
Su-24MK	24645 Black	416045*****	?	
Su-24MK	24646 Black	416045*****	?	
Su-24MK	24647 Black	416045*****	?	
Su-24MK	24648 Black	416045*****	?	
Su-24MK	24649 Black	416045*****	?	
Su-24MK	24651 Black	416045*****	?	
Su-24MK	24652 Black	416045*****	?	
Su-25K	6795 Black?	255081*****	?	Serial unconfirmed
Su-25K	8220 Black?	255081*****	?	Serial unconfirmed
Su-25K	25571 Black	25508107021?	?	Captured by US forces at H-3 AB in 2003
Su-25K	25585 Black	255081*****	?	Flown to Iran 1-1991; to IRGC as 15-245*
Su-25K	25590 Black	25508109041	?	Flown to Iran 1-1991; to IRGC as 15-245*
Su-25K	25591 Black	255081*****	?	Shot down during First Gulf War
Su-25K	25603 Black	255081*****	?	Flown to Iran 1-1991; to IRGC as 15-245*
Su-25K	25604 Black	255081*****	?	Flown to Iran 1-1991; to IRGC as 15-245*
Su-25K	25606 Black	255081*****	?	Flown to Iran 1-1991; to IRGC as 15-245*
Su-25K	25609 Black	255081*****	?	Derelict at H-3 AB in 2003
Su-25K	25611 Black	255081*****	?	Flown to Iran 1-1991; to IRGC as 15-245*
Su-25K	25612 Black	255081*****	?	Wfu Tammuz
Su-25K	25613 Black	255081*****	?	Flown to Iran 1-1991; to IRGC as 15-245*
Su-25K	25615 Black	255081*****	?	Flown to Iran 1-1991; to IRGC as 15-245*
Su-25K	25616 Black	255081*****	?	Wfu Tammuz
Su-25K	25631 Black	255081*****	?	
Su-25K	?	25508107019	?	Wfu Tallil AB
Su-25K	?	25508109043	?	Wfu Tallil AB
Su-25K	?	25508109051	?	Wfu Tallil AB
Su-25K	?	25508110306	?	Wfu Tammuz
Tu-16KSR-2-11	509 Black	?		Grey/green camouflage
Tu-16	547 Black	?		No.10 Sqn
Tu-16	548 Black	?		No.10 Sqn
Tu-16	558 Black	?		No.10 Sqn
Tu-16	559 Black	?		No.10 Sqn
Tu-16	560 Black	?		No.10 Sqn
Tu-16	561 Black	?		No.10 Sqn
Tu-16	562 Black	?		No.10 Sqn
Tu-16	563 Black	?		No.10 Sqn
Tu-16	566 Black	?		No.10 Sqn
Tu-16	638 Black	?		No.10 Sqn
Tu-124K	I.A.F. 634	5351609?		Red/white c/s. Became, see next line
	YI-AEY			Iraqi Airways livery. Destroyed al-Taqaddum AB ?-2-1991
Tu-124K	I.A.F. 635	5351610?		Red/white c/s. Became, see next line
	YI-AEL			Iraqi Airways livery. Destroyed Baghdad ?-2-1991
Tu-134K	YI-AED	9350916		Returned to the USSR ?-1971 as CCCP-65669

2. 'New Iraq' Air Force				
Type	**Serial**	**C/n**	**F/n**	**Notes**
An-32B	YI-401 (1)	3604		Test flown in bare metal 9-2010. Rejected by customer, not delivered; see next line!
An-32B	YI-401 (2)	3704		D/D 28-2-2011
An-32B	YI-402	3605		Seen Kiev-Svyatoshino pre-delivery 8-2011
An-32B	YI-403	3606		D/D 18-11-2011
An-32B	YI-404	3607		D/D 27-12-2011
An-32B	YI-405	3702		Seen Kiev-Svyatoshino pre-delivery 4-2012
An-32B	YI-406	3703		Seen Kiev-Svyatoshino pre-delivery 7-2012
Mi-8T	YI-571	?	?	Sand/tan/brown camouflage, 'Iraqi Army Aviation' titles, non-standard radar
Mi-8T	YI-572	?	?	Sand/tan/brown camouflage, 'Iraqi Army Aviation' titles, non-standard radar
Mi-17V-5	YI-251	784M11	?	
Mi-17V-5	YI-252	784M12	?	
Mi-17V-5	YI-253	784M13	?	
Mi-172	YI-254	784M14	?	
Mi-171E	YI-260	171E.00.05.440.2402.U		No serial originally
Mi-171E	YI-261	171E.00.06.784.2309.U		
Mi-171E	YI-262	171E.00.06.784.2310.U		
Mi-171E	YI-263	171E.00.05.440.2403.U		
Mi-171E	YI-264	171E.00.05.440.2404.U		
Mi-171E	YI-265	171E.00.*****.****.U		Upgraded by Yugoimport SDR
Mi-171E	YI-???	171E.00.05.440.2401.U		No serial originally
Mi-171E	YI-???	171E.00.06.440.2408.U		
Mi-171E	YI-???	171E.00.06.440.2409.U		
Mi-171E	YI-???	171E.00.06.784.2805.U		
Mi-171E	YI-???	171E.00.784.07.3604.U		Purchased via UAE
Mi-171E	YI-???	171E.00.784.07.3605.U		Purchased via UAE
Mi-171E	YI-???	171E.00.784.07.3606.U		Purchased via UAE
Mi-171E	YI-???	171E.00.784.07.3607.U		Purchased via UAE
Mi-171E	YI-???	171E.00.784.08.3608.U		Purchased via UAE
Mi-171E	YI-???	171E.00.784.08.3609.U		Purchased via UAE
Mi-171E	YI-???	171E.00.784.08.3610.U		Purchased via UAE
Mi-171E	YI-???	171E.00.784.08.3701.U		Purchased via UAE
Mi-171E	YI-???	171E.00.784.08.3702.U		Purchased via UAE
Mi-171E	YI-???	171E.00.784.08.3703.U		Purchased via UAE
Mi-171E	YI-???	171E.00.784.08.3704.U		Purchased via UAE
Mi-171E	YI-???	171E.00.784.08.3705.U		Purchased via UAE
Mi-171E	YI-???	171E.00.784.08.3706.U		Purchased via UAE
Mi-171E	YI-???	171E.00.784.08.3707.U		Purchased via UAE
Mi-171E	YI-???	171E.00.784.08.3708.U		Purchased via UAE
Mi-171E	YI-???	171E.00.784.08.3709.U		Purchased via UAE
Mi-171E	YI-???	171E.00.784.08.3710.U		Purchased via UAE
Mi-171E	YI-???	171E.00.784.08.3801.U		Purchased via UAE
Mi-171E	YI-???	171E.00.784.08.3802.U		Purchased via UAE
Mi-171E	YI-???	171E.00.784.08.3803.U		Purchased via UAE
Mi-171E	YI-???	171E.00.784.08.3804.U		Purchased via UAE
Mi-171E	YI-???	171E.00.784.08.3805.U		Purchased via UAE
Mi-171	YI-???	59489619691	?	No serial originally
Mi-171	YI-???	59489619708	?	No serial originally

Israel

Israel was never a customer for Soviet/Russian military equipment, being perpetually at war with the neighbouring Arab nations which were supported by the Soviet Union; in fact, the latter broke off diplomatic relations with Israel in 1967 after the Six-Day War, and these were not restored until October 1991, shortly before the Soviet Union ceased to exist. However, the Israeli Defence Force/Air Force (IDF/AF, or *Heyl Ha'avir*) evaluated several Soviet combat aircraft types – mostly captured during the numerous Arab-Israeli conflicts.

The first of these was an Egyptian Air Force Mikoyan/Gurevich MiG-15*bis* *Fagot-B* which ditched in Lake Bordavil (or, to use the Israeli name, Lake Sirbon) near el-Arish on the Sinai Peninsula after being damaged by an IDF/AF Dassault Mystère IVA fighter on 31st October 1956. The aircraft was recovered by the Israelis and studied at Hatzor AB; later, the aircraft was preserved as a war memorial at the base.

Additionally, Israel obtained a Mikoyan/Gurevich UTI-MiG-15 *Midget* trainer in good condition – very probably as war booty; since the abovementioned MiG-15*bis* was not made flyable, the reports that 'IDF/AF pilots logged a total of 500 hours in the MiG-15' must apply to the trainer. The aircraft was preserved in the IDF/AF Museum at Hatzerim AB, Jerusalem, wearing fake Soviet markings as '303 Red' for a while; it is now painted in pre-UAR Egyptian Air Force markings with no serial.

On 12th August 1968 the Israelis captured two Syrian Air Force Mikoyan/Gurevich MiG-17F *Fresco-Cs* (serialled 1033 and 1041) when the fighters landed at the IDF/AF airbase at Bezel because of a navigation error. Some sources, however, maintain that this was a planned defection. The machine serialled 1041 was a Polish-built PZL Lim-5 (c/n 1C 07-18) The MiGs were carefully examined and at least one of them was test-flown by the Israelis.

Several Mikoyan/Gurevich MiG-21s of different subtypes fell into Israeli hands in the series of wars with Egypt, Syria and Iraq in the 1960s and 1970s. On 6th June 1967 the first six of the 20 Algerian Air Force MiG-21F-13 *Fishbed-Cs* dispatched to Egypt to assist in the Six-Day War landed at el-Arish AB which, unbeknownst to the pilots, had recently been seized by the Israelis. One fighter was destroyed by its pilot but the other five were captured intact. Of these, four were later sent to the USA. Another MiG-21F-13 (an Iraqi Air Force example serialled 534 Black) was surrendered to Israel on 16th August 1966; it was flown to Hatzor AB by a defector, Capt. Munir

Two views of a former Syrian Air Force MiG-17F being evaluated by the Israeli Defence Force/Air Force in 1968. An IDF/AF Dassault Mirage IIICJ provides scale.

Habib Jamil Redfa, who had been bribed by the Israeli intelligence service, Mossad. Painted in IDF/AF markings and eloquently serialled 007 (James Bond was already around by then!), the aircraft was thoroughly tested before reportedly being shipped to the USA; the MiG-21F-13 '007' now on display at the IDF/AF Museum is said to be a different one.

There was a rumour of a so-called Soviet Squadron of the IDF/AF. It operated three former Syrian MiG-17Fs, an ex-Egyptian Sukhoi Su-7B and the ex-Iraqi MiG-21F-13. These aircraft were not sent into combat against their former owners but were used for familiarise pilots with these types and developing tactics to use against them. Another possible knock-on effect of their capture is that the squadron's suggested existence caused the Soviets to have second thoughts about sending their latest equipment to an ally who cannot guarantee their security.

Additionally, three MiG-21s were used by Israel Aircraft Industries (IAI) as upgrade demonstrators. One of these was an ex-Romanian Air Force MiG-21MF *Fishbed-J* (ex-5902 Red, c/n N96005902, f/n 96-04-24) converted as the MiG-21-2000 upgrade demonstrator, receiving an EL/M2032 fire control radar developed by Elbit Electronics (a division of IAI), new cockpit instrumentation and a wraparound birdproof windscreen replacing the standard unit with a flat bulletproof windscreen and curved sidelights. The grey-painted aircraft with a red/white striped rudder carried the numbers 252 and 5902 on the fin, along with IAI and Aerostar logos (Aerostar is a Romanian company that was to upgrade operational MiG-21MFs to the new standard).

A MiG-21*bis* *Fishbed-L* bought from Nigeria was used by IAI for development work; the silver-painted aircraft wore the IAI logo and the serial 802 on the tail. An unusual feature was the aft-pointing chaff/flare dispensers mounted low on the rear fuselage sides. Another MiG-21*bis* converted to MiG-21-2000 standard (c/n N75085304) that was to be delivered to Namibia, but eventually remained undelivered, wore a white/red/black demonstrator colour scheme with IDF/AF insignia and the serial IAI 304.

On 11th October 1989 the Israelis received another 'gift' when a Syrian Air Force pilot, Abdel Bassem, landed at Megiddo in his Mikoyan MiG-23MLAE *Flogger-G* fighter serialled 2786 Black (c/n 0390324522) and requested asylum. Again, the fighter was thoroughly evaluated by the IDF/AF and is now on

MiG-21F-13 '007' No.1 undergoing tests in Israel. The spine is black-striped, while the nose and parts of the tail are Dayglo orange.

The second Israeli MiG-21F-13 was also serialled '007' but sported a more eyecatching test livery with lots of Dayglo orange.

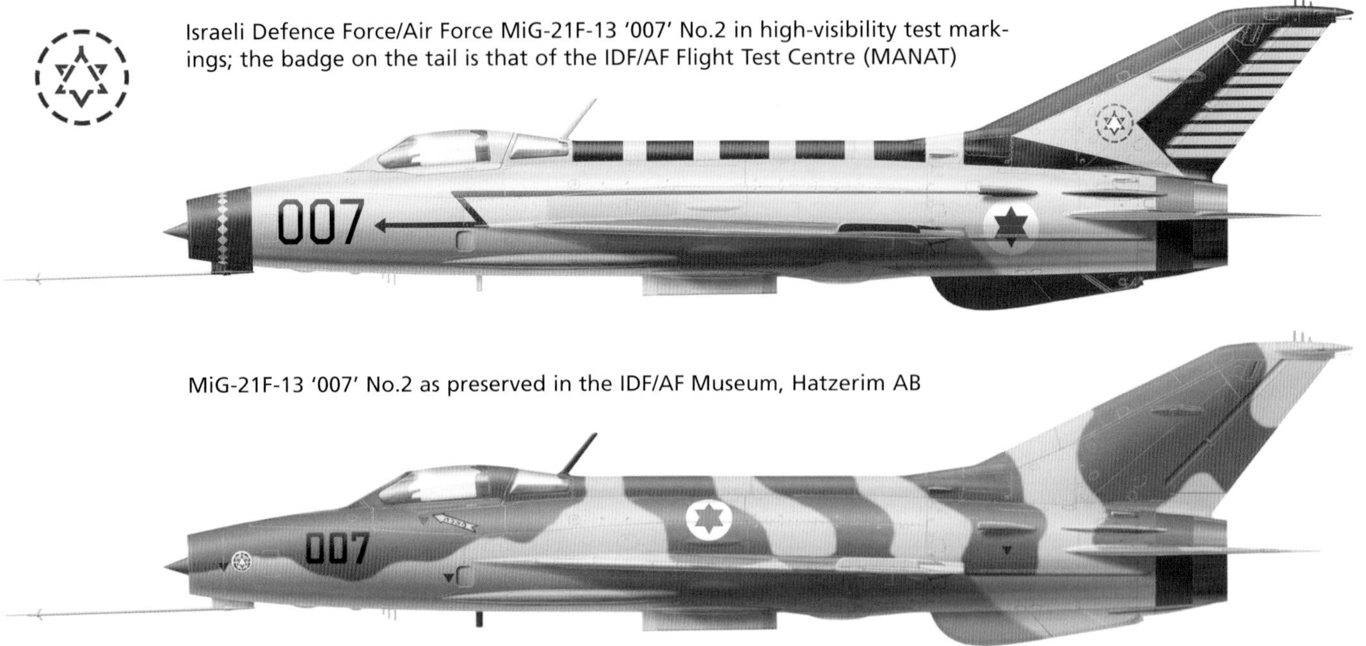

Israeli Defence Force/Air Force MiG-21F-13 '007' No.2 in high-visibility test markings; the badge on the tail is that of the IDF/AF Flight Test Centre (MANAT)

MiG-21F-13 '007' No.2 as preserved in the IDF/AF Museum, Hatzerim AB

The same aircraft as it looks now. '007' No.2 is on display at the IDF/AF Museum in a typical Israeli camouflage scheme.

MiG-23MLA '2786 Black' was another ex-Syrian aircraft evaluated by the Israelis. Here it is seen in a test flight wearing both Syrian Air Force and IDF/AF markings. Note how faded the Syrian roundels are.

A dramatic view of the Israeli MiG-23MLA as it climbs in full afterburner.

display in the IDF/AF Museum at Hatzerim AB, wearing Israeli roundels.

In April 1997 the IDF/AF loaned two Mikoyan MiG-29s from the Polish Air Force's 1st Fighter Regiment (1.PLM) for two weeks for evaluation purposes. These included *Fulcrum-A* (*izdeliye* 9.12A) '105 Red' (c/n 2960535105, f/n 4414). The trials took place at Sedom AB in the Negev Desert in southern Israel. The two units conducting the trials were No.601 Sqn (part of the IDF/AF Flight Test Centre, or MANAT) at Tel Nof and No.253 'Negev' Sqn at Ramon operating Lockheed Martin F-16A/B Fighting Falcons (known locally as the Netz). No.601 Sqn examined the MiG-29's systems and explored its flight envelope, while No.253 Sqn was responsible for dissimilar air combat training (DACT) evaluation. The aircraft retained the standard two-tone grey camouflage with the Polish 'chequerboard' national insignia and the 'Syrenka' (Mermaid) unit badge of the 1.PLM painted over in a lighter shade of grey; the red/white badge of No.253 Sqn was carried on the fins but the IDF/AF roundels were not applied.

The tests posed a fair share of problems at the preparatory stage. All the technical manuals had to be translated into Hebrew and the warning lights and critical switches in the cockpit provided with Hebrew-worded labels; the messages issued by the audio warning system could not be translated, of course. After a session of lead-in training, each of the Israeli pilots involved flew 20 DACT sorties in the MiG-29 against the McDonnell Douglas F-4E Phantom II (known locally as the Kurnass), the McDonnell Douglas F-15A/B (known locally as the Baz) and the F-16A/B. The Israeli pilots

MiG-23MLA '2786 Black' taxies with the wings folded back to 72° maximum sweep.

Polish Air Force MiG-29 '105 Red' during evaluation in Israel in 1997

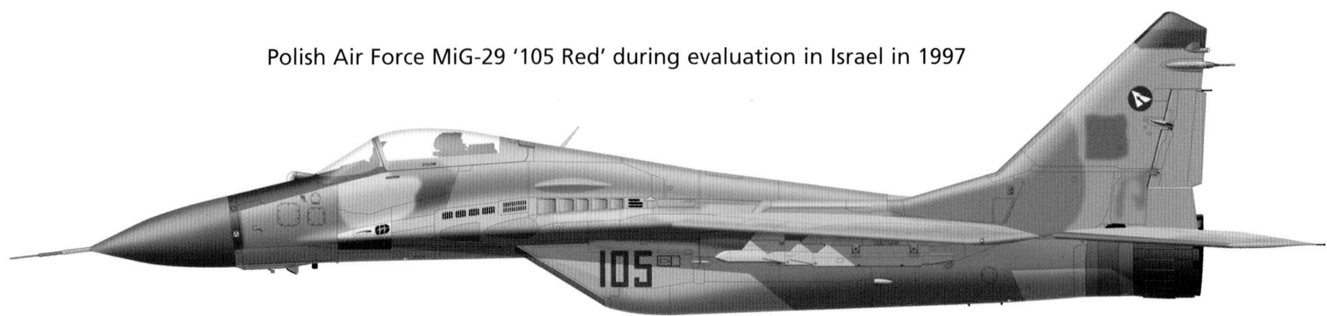

rated the *Fulcrum* as excellent and a dangerous adversary in a dogfight; the Shchel'-1UM (Slit) helmet-mounted sight proved to be on a par with the ones developed in Israel for the F-16C Barak/F-16D Brakeet and the F-15.

An Israeli military spokesman was quoted as saying that the IDF/AF was not planning to buy the type; the objective of the evaluation was to consider upgrade possibilities for IAI. Elbit Electronics had some experience with Soviet/CIS aircraft by then, having successfully upgraded the MiG-21MF and MiG-21UM for Romania (known as the Lancer A/Lancer C and Lancer B respectively in upgraded form) and the Antonov An-72P *Coaler-C* border patrol aircraft. However, the real objective was to develop anti-*Fulcrum* tactics in case the IDF/AF would wage war against any of the Arab nations operating the type. As a result, the IDF/AF fielded new models of helmet-mounted sights which, together with the indigenous Rafael Python 4 and US-supplied AIM-120 AMRAAM missiles, would enable Israeli pilots to emerge victorious from dogfights with the latest Russian fighters.

Israeli experts judged that the MiG-29 to be at least as good as (and in some respects better than) the F-15 and F-16 as far as aerodynamics and performance are concerned; they were also impressed by its rugged design and low maintenance requirements. The avionics suite, on the other hand, was found to be less capable than that of Western fighters. IAI was said to be discussing possible upgrade programmes with many MiG-29 operators, including Poland, Romania, Slovakia and the Ukraine.

There have also been unconfirmed reports that in 1990 the IDF/AF took possession of a Syrian Air Force MiG-29 (*izdeliye* 9.12B) whose pilot defected to Israel.

Soviet helicopters have also fallen into Israeli hands in various ways. The first of these was an Egyptian Air Force Mil' Mi-8T *Hip-C* serialled 1208 Black which was captured on 16th October 1973 after making a hard landing in a canyon 13 km (8 miles) from Abu Rudeis on the Sinai Peninsula and being abandoned by its crew. The helicopter was evacuated to Bir Gifgafa, repaired and evaluated. It retained the beige desert camouflage typical of the EAF *Hips*, and even the Egyptian serial applied in Arab characters was left intact; the only change was the substitution of the Egyptian roundels for Israeli ones. In the course of the evaluation the helicopter came

MiG-29 '105 Red' was loaned by the IDF/AF from the Polish Air Force in 1997. Note the badge of the No.253 'Negev' Sqn on the fin and the over-painted Polish AF insignia below it.

to grief, striking an obstacle with the nose landing gear unit, which snapped off completely. To enable a safe landing the ground crew had to get a huge heavy-duty tyre (probably from a tractor or loader) so that the pilot could manoeuvre the helicopter into position and gingerly rest the Mi-8's nose on the tyre. When the trials had been completed the Mi-8 was preserved in the IDF/AF Museum in 1978 but sold to the USA for US$ 1 million in 1983.

Another example operated by the Israelis was a second-hand Mi-8MTV *Hip-H* (c/n 94849) in armed configuration of unknown provenance that was converted into the Mi-17 'Peak 17' avionics/weapons upgrade demonstrator in 2001. The tactical upgrade package was developed by IAI's Tamam division acting as systems integrator. This involved installing Tamam's Helicopter Mission Optimised Stabilised Payload (HMOSP) surveillance/targeting system comprising low light level television (LLLTV) and forward-looking infrared (FLIR) channels – the heliborne version of the MOSP that was already fitted to some of IAI's unmanned aerial vehicles. The neat HMOSP 'ball turret' was mounted centrally under the nose, replacing the lower centre glazing panel. It worked with an integrated 'smart' helmet featuring a Vector day/night helmet-mounted sight (compatible with night vision goggles developed by IAI's Mata division) and a helmet motion sensor. The latter allowed the pilot to aim the HMOSP by simply turning his head. The conventional electromechanical flight instruments gave place to large multi-function displays (MFDs) likewise developed by Mata. The digital mission map allowed the mission data to be updated in real time in flight. The helicopter was equipped with a new ECM/IRCM suite developed by IAI's Elta Electronics division and able to carry air-to-ground weapons of Israeli manufacture.

Ex-Egyptian Mi-8T '1208' with Israeli roundels is making an unconventional landing, using a large tyre as a substitute for the missing nose gear unit.

The same machine a few minutes later. Note that the sliding cockpit windows are missing too.

When it was unveiled in 2001 and presented to India (the most likely customer), the helicopter was painted flat dark green overall, bearing the IAI/Tamam logo and the apt serial IAI 817. By June 2007 it had been repainted in a dark blue/silver/red demonstrator colour scheme, appearing at the 47th Paris Aerospace Salon at Le Bourget as the Mi-8 Mission Plus.

In the late 1990s IAI's Tamam division offered another upgrade package for a Soviet helicopter – the Mi-24 'Mission 24'. A single demonstrator was converted from a Mi-24V whose c/n has been reported as 14792; this means the full c/n is 3532421014792 or 3532422014792 (if the helicopter was built in Arsen'yev) – or 34035114792 (if it was built in Rostov-on-Don). The avionics suite giving the Mi-24 round-the-clock capability was broadly similar to that of the Mi-17 'Peak 17'; this time the HMOSP 'ball turret' was installed on the starboard side of the nose and the USPU-24 gun barbette in the nose was slaved to it,

IAI 817, the Mi-8 'Mission Plus' upgrade demonstrator, in its 2007 Paris Air Show colours. Note the undernose HMOSP 'turret', the non-standard blade aerial on the tailboom and the new IRCM flare dispensers.

allowing the WSO to aim the machine-gun by turning his head. Both cockpits were equipped with MFDs (one for the pilot and one for the WSO), and the avionics included an inertial navigation system (INS) and satellite navigation equipment. The standard YakB-12,7 machine-gun was retained but, in addition to the standard Soviet 9M114 Shtoorm ATGMs, the helicopter could carry Israeli Rafael Spike ATGMs and Western unguided rockets. The avionics and weapons were controlled by a central mission computer. No changes had been made to the powerplant, rotors or power train.

Painted in a rather yucky swampy green camouflage, the unserialled Mi-24V 'Mission 24' made its debut at the 43rd Paris Aerospace Salon in June 1999. Surprisingly, IAI's display stands and press releases at the show contained not the slightest hint at the helicopter's Russian origins. Made in the Holy Land, period.

The Western press treated the Mi-24V 'Mission 24' as a sensation. So did the Russians – but, understandably enough, their reaction was different. The Mil' Design Bureau and the Russian media were outraged by IAI's violation of the original equipment manufacturer's proprietary rights to the Mi-24, since the upgrade had been done without as much as a by your leave, and tampering with the helicopter's systems could jeopardise flight safety and damage the reputation of the Mi-24 and the Mil' Company in general. In reality the Israeli upgrade was nothing unexpected. IAI has a long history of upgrading both Soviet and Western military aircraft. Since the Mi-24 is one of the most popular combat helicopters, the many *Hinds* operated outside the CIS could bring upgrade contracts worth hundreds of millions of dollars; small wonder that IAI wanted to get a piece of the pie.

Jordan

The Hashemite Kingdom of Jordan was likewise not among the traditional customers for Soviet hardware. Nevertheless, the Royal Jordanian Air Force (RJAF, or *al Quwwat al-Jawwiya al-Urduniya*) operated three Antonov An-12BP *Cub* transports in 1981-84. The transports, which were loaned from the Iraqi Air Force, served with the No.3 Sqn in Amman alongside three Lockheed C-130B and four C-130H Hercules. Their missions reportedly included the delivery of spares for Chinese-made fighters from China to Iraq.

In 2007 the RJAF purchased at least one Antonov An-32B *Cline* tactical transport from the Antonov Design Bureau. This aircraft, and possibly two other An-32s, belongs to No.31 Sqn of the Prince Hashim bin Abdullah II Aviation Brigade which is the support unit of the Jordanian Special Forces. In November

A fine study of JY-JID, the first IL-76MF delivered to Jordan International Air Cargo.

Below: JY-JIC, the other Jordanian IL-76MF, makes a pre-delivery test flight at Zhukovskiy.

Royal Jordanian Air Force and paramilitary aircraft of Soviet origin				
Type	**Serial/registration**	**C/n**	**F/n**	**Notes**
An-12BP (+)	351	6344305		Ex/to Iraqi Air Force YI-AES (or possibly to the Soviet Union as CCCP-11650)
An-12BP (+)	352	6344306?		Ex-Iraqi Air Force YI-AGD, to Iraqi Air Force 352 Black?
An-12BP (+)	353	?		Previous identity unknown
An-32B	3010	3001		Ex-Antonov Design Bureau UR-48083; previously operated by Air Mark Indonesia
IL-76TD 'Falsie'	JY-JIA	0023437093	2804	Ex-Botir-Avia EX-86911, converted (demilitarised) IL-76MD with tail gunner's station in place; in service 4-2005
IL-76TD	JY-JIB	1023413438?	8610?	Ex-Click Air EX-100?, operated 2006; sold to Click Air as EK-76400
IL-76MF	JY-JIC/360	1063421724	9401	Ex-[RA-]76953 (test registration), D/D 29-6-2011; c/n as per factory list but should be 2113421724!
IL-76MF	JY-JID/361	1063423808	9602	Ex-[RA-]76954 (test registration), D/D 30-6-2011; c/n as per factory list but should be 2113423808!

2008 the An-32 in question suffered a starboard main landing gear collapse while parked, sustaining damage to the starboard wing, but was apparently repaired and still active in 2010.

Additionally, Jordan International Air Cargo (JIAC), an airline based at Amman-Marka airport and apparently operating as the commercial division of the RJAF had four Il'yushin IL-76 transports. Two of these were second-hand IL-76TD *Candid-As* acquired in Kyrghyzstan (one has since been resold). The other two are the only production examples of the stretched and re-engined IL-76MF; they were ordered in July 2007 and test flown in 2010 and 2011. Delivered in full JIAC livery with civil registrations in June 2011, the IL-76MFs gained additional Air Force serials in 2012.

Lebanon

Under a contract signed in late February 2010 Russia was to donate a batch of six (some sources say ten) Mil' Mi-24 *Hind* attack helicopters from Russian Air Force stocks to the Lebanese Air Force (*al Quwwat al-Jawwiya al-Lubnaniya*). This replaced a previous offer of Mikoyan MiG-29 *Fulcrum* tactical fighters. The helicopters were to be delivered before the end of the year, but so far there is no evidence that deliveries have taken place.

Palestine

In 1994, as the Middle Eastern peace process progressed to the point of Israel allowing the wannabe-sovereign Palestinian state to have its own aviation, the Palestinian National Administration (PNA) received two ex-Yemeni Mil' Mi-8 *Hip-Cs* – a Mi-8T utility helicopter and a Mi-8PS VIP helicopter – which had been operated for Palestine Liberation Organization (PLO) up to then, as it was. Under the arrangement agreed upon by ICAO the helicopters were placed on the Egyptian civil register in the out-of-sequence SU-YA... block reserved for Palestinian aircraft; there have been speculations that 'YA' stood for Yasser Arafat, the long-time leader of the PLO! Two more VIP helicopters, this time Mi-8MT *Hip-Hs*, joined the fleet in 1996, and a fifth (also a Mi-8MT) was added shortly afterwards. Regrettably two of the three Mi-8MTs were destroyed at Gaza Strip airport on 3rd December 2001 in an Israeli punitive attack on the Gaza Strip launched in the wake of PLO terrorist attacks against civilian targets in Haifa and Jerusalem.

Additionally, a single Antonov An-24RV *Coke* airliner bought or leased from the Romanian flag carrier TAROM was used as Yasser Arafat's personal aircraft; it was placed on the register of Guinea-Bissau. In April 1992 this aircraft crashed in a sandstorm while carrying Yasser Arafat; the latter was unhurt but the aircraft was a write-off.

Syria

Though formally declared an independent republic on 27th September 1941, Syria effectively remained a French protectorate until 17th April 1946 when the last foreign troops were withdrawn. Diplomatic relations with the Soviet Union were established in 1944. The Syrian Arab Air Force (*al Quwwat al-Jawwiya al-Arabiya as-Suriya*) was established in the early 1950s. On 1st February 1958 Syria, together with Egypt, formed the United Arab Republic (and accordingly the Syrian Air Force was integrated into the United Arab Republic Air Force, although the existing squadrons remained intact). Soon enough, however, resentment with Egyptian policies began to develop in Syria; on 28th September 1961 Syria seceded after a military coup d'état, and the two countries went their separate ways, leaving a shared enmity with Israel as their

Palestinian National Administration aircraft of Soviet origin

Type	Registration	C/n	F/n	Notes
An-24RV	J5-GAE	77310810		Ex-YR-AMW, bought 1983. Became, see next line
	J5-GBE			Reregistered 1989. Became, see next line
	J5-GAE			Crashed 7-4-1992
Mi-8PS	SU-YAA	10710	?	Ex-Yemeni Air Force '710', D/D 12-1994
Mi-8T	SU-YAB	10722	?	Ex-Yemeni Air Force '722', D/D 12-1994. Crashed 31-8-2006
Mi-8MT	SU-YAF	202M08	?	C/n suggests diverted from Chinese order; ex-4K-13208, D/D 1996. Destroyed Gaza 3-12-2001
Mi-8MT	SU-YAG	341M16	?	Ex-4K-15416, D/D 1996. Destroyed Gaza 3-12-2001
Mi-8MT	SU-YAL	324M45	?	C/n suggests the helicopter was diverted from an Ethiopian order

only common cause. After the revolution on 8th March 1963 which brought the Ba'ath Socialist Party to power, Syria became a staunch ally of the Soviet Union.

Syria ordered its first 25 Mikoyan/Gurevich MiG-15*bis* *Fagot-B* fighters in 1955. The following year Czechoslovakia supplied 20 licence-built *Fagot-Bs* (Aero S-103s), along with at least four licence-built UTI-MiG-15 *Midget* trainers (Aero CS-102s), to Abu Sueir AB in Egypt where the Syrian pilots were taking their training. One of the CS-102s crashed at Dekkelah AB, Egypt, during a post-delivery checkout flight on 16th August 1956, killing the Czechoslovak pilot. All the others, except four *Midgets*, were destroyed on the ground at Abu Sueir by Royal Navy Westland Wyvern attack aircraft on 1st November 1956 without ever flying a single sortie. Further *Midget* deliveries came when the Polish Air Force supplied five CS-102s in 1969, followed by five PZL SBLim-1s – that is, Lim-1s (Polish-built MiG-15 *Fagot-As*) converted to UTI-MiG-15 standard – in 1972.

The fighters and trainers were operated by the Nos. 1 and 2 Squadrons (both based at Hamah and then at Minakh); No.2 Sqn later moved to Almaza AB near Cairo in UAR days and subsequently became the No.204 Sqn. Syrian MiG-15s took part in all subsequent conflicts with Israel, but most of the aircraft lost in these conflicts were destroyed on the ground, not in the air. One squadron of UTI-MiG-15s remained active by early 1987; more than 25 aircraft were reportedly still operational in late 1991.

In November 1956 Syria signed an agreement with the Soviet Union for the delivery of 60 Mikoyan/Gurevich MiG-17F *Fresco-C* day fighters. Twenty Syrian pilots were sent to the USSR to take their training; another 18 went to Poland and still others were trained *in situ*. MiG-17F deliveries began in January 1957, when there were still no pilots qualified to fly them, and were completed in August. An unspecified number of MiG-17PF *Fresco-D* radar-equipped all-weather interceptors were also delivered. The MiG-17s formed the Syrian component of the UARAF in 1958-61. Like the Egyptian MiGs, they were hastily camouflaged as a result of lessons learned in the Six-Day War. An additional seven MiG-17Fs, including four Polish-built PZL Lim-5s, were supplied by East Germany in 1968. Though largely

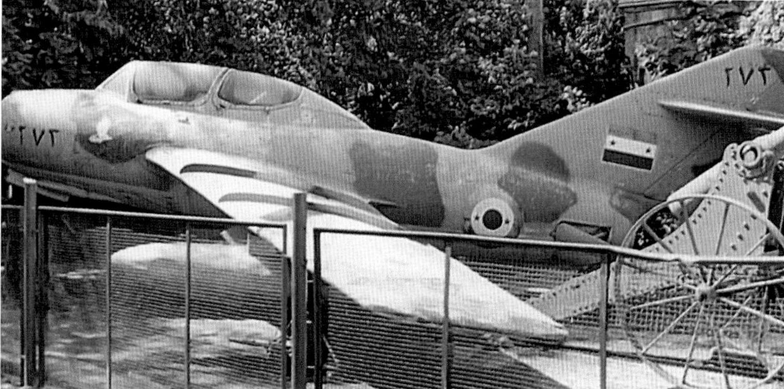

Top: Syrian Air Force (UARAF) Aero CS-102 '273' on display at the Military Museum in Damascus in authentic (if rather faded) colours.

Above: The same aircraft as it looks today. The paint is fresh but the spirit is gone.

A Syrian Air Force UTI-MiG-15

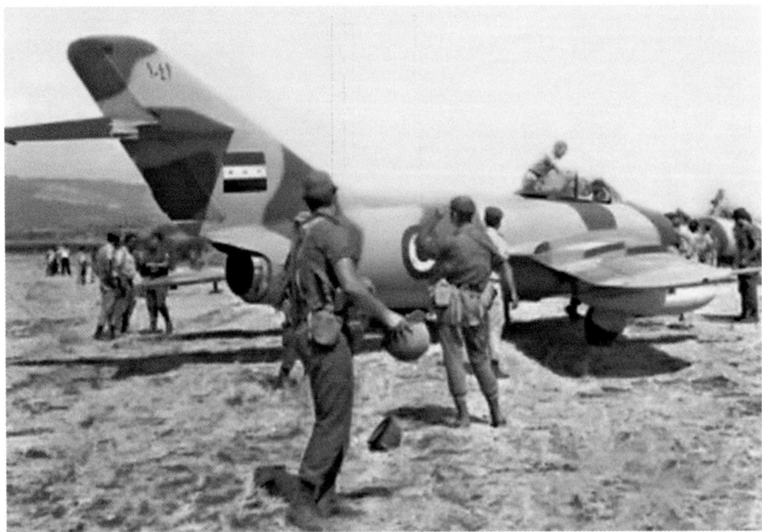

Top: Syrian Air Force MiG-17F '939 Black' in natural metal finish. The full serial is carried on the fin, the last two digits being repeated on the nose.

Above: Camouflaged Syrian Air Force MiG-17F '1041 Black' at a forward airfield.

replaced by more modern fighters, more than 30 MiG-17s were reportedly still in service as tactical trainers in late 1991.

Syria joined the 'supersonic club' when it became the second non-Warsaw Pact nation to operate the Mikoyan/Gurevich MiG-19S *Farmer-C*. 40 of these fighters were delivered from the Soviet Union in 1958-62. According to other reports, the aircraft were obtained second-hand from Egypt.

In 1965 the Syrian Air Force took delivery of the first of an eventual 40 or 45 Mikoyan MiG-21F-13 (*izdeliye* 74) fighters. The *Fishbed-Cs* equipped three squadrons – Nos. 8, 10 and 11. Following the Six-Day War of 1967 and other wars with Israel, more MiG-21F-13s were urgently supplied by Czechoslovakia (12 Aero S-106s in 1973), Hungary (ten) and Iraq (four) as attrition replacements in addition to the Soviet deliveries.

36 MiG-21PF (*izdeliye* 76) *Fishbed-D* fighters arrived in 1966, but many were lost in the Six-Day War, after which the Soviet Union supplied a further 24 in 1968. The next version delivered was the MiG-21PFM (*izdeliye* 94A) *Fishbed-F* in 1968; the first batch of 40 was followed by a second of 60. Some of these aircraft were MiG-21PFS (*izdeliye* 94A) *Fishbed-Ds* which differed from the MiG-21PFM in having blown flaps and retaining the old forward-hinged canopy.

In 1971 the Syrian Air Force took delivery of twenty-one MiG-21MFs (*izdeliye* 96F) *Fishbed-J* fighters, followed by 40 more in 1973. So great were the losses in the Yom Kippur War and the skirmishes with Israel preceding it (about 180 Syrian fighters of all types were destroyed) that the USSR supplied a further 75 MiG-21MFs in late 1973. In an effort to hide their losses from casual observers, the Syrians changed the serials on their aircraft time and time again; thus, many new MiG-21MFs inherited the serials of older destroyed fighters. In October 1973 twelve MiG-21M (*izdeliye* 96) *Fishbed-Js* were bought

This view shows the pre-UAR Syrian markings on a MiG-17F, the green/white/black roundels and fin flash featuring three red stars.

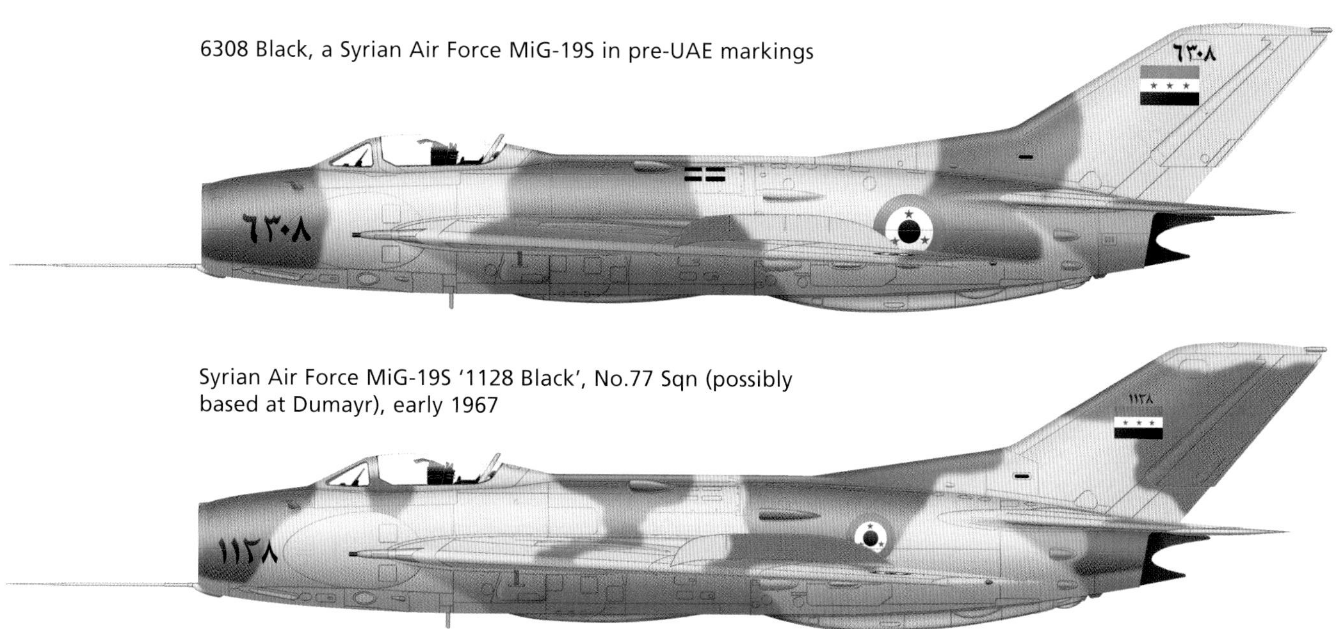

6308 Black, a Syrian Air Force MiG-19S in pre-UAE markings

Syrian Air Force MiG-19S '1128 Black', No.77 Sqn (possibly based at Dumayr), early 1967

from East Germany as attrition replacements. These were similar to the MiG-21MFs, except for less powerful engines and less capable radars.

In the 1970s six MiG-21R (*izdeliye* 94RA) *Fishbed-H* tactical reconnaissance aircraft were delivered; some served until at least 2000. Only one aircraft has been identified.

To replenish the stock and allow the withdrawal of obsolete types, in the 1980s the Soviet Union supplied 198 MiG-21*bis* (*izdeliye* 75A) *Fishbed-L* fighters. By 1990 the Syrian Air Force had 178 *Fishbed-Ls* in 12 squadrons plus 61 older variants in reserve. The MiG-21*bis* numbers were down to 172 in 1990, 160 in 1995 and 102 in 2005 (in seven squadrons).

Little information is available concerning the deliveries of the MiG-21's trainer versions to Syria. About eight MiG-21U *Mongol-As* were delivered in the 1960s, followed by 20 MiG-21UM *Mongol-Bs* around 1973.

In 2007 the MiG-21 was still in service with eight squadrons – No.8 Sqn at Deir-az-Zor, No.12 Sqn at Tabqa, Nos. 679 and 680 Sqns at Hamah (all operating MiG-21MFs), Nos. 825, 826, 945 and 946 Sqns (all based at al-Qusayr and equipped with MiG-21*bis*). The total number, including trainers, was about 200 aircraft.

In 1973 the Syrian Air Force introduced the Mikoyan MiG-23 'swing-wing' fighter. The first four machines – two MiG-23MS *Flogger-E* fighters and two MiG-23UB *Flogger-C* trainers – were delivered on 14th October 1973, arriving in two Soviet Air Force Antonov An-12B transports. A total of sixty MiG-23MSs and twenty MiG-23UBs were delivered in 1973-76. The next tranche came in 1980-81 came twenty MiG-23MF *Flogger-B* fighters (some sources suggest these arrived in 1978) and five additional MiG-23UBs. A number of Syrian MiG-23s were shot down during the fighting in the Lebanon in 1982. These losses were made good by deliveries of about 20 MiG-23MSs from Libya. Shortly afterwards, fifty MiG-23MLAE (*izdeliye* 23-19B) *Flogger-G* fighters – sometimes misidentified as MiG-23MLD *Flogger-Ks* – were delivered from the Soviet Union.

In Syrian Air Force service the MiG-23MS was operated by the No.54 Sqn at Dumayr, No.77 Sqn at Marj Ruhayyil, No.678 Sqn at Abu ad-Duhor and No.697 Sqn at Saiqal. The MiG-23MFs served with the No.8 Sqn at Deir-az-Zor, No.12 Sqn at Tabqa, No.675 Sqn at Shayrat and No.678 Sqn. A further (unidentified) MiG-23 unit was based at Blai. The MiG-23MLAEs served with the No.77 Sqn and an unidentified squadron at Dumayr (possibly No.54).

The Syrian Air Force took delivery of approximately 16 Mikoyan MiG-25PD *Foxbat-E* interceptors, eight MiG-25RB *Foxbat-D* reconnaissance/strike aircraft and two MiG-25PU *Foxbat-C* trainers. The aircraft saw service with the Nos. 1 and 5 Sqns at Tiyas AB, also known as T4, located north-east of Damascus, No.7 Sqn at Shayrat, and No.9 Sqn at Dumayr. Later, all four squadrons were reportedly concentrated at Tiyas.

Syrian MiG-25s have been used to intercept Israeli aircraft on many occasions but with

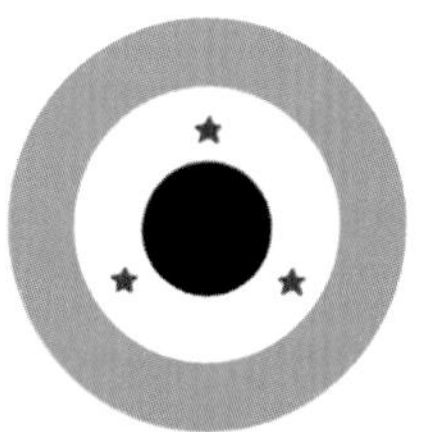

The original (pre-United Arab Republic) insignia of the Syrian Air Force.

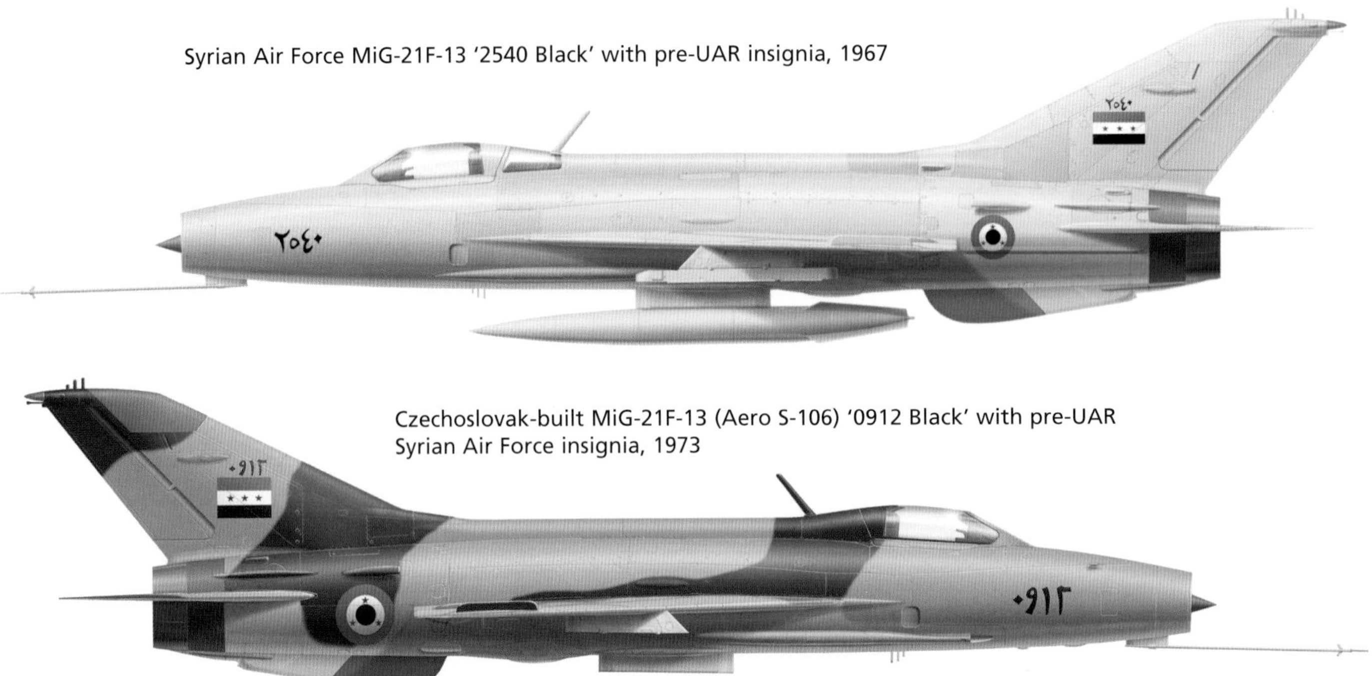

Syrian Air Force MiG-21F-13 '2540 Black' with pre-UAR insignia, 1967

Czechoslovak-built MiG-21F-13 (Aero S-106) '0912 Black' with pre-UAR Syrian Air Force insignia, 1973

Syrian Air Force MiG-21F-13 '1864 Black' is on display at the Army Museum in Damascus. Contrary to some reports, it is a genuine Soviet-built example, not an S-106.

scant success; this was largely due to lack of experience on the part of the Syrian airmen and ground controllers. Moreover, at least two MiG-25PDs have been shot down by Israeli F-15s.

Syria became the second export customer for the MiG-29, signing an order for 150 in April 1987. Deliveries commenced quickly; the first aircraft – single-seat MiG-29 (*izdeliye* 9.12B) *Fulcrum-As* and two-seat MiG-29UB *Fulcrum-Bs* – were handed over to the Syrian Air Force in July 1987. The first MiG-29 squadron became operational in October 1988. A second tranche was delivered by the end of the year, bringing the total strength to three squadrons. These are the Nos. 698 and 699 Sqns and probably the No.697 Sqn, all based at Saiqal AB.

In 1988 military co-operation between the Soviet Union and Syria was interrupted, with the result that half of the MiG-29 fleet became unserviceable during the following decade. There have been no confirmed reports of Syrian *Fulcrums* in action against Israeli jets. Rumour has it that a Syrian MiG-29 pilot defected to Israel in 1990 and that at least one more MiG-29 was lost in a shootout with IDF/AF fighters in early 1991. What *is* known, however, is that Syria never received the full number of 150 MiG-29s originally ordered; it is generally believed that deliveries stopped at 80. These include 48 *Fulcrum-A/Bs* in the first shipment delivered in the late 1980s, plus

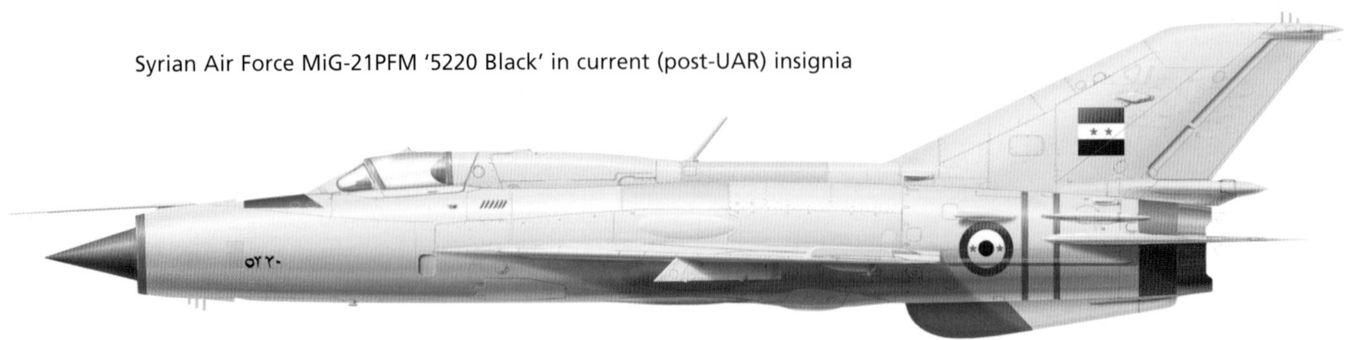

Syrian Air Force MiG-21PFM '5220 Black' in current (post-UAR) insignia

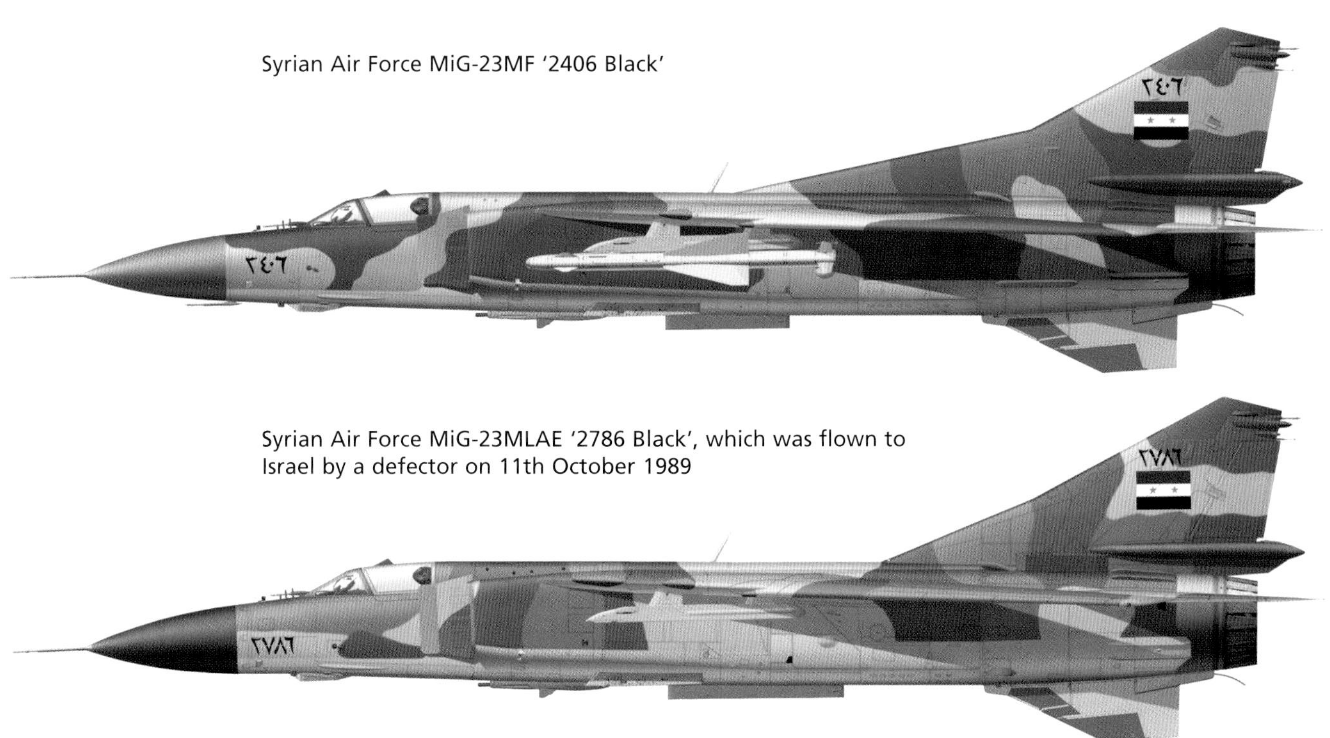

Syrian Air Force MiG-23MF '2406 Black'

Syrian Air Force MiG-23MLAE '2786 Black', which was flown to Israel by a defector on 11th October 1989

another 14 aircraft (12 single-seaters and two MiG-29UBs) diverted from an embargoed Iraqi order in 2000 after the resumption of military co-operation with Russia, plus 22 second-hand examples bought in 2001-02.

The Syrian Air Force received a total of 60 Sukhoi Su-7BMK *Fitter-A* fighter-bombers and Su-7UMK *Moujik* trainers after the Six-Day War. Aircrew training took place *in situ* from August 1969 to March 1970 under the guidance of a Czechoslovak instructor, Maj. Zdeněk Brych. The units equipped with Su-7s redeployed to new locations every now and then – obviously to avoid the attentions of Israeli forces. Nonetheless, by 1973 the Syrian Air Force had lost 35 of the original 60 Su-7s in skirmishes with Israel; a further 13 were destroyed in the Yom Kippur War. The few surviving examples serving at Deir-az-Zor AB and Khoms AB were retired in the mid-1980s.

In 1973 Syria started re-equipping with the more modern variable-geometry versions of the *Fitter* family, reportedly purchasing 40 Sukhoi Su-20 *Fitter-C* fighter-bombers and an unknown number of Su-22M *Fitter-H* and Su-22M4 *Fitter-K* single-seaters, as well as Su-22UM3 *Fitter-E* trainers. Of the latter types, 22 were delivered in 1990. As many as 96 'swing-wing' *Fitters* were reportedly operational in 2004; some sources, though, give a more modest (and more realistic) figure of 60 Su-20s/Su-22s in mid-1995. The Su-22 variants saw service with four units – the Nos. 677 and 685 Sqns at Shayrat, No.827 Sqn at Tiyas AB and an unidentified squadron at Dumayr.

Concurrently with the *Fitter-C* the Syrian Air Force introduced another 'swing-wing' fighter-bomber – the Mikoyan MiG-23BN *Flogger-H*. At least two batches were delivered: the first, comprising 60 aircraft, arrived in 1973-76 and the second batch of ten followed around 1980. The type was operated by the 695th and 698th Squadrons, both based

A Syrian Air Force MiG-23BN delivers a pair of 500-kg bombs.

Syrian Air Force MiG-25RB '2715 Black'

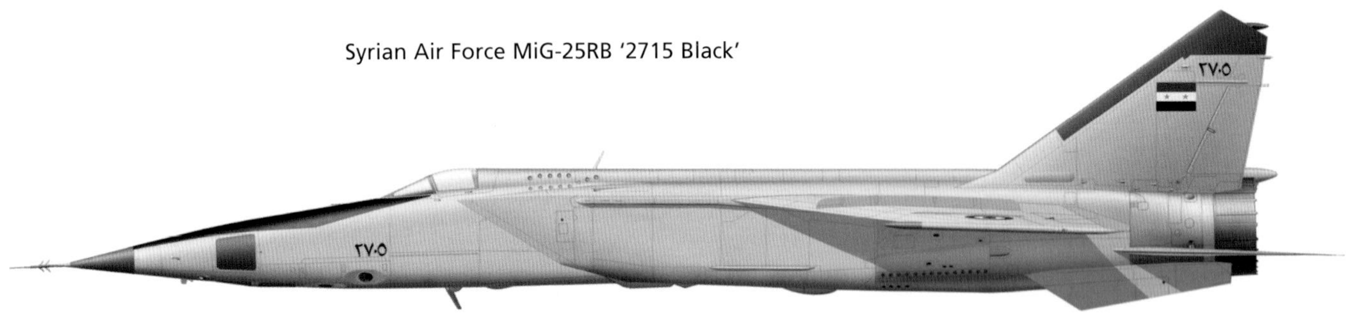

at an-Nasiriyah, plus a detachment at Shayrat.

The Syrian Air Force's first specialised strike aircraft were six Il'yushin IL-28 *Beagle* tactical bombers received from Egyptian stocks in the mid-1960s. Two of them were destroyed by Israeli attacks during the Six-Day War. Much later, at the end of 1989, Syria took delivery of 20 (some sources say 22) Sukhoi Su-24MK *Fencer-D* tactical bombers, becoming the third export customer for the type. Most reports indicate that there were 20 in service at the beginning of 2004, serving with No.819 Sqn at Tiyas AB; the type is also reportedly operated by an unidentified squadron at Hamah.

In January 2012 Syria placed an order with the Russian arms trading company Rosoboronexport for 36 of the latest Yakovlev Yak-130 *Mitten* advanced jet trainers; the deal was worth US$ 550 million. The next month, however, unrest began in Syria, quickly escalating into a full-scale civil war which is still in progress as of this writing; hence the Syrian contract had to be suspended.

The current (post-UAR) insignia of the Syrian Air Force.

In 1964-67 the Syrian Air Force purchased ten Il'yushin IL-14P *Crate* airliners, including four second-hand aircraft supplied by East Germany; some of them were apparently in VIP configuration equivalent to the Soviet-built IL-14S. Some of them wore a green/brown camouflage, indicating they were operated after 1967 when camouflage colours were introduced in the wake of the Six-Day War.

As a successor to the type, two Antonov An-24B *Coke* twin-turboprop regional airliners were delivered in 1968 – apparently again in VIP configuration (An-24B 'Salon'). In 1975 the Syrian Air Force took delivery of four Antonov An-26 *Curl* tactical transports, adding a further two built to An-26B standard in 1981. The Antonov turboprop twins are operated by the No.522 Sqn based at Damascus International airport. All of them are quasi-civil, operating in the full old livery of Syrianair (Syrian Arab Airlines), the sole national airline; in spite of this, at least one of the *Curls* is outfitted as an An-26RTR electronic intelligence aircraft with huge blade aerials on the forward and centre fuselage revealing its mission.

In the 1970s, heavier military airlift duties were performed by Antonov An-12 *Cub* four-turboprop transports. Only one has been identified so far, wearing a civil registration that passed to one of the An-26s in 1975. In 1979 the Syrian Air Force took delivery of its first two Il'yushin IL-76M *Candid-B* four-turbofan transports. They were quasi-civil and nominally operated by Syrianair, with appropriate titles in English and Arabic on the rear fuselage; initially they wore a distinctive colour scheme with a dark blue triple cheatline and a white tail bearing the Syrian flag. Two years later they were joined by two IL-76M 'Falsies'; unlike the first two, these had no gunner's station and wore Syrianair's full then-current livery featuring a single bright blue cheatline outlined in the same colour and bright blue tail with stylised bird logo. Subsequently, in the 2000s, the first two machines were converted to IL-76T *Candid-A* standard in the course of an overhaul, exchanging the gunner's station for a 'solid' commercial tailcone; they also gained Syrianair's new livery with an all-white fuselage, a darker shade of blue on the tail and bolder titles. The *Candids* likewise belong to the No.522 Sqn.

Syrianair operated six Tupolev Tu-134B-3 *Crusty* short-haul airliners. Three of them were built as Tu-134B-3 'Salon' VIP jets featuring a rear entry door and integral airstairs in the manner of the Tu-134AK. However, both these aircraft and the other three, which lack the rear entry door and were apparently built as 80-seaters, are listed for the Syrian Air Force's No.585 Sqn based at Damascus. In 1998 Syrianair began a large-scale fleet renewal programme. The Tu-134B-3s and the airline's three Tu-154Ms were replaced by six Airbus Industrie A320-232s, though at least three of the *Crustys* served long enough to receive the airline's current livery; by March 2001 Tu-134B-3 YK-AYE was Syrianair's last operational Tupolev aircraft.

Syrian Air Force MiG-25PD '2519 Black' armed with R-40RD and R-40TD AAMs

A rare picture of a Syrian Air Force MiG-25PD serialled '2519 Black'.

The Syrian Air Force took delivery of eight Yakovlev Yak-40 *Codling* feederliners (one in 1974, two each in 1975 and 1978, and three in 1979). The trijets entered service with No.565 Sqn at Damascus International airport. At least two of them were Yak-40 'Salon 2nd Class' VIP aircraft; the last four were in the Yak-40K convertible version with a cargo door, and the other two were in standard airline configuration and were operated on Syrianair's domestic services. On 19th March 1976 one of the Yak-40s was destroyed at Beirut airport as a result of a terrorist attack. Just as the passengers were disembarking, a gunman fired two rocket-propelled anti-tank grenades at the jet; the first one missed but the second round hit home, setting the tail section on fire. The passengers escaped unhurt but the aircraft was damaged beyond repair.

The first Soviet helicopter type delivered to Syria was the Mil' Mi-4 *Hound* utility helicopter; no information is available on how many were delivered and what units they served with. In 1982 the Syrian Air Force took delivery of at least ten Mil' Mi-2 *Hoplite* light helicopters in armed assault configuration.

More than 100 Mil' Mi-8s, at least some of which were ex-Soviet Army Aviation aircraft, were delivered to Syria. Versions operated by

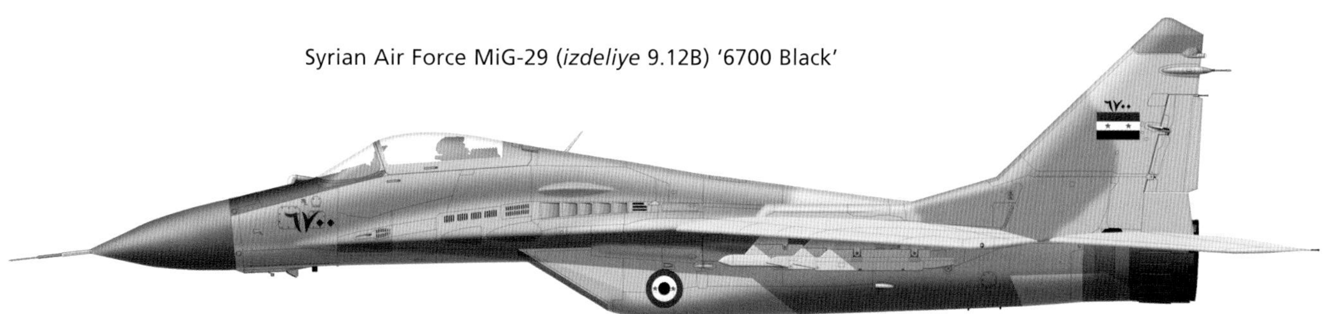

Syrian Air Force MiG-29 (*izdeliye* 9.12B) '6700 Black'

A very shaggy Israeli reservist examines the wreckage of a Syrian Su-7BMK downed at El Kuneitra. Note the half-empty UB-16-57 FFAR pod.

the Syrian Air Force include the 'first-generation' Mi-8TV *Hip-C* transport/assault version, the Mi-8PPA *Hip-J* ECM version based on it, the 'second-generation' Mi-17 *Hip-H* and the Mi-17PP ECM version. The Mi-8/Mi-17 is in service with the Nos. 253 and 255 Sqns based at Afis, the Nos. 525, 527 and 909 Sqns based at Marj-as-Sultan, the No.532 Sqn at Qabr-as-Sitt and a further squadron based at Nayrab near Aleppo. On the heavier end of the scale, more than ten Mil' Mi-6 *Hook* heavy-lift helicopters were delivered.

50 Mil' Mi-24D/Mi-25 *Hind-D* attack helicopters, at least some of which were ex-Soviet Army Aviation aircraft, were handed over to the Syrian Air Force. Of these, 36 remained

The spoils of war: this tail section of a downed Syrian Su-7BMK is on display in an Israeli museum.

operational in November 2000. A number of Mi-24V/Mi-35 *Hind-Es* were delivered subsequently. The *Hinds* were operated by the Nos. 765 and 766 Sqns at as-Suweidaya AB, though this may be no longer current as of 2012, and two further squadrons (including No.767 Sqn) at Marj Ruhayyil.

The Syrian Navy, too, operates Soviet helicopters. The No.618 Sqn based at Latakia on the Mediterranean coast has a number of Kamov Ka-28 *Helix-A* and Mil' Mi-14PL *Haze-A* anti-submarine warfare helicopters and Mi-14PS *Haze-B* search-and-rescue helicopters.

Syrian Air Force in action

The first episode in the Syrian MiGs' combat history was the incident which happened near Damascus on 14th February 1958. A Royal Jordanian Air Force de Havilland DH.104 Dove liaison aircraft (possibly serialled D-101) was winging its way from Amman to Europe, captained by none other than His Majesty King Hussein bin Talal; the 23-year-old monarch intended to spend his three weeks' vacation in Europe. The aircraft's route lay across Syria, but no one had taken the trouble to obtain the required overflight permission via diplomatic channels. Hence, when the DH.104 entered Syrian airspace it was promptly challenged by the air traffic controller at Damascus airport who ordered the pilots to land there.

Defying the orders, King Hussein gave the controls to his more experienced British co-pilot Jock Dalgleish, an RAF Wing Commander, who set course back towards Amman. Minutes later, however, the aircraft was intercepted by two Syrian Air Force MiG-17Fs. Then, acting against their orders, the fighter pilots opened fire (they said afterwards they had requested permission to fire but received no response and thus acted on their own); yet, Dalgleish repeatedly took evasive action and pressed on towards the Jordanian border, eventually landing safely at Amman-Marka airport. It is not clear if the fighter pilots saw the royal standard painted on the DH.104's tail.

The intercept created a huge scandal and strong anti-Syrian sentiment in Jordan. However, the UAR provided clear evidence that the DH.104 had entered Syrian airspace without clearance and, being regarded as an intruder, had been legitimately intercepted. A Jordanian investigation ended in embarrassment: it turned out that the flight plan had been duly filed – but not the overflight clearance. The Jordanians had assumed the flight

A Syrian Air Force Su-22M passes overhead, showing the unpainted portions of the outer wings exposed at minimum sweep.

had been cleared to cross the border via the UN representative in Amman – which was not the case.

On 14th February 1959 Syrian MiG-17Fs shot down a 'visiting' Israeli Defence Force/Air Force Dassault Mystère IVA near the Syrian border. In February 1960 four Syrian (UARAF) MiG-17Fs were attacked by IDF/AF 105th Sqn fighters but neither side suffered any losses.

On 27th September 1960 a Syrian (UARAF) MiG-17F crash-landed in northern Jordan, possibly as a result of navigation error. A similar incident involving a MiG-17F serialled '48 Black', which belly-landed in the desert near Amman, occurred just a few days later, on 4th October; this time it was a planned defection, the pilot, Adnan Madani (also reported as Adnan Malki), seeking political asylum in Jordan. The aircraft was returned to Syria a year later, after it had been thoroughly examined by British and US specialists.

As mentioned in the Egyptian section, by the spring of 1967 skirmishes on the Israeli-Syrian border in which both sides used heavy weapons and aircraft were becoming increasingly more frequent. In particular, on 7th April a group of Syrian MiG-21s (presumably mostly MiG-21F-13s) clashed with IDF/AF Dassault Mirage IIICJs over the Golan Heights; in the resulting furball six MiG-21s were shot down.

The combined air forces of the Arab nations outnumbered the IDF/AF almost three times, so it was decided to destroy them on the ground rather than tangle with them in the air. The first Israeli air strike was directed against 19 Egyptian airbases. Once the Egyptian Air Force had been neutralised by 1400 hrs, the Israeli strike force would be redirected at Syria, Jordan and Iraq. The Arabs' bombers (49 to 56 IL-28s, including six in Syria, and 36 Tu-16s) were priority targets.

On the morning of 5th June 1967 Israel launched a massive assault against Arab airbases, starting the Six-Day War. Syrian losses in

A trio of Syrian Su-22Ms in V formation.

A specialist of the Komsomol'sk-on-Amur Aircraft Production Association (KnAAPO) examines a Syrian Air Force Su-22M serialled 325 White.

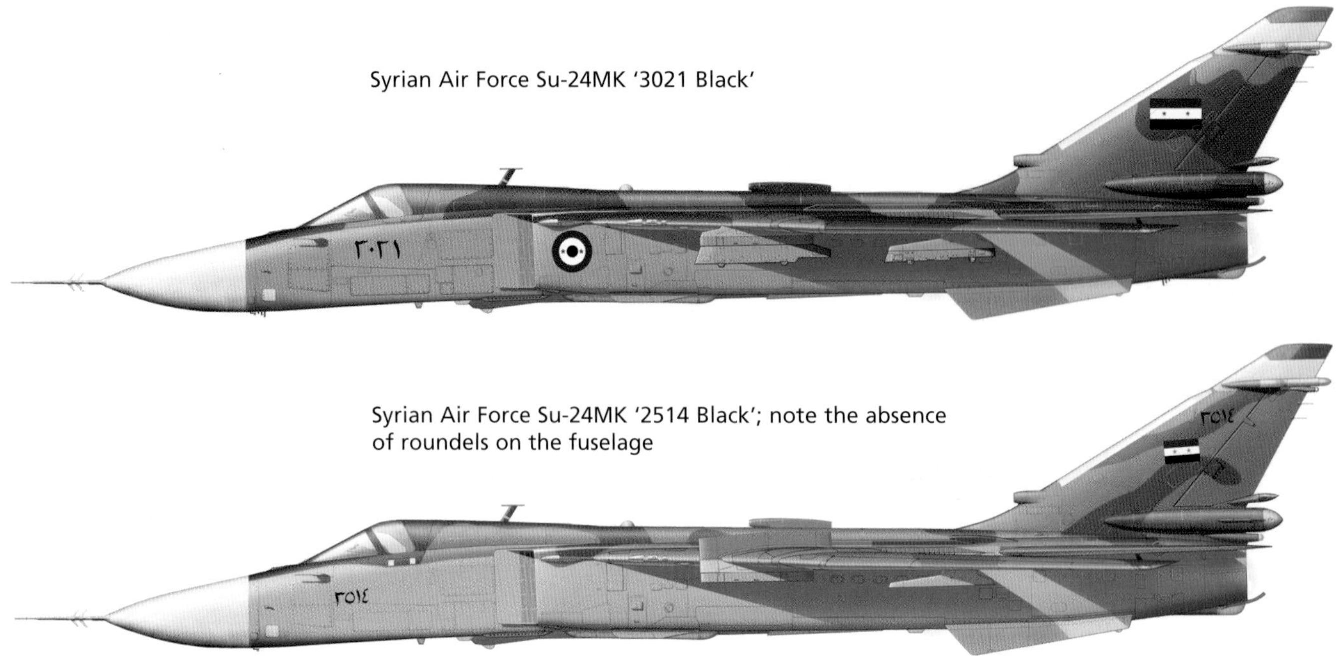
Syrian Air Force Su-24MK '3021 Black'

Syrian Air Force Su-24MK '2514 Black'; note the absence of roundels on the fuselage

the Six-Day War were substantial. Among other things, 20 MiG-15*bis* fighters and two IL-28s were destroyed on the ground; also, more than half the Syrian MiG-21 fleet (32 out of 60) was destroyed. (Some sources give different figures: five MiG-15*bis*, 16 MiG-17Fs, 23 MiG-21s (out of 45 available) and two IL-28s destroyed on the ground plus two MiG-17Fs and seven MiG-21s shot down on Day One alone.) On the other hand, the Syrian Air Force was more aggressive; four groups of MiG-17Fs escorted by MiG-21s attacked Israel on 5th June just as Israeli jets were attacking Egypt. Because of factionalism in the Syrian government these strikes were delayed and were 'too little, too late' to have any significant impact on the course of the war. Moreover, most of the strikes missed their assigned targets, hitting civilian objectives by mistake; they also played into the hands of the enemy, giving Israel an excuse to strike back, on the grounds that there had been an unprovoked aggression.

The air war over Syria on 5th June included an episode when Capt. Adnan Ahmad Hussein flying a MiG-21FL shot down several IDF/AF fighters before he, in turn, was downed by a Mirage IIICJ flown by Capt. Ehud Hankin. The MiG exploded so violently that debris damaged Hankin's aircraft, and eventually the Israeli pilot was forced to eject. That same day IDF/AF SO.4050 Vautour IIAs escorted by

Syrian Air Force Su-24MK '2514 Black' awaits refurbishment at Rzhev, Russia, alongside a camouflaged Russian sister ship.

A trio of Syrian Su-24MKs in V formation.

Mirages bombed Dumayr AB just as a flight of four MiG-21FLs was scrambling, one of the fighters being hit by the fragments; in the ensuing dogfight one Vautour was shot down, crashing near Lake Jeiroud north of the base. Overall, the Syrian Air Force avoided all-too-heavy losses by evacuating part of the fleet to remote bases, although many Syrians later deemed this to be one of the contributing factors to the loss of the Golan Heights, and remained active throughout the war, flying 116 sorties.

The Syrian Su-7BMK fighter-bombers joined the action after the Six-Day War. In the inter-war period the Syrian Air Force suffered considerable losses, 35 of the original 60 *Fitter-As* being shot down in skirmishes with the Israeli forces or written off in accidents. For example, on 9th September 1972 two Syrian Su-7s were shot down by Mirage IIICJs and a third by a McDonnell Douglas F-4E Phantom II.

Even so, Syria was quite well prepared for action; in the autumn of 1973 it had 25 Su-7BMKs, augmented by 93 MiG-17Fs and 15 of the latest Su-20s which even the Soviet Union's Warsaw Pact allies did not yet have. The fighter-bombers were operated by two air brigades based at Blei, Dumayr and Daouli near Damascus. The combined fighter-bomber force of Syria and Egypt was twice that of Israel. The Soviet advisors assessed the Syrian pilots and technicians as quite professional; the pilots were brave and well motivated. By the outbreak of the Yom Kippur War most of the pilots had been trained for group strikes against ground targets, using all available weapons, and for ultra-low-level flying in order to get below the Israeli AD radar cover; anti-air defence manoeuvres were also practiced.

Each Syrian airbase had hardened aircraft shelters and up to four auxiliary dirt strips in case the main runway was cratered; additionally, two highway strips had been built near Damascus. Reserve command posts were built near the Golan Heights and along the Lebanese border. On the down side, the Syrians had no aerial reconnaissance assets; also, the Syrian Air Force had a rigid chain of command which discouraged initiative. As if that weren't enough, the Israelis were well equipped to cope with intruders, having built a chain of air defence radars and ECM instal-

Syrian Air Force Su-24MK '2518 Black' has been dismantled and loaded on special dollies for airlifting by an Antonov An-124.

Syrian Air Force IL-14S '1126 Black' visiting Berlin-Schönefeld.

lations on the high ground on Mt. Jebel Sheikh, at Tel Abunida, Hebron and Tel Foras which commanded a good view of the Syrian airbases.

The Syrian Air Force stepped up its activities near the Israeli border, especially when Israel invaded Lebanon on 12th May 1970. That day a group of IDF/AF Douglas A-4E Skyhawks headed into Lebanon was attacked by six MiG-17Fs. The MiGs had two of the Skyhawks ready for killing, and these would almost certainly have been shot down, had not the Mirage IIICJs flying top cover descended on the attackers, destroying three of them. In the afternoon the Syrian MiG-17Fs strafed Israeli troops twice, suffering no losses. These attacks caused the Israelis to concentrate on hunting Syrian aircraft, which left fewer aircraft available for close air support.

Between the end of the Six-Day War and the end of the War of Attrition Israeli pilots claimed to have destroyed 25 Syrian MiG-21s; in turn, Syrian MiG-21 pilots claimed three confirmed 'kills' and four probables. In mid-September 1973 a furious air battle took place: two RF-4E reconnaissance jets escorted by two F-4Es, with four Mirage IIICJs lurking some distance behind, approached the Syrian coast and four MiG-21PFs took off from Abu al-Dahur AB to intercept. In the ensuing dogfight two MiG-21PFs and one Mirage IIICJ were shot down. Both sides called in reinforcements; a further four MiG-21s arriving on the scene were bounced by four newly arrived Mirages, three of the MiGs and a Mirage being shot down. A Sikorsky CH-53D helicopter, with Mirage and Phantom II escorts, appeared an hour later to rescue the Israeli pilots who had ejected and the Syrians, bent on revenge, took the opportunity to prolong the melee. They succeeded in shooting down one Phantom at the cost of several MiG-21s. After the battle, the Israelis claimed a total of 12 MiG-21s destroyed for the loss of one fighter; the Syrians claimed eight 'kills' and admitted five losses. Most historians estimate the actual losses as three Israeli and 12 Syrian aircraft.

Syria also attacked Israel on 6th October 1973, the first day the Yom Kippur War. At the time the Syrian Air Force had ten squadrons operating MiG-21s, with about 100 aircraft –

A Syrian Air Force IL-14T in two-tone 'Middle eastern' camouflage.

Soviet personnel pose with a Syrian Air Force An-12B registered YK-ANC. The base colour is obviously grey, as was standard for Soviet Air Force An-12s; unfortunately the colours of the cheatline are open to conjecture. Note the odd presentation of the letter K which seems to be painted on upside down.

mostly MiG-21F-13s plus some MiG-21PFs, 'PFMs and 'PFSs and 21 MiG-21MFs. To avoid exposing greenhorn pilots to the battle-hardened Israelis, only pilots having the rank of captain or higher were allowed to fly supersonic jets. On the opening day, the first wave of fighter-bombers (more on these below) and the escorting MiG-21s suffered no losses. The second wave, however, was jumped by Israeli fighters: three MiG-21MFs of 5 Sqn were shot down by IAI Nesher fighters of 144 Sqn.

At the start of the war, the Syrians outnumbered the IDF 9 to 1 in manpower and 7.2 to 1 in tanks; unsurprisingly, therefore, they made substantial gains on the first day. With the arrival of Israeli reservists, the Syrian advance slowed down on the second day, prompting them to rely on S-125 SAMs for air defence rather than risk their MiG-21s. Instead, they planned to use the latter to lure the Israeli fighters into a trap. The SAM sites were repositioned under cover of darkness, carefully camouflaged and instructed not to activate the radar at the first sign of the enemy. Several pairs of MiG-21s lurked nearby, ready to pounce on the attackers. A first wave of well-escorted F-4E Phantom IIs had spread out in search of targets, only to be met by a fusillade of missiles. As they attempted to dive below radar cover, they were attacked with radar-controlled anti-aircraft guns; five were shot down by ground fire. The survivors were intercepted by No.5 Sqn MiG-21MFs and one Phantom was destroyed before the escorting Neshers shot down two MiG-21MFs. Another pair of F-4Es were bounced by more MiG-21MFs, one of the latter scoring a 'kill' before two Phantoms bringing up the rear destroyed a MiG-21MF. Whilst the IDF/AF admitted both of these two losses, neither was claimed by Syrian fighters. On the same afternoon, three Mirage IIICJs and an A-4E were shot down without loss but three MiG-21MFs were downed by AAA and SAMs in a 'friendly fire' incident.

The Israelis mounted an immense strike to halt the advance of Syrian tanks over the Golan Heights. Not only did they succeed in stopping the Syrians as they approached Nafah where the HQ of the Israeli 7th Armoured Brigade was, but from this point the Syrians were slowly but surely pushed back. The IDF/AF suffered huge losses in so doing: 23 aircraft were shot down and 40 damaged, mostly by ground fire (three F-4Es were destroyed by MiG-21PFMs); in contrast, the SyrAF lost 13 aircraft to Israeli fighters. However, on 10th October the last Syrian troops left the Golan Heights and the Israeli Army flooded deeper into Syria to approach within 40 km (25 miles) from Damascus, forming the so-called Bashan Salient. Aided by 30,000 Iraqi soldiers, the Syrian Army counterattacked and halted the Israeli advance but failed to dislodge them from the salient. A UN-brokered ceasefire came into operation on

IL-76M YK-ATA in early colours with a distinctive triple cheatline and small Syrianair titles on the rear fuselage.

26th October 1973. In the war the Syrians claimed 30 confirmed kills by MiG-21s for the loss of 29 MiG-21s.

On 6th October 1973, 20 Su-7BMKs assisted by 16 MiG-17Fs and escorted by six MiG-21MFs bombed three Israeli radar sites on the Golan Heights. The Syrians were unable to join the action straight away because of a sandstorm which kept their aircraft on the ground for a while. The first strike was aimed at the IDF/AF control centre at Hebron, three AD radar sites and Israeli strongholds and lines of communications on the Golan Heights and along the River Jordan. That day the Syrians flew a total of 270 sorties, sustaining no losses; among other things, the strategically important bridge across the River Jordan at Deganiyah and the command post on Mt. Jebel Sheikh were destroyed. This allowed the Syrians to make an airborne assault, the commandos capturing and destroying Israeli ECM equipment. The Israeli propaganda tended to downplay the scale of these operations, reporting that 'only 25 sorties' had been flown.

In the subsequent days the Syrian Su-7BMKs flew CAS sorties; these were made by groups of six to 12 aircraft covered by MiG-21s. This was no vain precaution, as IDF/AF fighters would pursue the *Fitters* as they returned home. Soon the Su-7s started operating in pairs or flights to improve tactical flexibility. On 8th October the Su-7BMKs attacked the command post at Kiryat Shmon in Israeli territory. The IDF/AF mounted a retaliatory strike but lost four McDonnell Douglas F-4E Phantom IIs to the Syrian air defences.

On 9th October the Su-7s bombed the oil refinery in the suburbs of Haifa. The jets approached covertly at low level and zoomed to an altitude of 200 m (660 ft) immediately before the target, releasing ZAB-250-200 incendiary bombs and OFAB-250-270 HE/fragmentation bombs. The attackers suffered no losses. Three days later, however, Shlomo Levi flying an IAI Nesher interceptor managed to shoot down two Syrian Su-7s.

Apart from these types of bombs, the Su-7s' main weapons were S-5 FFARs, S-3K and S-24 HVARs, and the highly effective

Syrian Air Force IL-76M YK-ATB, No.522 Sqn, Damascus International airport

In contrast, IL-76M 'Falsie' YK-ATD wore the full old Syrianair livery.

RBK-250 cluster bombs loaded with 2.5-kg (5.5-lb) PTAB-2.5 shaped-charge armour-piercing bomblets. The pilots made good use of the hilly terrain to escape detection by the enemy during target approach. Attacks were usually made in level flight or a 10-12° dive from 100-300 m (330-980 ft). Steeper dives were ruled out because of the altitude limit – commencing the attack at higher altitude resulted in being promptly targeted by the air defences. On the way back the *Fitters* scattered to throw the pursuing Israeli jets off course. The Israelis would often follow a group of fighter-bombers and try to attack the bases' air defence installations; the air defences were often unable to fire in this situation for fear of hitting 'friendly' aircraft. The IDF/AF made a total of 52 raids against Syrian bases, including five at Daouli, six at Dumayr and nine at Blei; 19 Syrian aircraft were destroyed on the ground but there were no Su-7s among them.

On the night of 20th October a new attack was made on the refinery at Haifa, the Syrians losing a single Su-7BMK to ground fire. All in all, the Syrian *Fitter-As* made 203 sorties in the Yom Kippur War.

The pilots had a hard time pinpointing small targets and were forced to circle over the battle area, which made them vulnerable to Israeli air defences. This was due to the fact that the Syrians had no forward air controllers to assist the pilots. Four or five aircraft were shot down daily – mostly during repeat attack runs or if the pilots grew careless on the way back. The Israelis destroyed 13 Syrian *Fitter-As* during this war, virtually exterminating Syria's Su-7 fleet. On the other hand, unlike Egypt, Syria suffered no non-combat losses of Su-7s in the Yom Kippur War.

The Syrians had the distinction of being the first to use the Su-20 in real combat. The *Fitter-Cs* fired in anger for the first time in 1973 during the Yom Kippur War. At the start

Here YK-ATA is seen after conversion to an IL-76T and repaint in Syrianair's current colours.

of hostilities the Syrian Air Force had 15 aircraft of this type. On the first day of the conflict, 6th October, 12 Syrian Su-20s escorted by eight MiG-21s launched a strike on the Israeli air control centre at Hebron. On 6th and 7th October groups of six or 12 Su-20s attacked targets deep in the Israeli rear. After 7th October smaller groups of two to four fighter-bombers were used. The aircraft approached their objectives at ultra-low level, changing altitude, heading and speed to frustrate the air defences. As the latter were bolstered, GCI command centres and radar sites were increasingly often chosen as targets.

The main weapons used by the Su-20 against Israeli strong points were FAB-250 and FAB-500 HE bombs. These were delivered in a shallow dive from about 300 m (990 ft) after a steep climb or a combat turn, or in level flight at low altitude with a brief (8- to 10-second) climb followed by a dive and an anti-air defence manoeuvre. Troops and military equipment were usually attacked with OFAB-250 HE/fragmentation bombs or S-24 and S-5K rockets, the latter featuring shaped-charge warheads. The strikes were made from level flight or in a shallow dive at angles of 10-12° from a height of 100-200 m (330-660 ft). RBK-250 cluster bombs filled with PTAB-2.5 SCAP bomblets were used against tanks; the cluster bombs were delivered, using the toss-bombing technique. Unguided rockets were launched in level flight at a height of 25 to 50 m (80-164 ft). In the raid on the oil refinery at Haifa ZAB-250 incendiary bombs and OFAB-250 HE/fragmentation bombs were used; these were delivered in level flight at 200 m (660 ft) after a short preliminary climb.

The fighter-bombers suffered their greatest losses when pulling away from the target and during attacks when the aircraft had climbed to 200 m (660 ft) or higher. In the course of the Yom Kippur War the Syrian Su-20s flew 98 sorties, in which eight aircraft were lost. All of these losses were ascribed to AAA or SAMs, although Israeli pilot Ariel Cohen flying an IAI Nesher fighter is known to have shot down a Syrian Su-20 on 8th October 1973. At the closing stage of the war, on 19th (other reports say 20th) October 1973, another IDF/AF Nesher pilot, Giora Aven (Epstein), shot down two Egyptian Su-20s in one day.

As they had done in the previous war, the Israelis tried bombing and mining the runways at Syrian airbases. For example, on 11th-16th October Mezze AB near Damascus was raided by Israeli Phantoms several times a day. They succeeded in destroying one UTI-MiG-15, one MiG-17F, one Mi-8T helicopter and one An-24B airliner parked in the open, and two more Fresco-Cs were damaged by unguided rockets which flew into open HAS doors. However, this cost the IDF/AF six Phantoms shot down by AA fire, and bombing accuracy was greatly reduced because of the need to take evasive action.

Syrian MiG-23s also had their share of the action. Arriving on the scene in mid-October 1973, the first MiG-23MSs were too late to participate in the Yom Kippur War. In fact, Syrian SAM sites took a heavy toll on Israeli warplanes, with forty destroyed in the first 48 hours of the war. This had two important implications. Firstly, the Syrians became over-confident in, and overly reliant on, SAMs; secondly, the IDF/AF became determined to find ways to destroy them.

On 19th April 1974 the Syrian MiG-23MS received its baptism of fire. Capt. al-Masry was on a weapons test mission when, to his surprise, he spotted a formation of eight Israeli McDonnell Douglas F-4E Phantom IIs. Unable to contact his base because of heavy Israeli ECM, he acted on his own; accelerating hard, he made a tight turn and was able to manoeuvre into position immediately behind the Israelis. He launched three missiles, destroying two of the Phantoms, and was about to make another attack, this time with cannon fire, when his own aircraft was struck by a misguided SAM fired by a Syrian battery. Very badly wounded, he emerged from a coma one month later and never did discover how he managed to survive. Although he recovered from his wounds, he was no longer fit for flying but was rewarded by being promoted to major (he eventually rose to lieutenant-general) and awarded the 'Hero of the Syrian Arab Republic' title.

After a ceasefire was declared at the end of April 1974 the confrontation between Syria and Israel continued in the form of Israeli reconnaissance flights over the Lebanon, followed by attacks on Palestine Liberation Organisation (PLO) training camps. On 26th April 1981 an attack on a camp in Sidon by two Israeli Douglas A-4E Skyhawks was in progress when Syrian ground-controlled intercept stations detected the attackers and alerted two patrolling MiG-23MSs, which swooped in and destroyed the Skyhawks.

On 13th February 1981, two IDF/AF RF-4E reconnaissance aircraft acted as bait, intruding into Syrian airspace and luring a Syrian Air Force MiG-25PD into pursuing them. The interceptor was then ambushed by two F-15As which had

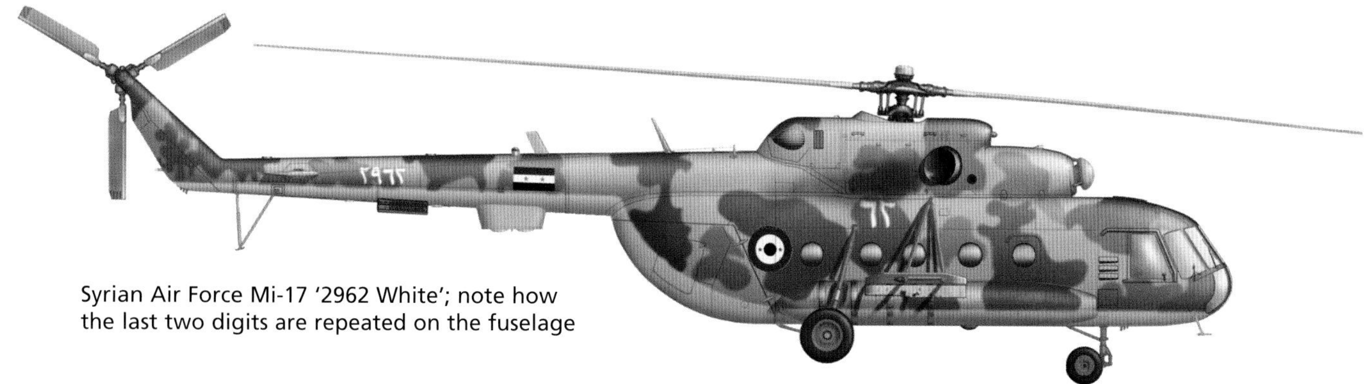

Syrian Air Force Mi-17 '2962 White'; note how the last two digits are repeated on the fuselage

been hiding from Syrian radars behind a mountain range. One F-15 popped up from behind a cloud of chaff, approaching the MiG from below so that its pilot could not see the Israeli jet, and fired an AIM-7M Sparrow missile which hit the MiG's port wing. Syrian ground controllers were unable to warn the pilot because the Israelis were heavily using ECM.

Shortly afterwards the roles in the cat-and-mouse game were reversed – but the end result was much the same. Two Syrian MiG-21s provoked a couple of Israeli F-15s, which gave chase. Two MiG-25PDs took off to intercept the Eagles; one attacked the F-15 head on, the other tried for a flank attack. The first MiG-25 failed to fire its missiles after losing target lock-on and was shot down by the F-15 flight leader. The other MiG destroyed the Israeli wingman with two R-40 missiles at about 40 km (25 miles) range. That was the last time Syrian MiG-25Ps engaged in combat.

In 1976 the surviving Syrian Su-7BMKs saw action for the last time when Syria intervened to stop the civil war in Lebanon. The Syrian Army moved in at the invitation of the Lebanese government – initially to protect Christian minorities caught in the struggle between Israel and one of its arch-enemies, the PLO.

Six years later the fifth Arab-Israeli war (aka the First Lebanon War) broke out because Syria gave support the PLO, whose guerrillas were based in Lebanon and systematically shelled northern Israel from there. After the PLO's failed attempt to assassinate the Israeli Ambassador to the United Kingdom, the Israeli Army retaliated by launching Operation *Peace for Galilee*, invading the Lebanon on 6th June 1982. Since the end of the Yom Kippur War there had been significant, if sporadic, air battles between Israel and Syria in which the IDF/AF shot down 33 confirmed Syrian aircraft, including 24 MiG-21MFs; the Syrian Air Force

2962 White, an armed Syrian Air Force Mi-17 in rather faded three-tone camouflage.

claimed eight confirmed 'kills', five by MiG-21MFs and three by MiG-23MSs. It was hardly a fight on equal terms; the Syrian jets were still armed with the old R-13M1 missiles, whose reliability was rather low, and stood little chance against the IDF/AF's McDonnell Douglas F-15A Eagles and General Dynamics F-16A Fighting Falcons armed with modern versions of the Sidewinder (the AIM-9D and AIM-9L). The carnage continued after the invasion began; between 6th and 11th June 1982 the Israelis shot down 79 confirmed Syrian aircraft, including about 45 MiG-21MFs (some were not positively identified as MiG-21s). In return, the Syrians scored three confirmed 'kills', two of them by MiG-21s, and claimed 15 probables. This time the Syrian pilots were experienced and soundly trained but, although they fought valiantly, it soon became clear that the MiG-21MF was outclassed, and from then on it was only used in air battles if no MiG-23MSs were available.

By the outbreak of the First Lebanon War the Syrian Air Force had received a squadron of the then-latest Su-22M fighter-bombers augmenting its Su-20s. These aircraft were initially held in reserve, finding use in a raid against the Israeli Army HQ in southern Lebanon on 11th June. Ten Su-22Ms had been covertly redeployed to Damascus; at dawn, carrying eight FAB-500 bombs each, they set out towards the target at low altitude. All precautions notwithstanding, the attackers were detected by an IDF/AF Grumman E-2C Hawkeye AWACS which vectored F-16As towards them. Seven of the *Fitters* were shot down before they had a chance to reach the target; still, the lead pair got through and placed their bombs squarely on the HQ building, which was destroyed, with high losses for the Israelis (the victims included the Deputy Chief of Staff who commanded Operation *Peace for Galilee*). The ceasefire order was issued that same day.

Su-22M3Rs equipped with KKR-1TE pods were also used to fly reconnaissance missions over the Lebanon. During the First Lebanon War, Syrian Su-22M and MiG-23BN fighter-bombers made 42 sorties, destroying 80 Israeli Merkava tanks and two battalions of motorised infantry. On the other hand, by the time the fighting ended in September the Syrians had lost 82 aircraft, including seven Su-22Ms and 14 MiG-23BNs.

The Syrian Air Force Mi-25s made their combat début in June 1982, engaging Israeli tanks that had entered the Lebanon. The Syrians' helicopter operations can be deemed successful. Together with Aérospatiale SA 342L Gazelles the *Hinds* flew 93 sorties, scoring most of the 55 'kills' against Israeli tanks claimed by the Syrian Air Force; they were especially successful in an operation against an Israeli armoured brigade near the mountain village of Aïn Zgalta. There were no Mi-25 losses during the summer campaign.

Syrian SAM sites had already started to move into the Lebanese Beka'a Valley in April 1981 and the influx continued after the Israeli invasion. This indicated to the Israelis that the Syrians did not want a full-scale war – otherwise they would have reinforced the defences of Damascus. Having found out the lethal power of the SAMs the hard way in the October 1973 war, the Israeli Air Staff was determined to eliminate the SAM sites in the Beka'a Valley, and government approval for this was obtained on 9th June 1982. Consequently, when the attack started at 1400 hrs that same day, an IDF/AF E-2C aircraft was employed for the first time ever in battle. The Hawkeye was able to pick-up signals 800 km (497 miles) away, monitor up to 200 aircraft at a time and control up to 130 aerial engagements. Additionally, an Israeli Boeing 707 modified for ECM duties was fielded to jam Syrian radar and communications. First, reconnaissance drones were sent into the Beka'a Valley to trick the SAM crews into switching on their radars. As soon as they did, the waiting Israeli F-4E Phantoms let loose with a salvo of anti-radar missiles, wiping out 17 out of the 19 SAM sites. Israeli F-15A and F-16A fighters were on guard all the while, but the overconfident Syrians had recalled all their fighters to their bases to create a free-fire zone; the fighters were not scrambled until after the damage had been done.

The remaining two SAM sites were destroyed the next day. During the two days of the attack, the Israelis claimed to have shot down 64 Syrian aircraft for no loss to themselves. Syrian sources admitted 21 aircraft lost but claimed that 25 IDF/AF aircraft had been destroyed – without mentioning the loss of any SAM sites.

The Syrians devised new tactics in the Lebanon, enabling their interceptors to take advantage of the F-15A's major weakness: it was unable to track more than one target at a time because its radar had to be concentrated into a narrower beam for missile guidance. The tactic involved using a team of four MiG-23MFs. The first was to lurk outside the area monitored by Syrian SAMs to detect a tar-

Syrian Air Force Mi-25 '2830 Black' shows off its faded tan/green camouflage. Note that the warning stencil on the tail-boom is in Arabic.

'2802 Black', another Syrian Mi-25. The wingtip rails for 9M17P anti-tank missiles are clearly visible.

get; then another MiG would present itself as a decoy, allowing itself to be tracked by Israeli fighters just outside range of the SAMs, allowing the third aircraft to make an undetected attack. The fourth acted as reserve in case other Israeli aircraft joined the party. The main drawback was that the Syrians had to use R-3S missiles, whereas the Israelis had Raytheon AIM-7F Sparrow missiles and, more importantly, the more manoeuvrable Sidewinders. Nonetheless, in the first few days the Syrians could claim some success for these tactics.

On 7th June Maj. Hallyak was leading a flight of three MiG-23MFs, with Capt. Said and Capt. Merza as his wingmen. Encountering a solitary Israeli F-16A, they shot it down but were immediately counter-attacked by two more. It was claimed that one of the latter was shot down as well, but not before a Syrian fighter also fell. The following day two MiG-23MFs piloted by Maj. Haw and Capt. Matuk were ambushed by IDF/AF F-16As but destroyed one of them before Haw was shot down; Matuk managed to disengage and return to base. On the morning of 9th June, two MiG-23MFs flown by Capt. Dib and Capt. Said claimed another F-16A but, again, one Syrian fighter was shot down. The Israelis denied these F-16A losses.

In late 1982 a multinational force of US, French and Italian soldiers arrived in the Lebanon and arranged the deportation of over 14,000 PLO combatants to other Arab countries. Israeli forces started to pull out from the newly set up Security Zone in May 1983, completing the withdrawal in June 1985. The Syrians finally withdrew from the Lebanon on 26th April 2005. Syrian fighter losses in the Lebanon War are estimated to be 54 MiG-21s and MiG-23s.

After the war, Syrian Mi-24s saw more action in the Lebanon – this time against militant right-wing Christian groups. Their missions included maintaining a naval blockade of the Lebanon in the areas controlled by the extremists. On 11th April 1989 a routine patrol mission ended in a tragic incident caused by mistaken identity: a pair of Syrian *Hinds* attacked two Soviet Navy support vessels – a tug and diver boat – 70 km (43.5 miles) west of the Syrian port of Tartous (where the Soviet Union maintained a naval base, and Russia still does). Both vessels were damaged and seven sailors were injured. Damascus acknowledged its fault and presented an official apology.

By 1985, Israel had largely withdrawn its troops from the Lebanon but continued to monitor it, using reconnaissance aircraft. On 20th November 1985 one of the latter was targeted by two MiG-23 fighters, but these were shot down by Israeli F-15As before they could approach within attack range. One Syrian MiG-23MLAE was presented to Israel by a defector on 11th October 1989.

On 14th September 2001 two Syrian Air Force MiG-29s were shot down by IDF/AF F-15s while intercepting Israeli reconnaissance aircraft flying along the Lebanese and Syrian coast. Both pilots (Maj. Arshad Midhat Mubarak and Capt. Ahmad al-Khatab) ejected safely and were rescued by Syrian ships.

As mentioned above, in February 2012 unrest broke out in Syria. The Libyan scenario was virtually repeated: what started as civic protests (for much the same reason) quickly turned into armed insurrection goaded and financed by the western powers and Saudi Arabia in a drive to remove President Bashar Assad. On 27th September Syrian government forces had their first major clash with the Free Syrian Army (FSA) guerrillas in the city of Rastan, Homs Province, which had been under opposition control for a couple of weeks. The Battle of Rastan continued until 1st October and was the biggest battle of the war up to then, the Syrian Army units being supported by tanks and helicopters. As a result, the FSA was forced to retreat from Rastan, crossing the border into Turkey.

A shaky ceasefire was concluded in the spring of 2012 but collapsed on 1st June, the rebels beginning a new nationwide offensives against the government troops. The pretext was what had been described as the Houla massacre by the rebels, who accused the government troops of killing innocent civilians, while the government argued that the victims had been armed guerrillas and President Bashar al-Assad vowed to crush the uprising. A new major battle began on 5th June, the government troops attacking the city of Latakia, using tanks and Mi-25 attack helicopters. In the course of the fighting the FSA has claimed several Syrian Air Force aircraft shot down, including a MiG-23 and a Mi-17.

Known Syrian Air Force aircraft of Soviet/Russian origin

Type	Serial/ registration	C/n	F/n	Notes
An-12	YK-ANC (1)	?		Seen between 1972 and 1975; see An-26 below!
An-24B 'Salon'	YK-ANA	87304203		
An-24B 'Salon'	YK-ANB	87304204?		Destroyed 13-10-1973 or 16-10-1973
An-26	YK-ANC (2)	3007		D/D 1975
An-26	YK-AND	3008		D/D 1975
An-26	YK-ANE	3103		D/D 1975
An-26	YK-ANF	3104		D/D 1975
An-26B	YK-ANG	10907		D/D 1981
An-26B	YK-ANH	11406		D/D 1981

IL-14S	1126 Black	?		Natural metal finish; also reported as an Egyptian/UARAF aircraft!
IL-14P	?	14803009		East German-built, ex-Interflug DM-SAC
IL-14P	?	14803015		East German-built, ex-Interflug DM-SAE
IL-14P	?	14803018		East German-built, ex-Interflug DM-SAG
IL-14P	?	14803024		East German-built, ex-Interflug DM-SAK
IL-76M	YK-ATA	093421613	1604	Standard version, white with triple blue cheatline and Syrianair titles. Converted to IL-76T (no gunner's station), full new Syrianair livery
IL-76M	YK-ATB	093421619	1605	Standard version, white with triple blue cheatline and Syrianair titles. Converted to IL-76T (no gunner's station), full new Syrianair livery
IL-76M 'Falsie'	YK-ATC	0013431911	2308	Full old Syrianair livery. Stored Damascus
IL-76M 'Falsie'	YK-ATD	0013431915	2309	Full old Syrianair livery. Now with 'IL-76T' nose titles!
Ka-28	3550 Black	5235004944508	?	Built in 1989
Ka-28	3553 Black	5235004944513	?	Built in 1989
MiG-15*bis*	?	613714		Czechoslovak-built (Aero S-103). Destroyed at Abu Sueir AB, Egypt, 1-11-1956
MiG-15*bis*	?	613715		Czechoslovak-built (Aero S-103). Destroyed at Abu Sueir AB, Egypt, 1-11-1956
MiG-15*bis*	?	613716		Czechoslovak-built (Aero S-103). Destroyed at Abu Sueir AB, Egypt, 1-11-1956
MiG-15*bis*	?	613718		Czechoslovak-built (Aero S-103). Destroyed at Abu Sueir AB, Egypt, 1-11-1956
MiG-15*bis*	?	613720		Czechoslovak-built (Aero S-103). Destroyed at Abu Sueir AB, Egypt, 1-11-1956
MiG-15*bis*	?	613721		Czechoslovak-built (Aero S-103). Destroyed at Abu Sueir AB, Egypt, 1-11-1956
MiG-15*bis*	?	613722		Czechoslovak-built (Aero S-103). Destroyed at Abu Sueir AB, Egypt, 1-11-1956
MiG-15*bis*	?	613723		Czechoslovak-built (Aero S-103). Destroyed at Abu Sueir AB, Egypt, 1-11-1956
MiG-15*bis*	?	613724		Czechoslovak-built (Aero S-103). Destroyed at Abu Sueir AB, Egypt, 1-11-1956
MiG-15*bis*	?	613725		Czechoslovak-built (Aero S-103). Destroyed at Abu Sueir AB, Egypt, 1-11-1956
MiG-15*bis*	?	613726		Czechoslovak-built (Aero S-103). Destroyed at Abu Sueir AB, Egypt, 1-11-1956
MiG-15*bis*	?	613727		Czechoslovak-built (Aero S-103). Destroyed at Abu Sueir AB, Egypt, 1-11-1956
MiG-15*bis*	?	613728		Czechoslovak-built (Aero S-103). Destroyed at Abu Sueir AB, Egypt, 1-11-1956
MiG-15*bis*	?	613729		Czechoslovak-built (Aero S-103). Destroyed at Abu Sueir AB, Egypt, 1-11-1956
MiG-15*bis*	?	613730		Czechoslovak-built (Aero S-103). Destroyed at Abu Sueir AB, Egypt, 1-11-1956
MiG-15*bis*	?	613731		Czechoslovak-built (Aero S-103). Destroyed at Abu Sueir AB, Egypt, 1-11-1956
MiG-15*bis*	?	613732		Czechoslovak-built (Aero S-103). Destroyed at Abu Sueir AB, Egypt, 1-11-1956
MiG-15*bis*	?	613733		Czechoslovak-built (Aero S-103). Destroyed at Abu Sueir AB, Egypt, 1-11-1956
MiG-15*bis*	?	613734		Czechoslovak-built (Aero S-103). Destroyed at Abu Sueir AB, Egypt, 1-11-1956
MiG-15*bis*	?	623739		Czechoslovak-built (Aero S-103). Destroyed at Abu Sueir AB, Egypt, 1-11-1956
UTI-MiG-15	224	?		Full serial should be 1224?
UTI-MiG-15	273 Black	?		Full serial should be 1273? Sand/green camouflage. Preserved Army Museum, Damascus
UTI-MiG-15	9380	?		Instructional airframe at Aleppo University, serial probably fake
UTI-MiG-15	?	612788		Czechoslovak-built (Aero CS-102), D/D 1956
UTI-MiG-15	?	612790		Czechoslovak-built (Aero CS-102), D/D 1956
UTI-MiG-15	?	612791		Czechoslovak-built (Aero CS-102), D/D 1956
UTI-MiG-15	?	612792		Czechoslovak-built (Aero CS-102). Crashed at Dekkelah AB, Egypt, 16-8-1956
UTI-MiG-15	?	522545		Czechoslovak-built (Aero CS-102), ex-Polish Air Force 545 Red?, D/D 1969
UTI-MiG-15	?	622033		Czechoslovak-built (Aero CS-102), ex-Polish Air Force 633 Red", D/D 1969
UTI-MiG-15	?	622036		Czechoslovak-built (Aero CS-102), ex-Polish Air Force 636 Red?, D/D 1969
UTI-MiG-15	?	722060		Czechoslovak-built (Aero CS-102), ex-Polish Air Force 760 Red?, D/D 1969
UTI-MiG-15	?	722080		Czechoslovak-built (Aero CS-102), ex-Polish Air Force 780 Red?, D/D 1969
PZL SBLim-1	?	1A 07-051		Ex-Polish Air Force 051 Red; D/D post 9-1972
PZL SBLim-1	?	1A 08-001		Ex-Polish Air Force 001 Red; D/D post 12-1972
PZL SBLim-1	?	1A 11-006		Ex-Polish Air Force 106 Red; D/D post 9-1972
PZL SBLim-1	?	1A 11-018		Ex-Polish Air Force 118 Red; D/D post 9-1972
PZL SBLim-1	?	1A 12-001		Ex-Polish Air Force 101 Red; D/D post 12-1972
MiG-17F	48 Black	?		Only last two digits applied? Natural metal, UARAF markings. Crash-landed in Jordan 4-10-1960
MiG-17F	912 Black/12	?		Full serial on fin and last two repeated on nose
MiG-17F	928 Black/28	?		Became, see next line

	1028 Black			
MiG-17F	933 Black/33	?		Became, see next line
	1033 Black			Camouflaged, captured by Israel
MiG-17F	936 Black/36	?		
MiG-17F	939 Black/39	?		Natural metal, pre-UAR insignia
MiG-17F	943 Black/43	?		Became, see next line
	1043 Black			
MiG-17F	944 Black/44	?		
MiG-17F	946 Black/46	?		Natural metal, pre-UAR markings
MiG-17F	950 Black/50	?		
MiG-17F	952 Black/52	?		
MiG-17F	957 Black/57	?		
MiG-17F	1196 Black	?		Preserved Army Museum, Damascus
MiG-17F	1228 Black	?		Teaching aid at Aleppo University
MiG-17F	2025 Black	?		Ex-Egyptian Air Force? Natural metal finish, red intake lip and rudder
MiG-17F	2051 Black	?		Ex-Egyptian Air Force? Natural metal finish, red intake lip and rudder
MiG-17F	2300 Black	?		Ex-Egyptian Air Force? Natural metal finish, red intake lip and rudder
PZL Lim-5	941 Black/41	1C 07-18		Ex-East German Air Force 707 Red. Became, see next line
	1041 Black			Two-tone camouflage, pre-UAR insignia. Captured by Israel 12-8-1968
MiG-17F	?	0112		Ex-Soviet Air Force?
MiG-17F	?	0115		Ex-Soviet Air Force?
MiG-17F	?	0130		Ex-Soviet Air Force?
MiG-17F	?	0314		Ex-East German Air Force 772 Red
MiG-17F	?	0327		Ex-East German Air Force 788 Red
MiG-17F	?	0337		Ex-East German Air Force 774 Red
MiG-17F	?	0338		Ex-East German Air Force 304 Red
MiG-17F	?	0427		Ex-Soviet Air Force?
MiG-17F	?	0446		Ex-Soviet Air Force?
MiG-17F	?	0503		Ex-Soviet Air Force?
MiG-17F	?	0510		Ex-Soviet Air Force?
MiG-17F	?	0654		Ex-East German Air Force 651 Red
MiG-17F	?	0657		Ex-Soviet Air Force?
MiG-17F	?	0681		Ex-Soviet Air Force?
MiG-17F	?	0863		Ex-Soviet Air Force?
MiG-17F	?	0873		Ex-Soviet Air Force?
MiG-17F	?	0895		Ex-Soviet Air Force?
MiG-17F	?	0911		Ex-Soviet Air Force?
MiG-17F	?	0926		Ex-Soviet Air Force? (possibly to Egypt)
MiG-17F	?	0932		Ex-Soviet Air Force?
MiG-17F	?	1017		Ex-Soviet Air Force? (possibly to Egypt)
MiG-17F	?	1021		Ex-Soviet Air Force? (possibly to Egypt)
MiG-17F	?	7019		Ex-Algerian Air Force
MiG-17F	?	7125		Ex-Soviet Air Force? (possibly to Egypt)
MiG-17F	?	7203		Ex-Soviet Air Force? (possibly to Egypt)
MiG-17F	?	7239		Ex-Soviet Air Force?
MiG-17F	?	7329		Ex-Soviet Air Force?
MiG-17F	?	7331		Ex-Soviet Air Force?
MiG-17F	?	7344		Ex-Soviet Air Force?
MiG-17F	?	8408		Ex-Soviet Air Force?
MiG-17F	?	8430		Ex-Soviet Air Force?
MiG-17F	?	0115304		Ex-Soviet Air Force? (possibly to Egypt)
MiG-17F	?	0315321		Ex-Soviet Air Force?
MiG-17F	?	0315333		Ex-Soviet Air Force?
MiG-17F	?	0415309		Ex-Soviet Air Force?
MiG-17F	?	0415310		Ex-Soviet Air Force?
MiG-17F	?	0415319		Ex-Soviet Air Force? (possibly to Egypt)
MiG-17F	?	0415342		Ex-Soviet Air Force?

MiG-17F	?	0415349	Ex-Soviet Air Force?
MiG-17F	?	0415375	Ex-Soviet Air Force? (possibly to Egypt)
MiG-17F	?	0415397	Ex-Soviet Air Force? (possibly to Egypt)
MiG-17F	?	0515314	Ex-Soviet Air Force?
MiG-17F	?	0515318	Ex-Soviet Air Force?
MiG-17F	?	0515363	Ex-Soviet Air Force? (possibly to Egypt)
MiG-17F	?	0615338	Ex-Soviet Air Force? (possibly to Egypt)
MiG-17F	?	0715305	Ex-Soviet Air Force?
MiG-17F	?	0815364	Ex-Soviet Air Force? (possibly to Egypt)
MiG-17F	?	0915306	Ex-Soviet Air Force? (possibly to Egypt)
MiG-17F	?	0915336	Ex-Soviet Air Force? (possibly to Egypt)
MiG-17F	?	0915394	Ex-Soviet Air Force? (possibly to Egypt)
PZL Lim-5	?	1C 07-26	Ex-East German Air Force 743 Red
PZL Lim-5	?	1C 08-23	Ex-East German Air Force 971 Red
PZL Lim-5	?	1C 09-11	Ex-East German Air Force 951 Red
MiG-17PF	452	?	In service 1973
MiG-19S	1127	?	
MiG-19S	1128 Black	?	Sand/tan camouflage, pre-UAR insignia. No.77 Sqn, 1967
MiG-19S	3878	?	
MiG-19S	6308 Black	?	Sand/tan camouflage, pre-UAR insignia. No.77 Sqn, 1967
MiG-21F-13	577	?	Noted 2001 derelict Aleppo
MiG-21F-13	0912 Black	?	Czechoslovak-built (Aero S-106). Camouflaged, pre-UAR insignia
MiG-21F-13	1073	?	
MiG-21F-13	1301	?	
MiG-21F-13	1864 Black	?	Tan/green camouflage. Preserved Army Museum, Damascus
MiG-21F-13	2190	?	
MiG-21F-13	2540 Black	?	Silver overall, pre-UAR insignia
MiG-21F-13	8842	?	
MiG-21F-13	?	740802	Moscow-built. Ex-Polish Air Force 802 Red, D/D 10-1973
MiG-21F-13	?	740803	Ex-Polish Air Force 803 Red, D/D 10-1973
MiG-21F-13	?	741212	Ex-Hungarian Air Force 212 Red, D/D 10-1973
MiG-21F-13	?	741214	Ex-Hungarian Air Force 214 Red, D/D 10-1973
MiG-21F-13	?	741215	Ex-Hungarian Air Force 215 Red, D/D 10-1973
MiG-21F-13	?	741216	Ex-Hungarian Air Force 216 Red, D/D 10-1973
MiG-21F-13	?	741222	Ex-Hungarian Air Force 222 Red, D/D 10-1973
MiG-21F-13	?	741302	Ex-Hungarian Air Force 302 Red, D/D 10-1973
MiG-21F-13	?	741306	Ex-Hungarian Air Force 306 Red, D/D 10-1973
MiG-21F-13	?	741311	Ex-Hungarian Air Force 311 Red, D/D 10-1973
MiG-21F-13	?	741314	Ex-Hungarian Air Force 314 Red, D/D 10-1973
MiG-21F-13	?	741320	Ex-Hungarian Air Force 320 Red, D/D 10-1973
MiG-21F-13	?	741324	Ex-Hungarian Air Force 324 Red, D/D 10-1973
MiG-21F-13	?	741810	Ex-Hungarian Air Force 810 Red, D/D 10-1973
MiG-21F-13	?	741812	Ex-Hungarian Air Force 812 Red, D/D 10-1973
MiG-21F-13	?	741906	Ex-Hungarian Air Force 906 Red, D/D 10-1973
MiG-21F-13	?	N74212007	Gor'kiy-built. Ex-Polish Air Force 2007 Red, D/D 10-1973
MiG-21F-13	?	N74212009	Ex-Polish Air Force 2009 Red, D/D 10-1973
MiG-21F-13	?	N74212019	Ex-Polish Air Force 2019 Red, D/D 10-1973
MiG-21F-13	?	N74212223	Ex-Polish Air Force 2223 Red, D/D 10-1973
MiG-21F-13	?	N74212315	Ex-Hungarian Air Force 2315 Red, D/D 10-1973
MiG-21F-13	?	360002	Czechoslovak-built (Aero S-106). Ex-Czechoslovak Air Force 0002 Black, D/D 1973
MiG-21F-13	?	360004	Czechoslovak-built (Aero S-106). Ex-Czechoslovak Air Force 0004 Black, D/D 1973
MiG-21F-13	?	360101	Czechoslovak-built (Aero S-106). Ex-Czechoslovak Air Force 0101 Black, D/D 1973
MiG-21F-13	?	360102	Czechoslovak-built (Aero S-106). Ex-Czechoslovak Air Force 0102 Black, D/D 1973
MiG-21F-13	?	460106	Czechoslovak-built (Aero S-106). Ex-Czechoslovak Air Force 0106 Black, D/D 1973
MiG-21F-13	?	560213	Czechoslovak-built (Aero S-106). Ex-Czechoslovak Air Force 0213 Black, D/D 1973

MiG-21F-13	?	560214		Czechoslovak-built (Aero S-106). Ex-Czechoslovak Air Force 0214 Black, D/D 1973
MiG-21F-13	?	560302		Czechoslovak-built (Aero S-106). Ex-Czechoslovak Air Force 0302 Black, D/D 1973
MiG-21F-13	?	269901		Czechoslovak-built (Aero S-106). Ex-Czechoslovak Air Force 9901 Black, D/D 1973
MiG-21F-13	?	269902		Czechoslovak-built (Aero S-106). Ex-Czechoslovak Air Force 9902 Black, D/D 1973
MiG-21F-13	?	269903		Czechoslovak-built (Aero S-106). Ex-Czechoslovak Air Force 9903 Black, D/D 1973
MiG-21PF	1401	?		
MiG-21PF	1411	?		
MiG-21PFS	8025	?		
MiG-21PFS	8070	?		
MiG-21PFM	1041	?		First aircraft of second shipment
MiG-21PFM	1072	?		
MiG-21PFM	1082	?		
MiG-21PFM	1461	?		First aircraft of first shipment
MiG-21PFM	1864 (1)	?		Preserved Army Museum, Damascus; see MiG-21MF below!
MiG-21PFM	2072	?		
MiG-21PFM	5220 Black	?		Natural metal finish, post-UAR insignia
MiG-21M	7501	?		Ex-East German Air Force 424 Red
MiG-21M	7601	962108		Ex-East German Air Force 415 Red
MiG-21M	7602	962101		Ex-East German Air Force 406 Red
MiG-21M	7603	960509		Ex-East German Air Force 582 Red
MiG-21M	?	962014		Ex-East German Air Force 402 Red
MiG-21M	?	962015		Ex-East German Air Force 403 Red
MiG-21M	?	962102		Ex-East German Air Force 407 Red
MiG-21M	?	962105		Ex-East German Air Force 412 Red
MiG-21M	?	962107		Ex-East German Air Force 414 Red
MiG-21M	?	962110		Ex-East German Air Force 418 Red
MiG-21M	?	960403		Ex-East German Air Force 532 Red
MiG-21M	?	960710		Ex-East German Air Force 610 Red
MiG-21MF	460	?	?	Preserved Tabqa
MiG-21MF	676	?	?	Preserved War Museum, Damascus
MiG-21MF	1487	?	?	
MiG-21MF	1571	?	?	
MiG-21MF	1864 (2)	?	?	Noted 2005 as active; see MiG-21PFM above!
MiG-21MF	2300	?	?	
MiG-21MF	2349	?	?	
MiG-21MF	1601	?	?	
MiG-21R	8506	?	?	
MiG-21*bis*	1074	N750*****	?	
MiG-21*bis*	1487	N750*****	?	
MiG-21U	513	?		
MiG-21US	1304	?		
MiG-21US	1603	?		
MiG-21US	1702	?		
MiG-23MS	1614	?	?	
MiG-23MS	1616	?	?	
MiG-23MF	2406 Black	?	?	
MiG-23MF	2407	?	?	
MiG-23MF	2487	03902*****	?	
MiG-23MF	3406	03902*****	?	
MiG-23MF	3478	03902*****	?	
MiG-23MLAE	2755	03903*****	?	
MiG-23MLAE	2781	03903*****	?	
MiG-23MLAE	2786 Black	0390324522	?	Flown to Israel by defector 11-10-1989
MiG-23BN	1650	03932*****	?	
MiG-23BN	1655	03932*****	?	
MiG-23BN	1661	03932*****	?	

MiG-23BN	2138	03932*****	?	To the USA for trials
MiG-23BN	2202	03932*****	?	To the USA for trials
MiG-23UB	2704	B103****	?	
MiG-23UB	?	B1037915	?	
MiG-23UB	?	B1038005	?	Seen on overhaul at 275th Aircraft Repair Plant, Krasnodar, Russia
MiG-23UB	?	B1038116	?	Seen on overhaul at 275th Aircraft Repair Plant, Krasnodar, Russia
MiG-23UB	?	B1038117	?	Seen on overhaul at 275th Aircraft Repair Plant, Krasnodar, Russia
MiG-25	808	?	?	
MiG-25PD	2519 Black	N840******	?	
MiG-25PD	2715 Black	N020******	?	
MiG-25	4101	?	?	
MiG-29	6700 Black	29605*****	?	Standard two-tone grey camouflage
Mi-2	?	567601042		
Mi-2	?	567602042		
Mi-2	?	567603042		
Mi-2	?	567604042		
Mi-2	?	567605042		
Mi-2	?	567606042		
Mi-2	?	567607042		
Mi-2	?	567608042		
Mi-2	?	567609042		
Mi-2	?	567610042		
Mi-4	3280			
Mi-8PPA	32	?	?	Wfu Gorelovo, Russia, 2008
Mi-8	52	?	?	
Mi-8TV	274	?	?	
Mi-8	276	?	?	
Mi-8	280	?	?	
Mi-8	296	?	?	
Mi-8	353	?	?	
Mi-8	354	?	?	
Mi-8	365	?	?	
Mi-8	371	?	?	
Mi-8	374	?	?	
Mi-8	376	?	?	
Mi-8	381	?	?	
Mi-8	382	?	?	
Mi-8	383	?	?	
Mi-8	390	?	?	
Mi-8	391	?	?	
Mi-8	392	?	?	
Mi-8	606	?	?	
Mi-8T	641	?	?	
Mi-8T	650	?	?	
Mi-8TV	1037	?	?	
Mi-8	1271	?	?	
Mi-8	1272	?	?	
Mi-8	1278	?	?	Preserved Army Museum, Damascus
Mi-8	1281	?	?	
Mi-8TV	1287 White	?	?	
Mi-8	1289	?	?	
Mi-8	1295	?	?	

Mi-8	1355	?	?	
Mi-8	1358	?	?	
Mi-8	1370	?	?	
Mi-8	1390	?	?	
Mi-8	1395	?	?	
Mi-8	1396	?	?	
Mi-8	2126	?	?	
Mi-17-1V	1285	?	?	
Mi-17-1V	2962 White/62	?	?	Last two digits repeated on the fuselage, camouflaged
Mi-17-1V	2963	?	?	
Mi-17-1V	2973	?	?	
Mi-17-1V	2974	?	?	
Mi-17-1V	2975	?	?	
Mi-17-1V	3932	?	?	
Mi-17PP	[*9]29	?	?	
Mi-14...	208	?	?	
Mi-14...	1282	?	?	
Mi-14...	1473?	?	?	Reported as 73
Mi-14...	1474?	?	?	Reported as 74
Mi-14PS	1475 Black/75	?	?	
Mi-14PL	1476	?	?	
Mi-14PS	1478 Black/78	?	?	
Mi-14PL	1481?	?	?	Reported as 81
Mi-14PL	1483?	?	?	Reported as such but carried only '83 Black' on the fuselage
Mi-14PL	1493 Black	?	?	
Mi-14PL	2383	?	?	
Mi-14...	2384?	?	?	Reported as 84
Mi-14...	2385?	?	?	Reported as 85
Mi-14PL	2386	?	?	
Mi-14...	2388?	?	?	Reported as 88
Mi-14PL	2392	?	?	
Mi-14PL	2396	?	?	
Mi-14...	6386	?	?	
Mi-14...	9296	?	?	
Mi-25	2800 Black	013178	?	Built in 1981
Mi-25	2802 Black	?	?	Sand/pale green camouflage
Mi-25	2808 Black	?	?	
Mi-25	2830 Black	?	?	Sand/pale green camouflage
Mi-25	2831 Black	?	?	
Mi-25	2834 Black	013254	?	Built in 1981
Mi-25	2839 Black	360428	?	Built in 1981
Mi-25	2840 Black?	360429?	?	Existence not proved but likely
Mi-25	2841 Black	360430	?	Built in 1984
Mi-25	2842 Black?	360431?	?	Existence not proved but likely
Mi-25	2843 Black	360432?	?	
Mi-25	2844 Black?	360433?	?	Existence not proved but likely
Mi-25	2845 Black?	360434?	?	Existence not proved but likely
Mi-25	2846 Black	360435?	?	
Mi-25	2847 Black	360436	?	Built in 1984
Mi-25	2848 Black	360437	?	Built in 1984
Mi-25	2851 Black	360588	?	Built in 1985
Mi-25	2852 Black	360589	?	Built in 1985
Mi-25	2853 Black?	360590?	?	Existence not proved but likely
Mi-25	2854 Black?	360591?	?	Existence not proved but likely
Mi-25	2855 Black?	360592?	?	Existence not proved but likely
Mi-25	2856 Black	360593	?	Built in 1985
Su-7BMK	813	?		Preserved Army Museum, Damascus; also reported as a Su-22!
Su-22M	140	?		To the USA for trials
Su-22M	143	?		To the USA for trials

Su-22M4	325 White	?		
Su-22M4	3214	?		
Su-24MK	2502 Black	416045*******	?	
Su-24MK	2511 Black	416045*******	?	
Su-24MK	2514 Black	416045*******	?	
Su-24MK	2518 Black	416045*******	?	
Su-24MK	3021 Black	416045*******	?	
Tu-134B-3 'Salon'	YK-AYA	(23)63992	6330	D/D 1982; old Syrianair livery. WFU/stored Damascus by 3-2001
Tu-134B-3 'Salon'	YK-AYB	(23)63994	6331	D/D 1982; old Syrianair livery, later new livery. In service 2012
Tu-134B-3	YK-AYC	(23)63989	6327	D/D 1982; old Syrianair livery. WFU/stored Damascus by 3-2001
Tu-134B-3 'Salon'	YK-AYD	(23)63990	6328	D/D 1982; old Syrianair livery. WFU/stored Damascus by 3-2001
Tu-134B-3	YK-AYE	(33)66187	6348	D/D 1983; old Syrianair livery, later new livery. In service 2009
Tu-134B-3	YK-AYF	(33)66190	6349	D/D 10-10-1984; old Syrianair livery, later new livery. In service 2011
Yak-40 'Salon'	YK-AQA	9411932		White with triple blue cheatline and Syrianair titles, later full old livery
Yak-40 'Salon'?	YK-AQB	9530443		White with triple blue cheatline and Syrianair titles, later full old livery, converted to airline configuration
Yak-40 'Salon'	YK-AQC	9531743?		White with triple blue cheatline and Syrianair titles. Destroyed Beirut International 19-3-1976
Yak-40 'Salon'?	YK-AQD	9830158		White with triple blue cheatline and Syrianair titles, later full old livery; converted to airline configuration?
Yak-40K	YK-AQE	9830258		White with triple blue cheatline and Syrianair titles, later full old livery
Yak-40K	YK-AQF	9931859		White with triple blue cheatline and Syrianair titles, later full old livery; repainted in new livery 2008
Yak-40K	YK-AQG	9941959		White with triple blue cheatline and Syrianair titles, later full old livery
Yak-40K	YK-AQH	9930160		White w. triple blue cheatline & Syrianair titles, later full livery. To Korsar Airlines in 1993 as RA-88298

United Arab Emirates

Though not a traditional customer for Soviet aircraft, the United Arab Emirates Air Force does operate a single Antonov An-124-100 Ruslan (*Condor*) heavy transport delivered in February 2004. Registered in the Ukraine as UR-ZYD (ex-UR-CCX, c/n 19530502843, f/n 03-03), this is the last Kiev-built Ruslan. Though nominally owned by Experts Commercial Agencies based at Abu Dhabi-International (the operator was renamed Maximus Air Cargo in September 2006), the aircraft is jointly operated with the UAEAF.

Speaking of which, Maximus Air Cargo's three Il'yushin IL-76TD *Candid-As*, which are also Ukrainian-registered (UR-BXQ/-BXR/-BXS), are probably not operated for the UAEAF, whose Lockheed C-130H Hercules fleet is apparently adequate for medium airlift jobs.

Yemen

Yemen… yeah, men – but which one? Both, as it turns out. Yemen, which had been part of the Ottoman Empire in the 16th century and an independent monarchy after an uprising in

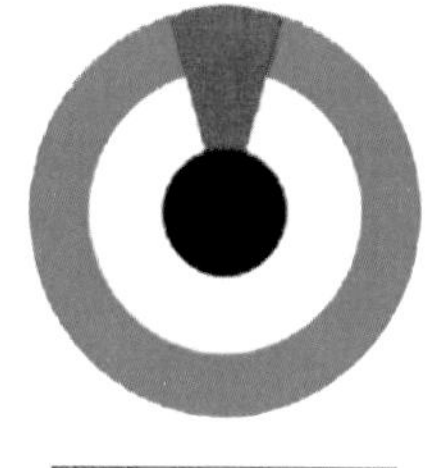

The United Arab Emirates Air Force roundel and fin flash.

UR-BXS, one of the three IL-76TDs operated by Maximus Air in this all-white livery.

the 17th century, was divided in the 19th century when Great Britain captured Aden in 1839, subsequently taking control of all the southern sultanates which became a British protectorate (Aden was declared a crown colony in 1937). North Yemen again formally came under Ottoman rule in 1872 and this status remained until 1919, when North Yemen became an independent kingdom (imamate) once again; it was officially recognised by Great Britain in 1934. On 26th September 1962 the newly crowned Imam al-Badr of Yemen was overthrown and the country became the Yemen Arab Republic (YAR). In the aftermath of the revolution the North Yemen Civil War between the royalists (backed by Jordan and Saudi Arabia) and the republicans (backed by Egypt) broke out, lasting until 1970 when the royalists were ultimately defeated and the Jeddah Peace Accord was signed.

Meanwhile, in southern Yemen the Federation of Arab Emirates was formed in 1959, changing its name to the Federation of South Arabia (FSA) in 1962. Five years later it, too, experienced a revolution and declared independence, becoming the People's Republic of South Yemen; Britain handed over sovereignty of South Yemen to the National Liberation Front on 30th November 1967 and the new government promptly embraced Marxist philosophy, becoming an ally of the USSR. Thus, in a reversal of the 'north-south schism' seen in Korea and Vietnam, North Yemen took the capitalist course of development while South Yemen opted for socialism. In 1970 the country was renamed the People's Democratic Republic of Yemen (PDRY).

The Soviet Union established diplomatic and trade relations with North Yemen as early as November 1928; South Yemen followed suit in 1967 immediately after gaining independence. Thus, in spite of their totally different political courses, the Soviet Union ended up supplying weapons to both Yemens, including aircraft for their respective air forces.

They say a house divided against itself cannot stand. Given the political differences between the two countries, North Yemen and South Yemen soon clashed in a border conflict in 1972; when the conflict ended, the belligerents signed a 'Yemeni Unity Agreement' that same year. Seven years later, however, a new deterioration of the North-South relationship occurred, culminating in the invasion of North Yemen by South Yemeni forces on 25th February 1979. Although militarily successful, the invasion caused widespread condemnation. International pressure forced the PDRY to back down, withdrawing its troops and restoring the status quo on 15th March 1979, and a peace accord was mediated by the League of Arab States.

In January 1986 internal power struggle in South Yemen's top political echelon led to a coup by a Soviet-backed dissident faction; this sparked a civil war and resulted in economic chaos. This war left 5,000 dead, destroyed $500 million worth of Soviet-supplied weaponry, and caused a major shift in South Yemen's leadership. Relations between North and South were normalised in 1987-88. Eventually, in November 1989 the governments of the YAR and the PDRY ratified an agreement concerning reunification of the country; the discovery of oil and natural gas in the border regions of the two Yemeni republics may have been a contributing factor to this decision. The united Republic of Yemen was proclaimed on 22nd May 1990, the North Yemeni capital Sana'a becoming the capital of the new state.

Imamate of Yemen

Even before the revolution, the Royal Yemeni Air Force received Avia B-33 piston-engined attack aircraft (Il'yushin IL-10 *Bark* built under licence in Czechoslovakia) from Czechoslovak Air Force stocks on 18th May 1957 (some sources say 20 standard B-33s and four CB-33 trainers). The B-33s were never used operationally; in fact, not all of them were even reassembled.

North Yemen (Yemen Arab Republic)

Established in 1957 as the Royal Yemen Air Force and growing stronger when North Yemen formed a confederation with the United Arab Republic in March 1958, the air arm was renamed the Yemen Arab Republic Air Force (YARAF) after the overthrow of the monarchy in 1962. Supported by the UAR (and supplied by the latter's chief ally, the Soviet Union), it began receiving Soviet aircraft. These included an unknown number of Mikoyan/Gurevich MiG-15*bis Fagot-B* fighters and about 30 Mikoyan/Gurevich MiG-17F *Fresco-C* fighters (reportedly supplied after the 1972 war with South Yemen). Nine *Frescos* were still in service in 1979 (some sources say twelve aircraft remained but were probably non-operational). Of these, according to *Interavia*, six were used in the advanced trainer role by early 1987 and were being withdrawn. One MiG-17F was lost in a crash on 25th February 1979.

Several UTI-MiG-15 *Midget* trainers were also supplied; four were reportedly in service by 1979. In early 1987 the YARAF was retiring the type.

The first Mikoyan/Gurevich MiG-21PF (*izdeliye* 76) *Fishbed-D* fighters were delivered in 1968 and followed by a further delivery of an unknown variant in the early 1970s. No details of these MiG-21s have survived, as in 1978 the YARAF began to receive Western aircraft, starting with Northrop F-5B Freedom Fighters from Saudi Arabia. The USSR supplied 45 MiG-21MF (*izdeliye* 96F) *Fishbed-J* fighters and MiG-21UM (*izdeliye* 69) *Mongol-B* trainers in 1979-80.

Strike aircraft were initially represented by six Il'yushin IL-28 *Beagle* tactical bombers received via Egypt in the mid-1960s. Unfortunately no serials or base details are known.

According to *Interavia*, as of late 1986, North Yemen operated 15 Sukhoi Su-22 *Fitter-F* fighter-bombers and five Su-22UM3 *Fitter-E* trainers.

The YARAF received a number of Antonov An-2 *Colt* utility biplanes. The type was based at Sana'a (al-Daylami AB); at least two examples were seen there in 1985, one of them no longer airworthy.

The YARAF operated at least four Il'yushin IL-14 *Crate* twin-engined airliners/transports. Some of them wore full military markings; two examples were delivered in IL-14S VIP configuration and operated by the government flight with civil registrations, although at least one of them subsequently received a military serial.

From 1978 onwards the IL-14s, which had become obsolete, were replaced by about four Antonov An-26 *Curl* twin-turboprop tactical transports.

On 24th November 1963 the YARAF government flight took delivery of an Il'yushin IL-18V *Coot* four-turboprop medium-haul airliner which had been only briefly operated by Aeroflot Soviet Airlines. Refitted to IL-18V 'Salon' VIP configuration, the aircraft bore a quasi-civil identity as YE-AYE and retained the basic livery worn by Aeroflot IL-18s pre-1973, albeit with 'Yemen Arab Republic Aviation' titles. In 1970 the Yemen Arab Republic changed its nationality prefix to 4W and the aircraft was reregistered again, becoming 4W-ABO. In addition to VIP transportation, it was occasionally operated by Yemen Airways on regular passenger flights. Finally, on 24th September 1984 the aircraft was sold to Balkan Bulgarian Airlines as LZ-BEU.

The first Soviet helicopters delivered to North Yemen were piston-engined Mil' Mi-4 *Hounds*. The first three, including a VIP-configured Mi-4S, were actually delivered to the Royal Yemen Air Force in 1957 and were quasi-civil; one of them was lost during the

The insignia of the People's Democratic Republic of Yemen Air Force (PDRYAF).

A row of six Yemen Air Force MiG-21*bis* fighters awaiting overhaul at the Odesavia-remservis plant in the Ukraine.

Yemen Air Force MiG-21*bis* '2231 White', '2232 White' and '2237 White', 2010.

North Yemen Civil War. The next batch of at least nine helicopters had overt military markings. Later, the YARAF received more than 30 Mil' Mi-8TV *Hip-C* armed utility helicopters and Mi-8PS VIP helicopters after 1982.

South Yemen (People's Democratic Republic of Yemen)

The South Yemen Air Force was created shortly after the British withdrawal in 1967. In 1970 this became the People's Democratic

This view shows that the Yemeni MiG-21s overhauled at Odessa have a standardised four-tone camouflage scheme with only minimum differences between individual aircraft. The fresh camouflage colours contrast with the pastel-coloured roundels, which are thus not weathered away but rather a low-visibility version.

Yemen Air Force MiG-29SMT '22 16' formates with a French Navy Dassault Rafale M over the sea. Note how the serial is divided by the YAF badge – a practice unique to the MiG-29s.

The insignia of the Yemen Arab Republic Air Force (YARAF).

Two Yemeni MiG-29SMTs (including '22 22') in front of their hangar.

Five MiG-29SMTs, including '22 13', '22 12' and '22 03', on the flight line at Sana'a. Many of the fighters bear the name 'Shafaq' on the fins and the nose.

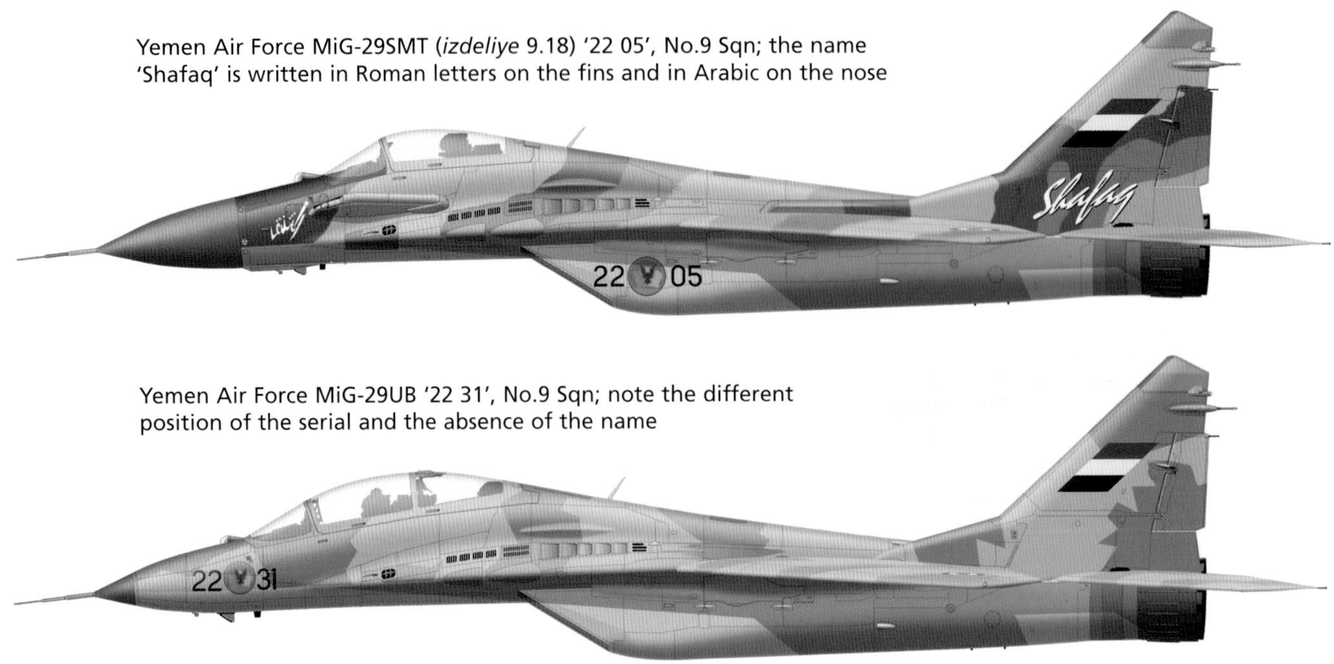

Yemen Air Force MiG-29SMT (*izdeliye* 9.18) '22 05', No.9 Sqn; the name 'Shafaq' is written in Roman letters on the fins and in Arabic on the nose

Yemen Air Force MiG-29UB '22 31', No.9 Sqn; note the different position of the serial and the absence of the name

'22 32' is a standard MiG-29S lacking IFR capability. Note also the serial positioned on the nose instead of the intake trunks.

'22 05' taxying at Sana'a shows the semi-retractable IFR probe added during the upgrade to MiG-29SMT (*izdeliye* 9.18) standard.

Republic of Yemen Air Force (PDRYAF). Again, it received an unspecified number of MiG-15*bis* fighters and UTI-MiG-15s trainers (three of the latter were reportedly active in 1979). *Flight International* stated that when the two Yemens merged in 1990, the united Yemen Air Force still had *four* UTI-MiG-15s!

In 1971 South Yemen took delivery of its first Mikoyan MiG-21F-13 *Fishbed-C* fighters from the USSR; according to some sources, more were supplied by Bulgaria, making it enough *Fishbed-Cs* to form a squadron. More MiG-21 fighters and trainers arrived later; by 1980 the PDRYAF had begun re-equipping with the more advanced MiG-21MF *Fishbed-J*. No details are known of the MiG-21 fleet's operations in those days.

In the 1980s South Yemen purchased 20 Mikoyan MiG-23ML *Flogger-G* fighters and five MiG-23UB *Flogger-C* trainers. However, there are no specific reports of their involvement in either the civil war of 1986 or the civil war of 1994. No MiG-23s were reported on strength in 2002.

In common with North Yemen, South Yemen operated the Su-22 fighter-bomber. In late 1986 the PDRYAF reportedly had 30 single-seat Su-22s and an unknown number of Su-22UM3 trainers.

Like its northern neighbour, South Yemen operated the IL-28 on a small scale in the mid-1960s, receiving 12 of the type. Only a single aircraft has been identified so far.

The PDRYAF was reported to have taken delivery of 25 Mikoyan MiG-23BN *Flogger-H* fighter-bombers. It is likely that the aircraft were only involved in the 1979 fracas. It is not known whether any MiG-23BNs survived the 1986 civil war to join the inventory of the new Yemen Air Force.

The South Yemen Air Force operated six Antonov An-12B *Cub* transports which had a civil-style colour scheme with a red cheatline, wearing both civil registrations and PDRYAF

Two views of Yemen Air Force MiG-29UB '22 31'. The MiG-29's sharply tapered fins dictate the odd shape of the fin flash.

'407 White', a North Yemen Air Force Su-22M in two-tone camouflage.

North Yemen Air Force Su-22UM3 '420 White' rests between missions. The support vehicles in the foreground are, left to right: an APA-35 ground power unit on a ZiL-130-76 chassis, a VZ-7.5-131 air/nitrogen charger and a UPG-300 hydraulics test vehicle (both on a ZiL-131 chassis).

serials. At least one aircraft also wore the titles of the South Yemeni airline Alyemda.

Tactical airlift duties were performed by eight Antonov An-26s supplied from 1980 onwards. Again, the *Curls* wore both PDRYAF serials and civil registrations; confusingly, the latter were reused several times, with multiple aircraft wearing the same registration (but different serials) at the same time.

The South Yemen Air Force received the Mi-8 ahead of its northern counterpart, with 15 such helicopters in service by 1982. The PDRYAF received at least 12 Mil' Mi-25 (Mi-24D) *Hind-D* attack helicopters.

The attempted coup d'état of 1986 led to a civil war in which 75% of the PDRYAF's aircraft fleet was destroyed.

Post-unification Yemen (Republic of Yemen)

After the merger of North Yemen and South Yemen on 22nd May 1990 the two countries pooled the remaining assets of their air arms to create the Yemen Air & Air Defence Force (YAF, or *al Quwwat al-Jawwiya al-Yamaniyya*). This continued the practice of buying aircraft from Russia and other former Soviet republics.

Among other things, the new YAF order of battle included four MiG-21 squadrons – No.6 and No.26 at Hodeida and two more at Ataq AB, a reserve base – comprising 47 MiG-21MFs and eight MiG-21UM trainers. By 2006 it was estimated that 21 MiG-21MF remained but few were airworthy due to a shortage of spares. However, other reports indicate that survivor figures could be as high as 60 fighters and 12 trainers; this includes second-hand aircraft supplied by the Ukraine (four in 2006 and 17 in 2007), including at least eight ex-Algerian MiG-21*bis* (*izdeliye* 75) *Fishbed-Ls* overhauled by Odesaviaremservis.

Since Yemen had defaulted on payments for Russian arms exports, in 1992 Russia stopped all further arms deliveries, forcing the Yemeni government to seek alternative suppliers. This did not take long; in mid-1993 Moldova sold three Mikoyan MiG-29 (*izdeliye* 9.13) *Fulcrum-C* fighters and one MiG-29UB *Fulcrum-B* combat trainers (some sources say eight single-seaters and two MiG-29UBs, or even 12 *Fulcrums*) – to the YAF via a third party. The aircraft belong to the No.4 Sqn at Sana'a, though there have been reports of Yemeni MiG-29s operating from al-Rayyan AB where a detachment with a mixed bag of aircraft is based.

However, it turned out that the aircraft were delivered incomplete and two were non-airworthy. In 1994 a violent civil war broke out in which the greater part of the MiG-29 fleet was destroyed; the survivors were eventually returned to Moldova.

Later the financial issues with Russia were apparently sorted out. This allowed Yemen to order 12 to 24 new MiG-29s from Russia in August 2001. These were MiG-29SE (*izdeliye* 9.12SE) *Fulcrum-As* and MiG-29UBs. Under the contract they were to be upgraded to MiG-29SMT (*izdeliye* 9.18) multi-role fighters with a 'glass cockpit', an upgraded radar, new weapons (including Kh-31 air-to-surface missiles) and IFR capability but with a *Fulcrum-A* style concave spine (known as 'the Yemeni version'). Deliveries took place in 2001-02. Later, six new-build MiG-29SMTs and two IFR-capable MiG-29UBT trainers were delivered in November 2004-July 2005. In December 2007, after two years of negotiations, Yemen ordered 32 additional MiG-29s. The Yemeni *Fulcrums* wear a three-tone desert camouflage; a curious feature of these aircraft is that the serials are divided in two by the circular

Yemen Air Force Su-22M4K fighter-bombers and Su-22UM3K trainers on the flight line at Sana'a.

YAF badge. In Yemen the MiG-29SMT has a local popular name, Shafaq ('dawn' in Arabic), which is writ large on most of the fighters.

Three Yemeni MiG-29s have been lost in accidents. One fighter crashed near Emran on 3rd July 2005 due to engine failure, the pilot Mohammed Thabet Dareem ejecting safely. Another was lost on 28th August 2005, and the third crash-landed at an auxiliary dirt strip at Saada some 230 km (142 miles) north of Sana'a on 7th March 2007; the pilot was injured but managed to get clear before the aircraft was consumed by the post-crash fire.

There have been reports that the Yemen Air Force took delivery of six Chengdu F-7M fighters (a Chinese derivative of the MiG-21F-13) in 2001 but this has not been confirmed. No deliveries were reported by China; however, the fighters could have been supplied by Iran or another Islamic country.

The surviving Su-22s inherited from North and South Yemen were augmented by deliveries of second-hand aircraft from the Ukraine, which sold Yemen four Su-22s in 1995 and a further four in 1996 (single-seat Su-22M4 *Fitter-Ks* and two-seat Su-22UM3 *Fitter-Gs*). According to press reports, it was a very advantageous deal for the Yemeni Air Force, since the last four examples were obtained for just US$ 500,000 apiece – quite an attractive price for a reasonably capable combat aircraft. The aircraft saw service with an unidentified squadron based at Sana'a.

After the unification the surviving An-24RV and An-26s were operated by the No.4 Sqn based at Sana'a, their serials being prefixed 'Y.A.F.'. It was easy to see which Yemen the An-26 had come from by the number of digits in the serial (three for South, four for North).

In the early 1990s the Yemen Air Force obtained three second-hand (but quite new) Il'yushin IL-76TD *Candid-A* transports. These served with the No.115 Sqn at Sana'a but were nominally owned by and jointly operated with the flag carrier, Yemenia (Yemen Airways Corporation). However, the identity of one IL-76 is open to doubt, so there may actually be four *Candids*.

The existing Mi-8T and Mi-8PS helicopters were supplemented by 25 newer Mil' Mi-17 *Hip-H* and Mi-171Sh armed utility helicopters; one of the Mi-17s crashed on 13th November 2000. The Ulan-Ude-built Mi-171Sh is available in several versions as regards airframe design, and the Yemeni examples combine the old fully glazed rounded nose with a one-piece cargo ramp. Currently Yemeni *Hips* serve with the No.8 Sqn at Ta'izz (Ganad AB) in the south of the former YAR and the No.128 Sqn (a composite helicopter squadron at Sana'a); the latter unit has the Mi-171Sh's.

At least 12 Mi-25s were reported operational with the united YAF in 1995. They were later augmented by six newer Mi-35 (Mi-24V) *Hind-Es*, some of which wear a rather unusual dark grey/green camouflage. The *Hinds* are operated by the No.9 Sqn at Ta'izz (*sic* – the

Yemen Air Force Su-22M4 '1725 White' with PTB-1150 drop tanks, No.6 Sqn, Hodeidah

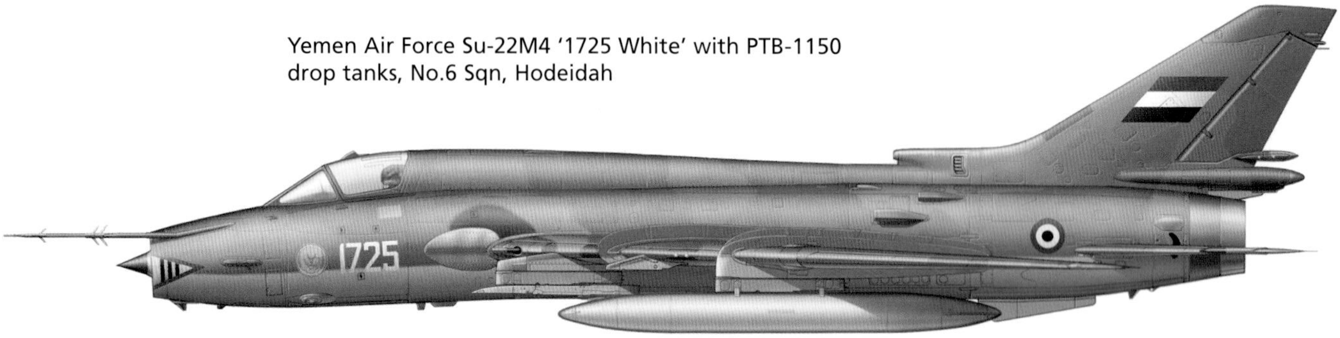

Su-22M4 '2214 Blue' wears a totally different camouflage with Yemen Air Force titles in English and Arabic; even the fin flash is different

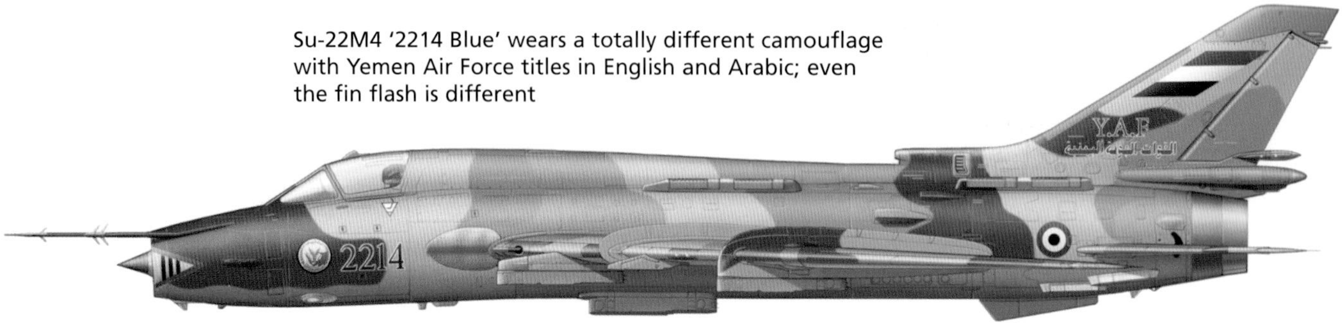

Yemen Air Force (No.6 Sqn) Su-22UM3K '825 White' wearing yet another camouflage scheme

Yemen Air Force Su-22M4s in different camouflage schemes at Hodeidah. Note that 2214 Blue (obviously refurbished by Odesaviaremservis – compare the colour scheme to the MiGs on page 256) has eight chaff/flare dispensers while 1725 White has none.

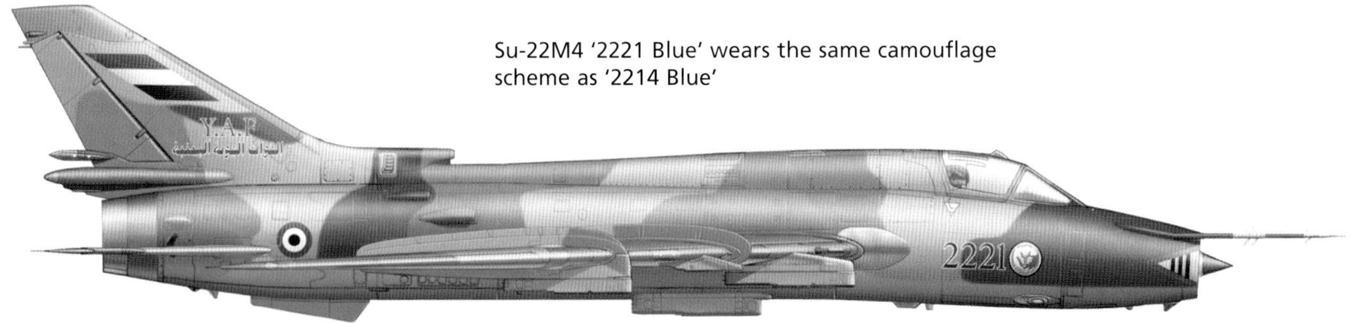

Su-22M4 '2221 Blue' wears the same camouflage scheme as '2214 Blue'

same squadron number is quoted for the MiG-29 unit at Sana'a!) and the No.128 Sqn.

The Yemeni Naval Aviation also operates Soviet helicopters – namely Mil' Mi-14PL *Haze-A* amphibians and Kamov Ka-28 *Helix-As* for ASW duties and Mi-14PS *Haze-Bs* for SAR duties. Surprisingly, these are reportedly likewise operated by No.128 Sqn at Sana'a, which is a long way from the Red Sea coast and even farther from the Gulf of Aden.

In action

While North Yemen and South Yemen have had quite a history of armed strife, there is no reliable evidence of the use of aviation in these border conflicts. Nor are details available on the use of aviation in the 1986 South Yemen Civil War – or the 1994 civil war which began when the south, where communist ideas were still strong, attempted to secede. This attempt was ruthlessly suppressed by the Sana'a government, the death toll reaching 10,000. A year later, Yemen had a tussle with Ethiopia which claimed rights to Hanish Island located in the Red Sea about half-way between the two shores.

It is known, however, that the YAF was involved in another domestic conflict which began on 19th June 1998. A wave of protests swept through Yemen's major cities and violence broke out in the rural regions dominated by various tribes. While there admittedly was a valid reason for this – massive unemployment, soaring fuel prices and the abolition of subsidies on flour and wheat, all resulting from the country's economic downturn – the conflict was fuelled by neighbouring Saudi Arabia. The latter, which is notorious for supporting various Islamic fundamentalist and extremist groups, had long been uncomfortable about Yemen's democratic secular form of government and had secretly sought to topple it (or at least destabilise it). When things started getting out of hand, Yemen government troops supported by Mi-35 and Mi-171 helicopter gunships were sent into the mountainous countryside to suppress the riots.

Yemen Air Force Su-22UM3 '415 White' taxies at Sana'a while a Northrop F-5E of the co-located No.121 Sqn takes off in the background.

North Yemen Air Force An-12B 7O-ABM/621 Black with Alyemda titles, registration and serial of almost illegible size

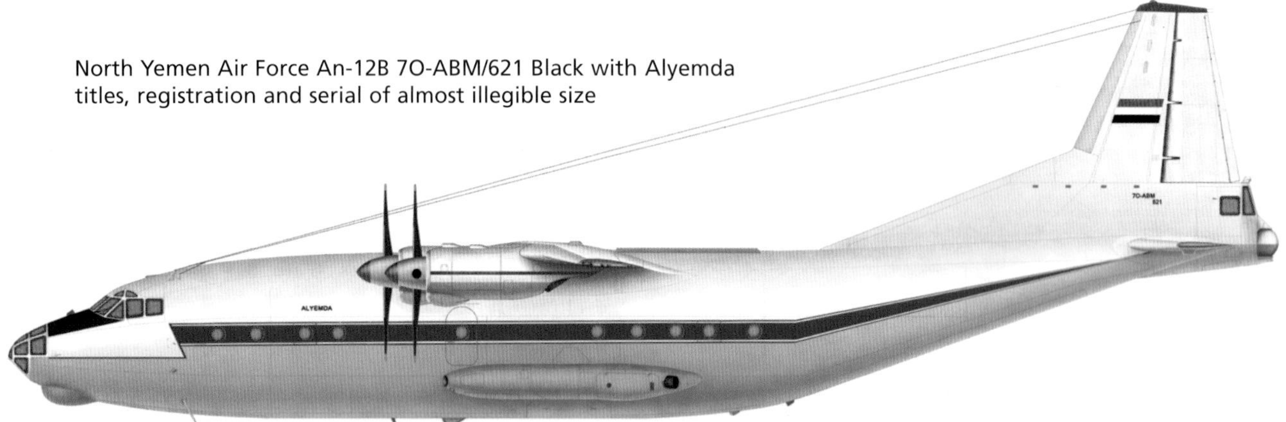

Later, Yemen Air Force aircraft (including Su-22 fighter-bombers) saw action in the Sa'adah Governorate in north-western Yemen, where the local dissident cleric Hussein Badreddin al-Houthi, head of the Shi'ite Zaïdiyyah sect, started an uprising in June 2004. The armed insurgency quickly spread to the neighbouring provinces. The Yemeni government alleged that the Houthis, as the rebels were known, were seeking to overthrow it and implement Shari'a religious law, and promised to use an 'iron fist' against the rebels. Hussein Badreddin al-Houthi was eliminated in the course of a hit operation in June 2004, but his brother Abdul Malik al-Houthi picked up the ball and carried on, prompting the government to resume operations against the rebels. A ceasefire was agreed in June 2007 but did not last long. In response to the fifth outbreak of the insurgency, on 11th August 2009 Yemeni armed forces launched Operation *Scorched Earth* to deal with the Houthis; the Air Force was also involved.

On 2nd October 2009 a Yemeni MiG-21 crashed on the way back from a mission against the Houthis. The rebels claimed they had shot it down, while the Air Force attributed the crash to technical problems. Three days later a Su-22 was lost in similar circumstances. On 8th November 2009 another Yemeni aircraft reported to be a 'Sukhoi' was lost; the pilot ejected and was recovered by friendly forces. Again the rebels claimed a 'kill', which the military denied.

In November 2009 the Houthis moved across the border into Saudi Arabia. The insurgency assumed such a scale that Saudi Arabia was forced to intervene, launching artillery attacks and air strikes against the Houthis – for once, helping the Yemeni government to suppress the rebellion when the situation became too hot for the Saudis' own comfort. Eventually a new ceasefire was negotiated, and in March 2010 President Ali Abdullah Saleh declared the war was over.

The latest conflict involving the YAF is the Yemeni Revolution that broke out in February 2011. What started out as protests against high prices and widespread corruption quickly

Yemen Air Force An-26 Y.A.F.1177 in grey/green camouflage. The red-tipped propeller spinners suggest the aircraft was bought second-hand in the CIS (coloured spinner tips are characteristic of Soviet/CIS military turboprops). Note how the blue colour extends to the underside of the radome; note also the dual presentation of the serial.

In contrast, An-26 YAF 612 is mostly white with a grey belly and smaller serial in European characters only. Note the black-tipped spinners, the absence of roundels and the rakishly tilted fin flash.

An-26 Y.A.F. 614 wears a two-tone green camouflage and a matching green colour on the radome.

Wearing the Yemenia logo but no titles, Yemen Air Force IL-76TD 7O-ADG is seen here being loaded at Sharjah in the late 1990s. It retains basic Aeroflot colours from its days as CCCP-76405.

Yemen Air Force Mi-171Sh '2251 Black' was built in the 'glass-nosed/ flatass' version. Note the YAF badge above the port entry door.

A Yemen Air Force Mi-35 escorts a Mi-171Sh over the mountains of northern Yemen.

grew into a major insurgency, the protesters demanding that President Saleh should resign. On 22nd September a Su-22 attacking the insurgents' positions was shot down by MANPADS; the pilot ejected and was captured. On 30th October the rebels attacked al-Daylami AB near Sana'a, destroying two or three bombed-up fighters prepared for a strike mission the following day, which reportedly included at least one MiG-29.

Known Yemeni military aircraft of Soviet/Russian origin
1. North Yemen (Yemen Arab Republic Air Force)

Type	Serial/registration	C/n	F/n	Notes
An-2	55	?		Seen 1985
An-2	99	?		Derelict Sana'a
An-24RV 'Salon'	4W-ACD	77310809		Ex-Aeroflot CCCP-47368? Became, see next line
	1190			
An-24T	2016	1022016?		Ex-Sudanese AF 966 Black? Delivered by 1-1985
An-26	1177	6507		
An-26	1178	?		
An-26	1188	6504		
An-26	119...	?		Last digit not known; reported as '119' but does not fit into PDRYAF An-26 serial range
IL-14S	YE-AAE	147001148		Ex-Aeroflot CCCP-Л1532 (SSSR-L1532), D/D 16-9-1958.Became, see next line
	1148	?		
IL-14S	YE-AAR			
IL-14	1131	147001131?		Wfu Aden by 1993
IL-14	1141	?		Not c/n 147001141, which is an Aeroflot IL-14
IL-18V 'Salon'	YE-AYE	183005905		Ex-Aeroflot CCCP-75870, D/D 24-11-1963. Became, see next line
	4W-ABO			Reregistered 1970. Sold to Balkan Bulgarian Airlines 24-9-1984 as LZ-BEU
IL-28	81	?		Derelict Hodeida

MiG-15*bis*	72	?		
MiG-21UM	207 Black	516999256	?	Stored Rostov-on-Don, Russia
Mi-4S	YE-AAP	?		
Mi-4S	YE-AAQ	?		
Mi-4A	YE-AAV	?		
Mi-4	101	?		Derelict Sana'a, 1992
Mi-4	102	?		
Mi-4	103	?		
Mi-4	104	?		
Mi-4	105	?		
Mi-4	106	?		
Mi-4	107	?		
Mi-4	108	?		
Mi-4	109	?		
Mi-8PS	710	10710	?	Ex-Romanian Air Force '710'; operated for the PLO, to Palestine National Authority 12-1994 as SU-YAA
Mi-8T	722	10722	?	Ex-Romanian Air Force '722'; operated for the PLO, to Palestine National Authority 12-1994 as SU-YAB
Mi-8	801	?	?	
Mi-8	802	?	?	
Mi-8	804	?	?	
Mi-8	807	?	?	
Mi-8	810	?	?	
Mi-8	811	?	?	
Mi-8	812	?	?	
Mi-8	813	?	?	
Mi-8	814	?	?	
Mi-8	815	?	?	
Mi-8	817	?	?	
Mi-8	818	?	?	
Mi-8	820	?	?	
Mi-8	821	?	?	Wfu Sana'a
Mi-8	822	?	?	
Mi-8	823	?	?	
Mi-8	824	?	?	
Mi-8	825	?	?	
Mi-8	832	?	?	

2. South Yemen (People's Democratic Republic of Yemen Air Force)

Type	Serial/registration	C/n	F/n	Notes
An-12B (+)	7O-AAW	401604?		
An-12B (+)	7O-ABH	?		
An-12B (+)	7O-ABM/821	?		Alyemda titles, red cheatline. Serial also reported as 802!
An-12B (+)	7O-ACI/626	?		
An-12B (+)	7O-ACJ/625	?		
An-12B (+)	623	?		Derelict Aden
An-26	611/7O-ABH (1)	9503		
An-26	612			Possibly had 7O-ABI allocated
An-26	613/7O-ABH (2)	9507		Reported derelict Sana'a, North Yemen, 3-2005
An-26	614	9509		
An-26	615/7O-ABN (1)?			Reported as such; possibly had 7O-ABL allocated
An-26	616/7O-ABM	9505		
An-26	617/7O-ABN (2)?	12303		
An-26	618/7O-ABO			
MiG-21MF?	101	?	?	
MiG-21MF?	105	?	?	
MiG-21MF?	108	?	?	
MiG-21MF?	112	?	?	

MiG-21MF	148 Black	?	?	Seen 1980
Mi-8	110	?	?	
Mi-8	126	?	?	
Mi-8	187	?	?	
Mi-8	523	?	?	
Su-22...	125	?		Exact version unknown; serial probably in Arab characters
Su-22...	401	?		Exact version unknown; serial probably in Arab characters)
Su-22...	403	?		Exact version unknown; serial probably in Arab characters
Su-22UM3	404	175323*****		Serial probably in Arab characters
Su-22...	406	?		Exact version unknown; serial probably in Arab characters
Su-22M	407 White	?		Serial in Arab characters
Su-22...	410	?		Exact version unknown; serial probably in Arab characters
Su-22...	412	?		Exact version unknown; serial probably in Arab characters
Su-22UM3	420 White	175323*****		Serial in Arab characters
Su-22M4	437	?		Serial probably in Arab characters. Sold to the USA for evaluation
Su-22M4	625	?		
Su-22...	725	?		Exact version unknown; serial probably in Arab characters

3. Post-unification Yemen (Yemen Air Force)

Type	Serial/ registration	C/n	F/n	Notes
An-26	Y.A.F. 612	?		All-white c/s, no titles
An-26	Y.A.F. 614	?		Two-tone green camouflage
An-26	Y.A.F. 1177	6507		Grey/green camouflage, serial in both European and Arab characters
Mi-8T	187	?	?	
IL-76TD	7O-ADF	1033418578	9005	D/D 11-1995, ex-RA-76380 No.1. Basic Aeroflot livery with Yemenia titles/logo, later full Yemenia livery
IL-76TD	7O-ADG (1)	1033415497	8805	D/D 11-1995, ex-RA-76361. Aeroflot cheatline but Yemenia logo until 1999; later all-white with 'YAF' titles
IL-76TD	7O-ADG (2)	1023412402	8601	D/D 1996, ex-RA-76405. Full Yemenia livery. Became, see next line
	7O-ADO			Reregistered by 2012
IL-76TD	7O-ADH	?	?	Existence not 100% confirmed
Ka-28	101	523500*******	?	Seen 2005
Ka-28	202	523500*******	?	Seen 2005
MiG-21MF	7749	?	?	Noted Hodeida 12-1997
MiG-21*bis*	2230	N75038147	75-25-**?	Ex-Algerian Air Force FA-**, D/D 2010
MiG-21*bis*	2231 White	N75038206	75-25-**?	Ex-Algerian Air Force FA-**, D/D 2010; sand/chocolate brown/grey/green camouflage, low-viz insignia
MiG-21*bis*	2232 White	N75038210	75-25-**?	Ex-Algerian Air Force FA-96, D/D 2010; sand/chocolate brown/grey/green camouflage, low-viz insignia
MiG-21*bis*	2233 White	N75038314	75-25-**?	Ex-Algerian Air Force FA-**, D/D 2010; sand/chocolate brown/grey/green camouflage, low-viz insignia
MiG-21*bis*	2234	N75038327	75-25-**?	Ex-Algerian Air Force FA-**, D/D 2010
MiG-21*bis*	2235	N75038399	75-25-**?	Ex-Algerian Air Force FA-**, D/D 2010
MiG-21*bis*	2236	N75036406	75-23-**	Ex-Algerian Air Force FA-**, D/D 2010
MiG-21*bis*	2237 White	N75052707	75-33-**?	Ex-Ethiopian Air Force, D/D 2010; sand/chocolate brown/grey/green camouflage, low-viz insignia
MiG-21*bis*	?	N75036395	75-23-**	Ex-Algerian Air Force FA-**, D/D 2007
MiG-21*bis*	?	N75038001	75-25-01?	Ex-Algerian Air Force FA-**, D/D 2007
MiG-21bis	?	N75038010	75-25-**?	Ex-Algerian Air Force FA-**, D/D 2007
MiG-21*bis*	?	N75044702	75-27-**?	Ex-Bulgarian Air Force 502 White, 6th Fighter Brigade, D/D 2007
MiG-21*bis*	?	N75051511	75-32-**?	Ex-Ethiopian Air Force 1052, D/D 2007
MiG-21*bis*	?	N75052786	75-33-**?	Ex-Ethiopian Air Force, D/D 2007
MiG-21*bis*	?	N75052808	75-33-**?	Ex-Ethiopian Air Force, D/D 2007
MiG-21*bis*	?	N75053045	75-34-**?	Ex-Ethiopian Air Force, D/D 2007
MiG-21*bis*	?	N75053407	75-34-**?	Ex-Bulgarian Air Force 92 White, 6th Fighter Brigade, D/D 2007
MiG-21*bis*	?	N75053569	75-34-**?	Ex-Bulgarian Air Force 93 White, 6th Fighter Brigade, D/D 2007
MiG-21*bis*	?	N75054147	75-35-**?	Ex-Bulgarian Air Force 85 White, 6th Fighter Brigade, D/D 2007
MiG-21*bis*	?	N75058180	?	Ex-Ethiopian Air Force, D/D 2007
MiG-21*bis*	?	N75059379	?	Ex-Ethiopian Air Force, D/D 2007
MiG-21*bis*	?	N75059405	?	Ex-Ethiopian Air Force, D/D 2007
MiG-21*bis*	?	N75059518	?	Ex-Ethiopian Air Force, D/D 2007
MiG-21*bis*	?	N75080645	?	Ex-Bulgarian Air Force 91 White, 6th Fighter Brigade, D/D 2007
MiG-21*bis*	?	N75084823	?	

MiG-21*bis*	?	N75084854	?	
MiG-21*bis*	?	N75088439	?	
MiG-29SE?	22 03 Black	29605*****	?	
MiG-29SE?	22 04 Black	29605*****	?	
MiG-29SMT	22 05 Black	29605*****	?	
MiG-29SMT	22 07 Black	29605*****	?	
MiG-29SE?	22 12 Black	29605*****	?	
MiG-29SMT	22 13 Black	29605*****	?	
MiG-29SMT	22 14 Black	29605*****	?	
MiG-29SE?	22 15 Black	29605*****	?	
MiG-29SMT	22 16 Black	29605*****	?	
MiG-29SMT	22 22 Black	29605*****	?	
MiG-29SE	22 32 Black	29605*****	?	
MiG-29UB	22 01 Black	N509030*****	?	
MiG-29UB	22 02 Black	N509030*****	?	
MiG-29UB	22 31 Black	N509030*****	?	
Mi-14PS	601	20601	?	Ex-ER-MGA
Mi-14PS	602	20602	?	Ex-ER-MGB
Mi-17	201	?	?	
Mi-17	203	?	?	
Mi-17	206	?	?	
Mi-17	224	?	?	
Mi-17	249	?	?	
Mi-17	659	?	?	Wfu by 12-2009
Mi-17	696	?	?	
Mi-17	697	?	?	
Mi-17	801	?	?	
Mi-171Sh	2250 Black	594896*****	?	No.128 Sqn
Mi-171Sh	2251 Black	594896*****	?	No.128 Sqn
Mi-171Sh	2252 Black	594896*****	?	No.128 Sqn
Mi-171Sh	2253 Black	594896*****	?	No.128 Sqn
Mi-171Sh	2254 Black	594896*****	?	No.128 Sqn
Mi-171Sh	2255 Black?	594896*****	?	Existence not proven but likely
Mi-171Sh	2256 Black	594896*****	?	No.128 Sqn
Mi-171Sh	2257 Black	594896*****	?	No.128 Sqn
Mi-171Sh	2258 Black	594896*****	?	No.128 Sqn
Mi-171Sh	2259 Black	594896*****	?	No.128 Sqn
Mi-171Sh	2260 Black	594896*****	?	No.128 Sqn
Mi-171Sh	2261 Black	594896*****	?	No.128 Sqn
Mi-171Sh	2262 Black	594896*****	?	No.128 Sqn
Mi-35	271 Black	?	?	Serial in Arab characters
Mi-35	273 White	?	?	Dark green/dark brown camouflage, serial in Arab characters
Mi-35	274 White	?	?	
Mi-35	275 White	?	?	
Mi-35	276 White	?	?	
Su-22M4	1025	?		
Su-22M4	1725 White	?		Tan/brown/green/dark green camouflage
Su-22M4	2211 Blue	?		
Su-22M4	2212 Blue	?		
Su-22M4	2214 Blue	?		Sand/chocolate/dark grey/green camouflage
Su-22M4	2215 Blue	?		
Su-22M4?	2217 Blue	?		Sand/chocolate/dark grey/green camouflage
Su-22M4	2221 Blue	?		Sand/chocolate/dark grey/green camouflage
Su-22M4	?	19716		Bought from the Ukraine in 2007; ex-Ukrainian Air Force Su-17M4?
Su-22M4	?	21803		Bought from the Ukraine in 2007
Su-22M4	?	21804		Bought from the Ukraine in 2007
Su-22M4	?	21607?		Bought from the Ukraine in 2007; third digit of c/n doubtful!
Su-22M4R	?	17613		Bought from the Ukraine in 2007; ex-Ukrainian Air Force Su-17M4R?
Su-22M4R	?	18715		Bought from the Ukraine in 2007; ex-Ukrainian Air Force Su-17M4R?
Su-22UM3K	415 White	175323*****		Tan/brown/green/dark green camouflage
Su-22UM3K	825 White	175323*****		Tan/brown/green/dark green camouflage
Su-22UM3K	1925	175323*****		

Map and Index

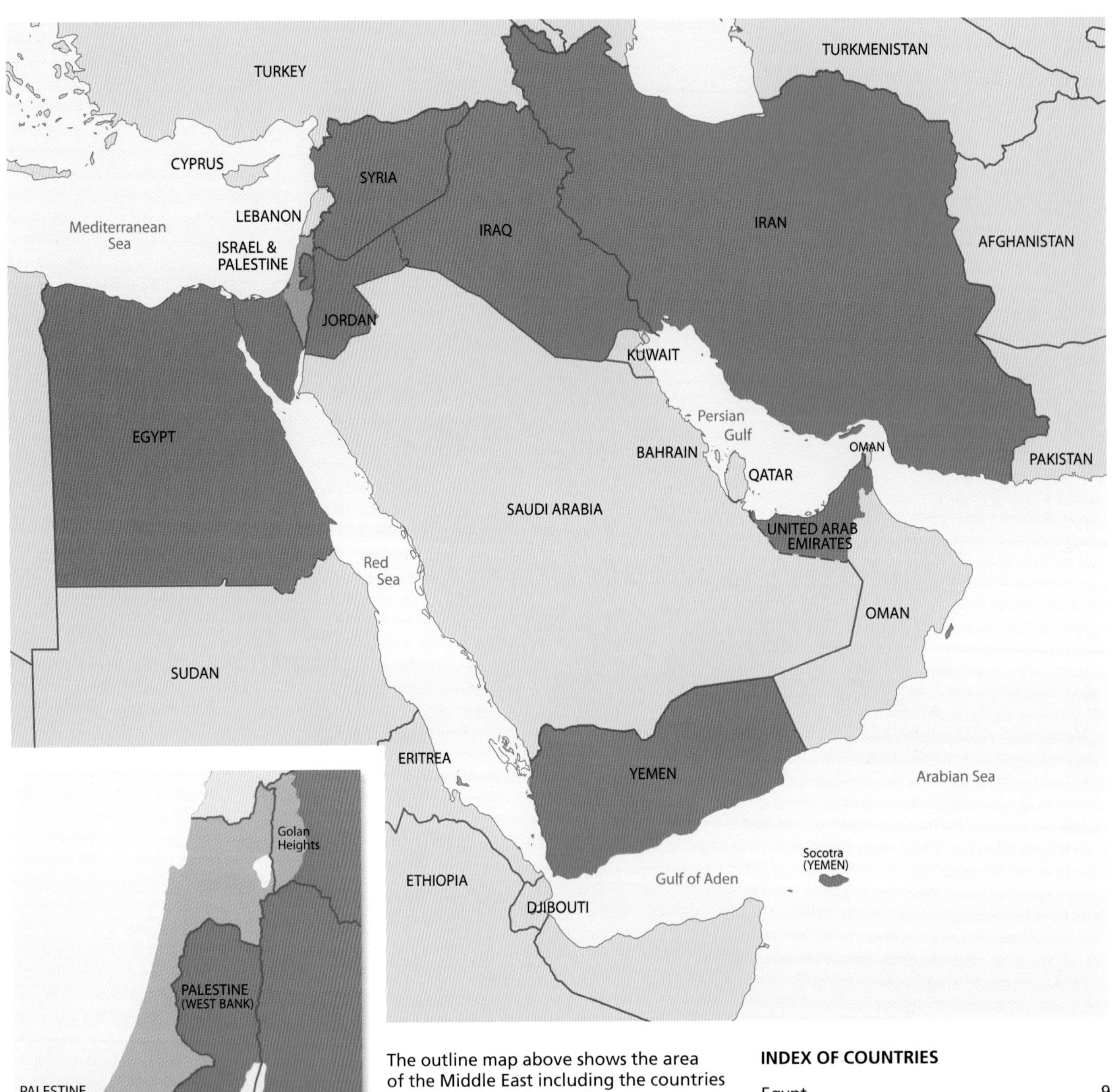

The outline map above shows the area of the Middle East including the countries covered in this volume. Those countries which have acquired and/or operated Soviet and/or Russian types are shown in red. Those which have had such types only for evaluation or development purposes are shown in blue.

The inset map to the left shows more detail of Israel and Palestine. Readers should please note that borders in the Middle East generally are prone to movement as a result of conflicts and in particular there are disputed territories between Israel and Palestine and much of the West Bank territories are now actually controlled by Israel, as are the Golan Heights, part of Jordan. These maps are not intended as any kind of political statement but merely as a general geographical guide to readers.

INDEX OF COUNTRIES

In this book, locations and units are not indexed, as the relevant entries are predominantly contained within each country's individual section and thus quite easy to locate.

AIRCRAFT TYPES

Soviet/Russian

Non-Soviet/Russian

MISSILES AND ROCKETS

NATO REPORTING NAMES

SOVIET AIR FORCE/NAVY UNITS